EVERYDAY
INITIATIONS

How to Survive Crises Using Rituals

EVERYDAY INITIATIONS

How to Survive Crises Using Rituals

RUEDIGER DAHLKE, M.D.

Translated by Petra Michel

In collaboration with
Margit Dahlke and Robert Hößl

SENTIENT PUBLICATIONS

First Sentient Publications edition 2025

A paperback original

Book design by Laura Waltje
Cover Design by Laura Waltje

Library of Congress Control Number: 2024948752
Publisher's Cataloging-in-Publication Data

Names: Dahlke, Ruediger, author. | Michel, Petra, translator.

Title: Everyday initiations : how to survive crises using rituals / Ruediger Dahlke, M. D. ; translated by Petra Michel.

Description: Includes bibliographical references and index. | Boulder, CO: Sentient Publications, 2025.
Identifiers: LCCN: 2024948752 | ISBN: 978-1-59181-348-4 (paperback) | 978-1-59181-349-1 (epub)
Subjects: LCSH Life change events--Health aspects. | Stress (Psychology)--Health aspects. | Rites and ceremonies--Psychological aspects. | BISAC BODY, MIND & SPIRIT / Healing / General | PSYCHOLOGY / Transpersonal | MEDICAL / Holistic Medicine | MEDICAL / Alternative & Complementary Medicine
Classification: LCC RC49 .D2513 2025 | DDC 616/.001/9--dc23

SENTIENT PUBLICATIONS
A Limited Liability Company
PO Box 1851
Boulder, CO 80306
www.sentientpublications.com

I am grateful to Andrea and Hermann Druckenthaner, Josef Hien, Christa Maleri and Dr. Helmut Oberhofer for their encouragement and corrections.

The photographs in the picture section are taken, with permission, from Lennart Nilsson: Ein Kind entsteht. Mosaik Publishers. Munich 1990.

Contents

Just as every blossom wilts and every youth
Yields to age, so too every stage in life blooms,
Every wisdom and every virtue blooms
In its proper time and cannot endure forever.
Each time life calls, the heart must
Be ready to bid adieu and begin again,
To give itself courageously and without grief
To others and to other relationships.
And a magic indwells every beginning,
Which protects us and helps us to live.

We should gladly stride from space to space,
Without clinging to any one as if it were a homeland,
The spirit of the world doesn't want to bind and
narrow us,
It wants to lift us, broaden us, step by step.
Hardly have we begun to feel at home in one circle of
life,
hardly have we begun to grow familiar,
when we're already in jeopardy of becoming soft,
Only he who is ready to depart and journey
Can avoid becoming lamed by habit.
Perhaps even the hour of death
Will send us new and youthful spaces,
Life will never cease calling to us....
Onwards, O Heart! Bid adieu and grow healthy!

Hermann Hesse, "Stufen" ("Steps")

Introduction: The Meaning and Might of Transitions

Although we have become increasingly adept at dealing with technological problems, it seems our ability to cope with natural phenomena continues to deteriorate. We are especially inept at handling transitions from one phase of life to the next. We rush through life, trying to save time wherever possible, and still end up having no time to spare, no time to devote ourselves to the essential stages of our own development.

The phenomenon of accelerated development can be traced in several different arenas. The transition from a hunting society to an agricultural society took thousands of years, but the transition into an industrial society took scarcely one hundred years' time. The Industrial Revolution occurred relatively slowly compared with the transition into the information society, a change that happened so fast many people hardly noticed it and were left behind, out of step with the rest of society. The next transition—into the consciousness society—is happening so fast and so subtly that few people are consciously aware of its onset and progress.

Transitions between the phases of an individual's life—marked by conception, birth, puberty, cutting the (figurative) umbilical cord to one's parental home, marriage, midlife crisis and death—are likewise experienced consciously by very few people. During conception and birth, the new arrival is seldom considered to possess any genuine awareness. Puberty is more or less muddled through, with parents hoping their adolescent will pass through the crisis years without offering any undue bother or challenge. The final separation from the parents at the end of adolescence is frequently absent entirely, or delayed as long as possible because of practical concerns or other reasons. Marriage is increasingly refused in favor of an allegedly more convenient single lifestyle, or serves merely as the continuation of a problematic relationship already begun with one's mother or father. Career has degenerated from true calling to mere job, a situation with which more and more people are feeling less and less satisfied, with the result that people tend to change jobs almost as often as they change underwear. The female half of the population doses itself with hormones in a misguided effort to evade the natural changes associated with menopause and midlife, while the male half tries its best to ignore or deny "male menopause." After all this denial and covering up, it comes as no surprise to learn that death, the last major crisis, all too often takes place under miserable circumstances and in an atmosphere rife with suppression and contempt.

As if we didn't have enough difficulties with these major, classical crises in life, new challenges are constantly arising. A large percentage of individuals cannot satisfactorily cope with these challenges since their roots lie in the failure to cope with major crises. One could almost say that, by ignoring the major transitions in life, we guarantee an abundance of minor long-term crises. Whenever the principle of transition is denied or misused, sand gets into life's gears and allows minor disturbances to grow into major crises. Instead of concentrating on and coping with the potential for crisis inherent in particular periods of transition, we collectively create a crisis-ridden world.

The abundance of "loss crises"—from loss of a partner to loss of a beloved pet—shows that we have trouble letting go. The retirement crisis reveals that life's evening (the long rest after a tough career) is seldom smoother than a single day's evening (the brief rest after a tough workday). Where earlier generations saw cause for celebration, we make ourselves miserable. The empty nest syndrome is a lament voiced surprisingly enough by emotionally healthy parents who have finally achieved the long-awaited reward. Their children have grown wings of their own and flown away, leaving their parents free to fly wherever their own wings choose to take them. Many old people today seem to have forgotten how to fly—or lost the desire to take flight. They continue to brood in the empty nest, trying to turn back the hands of time and tempting their nestling to return home. When that attempt fails, they become depressive and in need of care themselves.

Nowadays the opposite reaction is frequently observed in so-called "challenge crises." A move to new surroundings or change in place of employment can trigger a crisis of this sort. Basically, it has to do with a refusal to let go of what is old and familiar, often coupled with a refusal to accept anything new. The pattern In these crises corresponds to the pattern in the great crises of life. Whether one clings to one's old job "for dear life," or refuses to let go of an old theme (e.g., the idea that one must care for and support one's family), one is not receptive to new things that are long overdue. The old pattern may have functioned well enough in the past, but now the situation has changed and the old pattern is no longer appropriate. Persisting in it only leads to suffering.

It is obvious we have begun to change so rapidly we are no longer able to keep pace. To make matters worse, we must face the times of change in our lives without a safety net of rituals we can trust to catch and support us. Massive problems on all levels of personal and social life are the consequences of this deficiency.

This book illuminates these problems and crises from the standpoint of esoteric philosophy, and interprets the symptoms associated with these crises from a similarly esoteric point of view. The fact that I sometimes pitilessly push my fingertip into the sore spots and weak points of our society's efforts to deal with transitions does not mean I have better solutions to offer. Nor does my analysis of archaic societies, whose rites of passage made it easier for their members to deal with life's transitions, necessarily mean I want us to return to archaic ways of life. Just the opposite: esoteric philosophy has an inherent interest in evolution and progress—although in a different sense than generally conceived of by modern and "progressive" people.

The use of the word "esoteric" is not without its problems. The term *esoteros* can be traced to Pythagoras, who used it to refer to his inner circle of disciples. *Exoteros* described the larger, outer circle of students. The wisdom of the inner circle was traditionally reserved for a small group who guarded it carefully, not because they wanted to keep it for themselves, but because esoteric wisdom cannot benefit worldly people and might even pose some dangers for them. In this respect, nothing has changed since the days of Pythagoras. Secrecy was preserved less through the exclusion of others than through wisdom's inherent tendency to protect itself. Wisdom resists profanation. For example, even though the secret wisdom encoded in the Egyptian tarot is readily accessible to anyone with an ordinary deck of playing cards, it remains incomprehensible to the vast majority of casual card players. A similar situation exists with *The Revelation of St. John*. Because most people find it incomprehensible, it tends to be ignored and thus protected from misuse. Even books about astrophysics tend to remain "secret" simply because their mathematical foundations are too difficult for most people.

The esoteric wave of the past two decades has caused some fundamental changes in this situation. In order to make esoteric wisdom palatable to a wider audience, it has either been coarsely simplified—and thus falsified—or else more or less unwittingly turned upside down and presented in a ridiculous and often embarrassing way. Printed and distributed in thousands of copies, books of this sort sprinkle a bit of esoteric sugar and spice onto one or another of our society's most bitterly anxious themes. The recipe varies with the vicissitudes of the market. Charlatans promise spiritual sovereignty in one's career and relationships, material wealth through "correct" prayer, eternal youth and invincibility. The result is that people with a serious interest in the subject are increasingly hesitant to use the term "esoteric." This reaction is understandable, but we ought to bear in mind that esoteric wisdom itself is in no way responsible for the misuse of the term, just as medicine and religion cannot be held accountable for all the past and present crimes committed in their names. For this reason, I have chosen to continue using all three terms in their original senses here, just as I introduced them in my previous book *Illness as a Language of the Soul*. That book provides a reliable basis for interpreting the esoteric view of the world. Since a close relationship generally exists between symptoms and crises, a basic introduction has already been laid out in *Illness as Path* and *Illness as a Language of the Soul*, and in the corresponding publications about specific symptoms.[1] Conversely, life's unconquered crises often lead to a variety of pathological symptoms. This relationship is obvious from the names of some crises (e.g., puberty acne, puberty anorexia, involution depression, fear of death). However, other health disturbances (e.g., Alzheimer's disease, Parkinson's disease, and other illnesses associated with aging) can only be understood on the basis of a particular life pattern.

PART I

1. The Crisis

The Greek word *crisis* means more than just "crisis." It can also mean decision, divorce, conflict, separation, verdict, choice or test. The Chinese ideogram for "crisis" is identical with the one that signifies both danger and chance. If—as is typical in German and English usage—we limit our understanding of the word "crisis" to its negative aspect, our view of the situation remains correspondingly narrow. In medical contexts, however, the phrase "healing crisis" is sometimes used, and the decisive moment in the events surrounding an illness is referred to as the "crisis." If things go well, the critical moment is followed by the patient's recovery. Thus, the crisis is also the turning point on the path toward wellness. If, like the ancient Greeks, we add the idea of decision to our understanding of the word "crisis," we discover that we have a key to grasping the essence of all crises. By adding the Chinese connotation and understanding that every crisis also represents an opportunity, we can approach a crisis with an eye toward the perspectives it can unveil.

Karl Jaspers' definition also tends in this direction: "In the course of development, 'crisis' describes the moment when the entire situation undergoes a reversal, out of which a person emerges transformed: either revived with the new beginning of a resolution or crestfallen into hopelessness and despair." Jaspers continues, adding an idea that is especially important in this context: "The history of life doesn't proceed at a steady, unchanging pace; it divides its time in qualitative segments and pushes the development of experience to its peak, to a decisive point from which a decision must ensue. Only by resisting development do we make the futile attempt to cling to the moment of decision without actually deciding. In that case, the factual progress of life will decide for us. The crisis has its due time; it cannot be preempted or jumped over. Like everything else in life, it must ripen to maturity. It need not appear as a catastrophe but can, through a quiet process scarcely noticeable from outside, complete itself in an irrevocable decision."

Indeed, every crisis confronts us with an opportunity for choice: either we consciously accept the crisis or we use all our power to fight against it. This is the moment that determines whether a crisis will be a danger or an opportunity. Ancient Chinese thought, although revolving around the notions of yin and yang, can nevertheless discern the unity behind these two opposing possibilities.

Every clinical picture, every complex of symptoms, compels us to make a similar decision. Either we accept its message and transform the crisis into a therapeutic opportunity, or we fight against it and the crisis becomes an acute danger. The genesis of complexes of symptoms also progresses along this same path of decision. As soon as consciousness refuses to accept a challenge, its energy must make a detour into the unconscious. All too often that energy later embodies itself as a complex of symptoms. The original theme is represented symbolically by the individual symptoms. We are constantly deciding between consciously dealing with a crisis or delaying it for later handling under more difficult (because they are cryptic) conditions. Even if we are scarcely aware of having made such a decision because, by force of habit, we have chosen the apparently easier path of denial and suppression, the decisions are constantly being made for us.

As soon as we push a theme out of our conscious awareness and leave our body to deal with it on its own, we automatically create a gap between body and soul. If body and soul become too widely separated, the gap becomes unbearable, and the organism tries to help itself. The person either falls ill or is confronted by a different crisis that offers the chance to make a new decision about the unresolved theme. Both are attempts to bring body and soul together again, either by manifesting an illness or through an event in one's social surroundings. The best way to heal the gap is to consciously understand the drama that is being played out on the stage represented either by one's body or one's surroundings. Close examination of physical, psychological and social crises gives us the chance to interpret all three from the same vantage point, viewing them through the lens of esoteric philosophy. Karl Jaspers said every crisis has its proper time. Thus, if we want to view the crises in a temporal context, we must first occupy ourselves with the basic pattern of life; that is the *mandala*.

2. The Mandala as a Pattern of Life

A mandala is a circular structure whose every part is related to its center. Scientists describe it as possessing rotational symmetry. Many Eastern philosophies assume that the mandala arose from its center and that the entire mandala is contained within the central point. Indeed, one can imagine that a mandala is created by expanding a single point and letting space and time flow into that point.

The sketch depicts the southern rose window at Chartres Cathedral

Thus the mandala has a special role among symbols and images because it integrates all other symbols (and ultimately all of creation) within itself. Everywhere we look, from the smallest to the largest structures, we find mandalas. With its whirling dance of electrons around a motionless nucleus, every atom forms a mandala. This is true whether we choose Niels Bohr's old model or the newer one offered by quantum physics. Since all creation is composed of atoms, mandalas form the basic structure of all matter. The principle of a dance around the midpoint is shared by all atoms, although a striking characteristic of that central point is its uncanny ability to evade our comprehension. Even from a mathematical point of view, the center is not part of our world because the mid*point* has no extension in space and, by definition, cannot have any extension at all. If we were to draw it as a dot, that would already be too much because our depiction extends into space and reaches beyond the limits of the point. A point is one-dimensional and thus, in terms of geometry, is part of the unity. The *Tao Te Ching* describes the hub of the wheel (or rather the void at the center of the hub) as the decisive center around which everything revolves. The mythological dance around the void has been confirmed by our knowledge of the interior of atomic structures. The size of the nucleus is infinitesimal compared to the vastness of the electron cloud. If the latter were the size of St. Peter's Basilica in Rome (the largest church in Christendom), the nucleus would still be no larger than a speck of dust—yet everything revolves around this core, this nothingness.

In the cell, the building block of organic life, we encounter the same mandala structure. Here again, everything revolves around a fundamentally motionless core. All information needed for the life of the diverse cell structures issues from that center. Since all organic life is composed of cells, on this level as well, the mandala is the basis of life. Even in the inorganic realm, we find that many crystals are based on a mandala structure around which the crystal organizes itself.

When we consider the largest structures we have thus far been able to observe, we again discover mandalas. The earth as well as all other planets and celestial bodies correspond to the mandala pattern because each rotates around its motionless center, the point toward which gravity tends. The entire solar system likewise represents a mandala, as does each spiral nebula and the universe as a whole.

The spiral, itself a mandala, brings a special emphasis to the mandala form by stressing the element of motion inherent in mandalas. Everything issues from the center, remains related to that point, and tends back toward it. The universe arose out of its midpoint and will return there someday, as we know from Indian creation myths and, more recently, from the theories of astrophysicists. The life-giving light of the sun reaches us not along a straight path, but also along a spiral route. The spiral is also present in the microcosm, where matter is created. The subatomic particles that physicists observe indirectly in their cloud chambers often follow spiral trajectories. And precisely there, where organic life has its foundations, in the genetic material within the cellular nucleus, we find the double spiral of DNA in the center. The spiral pattern can be discerned at all life's decisive points. It is, therefore, not surprising to find the spiral plays an essential role in conception and death. The descent of the soul into the body is frequently experienced as a spiral movement, a vortex and, as we know from reincarnation therapy, the soul's departure at death follows a spiral path.

From the stupendously gargantuan dimensions of the macrocosm all the way down to the most infinitesimal dimensions of the microcosm, we continually encounter the mandala. In the intermediate regions where we experience our everyday lives, the mandala is also omnipresent. It gazes at us from the calyxes of flowers, from the eyes of animals and our fellow human beings. It whirls within every eddy and every whirlpool, in every tornado and every hurricane. We find it in seashells and snail shells and in every snowflake. When one considers that no two snowflakes nor any two ice crystals are identical, and that all of them are formed according to the same hexagonal pattern of the man-dala, one can begin to grasp its manifold possibilities and the role it plays within the framework of creation. Everything comes from the mandala. Even the Big Bang, as scientists describe it, forms a mandala. The mightiest mountain cliff eventually erodes into grains of sand, and thus into mandalas. Everything arises from the mandalas of atoms, and everything ultimately returns to these same mandalas. Nothing but time, that great illusionist, separates us from the mandala.

If everything is progressing along the path of the mandala, it should come as no surprise that human beings likewise follow this universal pattern. Life in the world of polarity begins to take form in the center of the mandala, in the fertilized egg, itself a mandala. From the boundlessness of free space, the soul is drawn into the narrowness of the body, which initially feels like a prison. The mid*point* of the mandala corresponds to the one-ness, to paradise, where no opposites yet exist. According to the biblical injunction to "have dominion over" the earth, the newly incarnated child strives again and again to get out of the center. Within its mother's womb, the fetus is still very close to the mid-point and thus close to the primal unity. Intimately connected to its mother through the umbilical cord, the embryo is constantly supplied with everything it needs. Its situation is comparable to the imaginary country of luxury and delight known in Medie-val times as the Land of Cockaigne. Through constant growth, the child irrevocably distances itself from this paradise, mov-ing deeper into polarity with each new phase of development. It soon becomes too large for its cozy nest. Painfully, under the pressure of powerful labor pangs, and regardless of whether the child is willing to be born, its mother presses it out of herself and into the world. Its first breaths of air bind it to the polarity of inha-lation and exhalation. The one heart divides itself down the mid-dle, and left and right chambers arise. Thus far its mother has done the breathing for herself and her child, but now the infant must breathe air by its own power. Thus far nourishment flowed automatically through the umbilicus into the child, but now the

8

infant must suck milk by its own power. Although it is still able to nurse, the breast (or bottle) is taken away. Once it is weaned, the baby takes yet another outwardly directed step toward polarity. It is still spoon-fed, but this too comes to an end and the child must feed itself. It then leaves the security of Mother Earth (whom it has thus far gotten to know while crawling on its belly) and learns to stand on its hind legs. Standing erect propels it into a fragile balance and hence still further into the insecurity of polarity. With its first "No!" the child continues on this path and begins to exclude things, a process that ultimately creates the shadows and oppositions whose contrasts cause polarity to appear in even sharper distinction.

With the advent of puberty, the young person has come a long way from the center of the mandala, thus putting an end to the relatively neutral existence of childhood. The (grammatically neutral) child must die so the (grammatically female) woman or (grammatically male) man can live. Cutting the ties to its parents after a successful adolescence is a further step toward independence, and the tensions of life constantly increase. Searching for her "better half" (a colloquial and accurate expression for one's spouse) often further exacerbates these tensions. With marriage and the founding of one's own family, the adult individual takes on added responsibilities and heavier burdens, but also experiences greater opportunities. Polarity is now tangibly evident. Things do not seem to be going the way one wishes. More and more often, the shadow rears its head to interfere with even the most positively intended enterprises. All other efforts to get a grip on life and "have dominion" over the earth only increase the tension and responsibilities. If a person succeeds in amassing much wealth, he has no choice but to administrate it and keep guard over it, thus increasing the tension still further.

Finally, at the periphery of the mandala, the point of irrevocable return is reached. The only possible step forward is, paradoxically, a step back. Even if most of us nowadays try to ignore or leap over it, the fact remains that this ultimate limit of life's pattern cannot be overcome. No human being nor any other creature has ever left life's pattern except through its central point. All attempts to cling to the periphery and deny the pattern of life's path are doomed to fail in one way or another, in debacles that range from spectacular to simple. At this point, Christ's words in Matthew 18:3 become especially significant: "Except ye be converted, and become as little children, ye shall not enter into the kingdom of heaven." At this juncture, all roads lead homeward, toward the center of the mandala, toward a leave-taking from polarity, into the unity of death. Every attempt during midlife to cling to the outer edge of the mandala is a hopeless effort to work against life, a senseless waste of energy in spasmodic and hopeless actions.

Since the goal of the path is the center, and thus also death, people who do not believe in the rhythm of life and death tend to have the greatest fear here. They do everything they can to avoid this point. Since that is obviously impossible, they at least try to avoid facing the facts, and thus our society allows death to degenerate into a miserable sham. Cultures (e.g., Tibetan culture) that put the mandala in its rightful place at the center of existence realize that death and conception are one and the same gateway, a portal that is simply passed through from two different directions.

The great religions use this basic pattern of all life as an illustration of life's path. The Christian religion immortalized it in Gothic architecture's magnificent rose windows. The parable of the Prodigal Son relates to it as well. The father, symbolizing God and the unity, lives with his two sons on his farm. When one of the sons rebels, demands his inheritance and renounces his father, the old man reluctantly agrees and allows him to go off into the world. The son leaves the center of the mandala and eagerly turns his steps toward its periphery. He falls into every imaginable variety of difficulty, gambling and carousing until he has spent his entire inheritance, until he finally sinks to the level of a mere swineherd. Only then does he remember his father and the unity he left behind. He returns home, where his father receives him with open arms. The father prepares a great feast to welcome the prodigal son, which angers the apparently "good" son who never left home. No one prepared a feast to reward him. This can be readily understood, however, from the perspective of the mandala. Why should a stay-at-home who has never left the nest be rewarded for his lack of courage? Every nestling must someday dare to leave the nest and try to live on its own. The reassuring thing about this parable is that we need only *try* (knowing it is all right to fail) as long as we remember the path and return, sooner or later, to our father and to the unity he represents.

Buddhism and Hinduism venerate the mandala much more explicitly. They build their temples on mandala-shaped floor plans, and consciously describe life's path as a mandala. They represent it in its classical form with four entry gates, each facing one of the four cardinal directions, along with a symbol of unity at its midpoint. This expresses the idea that there are many paths to the single goal in the one pattern. The Eastern description of the path "from here to here," which has been frequently misunderstood by people who assume it gives them an excuse to remain where they are and not evolve, finds its meaning and explanation in the mandala. The path leads from the middle to the middle or, to express it even more clearly, from the unconsciously lived middle to the consciously sought middle.

Myths and fairy tales likewise know about this universal pattern, and illustrate it in their own ways. The life of the hero Odysseus describes a complete pilgrimage through the mandala. Odysseus' journey to Troy represents the outward path. His victory occurs during midlife, and all the adventures recounted in the *Odyssey* illustrate his homeward journey to Penelope, his "better half."

Parzival, hero of the Grail, is kept at home (in the nest) for too long by his mother Herzeloide. She has already had bad experiences out in the wide world, where she lost her husband, Parzival's father Gahmuret. She dresses her only son in girl's clothes and gives him an education that does not prepare him for venturing into the outside world. But as soon as Parzival sees

11

his first knight, he turns his back on the maternal nest. He must pay his dues out there, where he commits error after error. He senselessly slays the red knight Itter and, when he comes to the Castle of the Grail, he cannot pose the redeeming question (whose answer is the shadow "What do you lack, Uncle?") because his mother has taught him never to ask questions. Only when he has reached the lowest point, and descended into hopelessness and desperation, does the return route appear to him. In *Excalibur*, John Boorman's film version of the tale, the redeeming answer that saves the realm that has fallen into agony is: "The king and his country are one." The king as symbol of unity represents the midpoint of the mandala and is identical with his realm, the field of the mandala, which can only develop from its midpoint and is unimaginable without it.

Typical fairy tale heroes (or heroines) must leave home, and thus also leave the midpoint of the mandala. This departure is frequently made easier for them by the presence of a cruel stepmother or loveless parents. The (male) protagonist must complete his tasks in the world in order to earn his anima, his feminine side. Once he has found, won and integrated that side of himself, the hero returns to his father's realm, where everyone lives happily ever after. This typical denouement indicates that we are dealing not with historical events, but timeless ones.

By way of summary, we can conclude that the stories told in myths, fairy tales and parables are meant as aids to help make life's pattern clearer and align us with that pattern. Because we modern people so often ignore these aids and forget the mandala as a fundamental map of the soul, we make it very difficult for ourselves to find our path in life, and especially difficult to progress along the transitional steps on that path.

All evolution occurs from one stage to another, in steps and phases, not smoothly and continuously as some evolutionary researchers (many of whom are still working and thinking in Darwin's shadow) would have us believe. It is no coincidence: there is a reason for so many missing links in the chain of evolutionary theory. Evolution happens in leaps. Ancient civilizations had rites of transition for each of these leaps.

3. Rituals as Keys to New Phases in Life

Enlightened Westerners are blithely unaware of a scarcity of rituals. Just the opposite, in fact: they tend to be glad civilization has finally freed them from such superstitions. Such individuals are liable to be surprised when they take a closer look at modern life and discover it contains just as many rituals as ancient life. The essential difference lies only in the degree of awareness. Although we continue to perform a wide variety of rituals, we are seldom aware of the fact. Anyone who has watched people leaving their cars at a large parking lot can observe an astonishing diversity of rituals related to security and closure. Even drivers whose cars are equipped with automatic locking systems conscientiously check each door, just to make sure it is indeed securely locked. Other drivers repeatedly return to the site of their "compulsive locking behavior." Still others circumambulate their vehicle, while others look over their shoulders ten times *just to be sure*. Similar rituals take place when people leave their homes to go on vacation. They check and double check everything, according to the old adage, "Better safe than sorry." Anyone who has ever watched adult human beings in a pedestrian-only zone has no doubt seen some who step only on the intersections of the pavement slabs, while others studiously avoid stepping on the cracks and carefully place their feet only in the middle of each slab. Among train travelers, we can find some who doggedly count each post as at rushes past the window. Others compulsively read every billboard and every advertising poster from start to finish. Other individuals have special washing rituals. Some make their toilet seats into veritable thrones, at which they celebrate impressive "letting-go" rituals. If, while away from home, foreign hygienic amenities (or the lack thereof) preclude the execution of any aspect of this familiar performance, the leading actor simply refuses to "let go," passing the remainder of the vacation in consternation and constipation. Some people have developed an especially elaborate cleansing ritual for themselves, others a corresponding rite of purification for their car. Still others unconsciously mark their territory by repeatedly touching particular corners and edges. Et cetera, et cetera, et cetera.

Alongside relatively harmless, yet unconscious and frequently annoying behaviors, there is also a wide range of rituals reaching levels that can only be described as pathological. A trained eye will have little trouble diagnosing a compulsive personality in our society. For many people, compulsive illness makes life a compulsively organized and repeatedly controlled hell. Anyone who feels compelled to perform hand washing more than a hundred times each day, and who experiences severe anxiety when the ritual is not performed, is suffering from a severe handicap. Such individuals are victims of a compulsive washing ritual whose real object is obviously not external dirt since the first ablution no doubt sufficiently removed any material impurities. Dirt and perhaps also blood perceived to be clinging to one's hands are the real issue. Within the framework of reincarnation therapy, the sources of such cleansing rituals can often be understood as originating from old, incomplete rituals that, once comprehended, can ultimately be released. No matter how effective the soaps or detergents, no exterior cleansing can possibly bring relief from compulsive washing disorders of this sort.

The various kinds of cleaning and scrubbing compulsions are similar. Whether it is a compulsion to cleanse one's body or one's surroundings, or a futile attempt to keep "everything under control," a disorder of this sort can become so severe it seriously interferes with one's daily life. Security rituals that were interrupted and never completed in the distant past are frequently found at the root of control compulsions. The unconscious attempt to repair the past by bizarrely controlling and checking irrelevant things cannot bring relief as long as the roots of the issue remain in the dark. Compulsive counting, for example, is often an indication of derailed ordering rituals, while compulsive religious behavior can result from failed rituals and bygone transgressions of the rules of a monastic order.

Other typical symptoms of compulsive behavior are the anxiety and fear that immediately arise whenever the ritual is not performed. While today's sufferers themselves inflict the punishment, in the original situation the sufferers often avoided the prescribed punishment for failing to perform or interfering with a particular ritual. Now they feel it is important to perform their compulsive rituals in secret—quite possibly because this was the manner in which the earlier rituals were conducted. Viewed from this perspective, we can recognize ill-performed rituals as the real source of a variety of neurotic symptoms. If we admit that almost no one is entirely free of neurotic characteristics, it seems likely that our enlightened, modern society is, in fact, nothing but a new and sicker form of the old ritualized community.

We need not rely solely on the psychiatric viewpoint to reach this conclusion. Nowadays we can readily find many socially significant rituals. Our system of justice is a prime example. Ever since its earliest beginnings, rituals have been an integral part of jurisprudence. Why would the (mostly male) judges wear ritualistic robes and sometimes even special wigs if they were not trying to slip into the symbolic role of the goddess Justitia? Why is one compelled to rise from one's seat and stand when the venerable judge enters the court? Why are all the rules conducted with such solemn, ritualized severity? Why can't a judge allow the defendant to remain seated?

The world of medicine likewise includes a wide variety of il-logical structures and rules that can only be understood from the viewpoint of ritual. Such rules are often defended with pe-culiar and sometimes false arguments. Because of some vague premonition (perhaps most inscrutable to the scientists them-selves), these illogical structures are steadfastly preserved.[1]

Ritualized structures are also found in businesses and in the palatial halls of government, at official visits by statesmen and politicians, at formal events and negotiations, in front of our bathroom mirrors every morning, and when we sit down to eat or get ready for bed. Why else would we seal a deal with a hand-shake? Monetary transactions, the backbone of our society, are ultimately a magical game of numbers played in a largely ritual-ized manner. Traffic on the streets, that loved and hated child of our mobile, industrialized society, follows strictly ritualized rules. We obey those rules, not because they are logical, but because "they are as they are." There is not a shred more logic to driv-ing on the right side of the road rather than on the left, but it is awfully dangerous to disobey the ritual and refuse to conform with its rules.

It is obvious: in the majority of important and less important areas of life, we use and need rituals. We tend to be unaware of all but a few of these rituals, even when they are as obvious as those associated with Justitia. Although we are mostly un-aware of them, they are effective nevertheless. There seems to be some mechanism inside us that urges us to unconsciously seek and find ersatz rituals to replace those we have discontin-ued or allowed to deteriorate.

We can readily identify the real issue by examining our own culture's ancient rituals. The seven sacraments of the Catho-lic Church, for example, are intended to accompany us at life's critical junctures. As their name implies, sacraments are holy acts with the goal of making human beings hale, whole and, ultimately, holy. The sacrament of **baptism** hallows us with water and inducts us into (Christian) life. As an encounter with Christ through His flesh (the communion wafer) and blood (the

17

sacramental wine), **first communion** allows us full access to the congregation of the faithful. This full participation is marked by our now being permitted to receive communion. **Confirmation** strengthens our contact with the Holy Ghost. Blessed by God, the sacrament of **marriage** hallows our partnership with another human being, while **ordination** to the priesthood hallows our partnership with God. **Extreme unction** prepares—unofficially in any case—the transition into the otherworld. At critical moments between these cardinal points in life, the sacrament of **confession** offers spiritual relief; it disburdens us of guilt and corresponds to a classical rite of purification. At least that was the original intent of confession, although it has all too often degenerated into an instrument of discipline and punishment.[2] But ignoring that aspect of it, confession still offers a chance to receive absolution for errors along the path of one's life, thus offering the soul welcome relief. Confession, in fact, is the original Christian ritual of return. One settles one's accounts, explains things and experiences *metanoia*, a turning around of one's attitudes that, in the Catholic context, is interpreted as rue or regret. In Germany, the seven sacraments gave life a ritualistic framework—at least until the Christian culture stopped linking people together and we stopped being a *cult*ure because we no longer shared in a binding cult.

Because we have devalued these rites of transition or allowed them to deteriorate, it stands to reason that a variety of ersatz rituals have arise to take their place. But as we have seen in our examination of compulsive rituals, ersatz rituals do not satisfactorily fulfill their intended functions. Despite constant repetition, they fall far behind their ancient models and seldom or never lead to the desired liberating effect. This phenomenon is even more obvious when we consider modern puberty rites. While a youth in a tribal culture needed to pass a test of courage only once in order to become an adult, in our society even hundreds of "dares" are unable to make an adult of the youth. To begin to unravel the mystery of all this, we need to look more closely at the background and structure of rituals.

Rituals and Their Effects

Actual lived experience provides the simplest access to ritual. But such experience has become problematic for people in our era, with its dogmatic faith in science, since science has thus far been unable to explain the efficacy of rituals. The official natural sciences cannot even offer us a promising intellectual approach. Jürg von Ins, whose dissertation deals with rituals from a scientific point of view, says, "Those who step across the threshold and enter ritualistic reality simultaneously step down from the throne of scientific objectivity."[3] Even if enthroned science can discover no access to them, scientists must nevertheless admit that there can be no reasonable doubt that profound effects can be achieved by ritualistic means. For example, by ritually exiling a member of the tribe who has broken a taboo, a shaman can effectively sentence the transgressor to death. Even when the banished individual is in perfect health, the exile usually dies within a few hours after the expulsion. Similar events have been documented in the context of voodoo and related religions. On the other hand, healings through rituals have been so thoroughly documented in diverse times and places that even scientists can no longer deny their existence. Ritual healings of this sort have also been frequently documented in Christian contexts (e.g., at Lourdes, where the events were observed under strict, scientifically controlled conditions).

The explanation that comes closest to a model acceptable to scientific thought derives from Rupert Sheldrake's discovery of morphogenetic fields.[4] Sheldrake put his own scientific discipline (biology) to the test. He devised a variety of experiments in his search for scientific explanations for a number of scientifically incomprehensible phenomena. In the course of his research, he discovered a series of phenomena that, although peculiarly inexplicable, nonetheless seemed to share a common logic. In one experiment, intended to determine whether or not learned behavior is heritable, scientists trained rats to quickly find their way out of a maze. The scientists crossbred the rats with one another and discovered that the untrained, second-generation rats were able to escape from the labyrinth just as quickly as their trained parents. The experiment seemed to prove that learned behavior can be inherited. Other scientists in another part of the world did not believe the results, so they repeated the experiment themselves. Using an identical maze, these scientists were astonished to find that their rats, even without prior training, escaped from this labyrinth with the same speed as the trained first-generation rats and untrained second-generation rats in the earlier experiment. The experiment was repeated frequently and the rats gradually improved their speed each successive time. The results were consistently remarkable: the world's laboratory rats were all endowed with the same level of skill, even though no conventional means of communication allowed them to share their knowledge with one another. In some logically and causally incomprehensible manner, they must be communicating with one another since the entire world community of laboratory rats all shares the same knowledge. (The Latin word *communis*, the root of both "communication" and "community," means "together.") After collecting a large number of other astonishing results, Sheldrake formulated his theory of morphogenetic (form-giving) fields that communicate information over vast distances without relying on material structures and without obeying the laws of time.

A similarly astonishing result comes from the annals of Russian military research. To test a communications system they hoped would be able to transmit and receive sensitive military information without being vulnerable to eavesdropping or jamming, the Soviets devised a brutal experiment. Shortly after their birth, baby rabbits were taken from their mother and put aboard submarines stationed in widely separated parts of the world. At predetermined times, the babies were killed and physiological tests were conducted on the mother animal. The data clearly showed that the mother was somehow able to sense the precise moment when one of her offspring was killed. Here again, it seems there must be some kind of connection that requires neither a material link between the communicators nor any time for the instantaneous relay of information. A discovery of this sort simply does not fit within conventional biology's scientific conception of the world.

In the human species, so-called "coenaesthetic" perception between mothers and their newborn infants represents a similar phenomenon. Even while asleep, mothers react to the slightest acoustic signals uttered by their babies, even when much louder noises from other sources go unheard. The American researcher Conden used highly sensitive, slow-motion videotapes to prove that when people are communicating they are linked to one another through so-called micromovements. Although visible in the film, these tiny movements are not consciously perceived by the communicators. Rather than reacting to what they were hearing from their interlocutors, the people were moving together simultaneously and harmoniously. The same patterns of instantaneous movement in unison have been observed in videotapes of all people except autistic children.

According to conventional scientific theories, none of these phenomena can possibly exist, yet all of them have been undeniably documented. Sheldrake proposed the idea of immaterial fields that communicate information and patterns. Although he offered no logical explanation for their existence, he nonetheless provided a description and a framework.

The idea that fields or images structure our reality helps explain a number of other previously incomprehensible phenomena. Many embryological observations, for example, can be more readily explained. Why do cells in artificial cultures grow wildly and without limits, while the same kinds of cells grow within their accustomed bounds when implanted into their appropriate tissues and organs? It would seem that the artificial culture does not supply them with the image or plan for the finished structure. The same idea also helps explain why saturated chemical solutions often do not crystallize, but do begin to crystallize explosively as soon as a single crystal is added to serve as a model.

21

The effectiveness of high-potency homeopathic medicines can also be understood according to this theory, as can the ability of inoculations to prevent illness, even when those inoculations took place so long ago that no antibodies can be found in the body of the immune individual. As in homeopathy, here too it seems that the presence of even a single antibody suffices as a model or as information. Once an image has been manifested in the world, it can obviously have effects that can influence the material realm—in a way that has thus far not been explained and that seems to subvert the laws of time since the ideas can be effective everywhere simultaneously. The mystery seems to lie in the in*form*ation: information carries contents across the *form* of time. An analogy is the plan for a house. In some cases, the plan exists nowhere except in the mind of the builder. Yet without the plan, the house cannot be built, even though the plan itself is entirely immaterial and never enters directly into the construction. It exists from the beginning to the end and is simultaneously effective in all parts of the house.

Sheldrake and his theory may well compel biology to take a step that the new physics took around the turn of 20th century when it abandoned causality in favor of synchronicity. Back then, physicists discovered that infinitesimal, so-called "phase-locked" particles (i.e., particles derived from the same event and from the same source) always appear in pairs and behave like mirror images of one another. If a scientist influences the attributes of one particle, its partner also changes correspondingly, even though nothing was done to directly influence the situation of that second particle. Each member of the pair does everything necessary to preserve the mirror-image relationship. As if that were not inexplicable enough, the discovery that the corresponding changes occur immediately, without allowing even an instant of time to pass, put a final end to the causal worldview of the old physics. Conventional means of communicating information simply could not explain the phenomena. At this point, many physicists abandoned their resistance to the dawning new worldview, accepted synchronicity as a determinative principle able to account for phenomena that causality could no longer explain. The Englishman John Bell proved this was not only valid for subatomic events, but was also true of the entire universe in general. If, as astrophysicists believe, the cosmos began in a single explosion (the Big Bang), then all its particles must be linked in a synchronous context. This, in turn, brings us to the realizations described by the Hindu Vedas and the Buddhist sutras that likewise assert that everything in creation is related to everything else and that this relationship is not causal, but synchronous.

Using these ideas as a basis, we can also explain the effects of patterns. Rituals begin by constructing fields that are existent and effective without material connections and that are independent of time. Each field obviously becomes stronger every time its corresponding ritual is conducted and precisely repeated. The energetic charge that arises from awareness no doubt plays an important role, as well. By means of consciousness, the ritual is constantly recreated within its predefined framework and, as we know from modern physics, every conscious perception influences that which is perceived. This explains why rituals we have borrowed from foreign cultures frequently have little or no effect on us. We cannot really perceive them because they are not yet real for us. At first we often lack the skills needed to conduct them precisely; the key does not quite fit the lock, and thus the door to the efficacious level remains unopened. Furthermore, the amplification that ensues through generations of repetition is also missing when we try to transplant a foreign ritual. Finally, the conscious charge is often impossible to achieve because the ritual's symbols evoke no resonance in the participants. It seems we have a natural access to the basic symbols of the culture into which we have been born. We find it easier to recognize and comprehend our culture's own symbols, and they alone are able to evoke that inner vibration in us that is essential to the efficacy of any ritual. Much time and a long process are necessary before we can create the necessary inner relationships that allow us to feel the potency of foreign symbols and patterns. In most cases, we do not spend enough time with foreign rituals simply because (at least at the beginning) they do not seem to produce the desired results.

The first step in the construction of a new field is always *the hardest step*, as the saying goes, and everyone knows the truth of that adage from personal experience. Once the field has been established, however, it becomes endowed with an impressive stability. Our first attempts to swim in a new, watery element are difficult, but once we have learned to swim, we remain swimmers for the rest of our lives. Even if we have not swum for ten years or more, the ability to swim is somehow, somewhere stored within us. The interesting question is this: Where is the skill stored? Not a single cell in our body survives from ten years ago; all of them have been exchanged for younger cells, and metabolism has even replaced all the building blocks within our nerve cells. Yet the pattern called "swimming" survives intact, without a material basis and relatively independent of the elapsed time. The time factor plays a partial, but ultimately subordinate, role—although if we refrain from swimming for many decades, the pattern does fade somewhat. A similar fading takes place with rituals that have not been performed (or not been consciously performed) for many years.

Awareness is the energy that fuels the ritualistic motor. This, too, corresponds to our experiences in daily life. A sequence of actions performed with a great deal of attention and awareness can be learned much more quickly than a sequence that is merely "aped," (i.e., mechanically imitated). But even imitative aping can result in reliable and enduring patterns, not only among the furry apes, but also among us "naked apes." Our actions quite obviously influence our inner reality as well as the external reality surrounding us. The influence on the inner world is clear in all learned skills; the influence on the outer world is evident in many other situations. No doubt it is a result of the collective field that (at least in Germany) the majority of people are most adept at the breast stroke and associate only that style of swimming with the word "swimming," even though the crawl stroke is a far more efficient style of swimming. People who have no experience with meditation, and even those who are not religious at all, are nonetheless able to feel the field that has been established within a temple or cathedral that has been used for many years and by many people exclusively for prayer and meditation.

The more coordinated and uniform our actions are, the stronger and more lasting are the impressions they make upon us, and the clearer and more enduring are their corresponding fields. As we saw in the swimming example, long-lasting fields are established only after a certain degree of awareness has been achieved and after a certain number of repetitions have been performed. It is difficult for us to define threshold values for these parameters because, especially in areas related to energy and the soul, we actually know much less than the average "primitive" medicine man or woman. It seems the point is reached only after the pattern has become *part of our flesh and blood*, as the saying goes. Fields only become natural and enduring after we no longer need to occupy ourselves with them on an intellectual level (i.e., only when we have the experience that *it* swims or drives our car, naturally and effortlessly). Neither this "it" nor the feeling of naturalness can be spatially localized. Fields are as much inside us as we are inside them. Since they remain spatially and temporally indeterminate, they are everywhere and nowhere simultaneously.[5] Nevertheless, one can enter a field much the way one enters a room, or plug oneself into a field much the way one plugs an appliance into an electrical socket. Whenever there is an affinity to them, wherever contact is made with them, they are effective. Likewise, when no one pays attention to them, they are often overlooked. It would be naive to claim that because no one notices them, they do not exist. That would be like a person who never used a radio denying the existence of radio programs. It would be more correct to say they do not exist for *that person* because she *has no antenna* for them.

In this way, each person lives in his own field. The tribesman who believes survival is impossible outside the tribe experiences exile as death. Perhaps we, too, only die at the end of our lives because death is what our reality field prescribes as taking place at life's conclusion. The fact that cells age is an argument from an entirely different and obviously lower level of reality. Cells obediently die in the body of the otherwise young and formerly healthy tribesman. We feel poorly after committing a misdeed because we are in conflict with our fields. Individuals differ in the degree to which these fields are more or less strongly influential on their lives and feelings. Conscience becomes active here, stepping in at precisely those moments when we have violated a pattern in our field.

Education sometimes consciously aims to create fields or attempts to instill the notion of a conscience. When a youth is growing up in a family of academicians, he is repeatedly asked, "*What* do you want to study when you go to college?" The question is never posed, "*Do* you want to go to college at all?" After a certain time has elapsed, the field called "going to college" begins to exist for this young person. Frequently this results from the parents' unconscious intention to prevent their offspring from even beginning to harbor unacceptable options. To a certain degree, we are all aware of how strongly our own expectations influence reality. Psychologists use the expression "self-fulfilling prophecy" to describe the fact that some people unconsciously behave in ways that ensure that prophesies come true in their lives. Once again we are witnessing the effects of a field when we see how someone with a strong personality can use the power of suggestion to influence other's minds. Every form of impression is also a step toward the formation of such a field.

Influencing is a well-known and much feared issue in therapeutic contexts. Academic psychologists go to great lengths to avoid influencing their clients, sometimes leading to clumsy attempts at so-called "non-directive" procedures. Ultimately, however, every form of psychotherapy is also a form of influencing—from both sides of the proverbial couch. It is basically a flowing together of energies. The only question is: How aware is the therapist that energies are mutually influential? Therapy creates a field, within which, ideally, a step toward healing is possible. Therapists know from experience that the right "vibes" are extremely important. They know therapy is much easier in a room where plenty of good therapy has already taken place, and they are aware of the role played by proper timing in the life of the patient, in their own lives, and even the time of day. All these factors influence the establishment of the therapeutic field, as well as apparently minor factors (i.e., the appropriate fragrance and relaxing music). The proper framework facilitates access to deeper layers of the soul, thus making it easier and safer to take evolutionary steps forward.

Intact Ritual Worlds

The rituals of archaic cultures provide a good preparation. They tend to place much emphasis on the establishment of proper surroundings. What we describe as "festive" or "ceremonial" they express as a matter of course through outward acts and inner attitudes. Outer and inner preparations are given the space they need and can thus create a safe and secure framework. Frequently lengthy dances and chants enhance inward focus to the point of trance. By painting their bodies and faces, through the use of masks and special clothing, priests and participants in the ritual outwardly manifest their awareness of the special temporal quality and the expected inner events. All of this occurs in service to the ritual itself—the pattern that all participants are acting together to endow with vital expression.

So-called "primitives" never feel the need to create something new or unique in the sense of an artwork. Their only goal is the imitation of already existent fields and the vivification of living, yet invisible, structures. In the most profound sense, they experience a repetition of the primal situation in the present moment, a kind of new creation. They never feel themselves to be the creators, but experience themselves as witnesses of creation. For them, everything is alive and already given, and they are fully occupied and satisfied with recognizing and participating in this lively pattern in each passing moment. Since they are authentically experiencing the *primo*rdial event in this very moment, they can never suffer from the boredom we moderns tend to feel during repetitious activities. Neither do they need written notes or written history. Rather than wanting to preserve the memory of some particular, unique, historical event, they are far more interested in lending vital expression to the eternal changes. Rituals are the most essential option for emphasizing and easing the progress through special moments in time (e.g., transitions from one level to the next). In everyday events as well as events of major importance, ritual offers them a possibility to give the event its appropriate framework and to integrate it in its corresponding pattern.

The enormous advantage for each individual member of the tribe lies in the fact that each person need not encounter problems of transition as personal difficulties, but can understand them as necessary steps in life. Ritual helps the tribal person generalize individual experiences, and thus integrate both the experiences and the individual in the cosmic order. Whereas youths at puberty or adults at midlife and menopause often imagine they are all alone with these anxiety-producing, concept-shattering problems, tribal people know that all these stages and transitions are integral parts of life and that everything is, in fact, entirely *in order*.

Another advantage of the conscious handling of rituals lies in the fact that, when a ritual is conducted in a well-targeted way, it can relieve much of the burden that otherwise falls upon parents and the community. Whereas in our culture, pubescent young people must create their own monsters for the necessary "battle with the dragon" (often putting their own parents in that thankless role), indigenous youths are offered the needed demons in the appropriate, traditional form. They need not use drugs to help them stage their death on the one level and their resurrection on the next. Insofar as drugs are necessary at all, indigenous youths are given the proper psychedelic substances

28

within the secure framework of their cult and undergo thorough spiritual and physical preparations in the competent hands of their shamans. They are thus never in danger of becoming addicted, but instead have the chance to switch over to the next stage of development.

As far as reality (with and without psychoactive substances) is concerned, an example from our own childhood may be helpful. Many children experience the pre-Christmas visit by Santa Claus in an impressive parental staging, one that seldom has lasting effects on their souls. If this ritual is not conducted and the children begin, as part of their role-playing, to improvise a ritual of their own, it will not have the same effectiveness and will merely reveal their need to experience a visit from heaven.

With respect to rituals of transition, adults have long since slipped into the role of needy children. Modern people experience the upheavals in their lives without the help of community, frequently in oppressive solitude. The nearest approximations to dealing with transitional situations come from attempts made in the therapeutic scene. Within the framework of reincarnation therapy, for example, it is possible to work with ancient rituals and participate directly in their effective fields, experiencing the corresponding emotions and feelings, and ultimately letting go of them. In this context, the American psychologist Paul Rebilot[6] has specialized on the issue of the modern hero journey and its rituals.

Healing Rituals

When a member of a tribe falls out of the cosmic order and falls victim to an accident or illness, a healing ritual is necessary. This is nothing other than an attempt to close the gap that the event has caused between the afflicted individual and the existing order. Just as a wound is closed by bringing the two edges of the wound together and closing the incision, the same action is performed in a transferred sense. Of course, the medicine woman or shaman does not rely solely on personal experience, but calls upon all possible higher powers for help in performing the act of restoring order or reunifying the sundered parts. Insofar as the healer is able to feel and perceive the fields that are important in his tribe's world, to that same degree the healer will be able to intervene. She does so through symbolic acts that are the appropriate means on the transferred level and that correspond to closing the edges of a wound in the physical body. Good healers have a highly sensitive "feel" that enables them to know just how far they are permitted to intervene. They say that they leave the decision to the spirits; we would say the decision is based on intuition or inspiration. Even when dealing with a physical wound, it can sometimes be dangerous simply to close the incision because that can increase the likelihood of infection. Only a clean wound is ready to be stitched closed. Similarly, only certain problems are ready to be smoothed over while others require an extra measure of attention and care.

Even though the participants in such rituals do not interpret the acts in an intellectual sense, they nevertheless become aware of how the event fits into their lives and what it is trying to tell them. It is almost impossible to imagine a significant event that is without meaning for archaic people. The only question is: Can we discover its meaning? Since these people always feel themselves to be under the wing of the Great Spirit or a comparable divine power, nothing that happens to them can be the result of accident or random chance. Archaic people spontaneously feel that *fate* is *slated*, that destiny is meaningful and related to their own growth. This whole structure and the faith grounded in the structure can often be the source of impressive healings.

Furthermore, archaic societies take it for granted that, on a higher but parallel level, the hierarchy of the tribe corresponds to the hierarchy of the gods. Just as the chief is the highest authority in mundane matters and the shaman is the utmost authority in religious affairs, so too the highest god is believed to possess all-encompassing competence. Hierarchy here is understood in its original sense as "rule by the sacred." Whenever something on earth falls away from its proper place in the world order, the shaman contacts a higher power in the divine hierarchy because things are still in order on that sublime plane. Orienting himself to this divine model, the shaman must try to restore the harmony between above and below. The idea that above corresponds to below should be familiar to Christians since the Lord's Prayer contain the words, "Thy will be done, on earth as it is in heaven." This viewpoint not only corresponds to ancient cultures that were consciously based on rituals, but also accords with the basic tenet of esoteric philosophy, "As above, so below." In recent years, even the austere eyes of natural scientists have begun to grant more respect to worldviews of this sort, especially since physics (as the most advanced scientific discipline) has discovered that the highest laws we are able to detect today are the laws of symmetry. Upper and lower levels that symmetrically mirror one another are the basis of both archaic and religious worldviews alike.

Looking at the whole situation from a psychological point of view, we could transfer all its events to the stage of the inner world, thus making it more easily comprehensible to Westerners. When Christians say the Kingdom of God is within, or when Buddhists say the outer world is a reflection of the inner world, they imply that everything occurs inside of us. Shamans, we could say, contact higher planes inside them and get the correct advice and inspiration there. Ultimately, and in accordance with the law of polarity,[7] both ideas are equally valid. What one's own point of view leads one to expect will be confirmed in the reality of one's own fields.

For healing rituals, it is very helpful if the healer is well-acquainted with the illness, although this familiarity can be entirely different from the sort we would likely expect. Whereas we assume that modern medicine men and women should be familiar with everything known about all the many ailments and their symptoms, people in archaic cultures believed it was much more important for the healer to have personally journeyed to the ailment, and become thoroughly acquainted with that sickness. Although this may seem unfamiliar to us, it is, in fact, entirely logical. If we were planning a trip, say, to Egypt, wouldn't we expect a guide who had already been there and who could lead our journey from personal experience to be more reliable than a guide who had read much about the country and who, full of dead knowledge, felt himself called to lead us through a foreign land?

To consider illness as a field of consciousness makes sense, and not solely in the context of archaic thought. Who among us can seriously doubt that illnesses have a consciousness-transforming quality? Who can doubt that illnesses can completely transform the way we feel about life? Some patients clearly feel how much they owe a new worldview to an illness they have overcome. If we assume illness represents a realm of consciousness all its own, then we can understand why shamans-in-training sometimes almost look forward to their initiatory illness, knowing that it will provide them with access to their field of work and that it has important things to teach them.

It is obvious that an attitude of this sort bestows a positive dimension upon illness, a dimension with which we are largely unfamiliar. When we admit that, along with its role as an expression of unconsciousness in general, an illness can serve as an initiation into a new field of tasks in life (as is the attitude of many ancient cultures and the basic approach described in *Illness as a Language of the Soul*), then our own personal attitude, as well as the attitude taken by society as a whole toward this issue, is bound to change. Sick people would no longer be isolated and shoved toward the fringes of society, but would be treated with respect and admiration since they are the ones with whom fate has chosen to come into special contact, whom destiny has focused itself upon in special and unmistakable ways. This attitude explains a phenomenon that is otherwise difficult for us to understand—namely, the particularly high level of respect shown in certain cultures to epileptics, mentally ill or handicapped people.

Rituals of Initiation

The essential difference between initiatory rituals and the various healing rituals lies in the fact that, in the former, the finger of fate comes not from above, but from the tribe and from the medicine men and women themselves. Responsibility for injuries or symptoms of illness occurring during the initiatory ritual lies in the hands of the shamans. Although, of course, fate plays a role here too by providing signs of physical and spiritual maturity that clearly show a change is due, it is essentially up to the specific individuals who are called upon to ensure that the necessary caesura is accomplished.

Viewed in this context, we can understand why the healer, shaman or medicine man sometimes actually harms the initiate. During the initiation into adult life, ritualistic measures presage the harshness that awaits the initiate in the adult field of consciousness. Sometimes the initiate receives physical injuries such as circumcision, a rite that also plays a role in cultures (e.g., the Jewish culture) that are more similar to Christianity. Other initiatory events include deliberately induced wounds or hair-raising tests of courage (e.g., being bound and forced to stand atop an anthill; being buried up to the neck and made victim to all sorts of insects; being exiled from the tribal community and made to spend extended periods of time in the terrifying realm of the wilderness, in trees or in isolated caves; being deliberately frightened by simulated nocturnal attacks by ghosts; and countless other similarly gruesome events).

These wounds, whether material or metaphorical, create the necessary caesura in life and bring the initiates into contact with the new level of consciousness that physical maturity has been preparing for them. The shaman then rushes to the scene and uses active or passive symbolic means to help the young people reconcile themselves with that new level of consciousness. Thus, in its second phase, the initiatory ritual is largely identical with the healing ritual. The interruption of continuity, the caesura,

33

comes from the shaman rather than from fate. In its structure and framework, the subsequent ritual of reconciliation with the new level fully corresponds with the structure and framework of the healing ritual. The task is to close the gap that natural processes of growth and maturation have opened between the old childhood consciousness and the incipient adult consciousness. Deliberately inflicted wounds also symbolize the unholy that will now be experienced. The hale and whole world of childhood, a kind of paradise, has been lost and must be left behind. Certain pains and anxieties are entirely normal here, and these are given their due place and time.

The enormous effect of fields of consciousness that are borne communally by all members of the tribe becomes especially evident after the conclusion of the ritual. Because the young people truly participate in the initiation, they become part of the adult world without having to learn its rules or behavioral norms and without having to undergo any other special training. This process no doubt takes place beyond the intellectual level, and thus also beyond the limits of rational understanding. The morphogenetic field accepts the new adults and continues to influence them from this moment onward. The field itself sets its own boundaries and determines its own values. For young adults who have undergone an initiation of this sort, falling back into childhood patterns is unthinkable.

Just as we find it difficult to comprehend the effectiveness of rites of transition of this sort, so too do indigenous peoples find it difficult to understand our problems with life's transitions. Their lives are fundamentally easier and freer of stress. Decisions in time of crisis are made for them by the tribe, and the changes follow unconsciously in the right directions. Becoming an adult is not seen as a personal achievement, but is viewed as natural in the same way that the physical processes of puberty are natural for us.

All members of the tribe stem from the same stock, just as the boughs of a tree share a common trunk, and each member relies on every other. On the level of its morphogenetic field, the tribe takes care of all who belong to it. Crises involving difficult, personal decisions are almost inconceivable, as are the concepts of independent development, innovations and progress. Each member, and all members together, communally follow the traditional path of the tribe. Pursuing an independent path is unthinkable because a severed limb simply isn't viable without the communal trunk. Anyone who veers off course and transgresses a taboo is simultaneously cut off from the tribe and from life itself. To be forced to exist on one's own, a task we find difficult but not impossible, is unimaginable to archaic people, simply because there is no space in their field for such a situation. Here lie the roots of their steadfast resistance to progress. Every innovation is simultaneously a break with tradition and is thus seen as a threat to the tribe and to life itself. To a very high degree, archaic people are sure of their goals within the scope of their existing field, yet they also find it difficult, to same degree, to evolve or progress in our sense of those words. For this reason, although enviable in some ways, they cannot serve as models for us.

Nonetheless, there is much we can learn from them that is relevant to our own path and our own task—to once more become like children. Of course, we should remember that there is a difference between "again becoming *like* children" and "*remaining* children." Archaic cultures' naiveté and ego-less membership in the group can serve as models for us, but on a higher evolutionary level. After having spared no attempt to penetrate deeply into polarity, we have lost our innocence. All we can do now is turn ourselves homeward like prodigal sons and daughters. Keeping our eyes on those who have never left home can help us find the right direction.

Temporal Qualities of Rites and Festivals

The difficulty we have comprehending rituals that archaic people readily understand is essentially due to differences in concepts of time. Nowadays, most Westerners consider time solely from a quantitative point of view, while primal people have always emphasized the importance of a qualitative approach to time. In the ancient world, these two aspects of time were described with separate names. *Chronos* with his sand-glass represented quantity, *Cairos* stood for quality. Our modern phrase "time is money" only emphasizes time's quantitative measure. Indeed, a large percentage of the population in modern industrial countries quite literally sells themselves (via their life's *time*) to their employers. The value of their work is calculated solely according to the number of hours worked, as measured by the tyrannical, mechanical punch-clock. Of course, even in industrial societies, people who work creatively are well aware that quality is an equally decisive factor. A single stroke of genius in an inspired moment can be much more productive than long, strenuous hours spent thinking and rethinking.

When we write history—an activity archaic people consider both strange and unnecessary—we agree on a compromise. We count the years quantitatively, as if each were the same as all the others, while also occupying ourselves more intensively with special years. Our notion of history focuses on the complicated intricacies within time, so that history, in a sense, becomes the story of the strata in time.

Archaic people consider only the quality of time. They live with their stories and legends in a temporal circle. They understand mythic events not as historically valid, but as timeless truths. Delving through the strata of story, they are interested only in the timeless core of things. This is how eternal myths evolve. Their festivals are not remembrances of ancient times, but always occur in the present moment. They thus immediately experience their myths—they both live them and live by them. Their stories are either alive or forgotten. In the evening, when the shaman recounts the ancestral myths, she reaffirms the pattern of the present moment for those who are alive now.

We can understand this when we consider the dreadful boredom of most history as it is taught in our schools. This is no surprise since what is being taught happened long ago and no is longer alive (i.e., it's a "dead story"). A good teacher tries to awaken the dead to new life and allows her students to witness the events with their minds' eyes. Only then does history become enjoyable, and remain vivid in students' memories. Only then can they actually learn something from the past—which, of course, was the intention in the first place. Our schools use mostly compulsive means and examinations to train students' memories in a short-term, and thus largely useless, way. In actuality, we learn "by heart." When we consider that familiar phrase more closely, we can see that, at least as a figure of speech, the connection to the only truly vital kind of learning still survives.

Religious history shows that legends can live, and can touch us deeply and inspire us as models for our own lives. The Christian holidays are not intended as historical, memorial festivals, but are meant to catalyze the shared experience of a living myth. When Angelus Silesius says, "Were Christ born in Bethlehem a thousand times, but not once in you, you would remain forever lost," he is referring to precisely this relationship between myth and the present moment. On the personal level, we are likewise familiar with the qualitative relationship to time. Again and again, we relive important events in life. We talk about *high* times and *low* points in our lives (i.e., we recognize special times and are superstitiously attentive to certain omens that we know from earlier experiences and that we believe will again serve as precursors of similar events).

4. The Year and Its Festivals

When we consider our year, we see it naturally represents a circle. The fixed points in the year, its "hold-fasts" as it were, are its festivals. Four fixed festivals (or "immovable feasts") divide the annual circle into four parts. On this level, one could say the attempt to "square the circle" has been successful. There is something strikingly objective about these four fixed points. The surprising thing about them is that even archaic civilizations were able to measure them quite accurately, as we know from many stone "documents" dating from the megalithic era,[8] as well as from studies of Egyptian and Aztec pyramids.

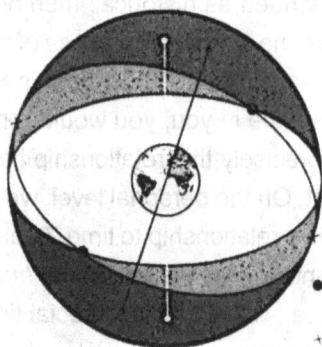

● Equinoxes

+ Solstices

The four fixed points are derived astronomically. The earth rotates about its axis, a movement that is most noticeable at the equator since this is the line of fastest motion. If one were to construct an imaginary plane through the circle of the equator, that plane (the celestial equator) would intersect at a 23 degree angle with the ecliptic plane, which is the name astronomers use to describe the plane along which the earth and the other planets move as they orbit the sun. The intersections between these two planes are the equinoxes, the points at which day and night are of equal length, which are also the points of greatest distance from the solstices.[9]Summer solstice is the longest day; winter solstice is the longest night.

Throughout history, these fixed points have always been celebrated. The field of these festivals was so strong that more recently arisen religions (e.g., Christianity) soon abandoned their resistance and agreed to abide by the timing of the old fixed festivals. After a few unsuccessful attempts to avoid doing so, the Church began to celebrate the Christmas festival during the same holy nights that previous cultures had already been celebrating—that mystical interval when light is weakest and hope is strongest.

The Year and Human Life as Reflected by the Sun

In the minds of archaic people, as well as in the minds of spiritually motivated individuals, the course of life is reflected in the course of the year, because the whole is found in each of its parts. In this context, the esoteric tradition talks about the *pars pro toto* principle. Nowadays, this law is also well-documented by science. For example, geneticists know that the information for constructing the entire human being is found in each individual cell. Chaos research has given us the now-familiar illustrations of the so-called "little apple man" from the Mandelbrot set. The fascinating thing about this figure is that the entire figure can be found in each individual structure. Naturopaths are now quite familiar with the concept, and consequently work on the reflex zones of the foot or ear as a means of treating the entire body. A technological analogy is the three-dimensional hologram, every part of which contains all the information needed to reconstruct the entire depiction.[10]

According to this law, every small unit contains the whole: the day contains the week, the month, the year, one's whole life, and the sum of many lives—all the way to liberation from the circle of rebirths. Consequently, the fundamental pattern of the mandala must also be contained within each of these structures. Indeed, by examining how a person begins his day, we can learn a great deal about how that person approaches his whole life. When we use the phrase the "evening of one's life," we relate the events of one day to those of an entire lifetime. Just as we shrink one or two centimeters in height during the course of a day (due to reductions in the interior pressure of the spinal disks under the weight of the upper body), so too does the combined weight of a lifetime of burdens cause us to lose a few centimeters in height as we grow older. Our spinal disks mostly regenerate themselves overnight, so that when we arise the next morning, we have regained our accustomed height. Looking at our entire lives, here too we shrink with age, only to regenerate once again during the resting phase that follows.

Most of the world uses the first day of January[11] as the starting point of the secular year. This date more or less corresponds to the winter solstice, the low point of the year. Christmas is the deepest night, and thus also the central turning-point in the annual cycle. The return occurs long before we humans notice it, just as we are seldom consciously aware of the moment of conception. Never is night more profound than in this night. It is during this deepest, most holy (i.e., most "whole") night, during this time of greatest darkness, that the seed of light is born. This corresponds to the moment of conception, when the soul immerses itself in the darkness of corporeality, even though its parents are usually unaware of its arrival.

From this moment on, the light grows steadily and secretly. Everything remains mostly veiled in darkness, but the days begin to grow longer. With the spring equinox, which corresponds to birth and sunrise, the year reaches the point when day and night are of equal length. Then light's victory march is clearly visible. As the sun gains in power, external growth begins. Through puberty (which corresponds to the early morning of life), the rising powers of light continue to adolescence (life's morning) and finally reach the highest point of the day and year. Midday and the summer solstice are distinguished by the highest ascent of the sun and the most intense light. It is the longest day, and the strongest light illuminates this high point, the climax of the year and of a life. It is the turning point, which corresponds to a fundamental change. Until now, everything has progressed upward; from this moment on, movement in the cycle of light is downward, even though this descent is not likely to be noticed for quite some time. Nevertheless, the change of direction is final. One can make it into a crisis in the negative sense but, negative or positive, it is inherently the moment of midlife. The periphery of the mandala has been reached. Westerners might feel that life's midpoint comes uncomfortably soon but, on the other hand, we call it "the change of life" and not the "change of days." The mandala pattern offers us plenty of change-over time during which to reconcile ourselves and grow accustomed to this change in the direction of life. Just as Christmas marks the year's nadir, so does the summer solstice mark its zenith.

Now begins the time of harvest, when the great power of the sun is reflected in nature's plump, ripe fruits. Although we tend to hate the changing years of menopause (both female and male), these years are, in fact, life's high point, the time of harvest, the season to enjoy life's fruits. If we weren't always rushing ahead in time, lost somewhere in the future, we would be able to fully enjoy this phase. Not until early autumn can we begin to enjoy the leisure we have longed for all our lives. This season of mellow ripeness lasts until the autumn equinox.

But pleasure is only one part of the story. Harvest also means that the ears of grain must die. The sheaves are left to rot in the field or are threshed *to separate the wheat from the chaff.* In the Bible, this image represents drawing up a balance sheet and taking stock. By giving up its grain as seeds for new plants, or as nourishment for other forms of life, the wheat plant sacrifices its best part and attains immortality in the cycle of living things. The now superfluous ear of grain is later plowed under the soil, where it decomposes to become the basic stuff for new life— burial and decomposition can both be understood as symbolizing the need to relinquish the ego.

Beginning with the moment of autumnal equinox, light begins to lag behind darkness, and the days become shorter than the nights. The cycle is moving toward the evening of life, although we should bear in mind that sundown and evening twilight are both lovely times of day. Giving up, losing weight, waning: these are the relevant issues—from both a physical and a metaphorical standpoint. The time has come to cast off ballast, to bid farewell. During late autumn, nature is dominated by severance and letting go, culminating in the ultimate passing away. Light grows steadily weaker, as does our vision (the "eye's light"), and the external senses become less acute. Colors in autumn flame one more time with outward brilliance, but only as a last fling before they withdraw entirely. Gray skies and gray hairs cause many of us to feel unattractive, but then comes white, the perfect color that contains all others within itself. It begins to dominate the scene by covering everything else beneath its silent blanket. The external light declines, but at the same time, the inner light grows ever stronger. Whereas growth and waxing were the themes from the moment of conception until midlife crisis, now a (healthy) shrinking is evident—until, at the end, nothing is left but the bare essentials. Darkest midnight and winter solstice are both the end and the beginning. They are both death and conception simultaneously: everything depends on the direction from which we approach the portal.

The Cycle of the Moon as a Developmental Mandala

In our patriarchal society, we are accustomed to orienting everything according to the radiant, masculine symbol of the sun. But we could just as well base everything on the receptive, reflective moon, the feminine symbol, since the month (from the Old English *monath, mona*, meaning "the moon"), no less than the day, likewise reflects the entire process. The new moon, the dark of the moon, is the point of most profound darkness, corresponding to the winter of the year and to old age and death in the cycle of a human life. This season is symbolized by the old gray or white crone, the wise woman, the grand(great)mother, as well as by the conception (of the new seed of light). The reappearance of the moon's light brings birth along with it. The waxing crescent moon embodies in its growth the growing child, the springtime, the virgin and the maiden. The half moon corresponds to half-grown, pubescent youth. The three-quarter moon corresponds to young brides and grooms. This lunar phase sheds its silvery light on the waxing growth of powers that will reach their apex at full moon.

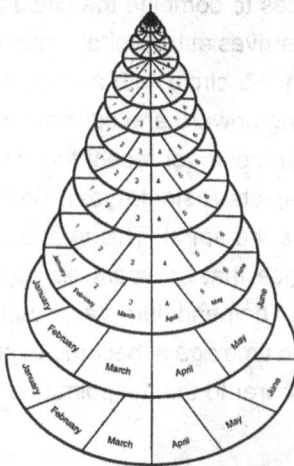

The spiral of years with its months.

43

This climax is symbolized by summer in the annual cycle, by the phase of motherhood in the cycle of life; and is also the turning point, the moment when the return journey begins, the midpoint of life. Anyone who passes this threshold must irrevocably progress toward the "change-of-life" years. From this point on, growth proceeds in a negative direction. The week from full moon until waning half moon corresponds to the time of integration and of beginning to deconstruct the ego, which should not only be understood in a spiritual sense, but also with an eye toward children and child-rearing. The waning half moon symbolizes autumn and the wise old woman. From half moon until new moon, we attain old age, the period of leave-taking and letting go. The new moon closes the circle and begins it anew.[12]

By considering things from the level of the mandala's circle, we have explored only one dimension, albeit a central one. The circle corresponds more closely to reality than the straight line, the arrow, the symbol of progress we so ardently pursue here in the West. Truth, however, ultimately lies in the middle. Cultures that relate only to the circle eventually go around in circles and undergo no evolution. Societies that are interested only in progress fall away from the cosmic order and endanger the entire world. When one tries to combine the circle and the arrow in a single symbol, one arrives at the spiral, the primal symbol of life. The spiral is basically a circle with a direction of motion. If we imagine it as tapering upward and culminating in a single point, we have an ideal symbol to represent the idea of evolution.

Each rotation depicts a single year, and the totality of the annual cycles forms the spiral. This image corresponds to the subjective experience that *as years go by*, each year seams shorter and shorter. The pendulum's arcs that have propelled us into polarity time and time again, become smaller and smaller as everything draws nearer to the midpoint and ultimate oneness\.

44

PART II

1. Conception and Pregnancy

*As on the day when you were given to the world,
when the sun stood to greet the planets,
you quickly thrived more and more,
according to the law with which you first appeared.
So too must you be: you cannot flee from yourself,
thus spoke the sibyls and the prophets.
No time nor any power can dismember
imprinted forms which vitally develop themselves.*
—Johann Wolfgang von Goethe, *Urworte. Orphisch (Primal Words. Orphic)*

*My father and my mother wished for a child,
and they conceived me.
And I wished for a mother and a father,
and I conceived the night and the ocean.*
—Khalil Gibran

Nowadays we encounter a number of problems when we try to determine the moment when life begins. Whereas spiritually motivated people believe life never actually begins but has always been and merely changes its level of manifestation, materially inclined people prefer to believe life begins after the third month of pregnancy, an attitude that offers certain "practical" opportunities that we will consider in the following pages.

Even if we assume that life, like everything else in creation, proceeds rhythmically and therefore (like a vibration) has neither a beginning nor an end, it is nonetheless relevant for our research into life's crises to begin our investigation with the beginning of bodily life (i.e., with conception). As soon as ovum and sperm cell unite, a common form arises, and consequently also a common content. Parallel to the onset of physical life, the life of the soul also begins. As cells divide, growth commences. The circular, female ovum and the arrow-shaped, male sperm cell come together. When circle and arrow unite, the primordial pattern of the spiral arises symbolically; and this same spiral pattern is sensually experienced when the soul descends into the body.

At first glance, many people do not consider conception as a crisis, simply because they know too little about it. Although we are highly skilled at preventing conception, we know very little about conception itself. We know how to practice contraception, but do not even know exactly what it is that we are contravening. Anyone who does not believe in the existence of the soul would say that preventing conception means nothing more than hindering the purely physical act of fertilization.

The discoveries made through in-depth psychotherapy provide a treasure-trove of material about this earliest epoch in life, material formerly available to us only through the symbolic imagery of myth and religion. Thanks to intrauterine photographs by Lennar Nilsson, we now have impressive photographic documentation from the earliest days of life after conception. Within the framework of reincarnation therapy, it is not only possible, but downright routine, to re-experience the time surrounding the moment of conception.

Prior to conception, the soul experiences itself in a state of expansiveness, weightlessness and freedom from attachments. Conception occurs when the wish for embodiment takes form, either because of unfinished tasks in life or, according to the Eastern view, because of karma. The soul experiences this as a kind of suction that pulls it in the corresponding direction. The soul clearly recognizes the two human beings who, motivated by love or for whatever other reasons, have found their way to one another. The actual moment of conception is generally experienced as a spiral-shaped suction that pulls the soul into the corporeal realm. Sometimes this path leads the soul first through a male body, sometimes the entry into bodily reality is perceived to take place immediately within the cavity of the uterus.

The soul experiences this plunge into material reality as a loss of freedom and the beginning of attachment, as a narrowing and, ultimately, as a step into the captivity of the body with all its accompanying limitations. Objectively, the tiny embryo has more than enough space. Subjectively, measured against the expanse and openness of its prior experiential space, the uterine cavity is experienced as restrictive. Relatively quickly, however, the soul grows accustomed to its new habitat, an environment warm and soft and by far large enough to accommodate the still minute but steadily growing bodily form. The watery world within the embryonic sac gradually develops. Seen from the outside, this seems like a small world, but from the perspective of the even smaller body within it, the embryonic sac is an expansive universe. On the one hand, the soul perceives everything going on outside it; on the other hand, it feels progressively more comfortable in the *maternal, material* world. (Both italicized words are derived from the same Latin root *mater,* meaning "mother.")

The soul is acutely aware of the moment when the mother discovers that she is pregnant or that a new soul has entered her body, and the soul is also quite sensitive to the experiences the parents associate with conception and pregnancy. Attempted abortions, or even the mere thought of abortion, are experienced in all their consequences by the newly embodied soul and can seriously disrupt that soul's feelings of safety and security in a warm "nest." Even when parents openly and joyously welcome the pregnancy, the strong desire for a baby of a particular (usually male) gender can place a severe burden on the intrauterine life. In half of pregnancies, the parental uncertainty and their hopes for a male child correspond to the unborn female embryo's certainty that it cannot but disappoint its parents simply because it belongs to the female gender. In this case, not only does life in the world of polarity outside the womb begin with disappointment, but a gloomy shadow is cast over the otherwise paradisiacal months inside the womb. Even at this early stage in life, the foundations can be laid for subsequent difficulties with one's gender role. Our era of ultrasound tests offers a number of advantages since it gives certain parents a reasonably early opportunity to reconcile themselves to the gender of their as unborn child.

If, rather than "sneaking aboard" as a stowaway, the soul is responding to both parents' open-hearted invitation, the intra-uterine sojourn passes blissfully and is experienced by the embryo as a time full of overwhelmingly positive experiences. The dominant impressions include oceanic feelings of limitlessness combined with free and weightless floating in the watery, inner world. Feelings like these foster the sense of oneness, and the unborn baby feels as though the entire world is embracing it like a mother. The limitlessness of the exterior universe is now re-experienced inwardly, although, of course, inside and outside are still mostly one and the same for the soul at this stage of development. A sense of trust and security accompanies the embryo's growth, adding still greater warmth to this first nest of childhood. Even without having to ask for it, everything needed for life flows toward the tiny but already complete creature. Ideally, the unborn baby need not do anything at all and the umbilical cord automatically keeps it fully supplied with everything it needs.

This is the time toward which adults' fantasies about the mythical Land of Cockaigne yearn. It is a land where milk and honey simply flow toward us—and it really does exist: at the beginning of life, in our mothers' wombs. Life in the spacious embryonic sac has a dreamlike quality. Nowhere does the unborn child encounter a hard boundary. Everything is soft and gently rocking. The mother's rhythmic heartbeat forms the acoustic background for a freely floating, carefree existence full of harmony between mother and child. Harmony reigns both within and without. The colors are as warm as the water, and the soft boundaries of this early universe elastically give way under the pressure of even the gentlest movements by the child. Because no harsh demands are placed on its senses, the embryo perceives everything with acute wakefulness and receptivity. If the mother's external situation is also in good order and if she is living in harmony with her surroundings, this can enhance the harmony experienced by the growing child. But even if this is not the case, an aware mother can largely shield her unborn baby from external threats simply by maintaining an attitude of unconditional acceptance toward the growing child. (See the first color illustration in the middle of this book.)

This phase of cozy security is so pleasant many adults yearn to return to it. It is so important that they may spend the rest of their lives trying to recapture it if it were too short or entirely lacking in the uterus. John Lilly's so-called "samadhi" or "isolation tank" is an attempt to give adults remedial access to this experience. Inside a huge, artificial "womb" (which, seen from the outside, bears a disquieting resemblance to a sarcophagus), the adult "baby" floats in a body-temperature saline solution. The environment is dark like a real womb, and even the intrauterine acoustic background can be imitated. In a very short time, the effects of the sarcophagus (from the Greek words *sarx,* meaning "flesh" and *phagein,* meaning "to eat") become noticeable. Although it does not actually eat the flesh like the sarcophagus at the end of our lives, this watery womb relieves the flesh of every burden. One no longer feels one's body. In this respect, the isolation tank may well be similar to the initiatory sarcophagi of the ancient world that likewise served to release the neophyte[1] from the bonds of corporeality. Oceanic feelings of limitlessness—so essential and so influential for our evolution—frequently occur in the weightless environment of the samadhi tank. It is possible to feel as though one were floating weightlessly in outer space or as though one had returned to one's mother's womb. The similarity between these two experiences is another indication of the analogous relationship between the microcosm and the macrocosm.

Experiences in the samadhi tank can also have a shadow side and the time spent in the tank can feel like a "bad trip" if the corresponding phase in one's life was rife with terrors. People who were forced to struggle against the sharply pointed tools of abortion during this early phase of life, or who were otherwise obliged to fight for survival, often feel threatened when they lie inside an isolation tank. Even if intrauterine events are not recalled in all their concrete, original vividness, the feeling of being in jeopardy often makes itself felt anew.

Experiences in psychotherapy lead us to conclude that this early time in the mother's womb gives rise to a feeling known as "primal trust" that is absolutely essential for our subsequent development. If this early time is overshadowed by threats, the feeling of primal trust may never arise and we are apt to suffer from its absence for the rest of our lives. There is nothing that can replace it. At best, we can try to compensate for its absence later on in life with external measures. Self-made safety nets and insurance policies can give us a feeling of safety but can never replace primal trust, for which they are merely pale imitations. Regressions experienced within the framework of psychotherapeutic sessions are a far more effective means of filling the deficit. Experiences of inner security are always helpful, even if they come from an entirely different context or are felt when we re-experience primal trust during regressions to prior incarnations.

Awe in the presence of the miracle of incarnation has largely disappeared from our civilization, where high-tech and "if it can be done, do it" reign supreme. We tend to regard this early stage in life from a naively materialistic point of view. Family planning and notions of efficiency dominate a field that requires feelings and emotions. From the standpoint of rational planning and the ubiquitous question about costs and benefits, it is almost a miracle that we continue to have children at all. In most cases, children ruin our ambitious plans and demand material sacrifices. Government subsidies to child-rearing families are intended as a consolation prize for those who, although they knew better,

nevertheless decided to make the "sacrifice of having children."
Society's egotism reflects each individual's egotism, and thus
it comes as no surprise that we tend to regard the whole thing
from the adults' point of view and not only avoid, but often even
deny, the possibility of seeing things from the embryo's point of
view.

Even if we have enough sensitivity to realize that the collective defensive magic of contraception is, in fact, an attempt to
prevent souls from incarnating, we nonetheless tend to see only
the *already conceived* souls. But the whole picture looks entirely different from the perspective of a soul who is *yearning to
conceive.* We suddenly discover that much suffering is hidden
behind our familiar technical and medical expressions.

From a soul's point of view, the attempt to find a body in which
to incarnate is almost a hopeless undertaking in a modern, industrial society like our own. During the years most favorable
to conception (i.e., during the third decade of a woman's life),
most young people have entirely different plans and desires
that have little or nothing to do with conceiving children. Modern medicine's contraceptive measures have become so reliable
that scarcely a soul is able to penetrate the defensive cordon of
latex layers and spermicidal foam. Conception also frequently
fails in a chronically irritated uterus that has been made inhospi-
table through the intentional insertion of a spiral-shaped foreign
body commonly known as an IUD. In some cases, hormone
pills have caused the potential passageways to become impass-
able. Or perhaps conception has been preempted at the highest
level by the hormones of the classic birth-control pill that—as
its German name "anti-baby pill" implies—is so much opposed
to babies that it counterfeits a pregnancy and thus disappoints
any not-yet-incarnated souls who might be seeking admittance
to corporeal life. If, despite all these precautions, pregnancy
nonetheless comes to pass, a shock treatment with the hormone bomb of a so-called "morning-after pill" can catapult the
newly incarnated soul back into oblivion. Pills before and pills
thereafter, diaphragms and IUDs: all these are familiar words

and utilitarian objects. But it is only the time factor that allows us to deal so casually with them all. We prefer not to think about the possibility of an "anti-person pill." Only at life's earliest beginning do we permit ourselves to be explicit with what Germans call the "anti-baby pill."

Concepts such as these suggest that, in our society at least, life frequently begins with a crisis. When a modern woman tells her gynecologist she is pregnant, his first question may well be, "Do you want to have the baby?" This in itself is already an expression of crisis in the form of a decision. This is something new and unique to our modern era. The majority of our ancestors had the feeling that the decision "to have or have not" was not theirs to make. We, on the other hand, believe it is our *right* to intervene and correct things as we see fit.

A soul who has managed to overcome the barriers described above is by no means sure our affluent society will allow it to keep its hard-won place as a conceived entity. Hunters refrain from shooting game animals during the breeding season, but no such prohibitions protect our own "young" during this vulnerable interval. Our newly conceived human offspring must first survive a three-month "trial period" during which they can, at any time, be given up to the lethal consequences of abortion. What seems practical from our point of view, what gives us a feeling of freedom and independence, is a period of extreme anxiety for the newly incarnated soul—and these feelings are often re-experienced in all their corresponding terror during subsequent therapy sessions. Our wish not to decide immediately puts the fully dependent creature within the womb through unimaginable tortures. For many fetuses, the life that has only just begun to take form comes to an abortive end. The little creature struggles against the threat by fleeing into the rearmost corner of its cave, but the retreat that in past centuries offered a chance of survival results in little more than a torturing delay in the face of today's modern techniques of abortion.

Although it is practiced routinely in thousands upon thousands of cases, to describe this procedure in detail is a taboo.

It simply is not done. Instead, we ignore it silently. It cannot really be all that terrible since, after all, it *is* legal, isn't it? But it is precisely the taboos that most clearly reveal the real problems in our society and expose the crises for which we have no answers. In order to understand the critical nature of conception, it is important to take a long, sober look at the procedures that are regularly used to reverse conception.

By the third month of pregnancy, the little human being is clearly recognizable as just that: a little human being. It has all its limbs and senses. All its organs are perfectly situated. Illustrations 2 and 3 in the middle of this book depict fetuses during this period of time. The extreme transparency of most of the body's structures is clearly visible. This transparency corresponds to the transcendental perception experienced during the first trimester of pregnancy. Although it is already quite profoundly anchored in material reality, the unborn child is still in a far better position to apprehend life's ethereal contexts than are its adult contemporaries. For example, the embryo regards it as entirely natural to feel the thoughts of its mother and her immediate surroundings.

In this situation, the child is acutely aware when a life-threatening foreign object intrudes into its perfect world, pierces the protective hull and siphons off its life's element—the essential amniotic fluid. Suddenly "high and dry," fraught with fear and terror, the unborn child is killed in either of two ways. While the mother has escaped into the unconsciousness of anesthesia and the father almost always distinguishes himself by his total absence from the scene, the gynecologists proceed with the bloody but legal craft that was formerly performed in Germany by so-called "angel-makers." After the water of life has been drained away, the abortionist uses strong-armed violence to destroy the little body. The minced, dismembered parts of the embryo's body are scraped from the maternal cavity with a so-called "sharp spoon." Finally, the placenta is likewise scratched away from the uterine wall and removed.

The other, and today more common method of aborting babies, uses a kind of vacuum pump to extract the little creature, its watery realm, umbilicus and supplying placenta. Although at first glance this vacuum-style abortion may seem cleaner, when one considers it more closely, it seems no less brutal than the first method. The living fetus is literally torn limb from limb under enormous pressure. Technological perfection makes it possible to exceed the brutality of the common medieval punishment of "quartering."

Experiences with reincarnation therapy,[2] as one would expect, provide more information about the older technique and leave little doubt that the unborn child remains fully aware throughout the entire tormenting procedure. That the child should be entirely conscious of tortures we find difficult to imagine is easily understood, even from the point of view of conventional physicians since they know from experience with countless births by cesarean section that the child is not rendered unconscious when the mother is subjected to anesthesia.

Even if the child manages to survive the first three vulnerable months unscathed (i.e., because its parents are eagerly awaiting its birth), the future of the little unborn person is by no means secure. If its parents are comparatively old or merely anxious or victims of the terrible kind of "new responsibility," they might permit the gynecologist to perform a *test* penetration of the pregnant belly. Amniocentesis involves withdrawing a sample of amniotic fluid; chorion biopsy involves extracting blood from a part of the placenta. For those of us who have already been born, this seems quite impressive as a skillful medical procedure, but from the standpoint of the unborn child, the test penetration is experienced with anything but appreciation.

While an enormous spear bores its way into the baby's protective enclosure and penetrates its no longer safe world, the embryo itself takes refuge in the rearmost corner of its nest. According to gynecologists, this escape attempt, that they can readily observe via ultrasound imaging, is the reason complications so rarely ensue during examinations of this kind. Indeed, the fetuses themselves are seldom pricked by the probes. The majority of problems are caused by "unavoidable" damage to the amniotic sac itself. The results of the examination—proudly announced, with emphasis on the refinement and safety of the method itself—nonetheless reveal the panic that spear techniques evoke in the fetus. It is a peculiar situation, especially when one considers that birth assistance was originally intended, first and foremost, to serve the best interests of the child. Of course, the idea behind examinations of this kind is to identify any possible birth defects early enough so that the embryo can still be aborted, which, in such cases, is legal until the fifth month of pregnancy.

The same methods of examination are (at least from our point of view) crudely misused in India, where they are not typically used to prevent the birth of hereditarily deformed offspring, but simply to prevent the birth of *female* offspring. Since many Indians regard girls as liabilities, embryos that ultrasound tests have revealed to be female are routinely aborted. What raises the indignation of those few Germans who are aware of the practice is quietly accepted in India as one of the few truly functional contraceptive methods. If one looks honestly at the situation, the difference between India and Germany is only a relative one. Some Indians are unwilling to accept babies of the "wrong" gender. We Germans, on the other hand, accept female babies but are often willing to intervene if we discover chromosomal errors that can cause abnormalities in the baby or if early ultrasound testing reveals deformed organs. In both countries, we adults have the audacity to decide which lives we believe are worthy—and which are unworthy—of sharing our planet with us. We make ourselves lords over life and death. Where this can lead is evident in a survey published in *Der Spiegel* magazine in 1993. According to that survey, eighteen percent of pregnant women in Germany would abort their babies if there were reason to suspect the child might suffer from obesity.

Late abortions (carried out until the fifth month) are technically more difficult to perform than the ones described above, simply because the fetuses are already so large. These babies are forced from the womb prematurely and are born in a mockery of the natural way. Births like these often have a brutal effect on the mother since her entire body is unprepared for the ordeal and can only be compelled to give birth by being injected with powerful, labor-inducing drugs. Births of this sort are so difficult that the babies do not survive—which, of course, was the intention of the whole awful exercise in the first place. It would surely place less physical stress on the mother to wait for the pregnancy to run its normal course, allow the cervix to open of its own accord and allow all of her tissues to become suppler and better prepared for the impending delivery. But this would mean that the child, which for one reason or another has been declared "unacceptable," would be born alive and protected by law. It would not be so easy to kill the infant at that point, which is why it is killed earlier—despite the tremendous stress an artificially induced, premature birth puts on the mother.

The whole situation looks even more terrifying from the point of view of the unborn child: no doubt it experiences the intruding lance as proof that its parents lack trust in it, that they are unwilling to accept it unconditionally, but will accept it only if it fulfills certain expectations and does not place undue demands on them. After the "test drilling," a waiting period begins that must be at least as terrible for the fetus as it is for the parents. Geneticists convene as a sort of jury to decide the fate of the unborn baby. In doubtful cases, the jurors in this kangaroo court generally rule against the accused (i.e., against the child whose life is at stake). The premature birth that is simultaneously its death sentence is an indescribably gruesome ordeal for the handicapped embryo. Future generations will no doubt judge our own era (one that some people earnestly believe to be an enlightened era) by these atrocities. The majority of people today seldom or never think about these procedures since, if they did, it would be very difficult to continue believing the lie that asserts that our modern society is a humane one.

For a variety of reasons, examinations of amniotic fluid are becoming increasingly commonplace. One reason that ought not be underestimated is our tendency to do in actuality whatever we can imagine. The official reason is the increasing average age of prospective parents. As parents grow progressively older, the risk of congenital defects (e.g., trisomie 21 or Morbus Down Syndrome, more commonly known as "mongolism") increases. Since we have such difficulty deciding, and since we prevent conception of countless children during the safest years for pregnancy, women facing the "now or never" dilemma around their fortieth birthdays try to make up for lost time. All these factors contribute to raising the average age of pregnant women, and hence to increasing the need for amniocentesis, at least from a gyneco*logical* point of view. This attitude, however, is only *logical* for people who have so distanced themselves from religion and from an understanding of the world that they share in natural science's belief that we mere humans can cheat fate. Although this belief is very likely our most prevalent superstition, not a single example can be found in either the secular or religious history of humanity to confirm its truth.

Why are congenitally handicapped children more frequently born to mature adults?[3] Fate seems to be saying that older parents are better equipped to cope with the challenges and learn from the tasks associated with raising a handicapped child. Scientific medicine tries to help us avoid life's harshness and challenges. Fate, on the other hand, wants us to learn, and does not shy away from confronting us with adversity and trials in order to teach us life's lessons. We can understand why medicine has moved so far toward the opposite pole and why it is evoking increasingly brutal consequences when we consider the so-called "shadow theory" that, to paraphrase the words Goethe put in Mephisto's mouth: "I am a part of that power that always desires the worst yet always creates the best." Science, paradoxically, has taken the opposite position: though it always desires the best, it all too often creates the worst.

From a superficial point of view, the increasing number of what conventional medicine calls "high-risk" pregnancies means that it is becoming increasingly dangerous to incarnate into an affluent society. The danger is exacerbated by conventional medicine itself and by a society that has progressively fewer scruples about life. Thus, the circle closes itself. Nowadays an older pregnant woman is considered "irresponsible" if she chooses *not* to undergo amniocentesis. The responsible[4] individual, at least in the sense of responsibility commonly understood in our society, is the one who does everything she can to avoid placing burdensome challenges upon either herself or her society. We want to prevent all harshness and adversity, even if it means preventing life itself.

Rituals of Greeting Versus Lack of Respect for Life

At present, universally applicable alternatives to the current practice of abortion cannot be meaningfully put into practice, at least not in ways that are accessible to our dynamic, materialistic society. Furthermore, the majority of the population in our modern, industrial nations is apparently satisfied with the status quo. The suffering caused by this practice falls upon children at the beginning of their lives, at a time when they are much too young to vote. If we look more closely, we can see that this pattern of projecting, of sloughing our own problems onto the shoulders of others, is a distinguishing characteristic of our entire society. To change that pattern would entail taking an enormous step toward individual responsibility. A least for the present, that step seems to lie far beyond our reach. If, considering the population's present state of consciousness, we were to prohibit legal abortions, we would do nothing more than transfer the site of the mayhem from sterile operating rooms into the uncontrolled back rooms of illegal abortionists, the so-called "angel-makers." Deliberate destruction of the fetus is bad enough; a prohibition on abortion would only exacerbate the dangers facing the mother seeking to terminate her pregnancy. Experience has shown that there is no reasonable way to prohibit abortions. Once a certain level of consciousness has been reached, abortions will prohibit themselves. If that level of awareness is beyond our reach, then there is simply no humane solution to the problem.

Only a fundamental alteration in consciousness, a change leading toward a universal respect for life itself, can transform the societal situation. Such a change can only come about if it is based on many individuals who have each discovered their own responsibility for life and who therefore no longer expect governmental assistance. It may sound cruel and harsh, but the fact is that at the moment the majority of our population places greater value on their own convenience than on unborn children's right to life. This means, for example, that this society compels its gynecologists to continually break the Hippocratic oath—even though its precepts ought to be binding upon all physicians. Society's guilty conscience shows itself in contradictory moments (e.g., when a doctor who openly performs abortions fails to adhere to laws regulating the abortion procedure and is subsequently punished either through revocation of his license to practice medicine and/or with imprisonment). On the other hand, the situation has escalated to the point that a doctor who wants to remain faithful to the Hippocratic oath can hardly become a gynecologist in Germany.

Of course, no one becomes a gynecologist because he wants to specialize in abortions. People who are trained to help women deliver babies would no doubt prefer to offer "birth assistance" rather than "death assistance." But since nowadays in many places the number of abortions performed exceeds the number of babies delivered, physicians who want to specialize in gynecology must learn how to perform both procedures. A gynecologist who refuses one option can hardly expect to be allowed to help with births, thus burdening other gynecologists with the task of "death assistance" (especially since, even though this euthanasia takes place at the beginning of life, it is no less unpleasant than euthanasia at life's end, which—at least for the time being—is still prohibited). This is one of the situations where medicine's shadow side (i.e., death) has its day, and physicians render—albeit unconsciously—their direct assistance.

On the other hand, alternatives for individualistic, conscious people are not only conceivable, but are taking place in ever greater numbers. Although it is not possible to fully withdraw oneself from the field of pragmatic disregard for life, space does exist for free, individual action, and a number of effective rituals exist to fill that space. In this context, it makes sense to withdraw oneself as far as is responsibly possible from the field that society and official gynecology have created. Nowadays we find gynecologists and obstetricians who see their task as limiting the physician's intervention in the birth process to the bare essentials. Moreover, there is a growing community of midwives who remain aloof from the compulsions of modern high-tech medicine, yet who do not ignore the options and chances it can offer.

In a free space of this sort it would be possible to follow in the spiritual footsteps of the Native Americans who celebrated the discovery of each new pregnancy and, for example, to revive their practice of initiating the unborn baby into the four elements. The great opportunity lies in the fact that, in our society as well, first only the mother, then, with her consent, also the father, are initiated into the mystery. Before any medical authorities are allowed to participate in the pregnancy, the "switches" would already be thrown in the right direction. Since the appropriate rituals have no corresponding fields in our society, the parents are entirely free to show their child our world, the one into which it has chosen to incarnate itself.

At this stage of its life, the unborn child is already mostly a part of the world of water. Initiation into this fluid realm could be a week's vacation at the seashore or in a lake region closely related to the watery "soulscape" of the liquid element. Initiation into the realm of earth could be supported by time spent on a farm or a by visit to an underground cavern. Initiation into the realm of air could take place—breathing deeply—atop a mountain peak on a windy day. The element of fire can be explored with help from the sun.[5] When a woman realizes she is pregnant, it is only natural that the unborn child should occupy the focal point. Special times when she mediates, bringing the outer world closer to her as yet unborn offspring, are initiations in the true and original sense of the word. Of course, they are also times of great significance for the mother since she, too, must rediscover and redefine her role in the world. Taking enough time for herself and her unborn baby can be a tremendous help with these tasks. The process is reciprocal: not only does one prepare the baby for entry into the world, one also prepares the world for the arrival of the newborn infant. Native American rituals place much importance on announcing to the world that the unborn baby is on its way. Thus, they conduct a ceremony to introduce each element to the baby. A child who has had its parents' help in commencing a healthy relationship with Grandfather Fire is likely to be on good terms with that element throughout life. Even if we cannot rationally comprehend why these rituals work so well, examples from a wide range of archaic cultures show they do indeed function astonishingly well.

We are not all that far away from this point of view. After all, don't many parents in our own society discover that things that were experienced during pregnancy have a formative influence on their children? It is a two-way street: the unborn child influences its mother (e.g., it can cause her to have an appetite for foods she avoided in the past) and the mother's preferences can obviously manifest years later as tendencies exhibited by her offspring. Observations of this sort can be made in even the most banal activities. For example, the children of a mother who enjoyed spending a lot of time in her car during pregnancy seldom have difficulty with automobile travel later in their lives.

No doubt a decisive role in all this is played by the degree to which the mother allows her child to take part in the life they share since, during pregnancy, the embryo experiences itself as wholly united with its mother, her perceptions and feelings. A mother who suppresses the pregnancy and continues to pursue all the activities of her normal, daily life without devoting much thought to the child inside her womb largely excludes her baby from their shared experiences. To a much greater extent than adults can imagine, the first experiences of the child's intrauterine world are influenced by feelings and cognitive associations. Children who have been excluded from these areas are limited to the experiential world within the uterus: they only become aware of their mothers' most extreme mood swings and of things they direct affect them. The route to the unborn child, like the paths to the newborn and the infant, is above all through feelings.

Even the uninvited intrusion represented by an ultrasound examination can be recast as a conscious ritual of greeting and introducing oneself to the world. It becomes a kind of first photo sitting. The difference lies quite simply in the inner attitude of all participants. *One* conscious ritual could well be enough, and then there would be no need to look inside again and again, to take photo after photo, simply because the appropriate technology and the corresponding apparatus are available. A growing seed is not unearthed again and again merely to check on the progress of its growth.[6]

The ideal attitude that would give the unborn child a healthy foundation would be a conscious, nine-month rite of initiation into its future world. That could include initiation into the realm of music by consciously attending concerts together (in one seat) or as a trio (in two seats). Naturally, the parents will be best able to introduce the child to areas with which they themselves are most familiar. On the other hand, pregnancy offers a lovely opportunity to explore new worlds—for oneself and together with one's unborn baby. Of course, these nine months of preparation are not going to be a long, uninterrupted vacation. But that, too, is necessary since initiations are not only related to life's pleasant sides, but can also include duties and even illnesses, as we shall see later when we discuss the initiatory illnesses suffered by neophyte shamans.

Pregnancy also offers the mother an excellent opportunity to use her growing sensibility in order to contact her inner voice and her inner physician, thus using this path as a means of

establishing another link with her child. Mothers who use meditation and inner journeys to access their souls' own inner landscapes usually find it easy to "hear" their unborn children's
expressions of emotion.[7] The mother's feelings and her inner
imagery can influence this phase and its rituals. Seldom is there
a more favorable time to make everyday life into one, great,
conscious ritual.

Problems During Pregnancy

Sensitivity to Odors

Problems that typically occur during pregnancy reveal the
shadow side of the aforementioned opportunities. Undue sensitivity to odors, which often exacerbates an already present nausea to a practically unbearable degree, is a negative version
of the enhanced sensitivity that naturally accompanies pregnancy. The unpleasant feeling of being "thin-skinned" is a similar shadow side of the enhanced perceptual acuity and empathic
depth that appear during pregnancy. If she feels as if everything
stinks, an expectant mother has the chance to create an appropriate atmosphere, to *follow her nose* and her other reliable
senses. The sense of taste is closely related to the sense of
smell, and here too a variety of changes are possible. It is obvious that the sense of taste aims to ensure that the growing child
receives the best supply of life-essential materials. One look
at the way we eat nowadays immediately shows that a radical
reorientation is urgently needed—for a great many mothers as
well as for their babies, large and small.

These days, most people treat their cars better than they
treat their bodies. The same people who have no qualms about
buying cheap groceries and questionable discount specials, or
even indulging in so-called "pleasures" that have been proven
poisonous would not dream of feeding their cars with low-quality

gasoline or old motor oil. Who would put ordinary gasoline into his car simply because that grade of gas is cheaper or because he happens to have pulled up to that particular pump when he knows full well that his car needs "super" grade gasoline? The fact that we seldom have compunctions about the quality of the food we put into our bodies proves that the time is overdue for whetting not our appetites, but our sense of taste. Anyone who eats unhealthily *gross groceries* rather than *delicate delicacies* not only damages her own health, but also has a negative effect on the health of the child growing inside her, a child who is even more acutely dependent on the quality of its nourishment.[8]

Drugs

This situation is especially obvious when we consider "guilty pleasures." Since every single cigarette drastically reduces circulation in the maternal organism, it also seriously limits the energy and nourishment supplied to the child because this supply depends on the degree of circulation in the placenta. This is the reason for the lower weights and other disadvantages observed from the earliest days of life in "smokers' babies." Nowadays, a pregnant smoker must consciously accept the fact that she is causing her baby to suffer. It would obviously be a blessing if her tastes would change, but nicotine's ability to cause addiction is strong and has caused many smokers to become so divorced from a healthy feeling for their own bodies that a change in one's tastes alone is not enough to persuade a person to quit smoking.[9]

The effects of alcohol and other drugs on the growing fetus are no less drastic. Since the effects of these and most other drugs are spread through the blood, the embryo fully experiences the high—and the low. Problems observed among infants born to alcoholic mothers readily reveal this. All too frequently, babies born to mothers addicted to heroin are themselves addicted at birth.

Nausea and Vomiting

On the bodily level, the nausea from which pregnant women frequently suffer is not only caused by their increased sensitivity to odors and tastes, but also by hormonal changes, especially the increasing level of estrogen, within them. The natural goal of these increased estrogen levels is to help the maternal, lunar archetype achieve its breakthrough and to shift that archetype into the midpoint of life. Women who already lived this archetype, or who were open to it prior to their pregnancy, have correspondingly fewer difficulties with the shift. Nausea during pregnancy is entirely unknown among women in archaic cultures. In our cultural milieu, the bodily shift to a new but not unexpected situation is quite naturally accompanied by a shift on the level of the soul.

If, on the other hand, a woman has felt that this pole of her existence was largely foreign to her, then the sudden increase in physical femininity can sometimes be experienced as an ambush or surprise visit. If the necessary shift cannot be accomplished on the level of the soul, symptomatic problems are liable to result from the discrepancy between body and soul. Nausea and the urge to vomit clearly show that the affected individual feels like throwing up and would like nothing more than to free herself of the situation and cough up the entity that has implanted itself within her. Of course, this resistance is not conscious since, if it were given space in her consciousness, she would not need to physically express the issue. The act of vomiting symbolically brings both levels closer together. On the one hand, it expresses her option of *spitting up* the new situation and thus freeing herself from it; on the other hand, it symbolizes the chance of *surrendering herself* to the new situation and positively accepting the tasks it entails.

The occasionally bizarre yearning for things that, prior to the pregnancy, held little attraction for the mother, is an especially clear indication of the fact that the mother must now feel, think and also eat for two—although "eating for two" should be understood in terms of the quality rather than the volume of food. In this way, the expectant mother broadens her horizons in every respect, not solely in the area of bodily experiences. This should provide a first impression of the initiation that every pregnancy signifies.

Dizziness and Weakness

The feelings of dizziness that frequently accompany pregnancy indicate that, on some level, the expectant mother is swindling herself. (The German word *Schwindel* can mean both "dizziness" and "swindle.") The prototype of dizziness appears aboard ship as seasickness whenever the information the eyes are sending to the brain no longer matches the data being sent by the organs of equilibrium inside the middle ear. When the seasick individual goes below deck to read, his eyes perceive no movement, although his inner ear clearly detects the rolling of the ship. This discrepancy makes itself felt as dizziness and shows that something is amiss. The problem solves itself as soon as one surrenders to the situation and admits to oneself that one is at sea. The surrender can take place physically either by closing one's eyes or else succumbing to one's nausea, going above deck, leaning over the railing and vomiting into the ocean. During the latter expedient, one cannot but admit that one is indeed on the ocean and not on solid ground. Similarly, a pregnant woman can overcome her nausea as soon as she surrenders herself to the pregnancy on all levels rather than trying to suppress the fact of the new situation. If, instead, she consciously continues to pretend everything is "normal" and unconsciously fights against the discrepancy, the swindle inevitably makes itself felt as dizziness and nausea.

Pregnant women also sometimes feel weak and powerless, which likewise indicates how unfamiliar they are with their own femininity and how much they unconsciously denigrate it. Feelings of weakness and powerlessness are the complement to typically masculine feelings of "dynamism" and "power." On the other hand, some women feel especially well and powerful during pregnancy; some even overcome past complaints (e.g., cold hands and feet) and experience heretofore unknown vitality, self-confidence and immunity to disease. In such cases, the body is showing that—consciously or unconsciously—these women have been yearning for pregnancy and are now discovering, in pregnancy, a previously unknown sense of fulfillment. The typical gait of women in their final weeks of pregnancy is an impressive and outwardly visible reflection of this inner change.

It is frequently the case that such women find it much easier to cope with all the consequences of becoming a mother than to cope with the never-ending and hopeless stress of trying to look perpetually elegant and beautiful. Of course, beauty and elegance need not be lost during pregnancy, but can flourish in a natural and relaxed way. Considered from the primal principles, it seems that women who have always given top priority to the Venus principle usually have greater difficulty inwardly accepting the lunar, maternal issue of pregnancy. When women whose primary issue is the lunar archetype become pregnant, they suddenly feel as if they have reached their goal, as if pregnancy has freed them from the Venus-stress patriarchal society places on women. When pretty little girls are the goal, motherly yearnings have a hard time. When a woman becomes pregnant, the pretty little girl archetype encounters massive problems; the maiden cannot but be left behind since the goal of pregnancy is to become a woman and a mother. The revivification of the pretty maiden can be difficult afterward since the years of maidenhood are now definitively gone.

Premature Labor

Compared with nausea and vomiting, the tendency to experience premature labor is a far more effective means of freeing oneself from one's unborn baby. Here the step has been taken from the symbolic level to the physical plane. Of course, these attempts are not conscious; the mere suggestion is rejected as a cruel insinuation and is vehemently denied. By the way, criticisms or insinuations should never be derived from the interpretations of symptoms. The fact that something is expressing itself through the body only means it is partly or entirely absent in conscious awareness. This should never lead to accusations or blame, judgment or condemnation. The issue is to interpret and understand the lessons these diseases and symptoms are trying to teach us.

Physicians' responses to premature labor are simple: either they sew closed the exit of the uterus in a so-called "cerclage," or they prescribe strict, often lengthy bed rest. Cerclage simply sews closed the "sack" to block the child's escape route, and the woman can remain as active as before without paying any special attention to the situation. For the child, who no doubt had reasons for its attempted escape, cerclage creates a kind of imprisonment. If the mother's excessively active or inadequately sensitive behavior were the chief reasons for the escape attempt, cerclage represents an intervention at the wrong location and at the weakest link in the chain.

On the other hand, the reason could lie in the mother's unconscious attempt to abort her baby and thus, although she does not consciously realize or admit it, she is in fact rejecting the child. For the unborn child, this creates a classical double-bind situation. On the one hand, it feels rejected and abandoned; on the other hand, modern medical technology has denied it access to the only avenue of escape.

Finally, premature labor can be an indication that the fetus is not viable, a situation that would lead to a natural miscarriage. In this case, the task of both mother and child would be fulfilled in a short time, and cerclage only compels both to suffer an unnecessary trauma.

Extended bed rest is the preferred therapeutic measure since it puts an end to the mother's hectic activity and gives her plenty of time to prepare herself for the arrival of the new baby. Bed rest is the sensible therapeutic response to the currently widely accepted practice of squeezing in the childbearing act somewhere alongside the career, according to the motto: "Take things a bit easier one month before the birth, then spend three months' vacation as ordered by the state and as paid for by your employer, then go back to work and continue as if nothing had happened." Some children are not satisfied with this situation, and thus they compel their mothers to grant them a longer "advent" period. Sometimes it is hard to resist the impression that the fetus is more comfortable with the no longer fashionable expression "to be expecting" than with the now more popular "check it off and get it over with" attitude toward childbearing.

Naturally it would be best if the mother would consciously and perhaps even thankfully accept the necessary bed rest as prescribed by her doctor and decided to take the child growing beneath her heart *to her heart* in a deeper sense. The associated restrictions could then be understood as opportunities since pregnancy is one of the few remaining occasions for a woman to truly become an adult. Furthermore, the long period of bed rest can help her realize she now needs another person to take care of her and thus relieve her of the cares associated with earning a living. When someone else *delivers* the goods, she can relax and focus her energy on the upcoming physical *delivery.* This is one of the chief problems facing today's "single mothers." Even in the past, mothers were all too often faced with the task of raising their children single-handedly; the work of earning a living for themselves and their families also frequently fell upon their shoulders. The novelty, then, lies only in the offensive enthusiasm with which "emancipated" mothers outwardly endorse the concept of single motherhood. But on the inside, as psychotherapy often reveals, things often look entirely different.

In other respects, too, single motherhood proves counterproductive for everyone involved. Despite elaborate and often demonstrative attempts to compensate, the mother cannot take as much care of her child as she could if she were free of material cares and also had a partner who relieved her of the burden of earning a living. On the other hand, the baby (who is now her one and all) often gets too much attention, especially the sort of attention that would be more appropriately lavished on a man. In one consultation, a single mother asked whether it was normal that her five-year-old could only fall asleep while lying on her naked body. The situation ultimately also damages the father, who misses out entirely and sometimes learns nothing at all—for example, when he has not even been informed about the "blessed event."

Surrendering oneself to bed rest as a therapy for premature labor ought not be underestimated as a way of taking time for oneself in an era when people so seldom allow themselves enough time for anything. An attitude of accepting the inevitable would also be most likely to give the mother adequate opportunity to "get back on her own two feet" later on. Experience has shown that, if she insists on continuing to work and merely transfers her workplace into her bed, she only succeeds in transferring the problems into bed with her since, in this symptom (as in all other symptoms), the ultimate issue is the inner aspect—in this case, her inner peace or lack thereof. The symptom of premature labor with extended bed rest as the appropriate therapy leads to a lengthening of the advent period, enabling the mother and unborn baby to consciously indulge in the ritual of (happy) expectation and granting each of them more time to become accustomed to the other. It should therefore be seen as an especially positive symptom, one whose inherent opportunities far outweigh its potential sorrows, especially since the labor pangs usually disappear entirely as soon as the mother assumes a horizontal position simply because the fetus, once it has asserted and been granted its right to peace and contemplation, usually abandons all exaggerated kicking and other attempts at escape from the womb.

Furthermore, bed rest usually puts an end to nausea and dizziness, and lying in bed means that weakness and tiredness are no longer serious problems. It would also be an ideal chance for the mother to grant herself the rest she needs, to prepare herself for the upcoming birth, and to consciously create a situation in which the unborn baby will feel tempted to stay in the womb until the time comes for it to be born. The aforementioned rituals of initiation into the future life, somewhat modified and mollified to conform with the mother's bed rest, could be a marvelous help here.

Looking Back at the Beginnings of Life

To sum things up: conception represents a severe crisis for most newly arrived souls. The difficulty of gaining acceptance into the womb is far greater than the difficulty of being granted acceptance into an Ivy League college 18 years and 9 months later. If we think that elite institutions of higher learning are unduly exclusive and choosy, we should take a closer look at the hurdles facing a soul at the inception of corporeal existence. Our affluent society exhibits the general tendency to seal itself off against new arrivals, whether they be new immigrants, refugees seeking asylum, foreign workers or children yearning to be conceived. We do not want to share our accumulated material wealth, and our behavior toward newcomers is correspondingly uninviting.

The problems surrounding conception, which we hardly even feel as a physical event,[10] are especially obvious in the social milieu. Our frequent inability to consciously perceive the moment of conception may be one factor contributing to our subsequent unwillingness to accept the fact that conception has indeed occurred. And the uncertainty surrounding the question "When does life begin?" could well have roots here. It is far more difficult to deny the existence of something that is clearly felt and perceived.

For a time, the majority of voters in New York State decided that life worthy of protection did not begin until the sixth month after conception. This concept, which leaves more free space and is thus even more practical for those who have already been born, ultimately failed because of resistance from physicians who simply did not have the nerves to endure the contradictions inherent in fighting for the lives of prematurely born babies on the one hand, and being called on the other to "dispose" of nearly mature embryos by abortion.

Even people who find such legally sanctioned atrocities acceptable will readily recognize the critical nature of conception when they consider the desperation accompanying the attempt by childless couples nearing the age of forty who, fraught with "now or never" panic, desperately try to conceive babies at almost any price. Even among younger people, the ever more severe problem of infertility is creating a critical situation. Fertility, especially among men, is currently in the midst of a dramatic decline. The simplest and most effective therapy for this situation lies quite simply in a lengthy and relaxing vacation for the childless couple. Alternatively, periods of sexual abstinence followed by well-timed intercourse can increase the chances of successful conception. The message of both practices is clear: if we want to become fertile again, we need to separate ourselves from the predominant hectic and haste, find our way back to ourselves, eliminate inessentials and become more *essential*.[11]

Hormonal therapies, artificial insemination, in-vitro fertilization and all the other elaborate measures taken by today's "if it can be done, let's do it" style of medicine only testify to the critical nature of this early period in life. When gynecologists specialize in treating post-menopausal women with hormones in order to allow them to become pregnant, that in itself is an expression of crisis and all too often of desperation. Hormonal therapies often lead to multiplying that which has been so long delayed. Considering the high frequency of multiple births in these situations, one cannot but recall the old adage: "Be careful what you wish for, because your wishes might come true." The problem becomes even more extreme when it leads to ever more highly technological solutions. Geneticists have already succeeded in cloning human embryos in the laboratory, which means they have produced several identical copies of the same embryo in order to increase the chances of a successful pregnancy for infertile couples. In the U.S., more than ten thousand embryos are already being kept quite literally "on ice"—each one is a potential human being left over from an artificial insemination attempt. Although they are no longer needed, one is loathe to simply throw them away, so they are being kept without legal rights in a wintry no-man's land, a liquid nitrogen hell where they await an uncertain future. Sperm banks and the eerie possibilities of genetic engineering foster the illusion that children can be conceived and born beyond the natural limits of the childbearing years and that the attributes of these children can be predetermined to the n'th degree.

If one assumes that the child is aware of fertilization and implantation and that the future course of events is already inherent in the sperm and egg (or that all successive events are fundamentally shaped by their own origins), then one cannot but suspect that the "superkids" from the sperm banks, despite their high IQs and exemplary anatomies, are not liable to be problem-free as far as their souls and emotions are concerned.

The time is ripe for us to admit that we have not yet come anywhere close to adequately comprehending conception, and that every medical breakthrough only makes things more complicated and, in most cases, worse as well. Before anything else can be changed, we need to change our understanding of the situation and develop enough compassion to recognize the wrongs that are currently being committed against these vulnerable and dependent souls. Many people have not the faintest idea of the misery being suffered by the souls of frozen embryos; instead, these people continue to believe that frozen embryos simply do not have souls. Only after we become aware of the reality of the soul can we (potentially) become a humane society and leave the darkness of the so-called "Enlightenment" behind us. At the moment, however, we are incapable of allowing the natural and intimate to occur at its proper time, nor are we able to decide in favor of conception and pregnancy at the appropriately early date. It is above all this indecisiveness that makes conception into a such an inordinately severe crisis.

Questions About Conception and Pregnancy

1. What is my situation with respect to my feelings of primal trust? How well am I able to relax and trust my sleep and my dreams?
2. What about caves? What was my relationship to them as a child, and how do I feel about caves today? Did I fear caves or did I always seek them out? Did I build artificial caves—for example, in my childhood playroom or bedroom?
3. When I enter a new environment, do I feel self-confident or must I create a sense of security through external means?
4. Do fantasies about the Land of Cockaigne play a role in my life?
5. Can I simply enjoy life, or do I need special reasons in order to be happy?
6. What role do blissful and pleasant experiences play in my life?
7. Have I ever experienced ecstatic, oceanic feelings?

Space for Practical Experience

1. Breath meditation: After intensive breath sessions, it is often possible to have feelings of ecstasy, a sense of limitless freedom and out-of-the-body experiences.
2. Warm-water exercise: An exercise can be conducted in body temperature water that can be nearly or equally as effective as experiences in a samadhi tank. If one puts water-wings on one's ankles rather than on one's upper arms, it is possible to experience oneself as floating effortlessly on the water's surface, gently rocked by the rhythm of one's own breath. The less air in the water-wings, the more deeply one's body submerges into the watery element. Of course, this exercise is only recommended for people who know how to swim.
3. Samadhi tank sessions with simulations of the intrauterine period.

4. Therapeutic experiences in the sense of immersing one-
    self in the limitless space prior to conception and in the
    still-free space following conception.

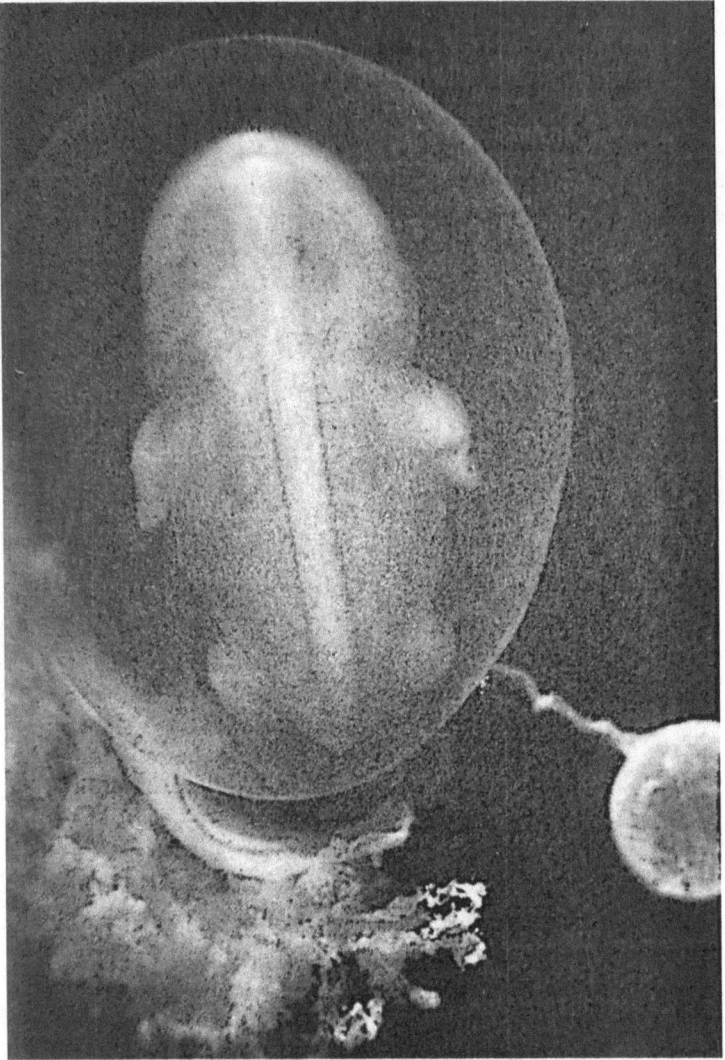

This six-week-old embryo is only 1.5 centimeters long. It is floating in the transparent ball of its amniotic fluid universe and already has an unmistakably human shape. Its spine and limbs are clearly recognizable. This is the time of oceanic feelings, amniocentesis and the majority of abortions.

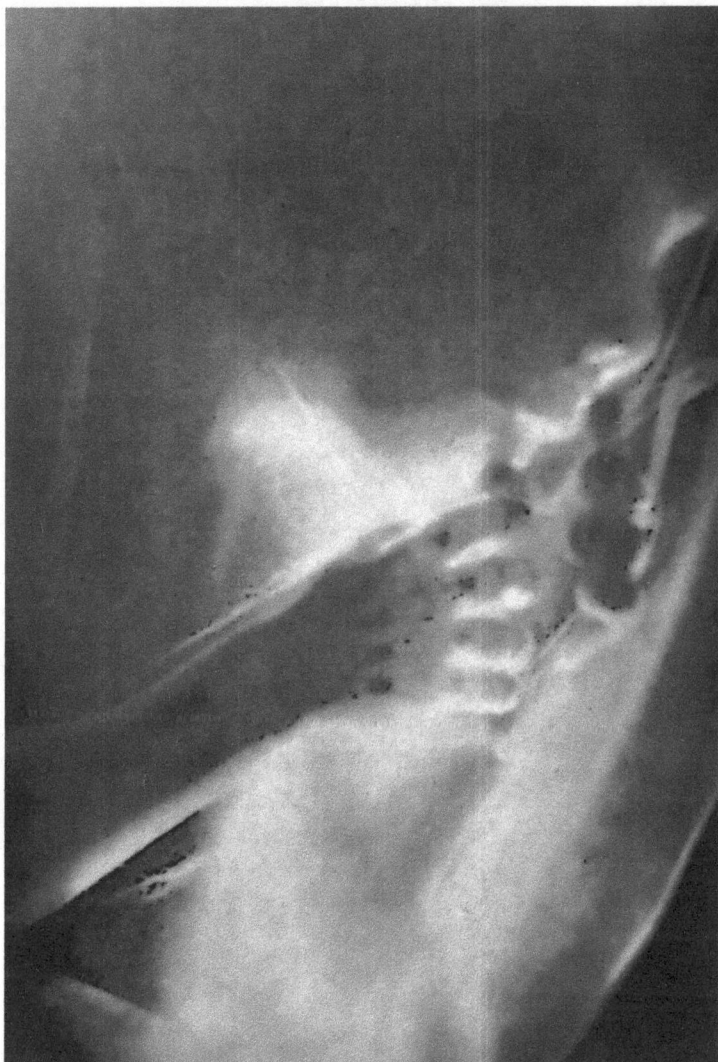

At twelve weeks, the bones of the arms and hands are clearly visible. The three-month-old, still wholly transparent human being gazes with open eyes into its world. It is enclosed within delicate membranes, yet nonetheless vulnerable and threatened.

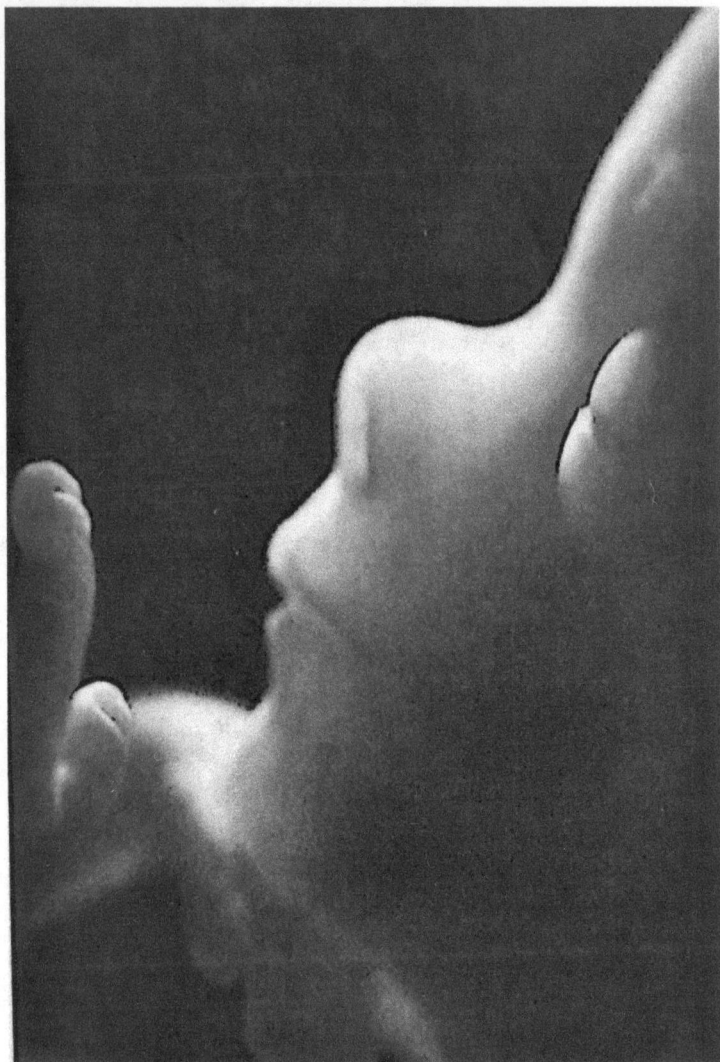

At thirteen weeks, the unborn child closes its eyes again and spends the next few months gazing within. Its features already reveal its individual facial expression. It plays with its fingers, on which fingernails are visible. The vulnerable interval of the first three months has been survived, but it is still not safe from abortion for another two months.

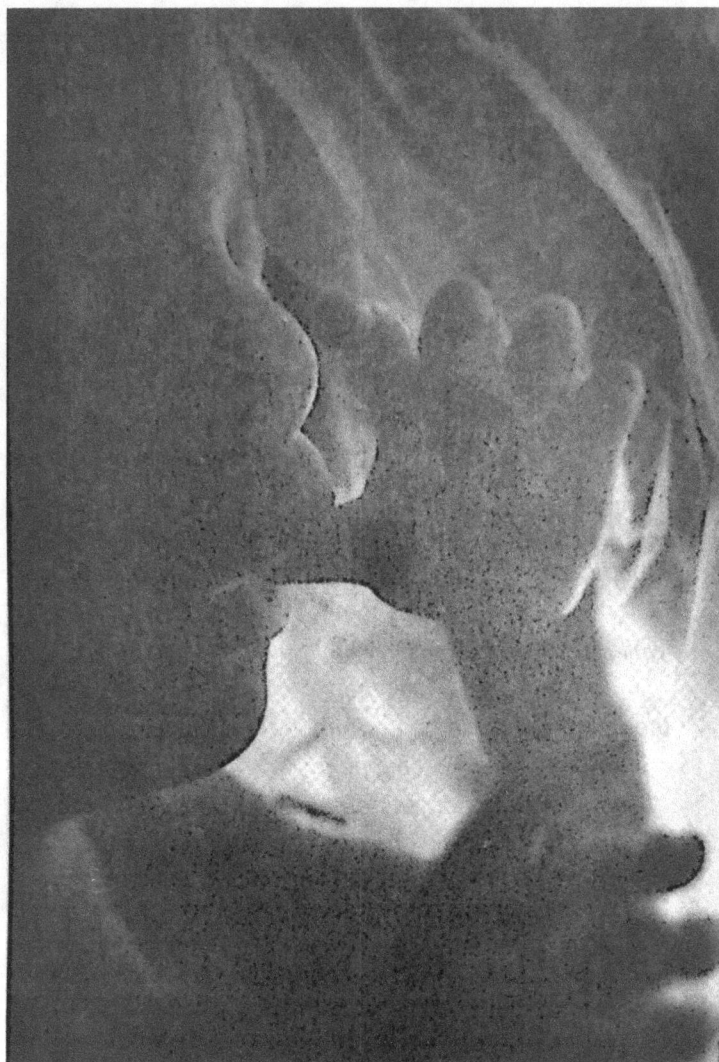

Eighteen-weeks-old and 20 centimeters long, the little creature dreamily sucks its thumb. The embryo moves about freely in its watery world and already has everything it needs for life, even though it has not yet passed the midpoint of its sojourn in the womb.

2. Birth

What seems like the end of the world to the
caterpillar
is, for the master, a butterfly.
—Richard Bach, *Illusions*

I am like a flag surrounded by distances.
I intuit the winds that come and I must experience
them
while the things below me have not yet been moved
by them:
the doors still close gently, and there is silence in the
chimneys;
the windows do not yet tremble, and the dust is still
heavy.

I already know the storms and I'm as excited as the
sea.
And I spread myself out and fall into myself
and throw myself down and am all alone
in the great storm.
Rainer Maria Rilke, Vorgefühl (Premonition)

When we are born, we cry that we are come
To this great stage of fools.
—William Shakespeare, *King Lear*

Just as every crisis in life sums up and takes stock of its preceding life phase, conception is an expression of the life experiences that have preceded it. This may not make much sense to people who deny the idea of multiple incarnations, but it will no doubt become clearer as we summarize the concept with regard to the issues of birth, conception and pregnancy. If pregnancy was characterized by feelings of acceptance and if the arrival of the child was eagerly awaited, then positive and optimistic expectations tend to facilitate the birth and make it less of an ordeal.

We find it easy to understand the critical nature of birth as a decisive step out of the womb and into the world. The simple fact that a book like Leboyer's *Birth Without Violence* is such a success is symptomatic of this attitude. Basically, though, the French gynecologist does little more than give quite natural tips about ways to greet each newly arrived little earthling. Only a society that has slipped unbeknownst away from what is natural would regard Leboyer's ideas as revelations. A look at the history of birth as it has been practiced in the twentieth century will show just how far away we have come from natural childbirth.

It begins with gynecology—a relatively new medical discipline and one with a certain eagerness to legitimize itself—pulling the rug out from under women and laying them *flat on their backs*. With the possible exception of the headstand, it is hard to imagine a less favorable posture in which to give birth. On her back, the pregnant woman finds it difficult to muster the strength needed to press her baby into the world; the child's head presses against her perineum rather than into the available opening. The only advantage of this supine posture is that it allows gynecologists to work in a comfortable, standing position and gives them a convenient view of their workplace. Even a man can readily understand just how inappropriate this position is for the task of childbirth if he considers how difficult it would be for him to defecate while lying flat on his back. Even a humble fecal sausage resists extrusion in this position: a newborn's head has commensurably greater trouble. Women in archaic cultures—the selfsame cultures we so falsely label "primitive"—have traditionally preferred postures such as the squat that allow them to bear down with the necessary pressure and give birth without the need for a perineal incision. Since tribal midwives do not cut the perineum and cannot safely care for the corresponding wound, the birthing women do not have much choice about this. Gynecologists, on the other hand, are so familiar with the procedure that they can sever a perineum more or less blindfolded, with the result that the procedure is routinely performed. In the Sudan, traditional "cord midwives" still hang a cord from the ceiling. The pregnant woman takes hold of the cord and gives birth while other women support her in a squatting position. Women in Borneo give birth while sitting on a preheated wooden bowl. On the Easter Islands, pregnant women give birth while standing with widely spread legs and leaning against their midwives. Mizteka Indian women in Mexico kneel with their legs apart on a straw mat specially woven for this purpose.

Before we place all the blame for our own clumsy birthing procedures on the shoulders of the gynecologists, we ought to consider that in our own predominant field and in our culture's typical "birth preparation," many women choose the supine posture of their own free will. Even if they have begun labor in another posture, after a certain time has passed they are often so completely exhausted they are happy to be able to lie down. At that moment, of course, helpers are needed, and we should be thankful they are so skilled in the techniques of their craft.

Even if much about the supine posture is understandable and "only human," it remains a symbolic problem that the baby's head is aimed at the wrong target from the beginning. Such children cannot but attempt to *ram their heads against the wall* and/or the perineum. Supine childbirth also results in more hemorrhaging and more loss of blood than would otherwise be necessary. The fact that our infants are, on the average, larger and heavier no doubt complicates things, but this is still no reason to choose such an unfavorable posture and routinely perform perineal section.

After being pushed *against the wall* (of the perineum) for so long, the newborn baby is finally squeezed through the bleeding wound of the vagina and the cut or torn perineum. Until recently, it was common practice to focus the bright lights of the operating room here, ensuring that the medical personnel had a clear view of the procedure but simultaneously blinding the newborn as a harsh welcome into the outer world—no doubt a painful ambush after nine months of darkness inside its secure cavern. At the same time, coming out of the womb must have been experienced as entry into a cold world since there was usually a temperature difference of some 15 degrees Celsius (25 degrees Fahrenheit) between the warmth of the womb and the ambient temperature of the typical operating room. Not especially cordial toward the newcomer, the medical reception committee did nothing to ease the transition from the peaceful atmosphere of linkage with the mother to the hectic haste of a modern operating room. On the contrary, all participants made it enduringly obvious that the nine months of security had come to an end.

Immediately after the welcoming torture by light, cold and hectic, the umbilicus that links the newborn with its mother is irrevocably severed. Newborns frequently feel pain when the still-throbbing umbilical cord is cut, even though modern physicians insist the absence of appropriate nerves in the cord makes this is impossible. The pain of that severance can be clearly re-experienced in the course of subsequent therapy sessions. When researchers finally discover the physical basis for the pain felt by the newborn, it will be a poor consolation for the millions of children who suffered this kind of shock upon arrival in the world.[12] Cutting the umbilicus so unduly soon also results in a sudden feeling of asphyxiation, which in turn causes an explosive inflation of the lungs, so that the newborn's first breath is experienced as a painful, burning sensation. All too often, poor breathing habits in later life have their origins in the trauma of asphyxiation and pain accompanying the first breath, according to the motto: "If inhalation is so dreadfully painful, then I'll never take another breath as deeply and as fully."

If, despite all these shocks and traumas, the newborn still has not begun to shriek, it is lifted by its feet, hung head downward and sharply slapped on its naked buttocks until it starts to cry. This helps it earn extra points in the so-called APGAR[13] scheme, a bizarre gynecological invention that is, unfortunately, fully in accord with the tenets of our achievement-oriented society. Incidentally, the basic esoteric assumption that everything is already evident in the beginning is confirmed here since this first test will surely not be the child's last, but represents the starting shot in a life-long competition for "brownie points." In the next stage of the ordeal, the eyes of the still-shrieking newborn were treated with an irritating solution of silver nitrate. This fluid has since been replaced by less irritating antibiotic eye-drops, but it still seems as though life in our society must begin with pain and torture.

As if that were not enough martyrdom, a sharp little skewer is now thrust into the newborn child's heel. Physicians who have perpetrated these tortures for decades have probably never realized that they have been playing the biblical role of the devil,[14] or more precisely, the role played by his accomplice, the snake. According to the Bible, the serpent is only interested in the heels of Eve and her daughters, but modern medicine has always tried to be somewhat more thorough. Of course, physicians have good scientific justifications to rationalize their chicanery. The puncture wound in the heel is needed to draw blood since, after all, it is essential to test the infant's ability to absorb oxygen and, of course, it is never too soon to begin searching for potential congenital diseases. Irritating the infant's eyes is intended to prevent blindness—just in case the mother was suffering from an undiscovered gonorrhea infection.

Although it seems hard to believe, we can all be certain that we, too, were victim to all these ordeals since they were part of regulations and were regularly conducted. Even if, as a whole, such actions by modern medical practitioners appear reasonable, there can be no doubt they concatenate to create the worst imaginable welcoming ceremony for a new little citizen of the planet. A more humane civilization would consider delaying the ordeal for a few hours or days at least. There can be only a few reasons the procedure has not been changed at all or, if changed, only reluctantly. The essential reason derives from the fact that the adults responsible for such harsh and insensitive theatrics believe it makes no difference since newborn babies cannot be consciously aware of it all anyway.

Reading about all these draconian measures, one is apt to feel one's ire rising. But one ought to bear in mind that birth is a crisis that must lead to a breakthrough. Aggression and/or Mars energy are needed to push through the narrow passage. Birth itself is not a primarily gentle event, but it could be better prepared for and accompanied by greater sensitivity, which, in turn, would make it easier for the mother to exert her own Mars energy. So-called "gentle birth" should only be understood as a reaction to the lack of gentleness that has surrounded the birth process in recent decades. Gentle birth, properly understood, has nothing to do with pacifying either the mother or the baby, nor does it reduce the strength needed by both. From the newborn's point of view, as well, birth is anything but a gentle event, although the moment of emergence is often experienced as an overwhelming relief and an indescribable triumph. Grof even talks about "orgiastic" feelings in this context. For the mother, a successful delivery ought ideally be accompanied by feelings of infinite relief, joy and victory, combined with the utter exhaustion of finally being able to let go. Shortly before, the feeling of unlimited power sometimes explosively discharges itself (together with the emerging baby) in a primal scream. What else can the *primal* scream in primal therapy signify but this first scream at the beginning, when everything—pain and relief, joy and triumph—can coincide?

Another possible reason for the decades-long practice of harsh births could be that gentle births, unlike typical brutal deliveries, tend to give one the (correct) impression that the physicians are mostly superfluous. In a hospital's delivery ward, I once met a mother who gave birth to her baby unassisted, in the hospital toilet, shortly before the moment when her baby was scheduled to arrive. The rather perplexed young woman returned from the bathroom carrying the tiny, entirely healthy infant in her arms. Because of her ideal position on the toilet (not very different from the old-fashioned birthing stools) and because of the pressing need to defecate, all the conditions for a natural birth were fulfilled, and the baby chose this comparatively intimate path into the world. The commotion and theatrics the doctors staged when they saw what had happened could hardly disguise the fact that their services were largely unnecessary and little more than an intrusive disturbance.

As if all these arrangements were not enough already, until recently it was common practice to show the newborn to its mother only briefly before shipping it off to one of the awful "baby wards." Here the newborns were free to scream and cry to their hearts' content, effectively preventing one another from sleeping, while their poor mothers lay alone, practically dying from unrequited yearning for their babies. Screaming, according to this type of obstetrics, was regarded as an exercise to strengthen the lungs and as a healthy vital sign. Pacifying the baby by laying it against the mother's breast was considered highly suspicious and not recommended.

Modern medicine had its typical reasons for both practices, reasons that were honestly researched yet seldom profound enough to make long-term sense. As far as breast-feeding is concerned, analysis of mother's milk has shown it is often severely contaminated with toxic substances. Even the milk of Native American mothers in Greenland, for example, contains concentrations of DDT that exceed acceptable limits. That substances such as DDT are even assigned an "acceptable limit" in human beings or their milk is in itself a bad sign. The discovery that mother's milk is present in such high concentrations that, if one were to handle the affair strictly, it would have to be disposed of as "toxic waste" is nothing short of shocking. The milk that remains after pumping a mother's breasts ought not to be simply poured down the drain, but should be disposed of in appropriate toxic-waste facilities. To conclude from all this that it is better to feed infants with artificially adapted ersatz mother's milk is a typical—and since exposed—medical error. The abominable fact of contamination is still the lesser evil compared to the gains in emotional security and the quite literal *influx* of love a child experiences while sucking at its mother's breast. As the German verb *stillen* (to nurse, to satisfy) suggests, the mother satisfies the child's inner need, stilling not only its physical hunger but also quieting and pacifying her baby. A wholly materially oriented medicine overlooks everything except calories and toxins.

Any reasonably sensitive human being can readily understand that crying in general is a sign of need and emergency, not an exercise for the lungs.[15] We need only imagine an adult (e.g., a gynecologist) in a comparable situation: rhythmically squeezed against a wall for hours by a hydraulic press, then harshly dragged through a torn opening and then, suffering serious pain and cut off from his oxygen supply, forced to undergo a trial by asphyxiation. Stark naked and chilled within a few seconds from 21 degrees Celsius (70 degrees Fahrenheit) to 6 degrees Celsius (43 degrees), blinded by bright spotlights, his eyes burning from a caustic solution and his heel smarting from a needle's prick, he is suspended head downward and slapped on his naked buttocks until he screams. Without consolation or comfort, emotionally abandoned, he is given a quick bath and subjected to several other functional examinations, then locked in a room with fellow sufferers. Who would have the courage to interpret his terrified crying as a "breathing exercise" to strengthen the lungs?

Thanks to American research, this routine of early separation from the mother, a practice for which modern medicine offers a host of learned arguments, has finally been discontinued. American scientists discovered that, in most cases, both mother and baby are much better off if they are allowed to remain together. This (re)discovery led to the development of a revolutionary procedure called "rooming-in," that caused quite a stir in the private hospitals where it was first practiced. The idea is simple: if one perseveres in a nonsensical practice long enough, then the return to normality can be celebrated (and marketed) as a great medical discovery. One older gynecologist laconically described "rooming-in" as the end of decades-old stupidity.

Once before in medical history, physicians made childbirth into a life-threatening adventure by infecting and unknowingly killing hundreds of thousands of birthing women with so called "childbed" or "puerperal fever." Unaware of the dangers of infection, they did not always wash their hands adequately after dissecting cadavers. Afterward, they sometimes transferred the deadly germs to birthing mothers and, thus, although they thought they were assisting at a birth, they were inadvertently lending their assistance to the Grim Reaper. Obstetrician Ignaz Semmelweis, the first physician to recognize the source of so much misery, was never honored for his discovery, but was reviled, humiliated and not exonerated his entire life. His life-saving realization was too insulting to the self-images of his medical colleagues. It simply could not be true that physicians themselves were responsible for such awful misfortune.

Nowadays gynecologists are still responsible for causing the soul to suffer much misery; as in the past, they are loathe to accept that fact. What many women and their newborn babies have always felt, what "primitive" people have always known, what midwives working beyond the confines of scholastic medicine have always simply allowed to occur: all this simply cannot be better than what the learned physicians have scientifically proven through decades of carefully controlled research. And yet, it is indeed better! We can only hope that the process of recognizing and acting on these realizations will not take quite as long and meet quite as much resistance as it did in Semmelweis' day. Just as hygiene in the delivery room has become a matter of course today, so too must awareness of the needs of the souls of mother and child likewise become a matter of course in the future.

The alternative to the horrific medical scenario of traditional hospital births is described by Leboyer in gentle and sensitive prose. His methods have since attained greater and greater acceptance among midwives and, more recently, among more enlightened gynecologists and obstetricians. Babies are even being born at home, which often involves the inestimably important advantage that no gynecologists are on hand to interfere and interpose their medical knowledge. Of course, this also involves a danger since obstetricians can save lives in the rare cases when their services are actually needed.

People contemplating home birth should, therefore, prepare themselves with particular care. Ideally, of course, the birth would be accompanied by an experienced midwife and a gynecologist who was mature enough not to feel constantly compelled to demonstrate all his skills. In Holland there has long been an exemplary system that in recent years, unfortunately, has gradually fallen victim to so-called "progress." Not long ago, however, some ninety percent of all Dutch babies were born at home, while the gynecologists kept themselves in the background, waiting in an ambulance "just in case." At that time, and as one would expect, infant mortality rates[16] in Holland were lower than they were in Germany. Although the practice of home births is on the decline in Holland, fully fifty percent of all Dutch births still take place at home today—without increasing risks to either the mothers or the infants.

Of course, "gentle births" can also take place in hospitals and that practice is on the increase. Fundamentally, however, we should realize that giving birth is not a sickness but an entirely healthy, natural event that, rather than requiring the services of a physician and the facilities of a hospital, requires above all the natural strength of mother and child. Many clinics now "allow" patients (at least those who are privately insured) to give birth in their own single-bed rooms or in special birthing rooms whose atmosphere feels safer and more cozy than that prevalent in old-fashioned, bright and loud operating rooms. Unobtrusive, soft lighting; relaxing music and relatively warm, infant-friendly ambient temperature are ensured. No labor-inducing drugs are injected. Everyone simply waits for nature to run its course in its own rhythm and with its own timing. This alone makes birthing much easier since the mother's bodily tissues are allowed to become suppler and more elastic in preparation for the event. The mother is also often allowed to give birth in whatever position she prefers. Some clinics have resurrected the old birthing chairs, and some even offer the luxury of underwater births. The latest invention is a so-called "birth wheel" the mother can adjust to any desired position. If the birthing mother has decided in favor of a squatting position, some gynecologists lie humbly on the floor and use a simple flashlight to observe the progress of cervical dilation. And, as one would expect, many women once again are giving birth without perineal incisions or tearing.

Some mothers have prepared themselves and their unborn babies so well they need no assistance at all and simply allow the event to take its natural course, guiding the process with their own strength. Phrases like "the festival of birth"—a cruel joke for three-quarters of the 20th century—suddenly seem appropriate once again. And to say that a pregnant woman is "expecting"— the German equivalent literally means "in hopefulness"—once again makes sense. Leaving the protective cavity of the womb is a decisive step in the life of every individual human being, comparable in its ramifications to prehistoric humankind's first wary emergence from the protective caves of Mother Earth. It is entirely appropriate to take these steps with sensitivity and awareness, and to greet them with celebration. Today, as in the distant past, emergence represents a quantum leap in the evolution from the troglodytic existence of the cavemen to the potential enlightenment of human existence in the sunlit world.

Whereas in the past, preparations for birth were mostly in the hands of medical personnel and were largely confined to rather functional breathing exercises and calisthenics, nowadays there is an increasingly broad spectrum of possibilities. In the stress of the birth process, the old exercises seldom made much of a useful contribution, sometimes even making the mother feel she was a failure.

An ever greater number of woman are taking matters into their own capable hands, undergoing therapy to clarify their own birth traumas and, thus, as a side effect, undergoing the best imaginable preparation for giving birth themselves. Using methods from rebirthing[17] and related therapies, it is not so difficult to find the most appropriate method of breathing, even if at first this requires a certain amount of courage and even though relatively few physicians are familiar with this technique. If a woman has contacted her powerful, deep breath long before the impending birth, then during the birth she will also be able to breathe fully, without the danger of experiencing the cramps physicians quite reasonably fear. Like the proper squatting position,[18] this type of breathing helps increase the strength of labor contractions. If the mother is able to stay connected to her own strength and to consciously endure the birth—both of which often require voluntary noninterference by the obstetricians[19]—then the act of giving birth can indeed come much closer to being a truly orgiastic event. The squatting posture means that obstetricians may have more difficulty seeing what is going on, but it also means they will likely have less work to do. They will simply have to accept the fact that, at least in this show, they are the supporting actors and by no means the leading lady or celebrated newcomer.

The unborn child, too, must be prepared for its birth. Contacting the fetus via the mother's inner voice or by other intuitive means can be an invaluable help in this process. It is equally important that both mother and her soon-to-be-born baby share the same optimistic, non-defensive attitude. It is advantageous for the mother to contact her inner voice, either through meditation or by other means, as early as possible and, in the best case, prior to the onset of her pregnancy. On the other hand, it is also entirely possible for the mother to feel her way into this realm of the soul's landscape after conception but still early in pregnancy. Once she has contacted her own inner voice, she can easily begin communicating with her unborn child.

Children who are prepared in this way can also be conceived differently. The child's initial reception into the intrauterine maternal world (i.e., at its conception) usually reflects its subsequent reception in the extrauterine material world (i.e., post partem). A look at extreme cases will help clarify this. A child conceived after years of longing, conceived and accepted in a loving atmosphere and nourished with love throughout nine months of pregnancy, is likely to be lovingly greeted at birth. On the other hand, a child conceived during a rape is unlikely to be nourished with love during pregnancy. Instead, its mother would be more likely to deny its existence and—assuming she does not terminate her pregnancy—would only allow it to come into the world more or less against her will.

A child born by the "gentle birth" method is not immediately separated from its mother. Before severing the umbilical cord, the infant is laid upon its mother's belly—while the umbilicus, still linking the two human beings, continues to nourish it. In most cases, once the cord stops pulsing, the infant begins to breathe of its own accord, without the shock of asphyxiation and the accompanying panic and pain. The separation of the one heart into two functionally separate heart chambers can occur more gently and more harmoniously. At this point, the now obsolete umbilical cord can be painlessly severed. Of course, the little person stays with its mother, experiences her warmth from the outside and, if it so desires, is free to make its first attempts at suckling. The old-fashioned practice of beginning life with one or two days of fasting is no longer compulsory, although it would seem that this practice has done no harm since otherwise the mother's milk would begin to flow sooner than on the second day after the birth.

The sum of all of these small changes creates an entirely different perinatal pattern. From the beginning, both mother and baby find it much easier to grow accustomed to one another. The first days are decisive for their subsequent relationship, so it is a good idea to use this time wisely. Among animals, the phenomenon of post-partem imprinting has long been the subject of thorough study. Everyone is familiar with the photograph of Konrad Lorenz and the goslings who have imprinted on him as their "mother," and who faithfully follow him in all conceivable (and some inconceivable) situations. It is hard to believe that gynecology continues to lag so far behind the science of animal behavior and that gynecologists still routinely separate mothers from their newborn infants. But times are changing, and it is above all the mothers themselves who are realizing that it is far better to begin this new phase of life in harmonious togetherness with their newborn infants rather than by allowing their infants to imprint on operating-room personnel or maternity-ward nurses. Even if a cesarean delivery is unavoidable, at least the father should be present in the operating room to take the newborn baby into his arms, although this expedient frequently causes the baby to develop into a so-called "papa's child." No research has been conducted to discover what effects, if any, are caused in the souls of children who imprint on and are then abandoned by medical personnel. Perhaps they develop into the kind of people who continually run from one doctor to the next!

This description, indeed, this commendation of "gentle birth," should not cause us to forget that, until just a few years ago, the first described, more brutal version was standard procedure—and continues as standard procedure for patients without costly, private health insurance. Readers who are shocked and dismayed by these descriptions can be fairly sure they were victims of similarly brutal births. Even people who were born at home are likely to have suffered through that era's typically insensitive medical scenario.

Today's "progress" deserves to be written within quotation marks since it is, in fact, a *regression* to older methods of childbirth dating from an era when birthing had not yet been surrendered to men's hands, when scientific research had not yet assumed priority over the well-being of women and their newborn babies. This is especially clear when we consider "rooming-in," the trend toward breast-feeding, the renewed popularity of home births and the trend toward creating medication-free and chemical-free zones surrounding the birth. The so-called "new discovery" of homeopathic childbirth preparation is really nothing more than a rediscovery.

Birth Problems

The fundamental perinatal problem, the one that causes it to become such a complex crisis, has two roots: on the one hand, the lack of primal trust; on the other hand, the lack of sufficient expulsive power. If too little or no primal trust has been developed during the intrauterine period, the unborn child cannot let go of a situation that has never given that child what it owes her. This may be easier to comprehend when we consider the situation at life's opposite pole. A person who has not created adequate material security encounters problems when the time comes to let go of the working world, and tends to cling to her job for better or worse. In an era when people are beginning to deal ever more sensitively with childbirth, but in which conception and the weeks of gestation are treated with increasing insensitivity, primal trust is difficult to establish. This makes it difficult for unborn babies to take the decisive step into extrauterine life. Such children have never felt adequately cared for *in* the womb, so they are less than eager to leave the nest when the time comes. One expression of this reticence could be the increasing number of high-risk births and cesarean sections.

On the other hand, a lack of expulsive power is less a result of inability to decide than it is a consequence of our unconscious dealings with Mars energy and aggression (from the Latin word *aggredi*, meaning "to step forward, to advance, to penetrate, to attack"). Healthy aggression is fundamental and indispensable for a successful birth. But since we have so often devalued the principle of aggression, we find it difficult to deal with it in a reasonable manner. Aggression is necessary: not only on the part of the mother, who needs it in order to motivate her labor contractions, but also on the part of the child, who needs it in order to dare the courageous, headfirst leap into life. The primal power of Mars, that makes possible every new beginning and that supplies the necessary energy, belongs at the inception of life. Mars is the "motor" of all births. The baby bird needs Mars energy to fight its way out of the egg, to hammer with its sharp little beak against its confining shell until the shell cracks and the nestling emerges. In that beak, we can see Mars' signature (i.e., everything that is pointed, acute and dangerous). It is the same point we find at the tip of every lance and every knife, at the front of every jet fighter and every rocket, but also at the tip of every bud and every sprout. Spring is the natural season of Mars and hence of birth. It is the season when most animals are born, when trees *sprout* leaves, when lettuce *shoots* up from the garden, when billions of seeds sprout roots that *pierce* and *penetrate* Mother Earth, when countless buds *burst* their husks. All this occurs *naturally*, without brutality or malevolence, but nonetheless full of Mars' *mar*tial, aggressive energy.

We human beings would also reap benefits from the more positive aspects of this principle, that Heraclitus called "the father of all things," if we could find more in Mars energy than merely war and brutality, and use martial strength to help us live more courageously, take decisive first steps in new areas, confront and address our problems and strike while the iron of life is still hot. We could transgress old cognitive limits and dare to explore new intellectual territories. But we have rejected aggression and also rejected its principle, Mars, together with the decisive take-charge attitude that goes along with martial energy. Consequently, we have made ourselves into enemies of aggression and created a host of problems for ourselves. This means that we become aggressive in the negative sense, and that we relegate healthy aggression to a shadowy existence—where it becomes truly dangerous. Instead of developing a culture of debate and confrontation, we try to avoid strife at any cost, with the result that we harvest precisely the opposite of what we have sown. Although we and all the world's peoples and politicians want peace and talk about peace, the world is buried beneath an avalanche of weapons.

No other illness is growing faster than allergies—those use-less (because they are hopeless) wars that a growing number of people are fighting within their own bodies. The "enemies" are essentially harmless substances such as pollen and cat hair, household dust, various foods and many other things. The efforts of all the world's allergic people have not helped to reduce the pollen count and never will. Their war and its goals are quite simply nonsensical. Suppressed and consequently unconscious aggressions are lived out on the battlefield of the body. But allergies are as senseless in the microcosm as are wars in the macrocosm. Wherever we look, we find examples of unresolved aggression that has been so thoroughly banished to a shadowy, unexamined area that we hardly recognize it for what it is.

Here, too, lies the more profound root of the increasingly frequent problems with giving birth. Measured according to the increasing numbers of high-risk births, academic medicine would say that giving birth is becoming an ever more dangerous event. We thus come closer to the basic motif of all developmental crises—namely, indecisiveness. We have a tendency to delay the moment when we finally rally the necessary energies and, thus, not long after, we harvest various unredeemed forms of the Mars principle. That principle is always involved (e.g., during perineal section, when a knife is used and blood flows). Martial energy is involved in cesarean section no less than in natural childbirth. The only difference is that, in the former procedure, the Mars energy is wielded not by the birthing mother but by the gynecologist. The fact that, in equally risky situations, German women are twice as likely as Swedish women to deliver their babies by cesarean section also means that Mars and martial energy are involved unconsciously twice as frequently in Germany. This unconscious presence is what makes Mars energy dangerous. Nearly every pregnant woman in Germany undergoes some incision (cesarean or perineal) in the course of her delivery. Every seventh delivery is by cesarean section, which amounts to fifteen percent of all German deliveries—more than 126,000 women in 1991. And the tendency is rising.

It is also interesting to note that statistics vary from hospital to hospital. There are certain hospitals with a twenty-three percent rate of cesareans, while other institutions have only a ten percent rate, which suggests that Germany could potentially have a situation like that in Sweden. No doubt the more careful physicians are most likely to opt for cesarean delivery since they are more apt to judge that the situation has become risky. Mars must make himself felt, either through courage or through the scalpel. It is only human that we try to avoid facing him, but this only makes him more threatening, ultimately giving one an especially unfavorable form of precisely that which one was trying to avoid. This is seldom so clearly evident as it is in childbirth.

Unfortunately, danger also lurks behind the growing trend toward natural childbirth. Nature has made birthing a highly aggressive event. When we fail to openly acknowledge this fact, the aggression must seek other paths. If a woman so thoroughly denies the martial principle that she produces no labor contractions, the gynecologist has little choice but to step in and artificially induce the necessary pressure. If no gynecologist is present because the mother has chosen to allow nature to take its course, then childbirth can become life-threatening for mother and child alike. This danger, of course, brings Mars into the picture again. Naturalness demands a large measure of holistic understanding. The exclusion of a fundamental energy (e.g., the Mars principle) necessarily compels it to find unexpected and unresolved paths through which to express itself—expressions we generally interpret as catastrophes. A similar pattern occurs when the lunar energies of the intrauterine period are ignored. An insufficiently maternal womb not only makes it difficult to let go, but is also sought in later life in the most inappropriate circumstances. One patient for whom this issue was particularly relevant was told by his boss: "We're a business, not a womb!"

Understandable counter-reactions to the functional, unfeeling procedures of academic medicine can create terrifying shadow sides of their own. Children are already suffering injury during alternative home births, and especially during underwater births, simply because the parents deliberately and as a matter of principle chose to exclude modern medicine from the scene. This is literally a case of throwing out the baby with the bath water. Although such problems are by no means as prevalent as academic physicians would have us believe,[20] they are no doubt too numerous compared with the variety of options available to prevent them.

A thoroughly well-meaning but, with respect to the Mars principle, naively approached birth unfortunately backfires all too often into a very tardy and all the more brutal attempt at abortion. If a woman cannot find her own access to Mars and his energy, she ought to gratefully accept the gynecologists' help since they *do* have access to his energy and are ready and willing to assist.

Birth is the decisive step into life. Its pattern is repeated in all of the subsequent "births" we undergo later in life. After all, from a symbolic point of view, every new beginning is a birth, as is every venture into uncharted territory and every step across a former limit. It is, therefore, worthwhile to know about one's own birth pattern in order to prepare oneself for dealing with the special individual problems one may have with new beginnings and breakthroughs.

Beyond this, the whole pattern of life is seminally concentrated in the pattern of birth as the beginning of life in polarity, much the way a seed already contains the entire life of the plant. That is the reason astrology chooses the moment one takes one's first breath as the starting point for decoding the framework and conditions of a person's life.

Psychotherapy can help us achieve a profound acquaintance with this first and most important phase of life. This is why a later re-experiencing of one's own birth plays such a central role in re-incarnation therapy. Reconstructing the birth process by tapping the mother's memory can likewise reveal the basic pattern and shed at least some light on these critical issues.

Birth Complications

Who can blame a child for avoiding the seemingly dangerous headfirst leap into life and choosing instead the apparently safer feet-first jump? The child cannot see where it is being pushed. It cannot see the "light at the end of the (birth) tunnel." The less adequately it has been prepared for the event by its mother, the more steadfastly will it resist the birth. Furthermore, children in this phase can sometimes still foresee the basic tasks awaiting them in their upcoming lives and may react to that vision by trying to withdraw in fear.

Finally, even the gentlest birth is a test of courage and a struggle that must seem threatening because of the unprecedented narrowness of the birth canal. Narrowness is connected with fear in many ways, as we can see by examining the Latin word *angustus*, which is the root of the German words *eng* (narrow) and *Angst* (fear or anxiety). Hence, even a natural and sensitively conducted birth is always an initiation into the realm of narrowness and anxiety. All situations in later life when one feels oppressively "boxed in" can revivify an unconscious birth trauma and call the corresponding anxiety to the surface.

Practically every birth represents a trauma. But traumas need not always be repressed, leading to a weakening of the individual. When they are consciously dealt with, traumas can make an important contribution toward strengthening the individual. The old saying, "If it doesn't kill you, it'll make you stronger" expresses this same realization. But the adage is only true if the situation is conscious. Otherwise, energy is constantly expended to keep the situation below the threshold of consciousness.

The typical birth trauma, one that can cause problems later on, generally takes place in the following manner: although the pain and labor contractions are growing increasingly severe, the child somehow has no more chance to oppose the situation. The expulsive force of the labor contractions and the efforts of the obstetricians are so overwhelming that the child must stop fighting and surrender to them. This surrender can either occur consciously or else as a kind of fleeing from an expulsive and painful body. In the latter case, the body is born, but more or less left alone, even abandoned. Only after the worst is over does the consciousness and/or the soul return to the body. The child's preparation in a sensitive environment and the mother's combined mental and emotional care can make it easier for the child to surrender to the inevitable. Not only do children understand a great deal more than we think, they are also especially sensitive to the language of emotions—a language adults have often forgotten or at least underestimated.

If the mother flees from the conscious experience into the painless sleep of general anesthesia, the child feels even more abandoned since its experience of the pain continues despite the mother's anesthesia. Every anesthesia is nothing other than the forced expulsion of consciousness from the body. The body's pain receptors remain fully functional, but no one is "at home" to receive their messages. This is why it is possible to consciously relive operations in a trance, and why the person in the trance perceives the events from outside her body. Perhaps this helps to explain why, despite anesthesia, operations are so strenuous for the organism. For the birthing mother, anesthesia has an added disadvantage: drugged into unconsciousness, she can hardly participate in the initiatory character associated with birth.

When a birth is experienced as so awful that the consciousness flees from the body, a corresponding experience is never gained. On the one hand, a person with an unresolved birth pattern tends to fear all "narrow" situations and new beginnings; on the other hand, he will unconsciously seek out such situations in order to learn to cope with them. This is the nature of the unresolved crisis: we consciously hate it and try to avoid it, yet we unconsciously seek it out again and again. In the school of life, as in elementary school, the same rules apply. If we never learn to read, we soon come to hate reading. And precisely because of that unresolved task we are continually confronted by this issue until we give up our resistance, bow to the inevitable and learn to read.

The fact that forms of therapy such as rebirthing are so successful in Germany indicates how many people in our society need to experience birth or rebirth so that, better late than never, they can finally reconcile themselves to their birth traumas.

This is also the point where we can find an explanation for the astonishing phenomenon that this therapeutic technique, which has grown increasingly popular among alternative therapists since the 1920s, continues to be reviled and treated as an illness by academically oriented physicians. What they describe as hyperventilation tetanus, what they fight against with calcium and valium injections, is identical with the situation psychotherapists deliberately encourage in their clients. The therapists gently yet consciously lead their clients through the feelings of narrowness and claustrophobia. Repeated experience of such anxious crises allows awareness to flow into suppressed traumas and, breath by breath, dissolve them. Academic medicine's response merely suppresses what fate has brought to light (i.e., the individual's natural self-therapeutic efforts) and uses medication to put an untimely end to the attempt. This only serves to bind yet another patient to modern medicine since the individual will repeatedly face such situations as long as the underlying anxieties continue to demand resolution.

This example helps us recognize the basic differences between academic, allopathic approaches and those that relate to healing in the true sense of the word. Whereas academic medicine helps us continue pursuing the affairs of life despite signals from psyche and soma, homeopathically motivated methods such as reincarnation therapy encourage us to accept and fulfill the learning tasks fate has in store for us.

The typical genesis of hyperventilation tetanus helps clarify this relationship. When people with unresolved birth traumas encounter anxiety-producing situations, they tend to deny their anxiety. What is given no space in conscious awareness takes the space it needs somewhere else. This is when forced breathing begins as an embodiment of the corresponding pattern. Everything feels narrower and the first cramps may begin. Now, through the narrowness of the body, the individual becomes consciously aware of the soul's anxiety. If she continues to breathe, the breath can carry her through the situation, and the individual can discover the openness that lies beyond the narrowness. When expansiveness and openness are felt, anxiety cannot continue to exist and it simply dissolves. If, on the other hand, the process is chemically interrupted as soon as the first cramps appear, the inner state of narrowness becomes permanently established. The patient's tendency to slip into this state again and again becomes greater with each successive crisis since fate never abandons its hope of carrying the individual through the narrowness of anxiety and into the *breath* and *breadth* of freedom. As the availability of allopathic medical care becomes greater and greater, fate's chances grow correspondingly smaller and smaller.

Fate, with its tendency to teach, and academic medicine, with its attempts to prevent learning at almost any price, are working against one another. A glance at history, and even at the history of science alone, should suffice to answer the question, "Who will win?" What we currently describe as a "paradigm shift" could give us reason to hope the two opponents might embark on a more conciliatory course in the near future.

Breech Presentation

The less adequately a baby is prepared for its birth, the more likely it is to refuse to take the courageous headfirst leap into life. In breech presentation, the baby refuses to assume the proper, courageous position. Instead, it turns itself in diametrical opposition to that position. This behavior can easily be understood when we consider it from the following viewpoint. Imagine yourself standing atop a ten-meter-tall diving platform above a swimming pool, looking down from above at an awfully tiny little puddle that your body must hit.[21] If this situation is new and if you have been poorly prepared for it, it is only natural to refuse to jump. If, however, every avenue of retreat is blocked, and if continually greater pressure is being applied to force you toward the edge of the platform, you might, despite your fears, leap feet-first since in this posture your anxiety is less than it would be if you leapt headfirst.

Rather than stretching its head toward life, the baby shows life its little backside. This posture expresses both refusal and protest. The gesture's meaning is obvious, and would be immediately understood in every other situation. But, as is so often the case, this attempt to say, "Kiss my ass" tends to backfire. The narrowness in the cavern grows ever more oppressive, the pressure of labor contractions grows ever more unbearable, until the birth begins—but the baby is in the wrong position. At first it seems that the refusal has been successful since the little pelvis slips easily through the birth canal. But then comes the widest portion of the baby's body—its own head. The crowning glory has by far the greatest diameter. As it enters the passage, its size blocks the way. And since the umbilical cord is also still there, the cord gets squeezed, too. This leads to feelings of asphyxiation that are far more dangerous than those that accompany premature severing of the umbilical cord. The child cannot breathe because its head, together with its mouth and nose, are still stuck in the birth canal. The longer this dangerous situation continues, the weaker the child becomes through inadequate supply of life energy, the more excitedly the obstetricians behave and the more desperately the mother struggles. Oxygen deficit can lead to severe problems, ranging from unimaginably severe feelings of being stifled, mortal fear and permanent brain damage. What the child has so strenuously sought to avoid has nonetheless come to pass: a life-threatening situation.

The avoidance of the Mars principle—expressing itself here in the refusal to take the courageous, headfirst leap—cannot be successful, but can only transform the principle into unresolved, and hence potentially pathological, forms. The situation atop the ten-meter-tall diving platform is similar. Here diving feet-first seems to be the lesser of two evils, but then the "fat end" (the head) only comes later. Water usually forces its way into the nostrils, and the stability during immersion is so poor that one risks a painful belly landing. Leaping headfirst may seem more dangerous but, in the final analysis, is the safer of the two alternatives.

The obvious pattern behind breech presentation is an early, anxious rejection of life. The child does not want to come into the world, and it clearly expresses this refusal through its body language. There is also a tendency to reject the planned pattern and insist upon one's own path, even if the price for this stubbornness entails jeopardizing one's life. To sum it up, breech presentation is the expression of a refusal based on fear, together with a certain stubbornness without regard for (one's own) losses. Furthermore, there is a refusal to accept the necessary surrender. The head refuses to move into the proper, downward position where it is entirely vulnerable. *Keeping one's head up* is a strategy that promises success in later life, but in the birth situation this exaggerated refusal to bow down is a sign of inappropriate stubbornness. The (fat) head insists on having things its own way and tries to keep itself safe, only to discover it has made a terrible mistake since the head is what suffers most when oxygen grows short during the ordeal in the birth canal.

Later life offers plenty of subsequent birth situations, all of which demand courage and a certain degree of assertiveness. The danger is that people who were born in the breech presentation will continue to turn their backs on life's challenges, will continue to insist on having things their own way, no matter what the costs.

This type of pattern is set at birth and nothing can make us release it, much the same way the positions of one's planets are set at birth and cannot be retroactively rearranged. But once one has understood the active principles, one need not continue to choose the unresolved variants. The Mars problems suggested by breech presentation could be handled differently if the individual learned to surrender and reconcile himself or herself to this principle. For example, the early refusal to accept Mars could be resolved by working for peace and fighting against war. Antiwar activists of this ilk would have the added advantage of knowing they are also working to overcome an individual problem. This would help them avoid much embarrassment with their surroundings, while enabling them to reconcile themselves to their own struggle with Mars. For example, they might realize how much fun it is to assume a position in the opposition or to engage in a righteous battle. Their strong sense of duty could be an asset since these are the people who (ever since birth) have refused to bow down their heads and surrender.

Finally, the child who is born in breech presentation tends to be bellicose and stubborn in both psyche and soma. Breech presentation creates dramatic situations during birth, situations that demand extra speed from the midwives, extra concentration and pressure from the mother. From the moment of their birth, these breech-birth children have compelled everyone around them to worry about them and their lives.

Transverse Presentation

The direct opposition of breech presentation is usually less dangerous than the crosswise posture of transverse presentation. When a person sets herself *crosswise*, as an unborn child can do, she is clearly refusing to participate. As long as a person stands in direct opposition to an effort, one is at least traveling in the same axis, albeit in the opposite direction. Opponents struggle with one another, but at least they are fighting over the same issue, and this unites them as adversaries. But when one of the combatants turns ninety degrees from the struggle, there can be no further progress in either direction. The refusal is complete. This is what the unborn child can do: unwilling to be born, it simply wedges itself into its cavern and refuses to come out.

Now and then, experienced midwives successfully turn the baby around and change its posture from either breech or transverse presentation into a more comfortable and serviceable position. Interventions of this kind are much more than merely mechanical repositioning. They are a fine art, based on much experience and much intuition and involving the bodies and souls of everyone present. If no such wise woman is at the birth, or if the child's resistance is so strong it cannot be repositioned, then there is often no other choice but to resort to the gross mechanical procedure of a cesarean section. From the child's point of view, the life-saving cesarean is a victory ensuing from its own self-destructive and uncooperative attitude. In this way, the infant avoids the tough fight for its own survival.

At first glance, cesarean section seems to have many advantages. Thanks to the gentle sleep of general anesthesia, the mother is spared the pangs of birth. The god Hypnos spreads his dark, velvety cloak about her and relieves her of all responsibility. The child can patiently wait until the maternal "curtain" is suddenly opened and gynecologists' sterile hands carefully lift it from its hiding place. It has insisted on having its own way and avoided the narrowness, trouble and potential anxiety of pushing its large head through the narrow birth canal. But long-term studies of people who were born by cesarean section have shown that this expedient is anything but advantageous. The procedure reveals just how intimately mother and child are bound to one another. One must assume that both of them have an inner investment in the situation. If the child refuses to accept responsibility, then the mother must also be absolved of responsibility and released into the unconsciousness of anesthesia. If the child will not take the leap into life, neither can the mother, who must be anesthetized. In this way, neither has the chance to fully experience the birth.

For gynecologists, of course, cesarean sections are undoubtedly advantageous since the procedure earns them esteem— and money. In fact, they must be able to prove that they have performed a certain number of cesareans in order to be granted a license as specialist. This regulation could well be partly to blame for the large number of cesarean sections regularly performed in Germany.[22] After all, it is a matter of judgment when to abandon other attempts and resort to the scalpel of cesarean section.

The pattern of the *cross-headed* child born by cesarean section is well expressed by the name for this surgical procedure. A Roman caesar was born by this imperial route into life, according to the motto: "I'll turn myself perpendicular to the normal path, and leave the problem of 'what shall become of me' to the others."

What seems like a convenient tactic at first, in later life can develop into a troublesome and dangerous pattern. After all, we cannot be sure there will always be well-meaning and competent helpers on hand to take all the risks and do all the work for us. The individual will continue to search for cunning, low-risk alternatives to cope with each new beginning, but the solutions will seldom be as elegant as the first time.

Despite its wish to tarry forever in the intrauterine Land of Cockaigne, the child failed at making its wish come true. The motivation behind this refusal to emerge is so regressive that, were it not for the saving grace of the gynecologist's scalpel, it would have led to a catastrophe. Mother and child would both have lost their lives as a result of the refusal. If no "birth assistants" are on hand in later life, the danger is that the person will again refuse to accept the imminent new beginning and will try to avoid facing her true tasks in life. People whose tolerance for frustration is so low they have never learned to push boldly onward despite narrowness and anxiety are liable to heap up such a vast stockpile of anxieties and fears that it threatens to suffocate them. Instead of facing the facts, such individuals tend to persist in the paralysis of resistance, remaining "fearful little children" all their lives and living life according to the motto: "Mommy or daddy, the nation, the society or somebody somewhere will take care of me."

The Mars issue, ubiquitous in the perinatal situation, insists on expressing itself. In the case of cesarean section, it expresses itself through the gynecologists' sharply pointed surgical instruments. Mars is entirely in his element when a tautly stretched belly is slit open, and far more blood flows during cesarean section than is ordinarily spilt during a natural birth. Mars is present at the birth, but absent in the mother and the child. The newborn never learns how to direct its energy toward mastering a new beginning, but learns instead that self-assertion is not really necessary. It has not used its own power to enter the new phase of life, and this pattern can later prove burdensome. If this strategy is to continue to be successful, the individual will always need a fully equipped operating room manned by a team of helpers eager to perform whatever subsequent operations present themselves during that person's later life. Such people frequently confront their environments with an imperial attitude: "I shall remain in a state of primal unity. After all, why should I beat my head against the wall or dirty my fingers with the filth of the material world? Let the others take care of polarity and its mundane demands."

Cesarean Section

Problems of the Mother

As a consequence of the anesthesia, cesarean section means that a mother has not been consciously initiated into being a mother. Despite even the most intensive efforts later on, there is no equivalent substitute for this essential initiation. Furthermore, the mother has missed the opportunity to imprint on her baby during the all-important first post-partem hours since she has spent them in the bonds of Morphius. In a very profound sense, she has overslept and missed the birth. Giving life to another human being ought to be an active process. It is almost as if she had arranged all the details for her baby's birthday celebration and then not been there at the actual party.

Some women realize this later, and the realization gives rise to their longing to give birth to their next baby without anesthesia. Unfortunately, many gynecologists adhere to the motto: "Once by cesarean, always by cesarean." Since they entirely ignore the ritualistic significance of birth, they have plenty of convincing, purely functional arguments to justify their acts. The first operation has left a scar in the uterus; the strenuous contractions of a normal birth could cause the old scar to tear open, creating a life-threatening situation. However, the uterus is a strong muscle that, like other muscles, heals well. After they have healed thoroughly, it is not uncommon for athletes who have suffered from torn muscles (such tears are usually far more serious than the clean wounds resulting from sharp cuts) to resume their careers in competitive sports.

In most cases, the conflict is resolved with a "low-risk" second cesarean. Sometimes, however, a real danger arises when neither of the opponents agrees to compromise. Women who are determined to experience this time around what they missed during the first birth face off against gynecologists who refuse to depart from their academically trained opinions. The confrontation inevitably creates unnecessary drama. In one case, a woman who had already had two babies by cesarean section gave birth to her third child by normal means in the company of her women friends on a little island far from the nearest gynecologist. That was a dangerously risky game, and the fact that everything turned out for the best shows how strong the uterus is and how well it is able to heal itself. But it also shows how stubborn obstetricians and their frustrated patients can be. "Experiments" like these are possible, but ought to be conducted in modern hospitals—just in case. Although there may be reason to doubt the need for a first cesarean, the need for a hospital during subsequent births can only be doubted by foolish and rash individuals for whom principles are more valuable than their own lives and the lives of their babies. Physicians in Germany

are generally uncomfortable about taking responsibility for anything outside the narrow limits of their customary procedures.
They might be advised to secure the woman's signature on a
document stating they have warned her of the risks. Moreover,
they ought to stay nearby during such high-risk situations.

Our high-tech medical establishment pursues its path to the
finish, according to the motto, "We've come this far already, so
there can be no turning back now." Once the physicians have
chosen an artificial path like cesarean section, they must continue with it and accept its far ranging consequences. A person
who has accepted an organ transplant and who, rather than taking medication to suppress the immune system's natural rejection of the foreign implant, insists on strengthening the immune
system (since this is the more natural alternative) is still exhib-
iting suicidal tendencies, even though his reasoning is correct.
In our case, both are right: the pregnant woman is right from a
psychological viewpoint and the gynecologist is right in terms of
her mechanistic worldview. Since we can hardly expect the expectant mother to be able to evaluate the physical factors of the
situation, it would be helpful if the physicians would try to appreciate the metaphysical aspects pertaining to the woman's soul
(and her baby's soul). In this way, at least one of the opposing
camps would be able to see both sides of the coin, thus allowing
a cooperative approach to arise. The more profound aspects of
the mother's point of view can only come to light when the rituals
of becoming a woman and becoming a man have been openly
discussed, along with an open discussion of the problems accompanying these maturational processes.

Problems of the Child

When the Unborn Child has Grown Too Large: There are
various reasons to explain why embryos sometimes grow excessively large inside the womb. The most frequent reason is
overly long gestation, which allows the child too much time in the
womb, and tarries too long in the Land of Cockaigne. The birth of

such overripe fruits is seldom pleasant—neither for the "fruit" nor for the "tree." On the other hand, it might be that the pregnant mother has been unwilling to give up the "fruit of her body." This inability to let go of her offspring when the time has come may repeat itself during the child's youth and adolescence.

Pregnancy is a time of incubation, a time of preparation for birth and a new life. The longer the period of incubation, the more powerful the subsequent eruption. Fear of an uncertain future can overwhelm a child who would otherwise have no compunctions about leaving its nest. The anxious unborn baby will be loathe to exchange the familiar, safe atmosphere for an incalculable risk. Or the embryo that has not been given enough of the Land of Cockaigne can be unwilling to leave it "so soon." By definition, post-term birth is always a delay beyond the proper time. If the right moment has been missed once, it becomes difficult to find the proper moment in later life. Such people tend to have problems with timing. The best thing to do is to choose the next best alternative and *take the bull by the horns.* For example, if the natural moment of puberty, the moment when hormonal changes occur, is missed, one can wait forever, but there simply will not be another natural turning point. An attempt at age twenty-five is preferable to one at age forty, but both attempts are undeniably tardy. Oftentimes the only thing that can help is pressure from a situation that is becoming increasingly unbearable.

Another important aspect of post-term birth is that the child is becoming unduly weighty. It has taken more time than is appropriate and it is becoming an increasingly *heavy* burden on its mother. Finally, her reserves of energy and capacity to open are exhausted, and there is no alternative except cesarean section. One pattern is that an especially lazy, self-serving child prefers not to leave Cockaigne voluntarily and insists on the seemingly more comfortable solution that cesarean delivery represents. Cesarean causes the infant no pain, but will later cause the mother all the more emotional pain. Similarly, a mother who will not let go, who holds onto her embryo longer than is really necessary, is making too much of herself and her own importance, thereby endowing the child with a weightiness that is dangerous for both mother and child.

When the mother holds onto her "fruit" for too long, the child is exposed to an increasingly claustrophobic situation. There is no escape from this too strait womb except through the brutality of surgery. A torn or cut perineum would be the lesser evil in this case.

Finally, an unfavorable relationship between the size of the child and the capacity of the mother's pelvis can result from a correspondingly unbalanced relationship in the genetic makeup or physical stature of the parents. To put things rather simply, one could say that an overly voluminous man has mated with an unduly tiny woman and, together, they have conceived a child who is too large for its mother. In such cases, a well-timed cesarean section is sometimes the only alternative, although in the majority of cases, such children find their way through the birth canal somewhat earlier by natural means.

An essential role is played by our "too good" diets. Just as diet contributes to the early onset of puberty (the so-called "acceleration" phenomenon), an over-supply of nutrients can also cause embryos to gain weight too quickly. Here again, prosperity has its revenge and leaves us no choice but to resort to the drugs and scalpels of modern medicine. Pregnant women who smoke heavily reverse this situation by keeping their embryos ill-supplied with adequate nutrients for proper growth.

The Uterus as a Trap—*placenta praevia*: In this rare situation, the placenta is located in front of the womb's exit and more or less blocks the way. This puts the child in a deadly trap from which it can only escape when gynecologists create an artificial exit through the skin of the mother's stomach. What may have begun as an unwillingness to release the "fruit of the womb" has developed into an inability to release it. Mother and child are chained to one another, and both must rely on outside help. The child sees no way out of the trap; outside intervention is the only alternative. If outside help arrives in time, the placental trap may have no further consequences for the child's subsequent development.

In order to cope with this pattern, it is important to get support and accept help—both during the birth and in one's later life. A person who inwardly expects and is prepared to accept outside help during transitional and breakthrough situations is likely to receive that assistance whenever he needs it to solve a problem. But the *placenta praevia* situation can make this pattern into an ongoing theme for one's entire life. The lessons for later life involve learning to ask for and accept assistance early, before the crisis becomes a catastrophe, and learning to organize competent helpers before rather than after the situation becomes urgent. The American pedagogue Al Siebert regards early asking and timely organizing as central attributes of the personality pattern he calls the "survivor personality."[23] People with this pattern are especially gifted with the ability to learn from crises and to emerge strengthened from a crisis. They can turn even apparently hopeless situations into victories, and regard life's difficulties as spurs to success rather than hindrances.

Later Consequences of Cesarean Section: From the beginning of their extrauterine lives, children who were born by cesarean never learn to deal with boundaries or to overcome them when necessary. They can develop a tendency to "wait things out," hoping someone else will take care of things. This can even go so far as to manifest itself in the most extreme Land-of-Cockaigne fantasies. Especially when parents yield to such demands, the children are done a disservice because they never learn to cope with difficulties on their own. Only when a person is challenged, is his development truly fostered. A person who never learns to bear and overcome frustrations repeatedly tends to flee from every problem—a pattern that, for example, can easily lead to addictive behavior.

The other possibility is that such people, after having had bad experiences with this pattern, tend to overcompensate, racing ahead in all areas as a way of proving their courage. This kind of behavior often seems contrived and demonstrative. Compensation, of course, is always possible and can also manifest among people born in the breech presentation. Esoteric philosophy posits that complementary things that lie at the opposite ends of an axis are inwardly related to one another. Hence, with respect to the deeper levels of their lives' issues, striking similarities can be discovered between insane people and psychiatrists, criminals and criminologists, teetotalers and alcoholics, chain smokers and fanatic nonsmokers.

Just as a defensive mother accuses her children of constantly waiting for her help, so too can we observe an excessive eagerness to help among physicians who readily opt for a cesarean section—a surgical procedure, by the way, that often does more harm than good, at least as far as the patients are concerned. The mothers have problems with letting go and separating to that of the children, who have difficulty letting go of their mothers. One major reason lies in the fact that both mother and child may not have consciously experienced the pregnancy as profoundly as they should have. One can only let go of something when has fully lived it and relished it.

Other Problems Involving Birth and Letting Go

Every birth is an enterprise that needs both offensive energy and surrender, a process that requires courage and energy coupled with primal trust. Just as the process of birth illustrates the way the child deals with the themes of aggression and Mars energy, so too the birth process reveals the mother's ability to give up and separate herself from the "ripe fruit"—or it can show that she yearns to be rid of it too soon.

Premature Rupture of the Amniotic Sac

When the amniotic sac ruptures prematurely, it suggests that the mother has brought the child *up for air* too soon since she has drained away the life-giving waters. Left, as it were, *high and dry*, the child is robbed of all sense of comfort and has no choice but to follow the amniotic fluid out of the womb. If it does not do so, then the birth must be artificially induced with labor-inducing drugs (as was common practice not so long ago). In most cases, the situation is not particularly dangerous since the child is usually mature enough to successfully take the daring leap into life outside the womb. The situation is like a somewhat early expulsion from paradise, and is generally less harmful than keeping the child in paradise for too long a period of time.

In the illegal abortions of the past, a common method was to pierce the amniotic sac. Once the fluid had drained away, the child was left with no choice but to follow the fluid, even if that choice spelled certain death, as it always does when an abortion is performed early in pregnancy.

When the amniotic sac ruptures prematurely (thus initiating a premature delivery), it often means that the individual will subsequently tend to make hasty and ill-considered decisions and will tend to become impatient with her surroundings. Such individuals belong in the category of people who "fall into the house when they open the door." Their plans and goals often seem not entirely matured, and they would do better to *brood* over things a bit longer, even though this is precisely the sort of behavior that has always been most difficult for them.

Premature Birth

Premature birth can indicate escapist tendencies on the child's part or an attempt by the mother to be rid of the pregnancy as soon as possible so she can return to her former independence. It is not uncommon to find both tendencies expressing themselves, which sometimes leads to so-called "precipitate deliveries." In such cases, neither mother nor child is able to wait a moment longer. The two are so eager to separate from one another that they regard taxis, airplanes, or even sidewalks as good enough places for a "crash landing" into life.

Such tendencies are obviously far less dangerous than their opposites (i.e., attempts to delay and exaggerate situations until they are more than ripe). When an start in life is attempted early, but not too early, the consequences are usually harmless. The lost cave of the womb must be replaced for a longer period of time by the artificial warmth of a mechanical incubator, a kind of "second womb" that human babies tend to leave only with regrets. The newborn human baby is no less of a "stay-at-home" than the laziest bird baby.

Very early arrivals (the tiny babies that physicians call "premies") must be placed in an artificial, external incubator that tries to replicate conditions in the womb. This situation suggests inadequate hospitality on the mother's part and/or undue impatience on the child's part. Such an unduly early start in life is of little use to the child since it only propels the infant out of a natural womb and into an artificial one. In fact, prematurely born children lose time since their development tends to lag behind that of their more patient comrades. The mothers are apt to suffer from a variety of problems derived from the radical shortening of pregnancy. The need for an artificial incubator creates a definite rift between mother and child. It means the infant must spend the first few weeks of life in the hospital—which, in turn, places considerable burdens on the mother, both in the early weeks of the child's life as well as later on. Themes such as the imprinting phase and breast-feeding play a less immediate role and are sometimes altogether absent against the frightening background of acute danger to the life of the premature child.

Extremely premature births can be life-threatening because certain organs are not sufficiently developed to support life in the realm of the air. The lungs especially must reach a certain level of maturity before they become capable of supporting life in polarity. The pattern corresponds to that which we have already seen in the case of premature rupture of the amniotic sac. The infants are not really "ripe" and have arrived too soon. This pattern repeats itself in later life, and such people are diametrically opposed to their opposites—namely, people who were carried in their mothers' wombs for too long. Just as the latter tend to be chronically late for appointments, adult "premies" frequently arrive far ahead of schedule, which can be equally annoying. Impatiently early and chronically late people share a common theme: problems in selecting the right time.

Premature Separation of the Placenta

This situation corresponds to the aforementioned patterns, although the danger here is more acute. Premature separation of the placenta cuts off the child's supply lines. This puts a sudden end to paradise since supplies are no longer replenished once they have been exhausted. Since the child relies on its mother for oxygen and cannot yet breathe on its own, the danger of asphyxiation is severe and immediate. Once again, the only hope lies in gynecological intervention. The mother's life is likewise in jeopardy because the tearing away of the placenta is generally accompanied by internal hemorrhaging. The child receives no fresh supplies of life energy and "starves" in terms of energy, while the mother's life energy drains away as internal bleeding.

Umbilical Cord Around the Newborn's Neck

The meaning of this problem is so clear that an interpretation is hardly necessary. From a medical point of view, the crucial factor is how tightly or loosely the cord is wrapped around the child's neck. Either it actually strangles the infant or it jeopardizes the infant by threatening to do so. Ultrasound examinations and intrauterine photographs have shown that unborn babies are capable of tugging at their umbilical cords. In most cases, such tugging causes the mother only a modicum of discomfort and can be compared to a master pulling on a bell cord to ring for a servant. But when the cord has become wrapped around the unborn child's neck, the image of self-directed aggression is patently obvious.

The situation suggests that, for the unborn child, something has cast a disquieting pall over the intrauterine period, a time ordinarily accompanied by pleasant, oceanic feelings. Energies directed against the embryo's own life suggest that the Pluto principle has forced itself to the fore at life's onset and impressed its stamp on life at this early stage. In this case, the strangulation is generally caused by the child itself, although in most cases damage due to poor circulation rather than successful intrauterine suicide ensues. This unfortunate pattern suggest the motto: "I'd rather kill myself than let go, surrender myself to the current and go with the flow."

As far as the mother is concerned, the maternal Moon principle (symbolized by the umbilicus) has transformed itself into a Plutonian snake that threatens to choke her baby. This theme can recur later on in the so-called "overprotection problem" in which the child is in jeopardy of suffocating from the mother's well-meaning but inappropriately dispensed "love."

120

Summary

As a portal of entry into polar life, birth is every bit as dramatic and decisive as conception. Birth looks very different from the point of view of the person who is being born than it does to the mother or other adults in attendance at the birth. Whereas conception is sometimes experienced as an limitation and even as an imprisonment in a physical body, birth (with its oppressive struggle through the confining narrows of the birth canal and the aforementioned "helpful" interventions by obstetricians) can seem like a dreadful violation. The newborn feels extremely vulnerable and helpless. Yet the selfsame events that newborns usually experience as terrifying are celebrated by the children's parents, and especially by the seldom-participating fathers, with joy and pride.

For the new arrivals, the time directly preceding the birth and the birth itself are the first terrifying encounters with narrowness and with the anxiety that accompanies the feeling of being trapped. All subsequent anxiety related symptoms are already potentially present in the basic pattern of the birth. These symptoms can be effectively treated through therapeutic reliving of the birth trauma.

It is possible to restructure the birth sequence, transforming it from the drama described at the beginning of this chapter into the festival of birth that it can be today, in our present era of growing awareness. However, the further removed the birth is from the old clinical procedure, the more essential it becomes that contact be preserved with modern obstetrical practitioners— just in case an emergency should arise. An ever-growing number of midwives is willing to assist at home births, and (whether voluntarily or simply because of a lack of patients) obstetricians are likewise becoming increasingly cooperative. *Hungry* physicians are a danger to society as well as to individual patients. If, however, they are dealing with healthily self-confident patients, physicians can make important contributions. In their heart of hearts, real "birth helpers" are happiest when they can truly help to meet the needs of mothers and their babies.

The best preparation a pregnant woman can make for giving birth is to relive and come to terms with her own birth trauma. Experiencing their own birth traumas should also be the most important step in training midwives and obstetricians since it would enable them to avoid projecting these problems onto the pregnant women who are their patients. Nothing is more dangerous at a birth than the unconscious fears the helpers still harbor from their own birth traumas. Experience has shown that people who have not yet fully reconciled their own birth traumas are likely to choose careers as midwives or obstetricians, just as people with psychological difficulties tend to study psychology. The fact that such approaches are still absent from conventional obstetrical training programs shows how dearly we love to handle problems as projections (i.e., as if the problems were other people's rather than our own), and how hesitant we are to confront and finally (re)solve the underlying issues.

Questions About Birth

1. Imagine that you've agreed to participate in an extended hike through a cave, but that after a few hours you're feeling tired, you've had enough, and you want to return to the daylight. Your guide, who has led you reliably thus far, says he knows a shortcut, an especially fast route out. The path is a narrow tube through which you must wriggle, so narrow you must get down on your elbows and knees and crawl on your belly like a reptile. Furthermore, you cannot see the light at the end of this narrow tunnel since the route leads first downward and only then turns upward. Your guide warns you not to breathe too deeply so you won't get stuck. When he sees you hesitating, he assures you that many others have crawled through here before you, that the mountain above you has remained unmoved for millions of years, and that the cavern is not

going to cave in at this most inopportune of all moments. Then he urges you onward.

- How do you feel when you think about crawling through the narrow tube, touching its walls as you inch your way through?
- Try to imagine crawling through, and feel whether or not you have enough trust to do so. Experience, in your mind's eye, this difficult route out of the dark, safe, but no longer pleasant cave and into the light of the world.
- Would you allow the narrowness and the associated anxiety to hinder your progress?
- Transfer these feelings to your experiences of your own birth and your path into life.

2. How do you begin the day? Consider this as a symbol of the year and of life as a whole.

- Do you find it easy to get out of bed, or is it difficult for you to leave behind the warm nest, the cave of the bed?
- Are you afraid, do you "choke" when you consider the tasks facing you in the coming day?
- Does the day seem like a mountain blocking your path, or does it draw you toward it with a magical attraction?
- Do you start the day with verve and élan or do you feel like you're driving with the hand brake on?

3. Do you like sunrises?

- When was the last time you saw the sunrise?
- Have you ever seen the sunrise or do you usually sleep through the beginning of the day—and through your life as a whole?
- How do you feel at this early hour of the day?
- Do you like to set out on journeys early in the morning?

Therapeutic Possibilities for Resolving the Trauma of Birth

1. Re-experiencing birth in an appropriate psychotherapy (e.g., reincarnation therapy), in which the birth can be re-lived and made conscious.

2. Therapy with forced breathing: the path through one's own narrow places, including possible cramps that force one to return to a fetal position, and the subsequent liberation.

Both of these methods are helpful in every developmental crisis. With the proper psychotherapeutic support, the individual is able to deal with the most acute and most pressing problem first.

Breath therapy automatically begins with the most severely acute energetic theme because life energy automatically chooses this path.

Finally, all of life's crises are births into new areas.

3. Symbolic birth exercises:

   • Bud exercise: One rolls oneself into the fetal position and gradually opens like an unfurling flower bud.

   • Womb exercise (for two people): One person embodies the womb; the other embodies the unborn child. The womb lies over the child, embracing it with arms and thighs. The unborn child gradually begins to free itself from the enclosing womb.

   • Digging out your car when it is stuck in the snow; bringing situations that have become stuck into movement again; exerting yourself to create breakthroughs on all levels.

3. Post-partem Crises and

Small Children's Crises

Your children are not your children.
They are the sons and daughters of Life's longing for
itself.
They come through you but not from you,
And though they are with you yet they belong not to
you.
You may house their bodies but not their souls,
For their souls dwell in the house of tomorrow,
which you cannot visit, not even in your dreams.
You may strive to be like them,
but seek not to make them like you.
For life goes not backward
nor tarries with yesterday.
You are the bows from which your children
as living arrows are sent forth.
The archer sees the mark upon the path of the
infinite,
and He bends you with His might
that His arrows may go swift and far.

> *Let your bending in the archer's hand be for*
> *gladness;*
> *for even as he loves the arrow that flies,*
> *so He loves also the bow that is stable.*
> —Khalil Gibran, *Of Children*

Children neither allow us to satisfactorily actualize some as yet unrealized dreams, nor are children appropriate projection screens for high-flying plans and wishes. But they are unequaled as mirrors of our own situation. Whatever has been missing in a relationship or in life—they bring precisely that to it. If we assume that destiny never makes mistakes but is always striving to work through our errors and bring us into closer contact with whatever has been lacking, then it should be clear that fate gives all parents exactly the right children, even if they adopt those children. In this sense, destiny is "heaven sent." The enrichment children bring with them often lies in areas where we least expect it, and even more often where we do not want to see it. If we were able to see and perceive it, they would be an enormous help to our own development and we would grow along with them in unimagined ways. It is hard to imagine better therapists than children. Genetically, each child is composed of half its parent; hence, they resemble us in pleasant (and sometimes embarrassing) ways. And, thanks to their intuitive understanding of their parents, they have the uncanny ability to put their little fingers right on our weak spots.

While children are growing up alongside us, our own growth can make astounding progress. This probably explains why so many parents are eager to see their children grow quickly, although a somewhat slower pace would, in fact, increase the parents' chances of being able to keep pace with their little ones. Just as children recapitulate the evolutionary history of the human race, they also reflect the developmental phases through which their parents have progressed. Problems frequently arise at precisely those phases where the parents themselves have gotten stuck, but have not admitted it.

Children are born with life issues, just as their parents were born with life issues a generation previously. In most cases, the children's lessons bear striking similarities to the lessons their parents incarnated to learn. The difference, however, is that the various themes are usually easier to discern since the children are not yet as skilled as their parents in using their favorite defense mechanisms (e.g., rationalization and projection). This is also the reason our children can aggravate us more easily than perhaps anyone else. It can be especially annoying to see our own problems in such a simple guise, as if our offspring were showing us a caricature of ourselves. It is all too easy to react with anger when we see our reflections in that uncompromisingly honest mirror, but the sole chance for development lies in recognizing the mirror phenomenon for what it is: a reflection. We should know from our experiences in front of the bathroom mirror each morning that it does little good to blame the mirror for the sour face we see staring back at us.

Certain Native American tribes believe that one's ancestors are standing behind him—the female ancestors on the person's left, the male ancestors on the person's right—and that these ancestors are hoping and yearning for obsolete family patterns to finally be resolved through the courageous life of the living descendant. This could be one of the reasons Native Americans exhibit far less of a tendency toward projection than do their Caucasian brothers and sisters. We "enlightened" modern people should not only want to change our children, but would be well advised to seize the opportunity to change ourselves, to grow and develop along with our children.

After the Birth

After birth and baptism (two entry rituals marking our arrival in polar life) a series of typical crises arises for everyone involved.

The mother's life undergoes a complete transformation as the child comes to occupy the focal point of her life. The father, who formerly enjoyed this central position, frequently faces a second crisis. But, especially for the mother, the need to cope with the new situation—as well as the anxieties and unaccustomed responsibilities that may accompany her new role—can sometimes lead to smaller or larger crises, or even become as severe as so-called "post-partem depression."

Post-Partem Depression and Puerperal Psychosis

As is the case in every depression, the disorder can lead to a turning away from life, which appears to the individual as overwhelming and overly difficult. The patient flees from the concentrated tension the child has brought into her existence and takes refuge instead in the pseudo-tension of depression. She neglects herself and everything else, shirking her responsibilities for the new situation and placing them on the shoulders of the people in her immediate surroundings. Depending on the severity of the depression, her thoughts can range from preoccupation with the threat posed by unavoidable restrictions, excessive demands and harshness, to morbid fascination with death. This tendency to flee from life is especially obvious when it manifests in the form of death wishes or suicidal tendencies. In such cases, it is likely that the mother was not inwardly prepared for the pregnancy and, above all, not prepared for the arrival of the newborn.

The mother has become preoccupied with the primordial Saturn principle, which is precisely where the solution should be sought—namely, in reconciliation with that principle's resolved levels. Indeed, the life with which she was familiar in the past must die. The former relationship to her mate must also die, at least in its old and accustomed form, so that it can be reborn on a new level. She needs to accept the coming limitations and the unavoidable restrictions that motherhood involves, perhaps even before the joys of this new phase in life become apparent. A certain discipline, as well as a certain harshness, are essential during the period that ensues. The mother must subordinate her desires to the needs of her baby, and this can sometimes cause her to neglect her own needs and interests. She may be compelled to fast—not to give up food, but to give up sleep—because the baby needs to be nursed during the night and, if the nocturnal feedings are delayed, the baby's screams will put an uncompromising end to the parents' peaceful night.

If the parents can consciously accept the demise of the old and familiar situation, the saturnine yet simple, natural and beautiful duties of the new situation can help create a new, different and more satisfying lifestyle. The sooner the mother assents to the overwhelming power of nature and its demands, the sooner this new phase can begin. The more willingly and eagerly she accepts the challenges of this new phase, the more likely it is that the experiences will be a source of strength for her. Once it has been inwardly accepted, the Saturn principle endows us with tremendous endurance and an astonishing degree of perseverance. Even the most strenuous things (e.g., chronic lack of sleep) seem less threatening when we accept them voluntarily as a kind of fast.

Post-partem psychosis, also known as "puerperal" or "nursing" psychosis, is similar to post-partem depression. As is the case in every psychosis, the disorder involves an attempted escape from a world one experiences as unbearable into an illusory reality that seems easier to bear. The onset of new challenges is experienced as so overwhelming and the mother's reserves of soul strength are felt to be so inadequate that her only escape seems to be in running away. The techniques of reincarnation therapy, as well as simple orientation exercises, can be used to retrieve the refugee and bring her back to reality. However, it is questionable how immediately one can offer her something that will persuade her to remain in this reality and accept the responsibilities of her maternal role because she still experiences both reality and motherhood as overwhelming. For-tunately, the child has such a grounding influence and mother-hood has such a powerful emotional charge that these refugees frequently return to reality even without therapy.

If she does seek treatment, one of the most important ther-apies is to ensure that she is able to sleep through the night. In many cases, it is the interruption or absence of essential dreaming phases that causes the psychosis in the first place. Research conducted in so-called "sleep laboratories" has shown that nocturnal dreaming is crucial to our mental health. If, under laboratory conditions, a person is prevented from dreaming by awakening whenever his REM phase[24] begins, in less than a week that person will begin to see dream images with open eyes. This simply means that the dream images that were not experienced at night have forced their way into waking aware-ness, where they begin to overlay waking consciousness. Psy-chiatrists describe this situation as "visual hallucinations." In a similar way, suppression of the inner voice can cause acoustic hallucinations.

Nursing can create a similar dream deficit since the infant demands its milk at regular intervals, thus preventing its mother from sleeping long enough to enjoy her dream phases. This sit-uation offers the mother the opportunity to become more con-sciously open to the thresholds of other realities and to confront the otherworlds to which her baby already has natural access. Of course, there are easier ways to open oneself to these re-alities than through the initiation posed by sleep deficiency and "dream fasting."

The parallelism becomes obvious when one considers that psychedelic drugs were often used as an aid during the initia-tion rites practiced in archaic civilizations, and that ergot alkaloid (closely related to LSD) played an important role in opening the doors of perception leading to other levels of reality. Albeit on a confused and unresolved plane, puerperal or nursing psychosis is nonetheless a kind of initiation into a new world for the soul, and sleep deprivation is a well-known method practiced in various traditions.

Loss of Sexual Desire

Other problems associated with this time period (e.g., loss of sexual desire) may seem comparatively harmless, but they can contain plenty of explosive charge. The father suddenly finds himself playing second fiddle. He is quite literally pushed away from his wife's bosom and bed. Especially if he also has unresolved problems with his role as father, this new situation can create serious difficulties that obviously lie not in the rational area, but in subconscious issues related to his sense of self-worth. A man who had primarily regarded his wife as his possession feels robbed. A man who had experienced her in the roles of provider and mother suddenly feels rejected, or at least "put on a back burner." And a man who had mostly viewed her as a pleasure object must suffer the painful realization that there are now more important things in her life, and that feeding and caring for the baby number among these priorities.

In many cases, the difficulties do not appear so directly, but only appear later in the form of sex-related disharmonies for which, of course, either or both partners can be responsible. More than a few couples discover that the birth of their first child has created a sexual bottleneck for them. If the man cannot or will not "perform" as he used to in the past, the reason could well lie in his image of women. This image is basically constructed from two archetypes: the Venus aspect of the lover and the lunar aspect of the motherly (house)wife. If the husband cannot integrate both aspects in a single picture, sorrow is sure to ensue. If, for example, he has become accustomed to a Venus woman as his lover and if he never reconciles himself with the motherly pattern, than the mere sight of "his woman" giving birth can call her so severely into question that he may no longer be able to do "it" (with her), perhaps because, on a deeper level, he no longer wants to.

Nowadays it has become quite commonplace for the father to be present at the birth, but this practice also has its shadow side. If the man does not dare to express his fears but merely remains by her side out of a sense of duty, the existential event of giving birth can overwhelm him. For many fathers, this experience of their own helplessness is difficult to bear, and some of them carry the scars for a long time. Obstetricians often joke that it is the father who is more difficult to care for than the leading actors in the birth show (i.e., the mother and her newborn baby). Perhaps it is the father's realization that he is at best a marginal figure that gnaws at his self-image during the birth of his child.

If the husband has been exclusively preoccupied with the maternal aspect of his wife, once she has given birth, he may feel he has "done his work" and no longer feel the inner need to do anything more. When she begins to nurse their baby, he may also find jealousy rearing its head—which can hinder or even destroy so much in a marriage. Even if the husband has not been entirely stripped of his role as child, he at least no longer finds himself at the top of his wife's list of maternal priorities.

An added difficulty may arise from the fact that the wife, looking back on their childless marriage, feels humiliated because she does not think her husband accepted her as a complete woman, but only as a lover or an ersatz for his mother.

If sexual desire wanes in the wife, it could mean that she has everything she always wanted and that she had unconsciously been using her Venus pattern only as a tactic to achieve her lunar, maternal purpose. When post-partem women feel degraded at the mere thought of the negligées they wore in the past, it is obvious they only played the game on the Venus level in order to achieve their real goal, namely the maternal role. To the degree that the women deceived themselves, to that degree their husbands are liable to feel disappointed. After so much illusion, disillusion cannot but follow.

Birth has brought the woman's life into a new temporal quality that sets new priorities. The husband, who has either not experienced the birth at all or, in any case, not experienced it in his own body, is sure to lag behind. If he insists everything continue for him as it did in the past, this new phase will soon teach him otherwise. The expression "making a baby for his wife" reveals this misunderstanding. A man eagerly deceives himself since he has also made a baby for himself, ignoring for the moment the all-important question of who actually made what! If the father outwardly projects the issue onto his wife and child, he soon finds himself ignored and is liable to suffer the consequences. If he succeeds in accommodating himself to his new role as father and if he can contact his own paternal archetype, then the experience can foster rather than frustrate his own development as a man. Feelings of being overwhelmed often derive from inadequate acceptance of the situation. The demands of fate can either challenge us or defeat us. The essential difference lies far more in one's own attitude and much less in fate.

Of course, for both mother and father, the real source of the problems can lie in something as simple as the physical exhaustion caused by countless night shifts. Or else the unfamiliar presence of a tiny voyeur in the marital bed can place restrictions on (or entirely put a stop to) erotic fun and games. When people feel they are being watched, they often encounter problems with their superegos. They may feel worried about emotionally overwhelming their child. And in the wake of the American tendency to find evidence of child abuse everywhere, the more anxious souls in Germany may begin worrying about later being accused of seducing their own children.

The Newborn Child's Problems

The life situation has changed for the parents, but the situation has undergone a far more drastic change from the newborn's point of view. In its own body and soul, the baby is making the phylogenetic step from aquatic to terrestrial life—a step that numbers among the most decisive in all of evolutionary history. A more drastic transformation could hardly be imagined. In general, every human being must repeat the decisive steps of evolutionary history in her own body.[25] Relatively little is given to us freely as a gift. Like all life, we begin as single-celled organisms, gradually growing into a multicellular aquatic creature. Even in later life, the whirlpool-shaped arrangement of our body hair continues to testify to our aquatic origins. Millions of years after our emergence from the primordial oceans, our bodies are still more than two-thirds water. The liquid in our cells has a similar composition to that which filled the basins of the ancient seas. Departure from the aquatic realm and the change onto dry land almost meant entry into the realm of air and entailed a gigantic evolutionary step forward, even if it merely enabled us to *land* on dry land as a reptile creeping along on its belly. Finally, we managed to get up onto all four legs, crawl forth and conquer the realm of mammals. The act of rising up onto our hind legs, the decisive step toward becoming a human being,[26] is one every toddler must repeat on his own.

Mothers in many archaic cultures ease the post-partem transition by binding the baby against to own belly, where it can continue to experience the intimacy and safety it had become accustomed to in the womb. In other cultures, newborns are tightly wrapped in swaddling clothes that, no doubt, remind them of the pre-birth situation.

A number of signs suggest that the adaptation does not come easy for newborns. So-called "cry babies" greet every new situation with a shrieking tantrum that can turn even the sweetest tempered parent's life into bitterest gall. It is impossible not to hear the aggression and desperation in the infant's screams, emotions that are all too often echoed in the hearts of the infant's frazzled family members.

So-called "three-month colic" follows a similar pattern, aggressively placing severe demands on the already stressed out parents. This situation clearly shows that the little newcomer cannot easily digest the new demands of its extrauterine life. The source of the problem probably lies in the difficulty of switching from the work-free supply situation (in the intrauterine Land of Cockaigne) to the work-intensive sucking needed for self-supply at the breast. These children's screams unmistakably express just how painfully they experience life in our world. That male infants suffer from this syndrome more frequently than female infants could be an indication that the male gender begins life with greater difficulties adapting to new situations, with more aggression to release, and at a greater distance from the *material* realm. Psychoanalyst René Spitz offers another level of explanation for three-month colic based on the observation that institutionalized infants seldom suffer from this syndrome. If a mother takes great pains to care for her child's every need, and especially if she nurses her baby "on demand" (i.e., offering her breast whenever the infant cries), then the chances are greater that this infant will suffer from colic. Researchers also discovered that cry babies exhibit greater muscle tension than their less vocal contemporaries. Spitz theorizes that cry babies are not actually hungry when they scream, but are merely looking for a way to release their tension. If they are always given a breast or bottle, they can suck (thus decreasing their muscle tension somewhat) and be pacified for a time, but this still does not solve their long-term problem since they are ingesting nourishment their digestive systems do not really need.

Nursing on demand can be quite good for some infants, but feeding ought to take place only as a response to genuine hunger. Feeding milk to babies who hunger only for a reduction in their muscle tension is the wrong answer and only "feeds" a vicious circle. Further support for the validity of this interpretation can be found in the observation that three-month colic is more or less nonexistent among indigenous babies who are carried against their mothers' bellies. Constant skin contact and continual rocking provide these infants with adequate opportunity to release their muscle tension.

One suspects that three-month colic is nothing more than the infant's attempt to get the (skin) contact it so desperately needs in order to grow and thrive. Why else would pacifiers or rocking cradles be so effective in quieting screaming infants? An institutionalized infant is not rewarded for screaming since its cries do not attract a worried mother eager to bring whatever she thinks it might need. Motherless infants are not subject to excessive or poorly timed feeding, and are consequently unlikely to suffer from three-month colic. According to Spitz, three-month colic generally cures itself as the child grows older simply because older infants develop other ways to free themselves from excessive muscle tension (e.g., rocking themselves).

Nursing Problems

The roots of nursing problems lie either in the mother, in the baby, or in both individuals. Like other post-partem difficulties, nursing problems can grow to critical dimensions. A mother who produces no milk is apt to feel inadequate since, quite obviously, her body is not adequately supplying her infant with food. The reason for her dry breasts can lie in her subconscious yet obvious attempt not to give herself to the child (i.e., not to nourish it). This interpretation is the only critical aspect of the situation since, from a purely material standpoint, artificial formula milk is healthier because it contains fewer toxins. But for the needs of the soul, artificial formula from the bottle is no substitute for genuine mother's milk from the breast.

In the rare phenomenon of inwardly directed nipples, the turning away from the outside world (at least as far as this sensitive part of the anatomy is concerned) is impossible to overlook. The buds at the tips of the breasts, so openly emphasized by the more daring fashions, have withdrawn inside. Although this defensive posture seems more allied with the breast's erotic role, the newborn is often able to solve the problem on its own. The baby's hunger for life turns the situation around and, by tirelessly exerting suction on the breasts, the baby compels its mother's nipples to come out of hiding and show themselves. Little plastic "prostheses" are another expedient that frequently help to solve the problem.

If the child will not nurse on its own, the blame can lie with the infant, although one ought to differentiate between babies who will not and babies who cannot nurse. Perhaps the infant is so weak or so immature that the sucking reflex does not yet function at all. In such cases, of course, one ought to try to interpret the situation causing the malfunction. If, on the other hand, a mature infant refuses to suck its mother's breast, the crisis is often preprogrammed. A mother who refuses to produce or dispense milk can escape into medical rationalizations, but an infant who will not nurse is making an unmistakable statement: this baby will not take anything from its mother, and really wants no part of her at all. Many mothers experience this rejection with great pain and feel spurned by their infants. The reasons for this rebuff might have their origins during her pregnancy, but they could just as well have roots in even earlier experiences.[27]

One Bed and the Other

The occasions and reasons little children find their way into their parents' beds are many and varied: during or after an illness (that incidentally teaches the child just how much it can gain by being sick); during vacations, when no separate room is available for the child; when it visits its grandmother, who does not mind a little company since she's feeling lonesome anyway, and so on. What begins as cute or even practical during nocturnal nursing can, in time, become increasingly irritating to the parents' nerves. Although the sweetness of an infant in their bed can become cloying and ultimately annoying, once the child has won access to the parent's bed, it tends to stubbornly insist upon its right to continue sleeping there.

Anyone who thinks small children have not yet developed an ego or an awareness of their own power learns otherwise. As is the case in later life, rights established by precedent are often defended with loud screams. If neither side submits, the battles can rage astonishingly long, teaching the parents unexpected lessons about their offspring's endurance and energy reserves. Oftentimes the cleverer combatants (i.e., the parents) capitulate, which means that, in order to avoid a crisis, they lose their first power struggle. But this also means they have preprogrammed the next crisis and, all too often, added potentially explosive issues to their own relationship, not to mention the sacrifices they make in loss of sleep and loss of opportunity for undisturbed sexual pleasure with one another.

Teething

The official onset of aggression in life occurs almost simultaneously on various levels. Although we cannot consciously experience the growth of the infant's immune system, we cannot help but share its woes when teeth begin to push through its gums. At first the offensive energy needed to defend the body against pathogenic influences was supplied by the mother in the form of antibodies. During the birth, the infant can complement its own vital energy by feeling the vitality of its mother's labor contractions. Later on, when the body's hardest substance (the tooth enamel) forces its way through the body's softest substance (the mucous membrane in the mouth), only a limited amount of outside help is available, and the infant is left more or less alone to cope with the problem as best it can. It is confronted with long-lasting pain, from which it tries to free itself by screaming long and heartily. At first the parents may be able to relieve their infant's discomfort with home remedies such as chamomile, clove oil or amber necklaces. But after several weeks have gone by during which the infant insists on being held and rocked all night long (even as it continues to scream), the adults have a sterling opportunity to test just how far and how consciously they've resolved their own aggression-related issues.

Chronic inflammation of the infant's gums reveals the fundamental conflict surrounding the issue of aggression. When teeth have to "bite their way" through the gums, a burning and biting sensation is felt in the mouth. In the Bavarian dialect of German, the verb "*zahnen*" (to teethe) also means "to weep."[28] Pain and inflammation both belong to the Mars principle, an issue with which many babies (as well as most adults) in our society tend to have a great deal of difficulty.

Weaning

Weaning may present a similarly difficult crisis. When children feel deprived of this last bit of the Land of Cockaigne, they are apt to fight back and may even resort to extortionist measures. As necessary and undeniable as the fetus felt its supply via the umbilical cord to be, just so naturally does the nursling feel its right to "belly up" to the maternal milk(bar). Looking at certain three-year-olds, one cannot avoid the impression that these little adults are eager to switch directly from the breast to the bar. Their demand for a drink has as little to do with real hunger as does a problem-drinker's demand for a drink have to do with actual thirst. Even the way the infant approaches its source of milk can shed light on the power issues involved. The parental front (in this case fathers tend to stand side-by-side with their wives, mostly because the father is the one who has most to gain when the infant is finally weaned) has only recently achieved a hard-won victory at home, when the child exerts its screaming weapon in the public arena to carry it to new triumphs, and the whole drama begins again.

Especially if the weaning drama is played out during the child's "spiteful" phase, the little warrior needs to learn that extortion will not bring it closer to its goals, that life goes on even when she does not get everything she wants, and that precisely this deprivation marks the threshold to her next phase of development.

The problems surrounding the issue of weaning lead directly to issues surrounding the theme of "doing without." If the yearning to suckle does not wane and disappear naturally, or if the child continues to stubbornly insist upon its assumed right to nurse, it could mean that the small child is feeling long-term deficits because, on some level, it has not been getting enough of what it needs. In such cases, the issue involves a tardy "rearguard action" during the expulsion from the Land of Cockaigne, and parents can expect to encounter resistance.

Small Children's Crises

Crawlers, Bookworms and Problems Learning to Read

Just how important each phase is often does not become apparent until somewhat later in life, and then only when problems arise. Nowadays, for example, we are fairly certain that crawling is important for the development and coordination of the two halves of the brain, and that unduly curtailing or interfering with the crawling phase can cause the child to have difficulty learning to read (or other difficulties) later on. Therapists have long been puzzled by the observation that children of ambitious parents are most likely to have problems learning the alphabet. It seems likely that the same parental ambitions prompted those children to get up onto their own two feet somewhat too soon. Later on, when reading disorder symptoms crop up, the parents take the child for therapy. Unduly early walking seems to be too much for the left brain to cope with, or else it does not give the right brain enough time to assemble an adequate stockpile of sense data. Physical contact with Mother Earth seems to be an essential foundation upon which to build in later life. Upstanding humility and the upwardly striving urge to achieve each have their proper seasons and each should receive due time to flourish. People who have trouble learning to read are not deficient in intelligence, but simply lack the ability to bring order to their confused "salad of letters." The latest therapies allow these children and young people the (essential) luxury of reliving the crawling phase, and this kind of therapy has proven quite successful. People who strive too soon toward Father Sky—before adequately reconciling themselves with Mother Earth—often encounter problems when they try to scale the heights of written culture. Crawling is not better than standing erect: each posture has its proper season and each ought to be given its due time.

Standing Up and Becoming Upstanding

Like the transition from the aquatic realm to the world of thin air, the struggle to stand on two legs recapitulates one phase of humankind's phylogenetic evolution. Children experience the struggle as a crisis; by observing this crisis, we can readily detect that its fundamental pattern is identical with the basic pattern found in all crises. What matters most is the decision to stand up. How much time it takes to put this decision into practice is comparatively irrelevant. The child is absolutely determined to conquer the crisis, stand up and learn to walk, and even the often lengthy series of failed attempts cannot discourage it.

The difficulties our ancestors must have faced when taking this decisive step are readily seen when we watch a toddler trying to stand and walk. These first attempts are extremely pregnant with meaning because the issues at stake are nothing less essential than the evolution of one's own righteousness and uprightness.

Even the most carefully trained animal is not expected to master the skill of uprightness. As long as a baby continues to crawl about on all fours, we generally do not expect it to meet our standards of upright behavior. But as soon as it has stood erect, the adults in its surroundings begin to expect more from it. In this aspect, too, rising up onto the hind legs is a decisive and unique step in the evolution of the human race. It is also the point when the child begins to say "I" and it probably corresponds with the moment when humankind began to develop egoistic consciousness.

At this point, many parents cling to their ambitions and (perhaps inadvertently) provide their offspring with more than enough early opportunities to discover that the world is full of hard, unyielding surfaces. One ambitious mother proudly declares, "Mine were able to walk by their first birthdays." Another mother says, "That's nothing; mine were walking on their own at nine months." If a convertible sports car were to drive past, we might expect its four-year-old passenger to lean out the window and calmly remark, "Who cares. I'm already four, but I still let them drive me around and carry me wherever I want to go."

The First "No" and the Spite Phase

Whereas rising onto the hind legs involves a crisis for the child, learning to say its first "No" may create a crisis for the parents. From this point on, the child refuses to be ignored. It demands to be heard, defends its own boundaries and verbalizes its will. It may have been happy to go along with most things in the past, but suddenly its willingness to compromise and "behave itself" have vanished. It increasingly tends to exclude things from its life, although so-called "eight-month shyness" can be seen as a precursor to this tendency. The path into polarity demands that the ego be constructed and expanded, and the process is nurtured above all by the child's efforts to exclude things and set itself apart. In the unity of paradise, in the center of life's mandala, there is no differentiation, no discrimination and hence no ego. But with the fall from paradise (which the Bible equates with "original sin"), human beings set themselves apart from the unity, begin to make decisions and draw boundaries. As life goes on, this issue becomes increasingly important. The child's first "No" marks the first clear manifestation of this all important phase, that reaches its acme during the so-called "spite phase."

As important as it is for the child to learn how to set itself apart and say "No," it is no less important that it also learns to lose some of the battles it fights during the spite phase. Children who always win these battles grow into young adults who suffer most from the lack of reliable limits and who are continually searching for those limits in their surroundings. The later the child begins to suffer from its own fat-headedness, the worse it is for the child. Ego development means learning to draw and defend one's own boundaries, but it also involves recognizing that the world is full of other egos with their own boundaries, that these boundaries must also be respected, and that failure to respect them is liable to be punished with a bloody nose.

Children who are not given clear limits—like the little victims of poorly understood antiauthoritarian upbringings—constantly provoke the people around them in the hope that this provocation will give them the boundaries for which they yearn. They are practically begging for a slap in the face. The ego needs boundaries in order to perceive itself, and it needs boundaries if it is to develop. Feeling these boundaries gives the ego something to hold on to. Failure to experience limits makes the ego feel "at sea," without handholds or footholds.

Apart from the dangers (e.g., the threat of succumbing to addictions in our ubiquitously drug-abusive society) facing children who have not undergone formative boundary experiences, overly permissive parents make their own lives difficult in the short term and their children's lives difficult in the long term. The child's "No" evokes corresponding "No's." If it does not get the "no's" it needs, it does not learn the important lesson that not everything in life necessarily goes exactly the way the child wants it to. If the individual's first serious frustrations are delayed until the time when the young person begins her career training (an area of life in which parental protection does not hold sway), it may be too late. These overgrown children often feel insulted; they pout and often escape from the unfamiliar situation of having failed rather than standing their ground and learning to pursue their chosen path with an appropriate combination of self-assertiveness and willingness to compromise. It need not always be escape into drugs, but the fact remains that a sizable number of drug addicts were once children in prosperous, middle-class families who, at an early age, fell victim to overprotection and were not confronted early enough and often enough with situations in which they were *not* allowed to have things their own way. The other large group of today's addicts is composed of people who experienced frustrations and received little or no counseling about how to live their lives.

In the long process of bringing up a child, it is especially important to be clear that crises cannot and should not always be avoided, but that each developmental crisis should be understood and given its appropriate response. The meaning and the intention of the spite phase is to teach the child that its soul can recognize and accept limits without dying from frustration and disappointment. These first, consciously experienced power games can teach the child how to cope with victory and defeat. If these lessons are not learned, the little despots and tyrants are all too often preprogrammed to fail in later life.

Classical Power Struggles

In general, the crises of early childhood reveal the central importance of aggression. Mars is the energy of new beginnings and first impulses, and thus Mars has a natural relationship to all fresh starts. There is no way to banish this primal principle from life altogether; neither a "gentle birth" nor antiauthoritarian upbringing can keep Mars out. The attempt to avoid this primordial principle only means that it has to search for another route to express itself and that its unresolved levels are likely to come to the fore.

Birth will always demand courage and offensive energy from both mothers and babies, just as early childhood will always demand self-assertiveness and energy. The positive chances in this realization lie in the opportunity to courageously implement the resolved levels of the Martian principle and, when the principle has "derailed," to get it back on track. Of course, a slap on the behind is a primitive and unresolved way of asserting one's authority, but it is a far less serious evil than a clenched fist that never finds its way out of one's pocket. A child knows how to deal with the occasional slap it may receive from an irate parent, and in most cases experience has shown that the child suffers no serious or lasting effects in later life. But the threatening, early morning promise made by a mother who cannot acknowledge her own aggression—"Wait till your father gets home!"—is a far more nefarious type of psychological terror since it prolongs the child's fear and apprehension for hour after hour. That evening, when the father (who, we assume, is better able to manifest his aggression) finally returns home to execute the long-pending punishment, there is no longer any immediate relationship between the child's misbehavior and the ensuing punishment. At this point and far too late, the unresolved side of the aggressive principle celebrates its victory—a triumph that can cause serious and damaging consequences.[29]

Most problems with small children center around three simple themes: either the little ones will not empty the (food) bowl; or they will not fill the (potty) bowl, or they will not go to bed when and how their parents wish. All three issues are classical power struggles that persist as long as both sides ossify their positions. Oftentimes the underlying theme is overlooked simply because parents cannot believe that such young children are already motivated by self-assertiveness and the will to power. This failure to identify the roots of the problem, in turn, derives from the parents' own inability to recognize their problems with power-related issues. It is only natural that they be unwilling to make use of the mirror their offspring is so eagerly holding in front of their faces. It would save so much wear and tear on the nerves if the adults would face up to the underlying mechanisms. Above all, they ought to bear in mind the fact that there are at least two sides to every power struggle. As the saying goes: "It takes two to tango."

The (Upper) Pot: Problems with Eating

Normally, a child nurses or eats whenever it is hungry. Only when it senses that eating has a more than natural significance for its parents does mealtime become a problem. Then it is no longer eating for itself, but is eating for its parents' sake, and sooner or later the child is sure to ask itself whether it wants to continue being so obliging to them. Parents who are particularly sensitive to healthy diets and who tend to ladle a spoonful of ideology into their children's bowls along with the mashed potatoes are especially vulnerable to puerile blackmail.

The solution is simple: as soon as the parents have recognized their own problem and withdrawn their contribution to it, the situation at the dining table can calm down again. Even older children who have had ample opportunity to learn the precise location of their parents' weak spots usually call a truce in the power struggle as soon as their parents have changed their own inner orientation. It is a good idea for parents to bear in mind that a child will not starve to death simply because it misses a few meals now and then. If it is not given anything to eat between meals, the child is likely to start eating what is on the table sooner rather than later.

If the parents were able to teach toilet training without the compulsive, achievement-oriented attitude that accompanied the way they teach eating habits, then the child would soon listen to reason and diapers would become unnecessary. When a child is hungry, it will eat and, of course, it will be most likely to eat the foods it likes best. This entirely natural behavior ought to represent an opportunity rather than a problem. Many adults still suffer under the mistaken notion that they must eat every last bite of whatever is put on the table. This compulsion derives from times when food was in short supply and every opportunity to eat had to be exploited to its fullest. Nowadays, we are facing the opposite problem: we ought to be glad to see our children developing tastes of their own at an early age; and we ought to be especially glad to see them exercise their freedom *to stop eating* when they have had enough. The flip side of that freedom, of course, means learning to wait until the next meal is served. Otherwise children can pervert the food issue into power trips and terrorism of their own.

Since at puberty (if not sooner) we begin to watch our weight and place emphasis on a healthy but slim body, it makes no sense to breed plump little butterballs in early childhood. All this accomplishes is to increase the number of fat cells and, hence, the likelihood of obesity in later life. The esoteric tradition is well aware that beginnings are of crucial importance, and this is also true with respect to subsequent development of the individual's figure and his tendency to be slender or chubby.

Seemingly clever feeding tricks ought to be subjected to a critical review. "A spoonful for mama and a spoonful for papa" is a clever but inappropriate way to link parental affection with eating against one's will. Eating as a way of proving one's love is obviously not a good plan for later life. Phrases such as "once is nonce" correspond to the child's magical style of thinking and are often effective, but remain problematic as tricks to tempt a child to eat.

In all crises related to the power struggles of early childhood, a good rule of thumb is simply to treat—and nourish—the little ones as if they were intelligent adults in their own right. In general, we are correct in our assumption that they understand far more than we think they do. In this context, a number of discrepancies, closely connected with the parent's own problems, become apparent. Even as the children are being encouraged to master many developmental steps at an unduly early age, they are also hindered from maturing and artificially kept at the baby level by parents who persist in talking "baby talk" and who continue to conduct obsolete feeding ceremonies.

Parents who notice that their children have made obvious advances in speech development but who find it difficult to bid adieu to the cute expressions of babyhood would be well advised to consider how those beloved expressions relate to their own inner child. They would be better off if they would allow their inner child to prate and prattle since it is this *inner* child who is loathe to give up the cute baby words. The flesh-and-blood child *beside them*, on the other hand, deserves every opportunity to grow and develop as quickly as it desires and as quickly as it can. It is especially hindering to the child's development when both phenomena come together: the parents refuse to stop talking baby talk at the same time they persist in conducting babyish feeding rituals. The right time is decisively important, and what may have been loving at one phase of development can be embarrassing and even harmful at the next stage.

The (Lower) Pot: Problems with Toilet Training

Problems with the second pot (the lower one) are similar to those encountered with the first one (the one on the table). Whatever goes in on top must necessarily come out again at the bottom. In most cases, digestion and excretion follow their natural rhythms without causing any problems. The risks surrounding this power struggle are as small as those involving the upper pot, as shown by the fact that breastfed children can go several days without moving their bowels.

In normal situations, when bowel movements are not subject to undue attention, everything moves smoothly. But if the entire family assembles around the child on its throne, eagerly awaiting the latest gift, it is only a matter of time before the child will begin to ask itself whether it wants to give its family such a marvelous present every day. The child will make the potty into its private throne, from which it reigns over its family. As desperation grows in that realm, the child may graciously dispense a hard little present, but will otherwise tend to be sparing in disbursement of its treasures. Expressions for a child's stool such as "great wish" and "mama's present" reveal just who is calling the tune here.

The child is quite right in viewing its stool as a valuable treasure. This view is confirmed by psychoanalysis and by fairytales (e.g., the one about the miraculous donkey "who shat golden ducats"). According to an old German folk tradition, a person who inadvertently steps in a dog's feces can expect to gain material wealth in the near future. After all, stool is the only material possession a small child can give as a gift. That alone suffices to transform feces into its most valuable treasure.[30]

The burdensome problem with a small child's lack of generosity usually disappears as if by magic as soon the parents stop focusing so much attention on it and postpone (or entirely abandon) their ambition of seeing their child toilet-trained according to some preconceived schedule. Ordinary, everyday experience has shown that practically all children outgrow the need for diapers sometime, and most do so by the time they are ready to begin school. This fact ought to ease parental worries. Patient parents will one day see their children begin to take responsibility and cooperate with the toilet-training process all by themselves.

Better than all training, exaggerated expectations and high-flying learning goals is simply the honing of one's own intuition. One can almost always see when a child is getting ready to pass a stool. If the little fellow is quickly led to the potty at this decisive moment, one achieves the desired effect without a lot of bothersome sitting and waiting. This sensitivity to knowing when the time is ripe is an entirely natural ability. If it has been lost, it can be regained, as the following anecdote clearly shows. A pragmatically oriented missionary asked an indigenous woman who had wrapped her baby in a piece of cloth how she knew when the child was getting ready to answer the call of nature. She looked uncomprehendingly at the missionary and asked him, "How do *you* know when *you* have to use the toilet?"

"Taps": Bedtime

Problems with the evening ritual of going to bed involve similar power struggles, but also have a deeper dimension. What makes people most weary and exhausted is their resistance to everyday life. If a person is enthusiastic about something, he seldom finds it as tiring as a comparable but boring occupation. People who have just fallen in love need hardly any sleep at all, yet they thoroughly enjoy every moment together. The more consciously and enthusiastically we live each moment, the less tiring our lives become. If we do feel weary, then it is a pleasant, healthy tiredness.

Many adults, however, spend the major portion of their days in resistance: they work at jobs which they do not really enjoy when they would rather be on vacation or enjoying a free weekend. Consequently, their thoughts are elsewhere: dreaming about the leisurely evening they plan to spend after work is over, or about the coming weekend or next vacation. This state of "not being in the moment" makes them tired and, when the longed-for leisure hours finally arrive, what they need most is peace and quiet. And this is precisely the moment when they are confronted by their little children, who have spent the whole day playing at whatever it is that provides them with the most fun during each passing moment. Immersed in the instant, it looks to adults as if the children have spent the day with one sort of enthusiastic nonsense or another. When evening comes, the children are not apt to be very tired and they prove this to their parents with an unending display of youthful vitality. The problem is exacerbated or manifests itself in a more unpleasant way if the children, like so many big-city kids, have not had an opportunity to exhaust themselves with healthy physical activity. They simply have not used enough of their abundant energy during the day. The children are perhaps just as tired as their parents, but the little ones do not want to go to bed because, like their parents, they are dissatisfied. They have seen too little of their parents, or else they cannot let go of the day because it still owes them their quantum of activity and pleasure.

Bedtime is less often determined by the hour on the clock than by the parents' nerves and by their longing to spend a quiet evening together without the little pests. A conflict of interests is obvious, and it manifests in quarrels and massive power struggles. If the parents turn night into day, recouping during the evening hours what they failed to experience during the day, it is only natural that their children will tend to imitate them and likewise attach special importance to the evening hours.

Above all on those evenings when the parents have plans for child-free diversions, their intuitive and power-conscious offspring are most likely to interfere with their parents' plans by steadfastly refusing to fall asleep, despite all the tried-and-tested tricks their frazzled parents desperately devise. The reason for the refusal lies in the fact that children pay far less attention to schedules and clock time than do their adult counterparts. Instead they tend to respond far more to intuition, feelings and moods. Even though daddy's wristwatch shows that he has already spent more than half an hour tucking the little fellow into bed, the child feels that hardly any time has passed. Why? Because the child intuitively senses that daddy's mind is elsewhere, perhaps already at the upcoming concert, and daddy is secretly hoping that the little guy will finally close those cute little eyelids and fall asleep. Each time the parents tentatively check to see just how tired their children are, the test only makes the children wider awake and even more acutely aware of their own position of power. And besides, in most cases, the children do not *want* their parents to leave them alone and (all too often covertly) slip away for an evening out.

The whole thing works best as soon as the parents achieve a state of truly relaxed indifference motivated by the certainty that bedtime problems really are not problems at all since every human being (large and small) must fall asleep sooner or later. Especially if one uncompromisingly awakens the child at an early hour each morning, thus helping it form *early to bed, early to rise* habits, a natural circadian rhythm will gradually establish itself.

There is no essential difference between children and adults with regard to sleep problems. So-called "sleepless" adults do in fact fall asleep, but unfortunately not at the moments when they wish they could. In this case, the power struggle is being waged between various factions within the adult's own psyche. The best alternative is simply to abandon all dogmatic views and accept that some people need more sleep and some people need less, some need a midday nap and others feel positively nauseated at the mere thought of lying down in the middle of the day. Phrases like "a person must have a minimum of so-and-so-many hours of sleep each day" are the source of unnecessary problems for people of all ages.

How many hours of sleep one's child needs is best determined empirically. Some people say the most important hours of sleep are the ones that come before midnight, but the people who say this are most often those who ignore their own advice yet consider that advice very practical when applied to their children. It is no surprise that intelligent children quickly see through the hypocrisy of such double standards. Of course it is salubrious to maintain healthy rhythms in life, but that holds true for human beings of every age.

Little Rituals Instead of Big Power Struggles

An appropriate and stable bedtime ritual can be a big help in the process of gently leading little children into the bonds of Morpheus. "When the sandman comes," lullabies and bedtime stories are all excellent for this purpose. Especially useful is a continuing story: the parent reveals another episode each night and the children look forward to hearing the next chapter before they drift into dreamland. A well-structured story begins with a summary of the action thus far, continues with an exciting development into new themes, and finally allows the action to become progressively calmer and more conducive to sleep.[31]

The conclusion could be a clever farewell and a release into the world of dreams.

Mealtime rituals can follow a similar pattern. Like all rituals, they can be more effective through the repetition of a fixed framework. Regular meal hours can help, as can a special place at the table that is occupied only by the child and only at mealtimes. Other aids could be particularly pretty silverware (e.g., a silver "pusher"[32] reserved solely for the child's use). For adults as well as for children, meals ought to be eaten without hurry, in a peaceful, relaxed atmosphere. A moment of introspection or (if appropriate) saying grace before the meal can be a substantial contribution to the effectiveness of the mealtime ritual. If the parents experience meals as something special, if they really understand that *groceries* aren't *gross* at all but are in fact precious gifts (if not from God, then at least from Mother Nature), this attitude is likely to communicate itself to their children, as well. Of course, it is important to ensure that all this thankfulness does not become unduly serious, overly sanctimonious or inappropriate for children.

Candles and soft music can help create the right mood for the evening meal. When the food is not only healthy but also attractively served and duly appreciated, the battlefield at the table can gradually become a scene of peace and familial harmony—especially if the vital Mars energy has had a chance to express and exhaust itself in other pursuits earlier in the day. Rarely do children create a battlefield under the Christmas tree: the atmosphere of awareness and respect that the adults have established prevents it.

A corresponding potty ritual can run the gamut from tiny to huge. Parents are most likely to appreciate (and share) in the ritual character of defecation. Turning on the water faucet and allowing the water to run is a widely practiced component of such rituals; its practicality and effectiveness are unchallenged. A similarly free-running piece of music, reserved solely as an accompaniment to the potty ritual, could have a similar effect. Small measures can lead to great effects because they help establish conditioned reflexes. The child becomes accustomed to letting go of its bodily wastes every time it hears that particular piece of music. It should be obvious why this piece of music ought to be reserved solely for its correspondingly conditioned activity!

The more naturally the parents deal with their own "letting go" rituals, the easier it is for their children to let go themselves. There are, however, a great many adults who exaggerate bathroom rituals. Not only do they assemble veritable libraries in the toilet, they also install especially soft and preheated toilet seats, and the "still, small spot" is redecorated to become the most important and most celebrated room in the house. Sometimes the toilet is the only quiet and private place in an otherwise loud and crowded apartment. Wouldn't it be a better idea to set up a meditation room or a reading room and leave the toilet to fulfill its own proper function? The name "still, small spot" implies that the business we do in the toilet, like many other affairs in life, needs a certain amount of peace and quiet to be accomplished successfully. Some adults are so enamored of these few moments alone on the throne that they extend their visits for minutes or even hours on end. Oftentimes, along with their stools, they also produce good ideas and useful concepts for other business affairs.

Naturally, children are well aware of all this, and it would surely be a mistake to exclude them from all toilet activities, especially since they are usually so curious to learn all the details. Their urge to imitate leads them to stage their own "letting go" in imitation of the way their parents do "it." If the parents use the toilet as a normal, natural act, without undue superstitions about imaginary filth or undue assistance from laxatives and enemas, the children are likely to do their own "business" with the same ease and naturalness.

Essentially, whether they have to do with hygiene and cleanliness or with any other thing in life, all rituals draw their efficacy and vitality from the consciousness with which they are performed. Awakening this awareness can begin with the smallest, most seemingly insignificant things. Washing the hands before coming to the table is a lovely little ritual that can help prepare everyone for the ensuing meal. Regardless of what (metaphorical or material) dirt may be clinging to them, it is a good idea to wash one's hands before sitting down to eat. Of course, the hygienic aspect is of only secondary importance. If hygiene were really at stake, we would have to wash our hands the way surgeons do before an operation: several minutes of scrubbing with an extra-hard brush under hot water, then a few minutes washing with a concentrated alcohol solution, after which the hands are still so unclean that surgical rubber gloves are necessary. The few seconds we spend washing our hands under lukewarm tap water with mild soap does not significantly improve their cleanliness.

Children think in magical ways, and magical thought is rooted in imagery. Consequently, children are particularly amenable to and thankful for inner images. Rituals give life a sense of security and structure. If they are practiced in a good way, rituals can give children the boundaries they so desperately need. Beyond that, it is probably the only way to awaken their interest in washing and in cleanliness in general.

Questions About the Age of Infancy and Young Childhood

1. How do I respond to new situations?
    - How do I react after moving to new surroundings (new country, new city, new dwelling)?
    - How do I react to a new position in my career, a new boss on the job, or new colleagues and coworkers?
2. How much do I expect to be taken care of by the government, by society, by my company, family or partner?
    - Would I feel more comfortable as a civil servant or as a freelancer?
3. How do I cope with being alone?
    - With being alone in my own dwelling?
    - With being alone at night in my bed?
4. How do I react when aggression comes into play?

5. How easy is it for me to assert myself?
6. Have I learned to accept other people's opinions and standpoints, and to accommodate myself if I cannot change a situation?
7. What role does power play for me?
8. Is it easy or difficult for me to give? Do I like to give presents? How valuable are they?
9. Do I know when enough is enough? Can I find a good way to conclude things? Do I go to bed at the proper time?
10. Do I allow enough time and space in my life for regeneration?

4. Childhood Crises

From the diary of a two-year-old:

Thursday, 8:10 a.m. Sprinkled eau de cologne on the carpet. It smelled good. Mama got angry. Eau de cologne is forbidden, a no-no.

8:45 a.m.   Threw cigarette lighter in the coffee. Got slapped.

9:00 a.m.   Went into the kitchen. Got thrown out. Kitchen is off-limits.

9:15 a.m.   Went into Papa's study. Got thrown out. Papa's study also off-limits.

9:30 a.m.   Took the key to the cabinet. Played with it. Mama couldn't find it. Neither could I. Mama scolded.

10:00 a.m.   Found a red marker. Scribbled on the wallpaper. Marker is a no-no.

10:20 a.m.   Took knitting needle from knitting basket and bent it. Stuck second knitting needle in the sofa. Knitting needles are also a no-no.

11:00 a.m.   Was supposed to drink my milk. Wanted water. Had a tantrum. Got slapped.

11:10 a.m.   Wet my pants. Got slapped. Wetting pants is a no-no.

11:30 a.m.   Broke open a cigarette. Found tobacco inside. Tasted bad.

11:45 a.m.   Followed millipede under the wall. Found wood louse there. Very interesting, but a no-no.

12:15 a.m.   Ate dirt. Interesting flavor, but a no-no.

12:30 a.m.   Spit out the lettuce. Tasted disgusting. Spitting out food also a no-no.

1:15 p.m.   Naptime in bed. Didn't sleep a wink. Got out and sat on top of the bed. Felt chilly. Feeling chilly is a no-no.

2:00 p.m.   Thought things over. Realized that everything is a no-no. Why have we been put here in this world anyway?

—Hellmut Holthaus

All subsequent crises are ultimately nothing more than enlargements of the birth pattern and, as such, are dependent upon the solution of prior crises. Unsolved problems are dragged along with us until they are solved. If a child is unable to let go during the birth process, if it would prefer to remain in its warm, familiar den, then chances that it will not be eager to leave its parental home later on, neither on the way to kindergarten nor on the way to occupational training or college. If the severing of the umbilical cord is fraught with difficulties at birth, it is a good idea to pay close attention to the next severance, namely, when the time comes to leave the safe nest of home.

Childhood Diseases and Inoculation Campaigns

How we feel about this theme tends to reveal our general attitude toward symptoms of illness and problems in general. Most of us would prefer not to know about unpleasant things. We wish we could magically do away with them all so that not even the faintest shadow would darken our bright illusion of a "brave new world" where children, and especially our own children, never suffer from any illnesses. Nowadays practically all childhood diseases are systematically preempted by multiple inoculations that "kill two (or more) birds (i.e., germs) with one stone (i.e., injection)." The illusion is that we can trade a variety of unpleasant infectious diseases for a single prick of the hypodermic needle. But this exchange does not take the shadow into account, and that shadow can only be pushed aside temporarily. Once it has been pushed aside, it reappears in forms that tend to be even more troubling than its original guise. Thoroughly inoculated children are immune to certain diseases, but this does not mean that they are healthy. True, they will not get the measles, but they frequently suffer for long periods of time from atypical mixtures of symptoms that, although not German measles or measles, are nonetheless bothersome and unpleasant.

Our grandparents knew that childhood illnesses are crucially important to the child, helping to strengthen the child's immune system for its lifelong battle in a world full of aggressive pathogens. Infectious diseases are confrontations: by overcoming these illnesses, the organism gains new strength and assertiveness. In the past we had enough faith in our children to allow them to do battle with childhood diseases. Nowadays, our modern academic medical establishment can prevent those diseases. In other fields of life, however, we recognize the importance of childhood diseases. Newly designed cars and new generations of computers are allowed to have "early childhood diseases." Once they have passed beyond that stage, they are "riper" and more reliable.

Of course, inoculations are a blessing that saves us from a great deal of misery. But this does not mean that every little conflict ought to be preempted before it can be fought. That would be like prohibiting an army from going out on maneuvers. In time, that army would degenerate and become incapable of responding to real emergencies. The situation is similar with inoculations: we should decide whether we want to aim our "magic bullets" against truly dangerous illnesses (e.g., tetanus and polio), or if we also want to inoculate against relatively harmless ailments (e.g., measles, mumps or influenza).

As far as fate and destiny are concerned, inoculations cannot help us avoid facing our life's real tasks. With or without immunizations, we will surely be called upon to learn whatever it is we incarnated to learn. We can, however, choose on which *level* we want to do our learning. Small pox and polio, for example, are two of the more dangerous diseases, so it is better to inoculate against them and let the children learn to assert themselves while fighting less dangerous diseases. The question remains: if we could completely prevent all infections, would our children find other options for exercising the healthy aggression and assertiveness that are essential for their development?

As always, the answer lies in the middle: inoculations are neither inherently good nor inherently bad. Sometimes they are appropriate, other times they are superfluous or even dangerous. Not to inoculate in a day and age when we can so easily immunize our children against truly dangerous diseases is not courageous—it is foolhardy. Why should we expose our children to greater risks than we would dare to face ourselves? We adults have been inoculated against practically everything; not immunizing our children *on principle* is as questionable an approach as is the other extreme (i.e., immunizing them against everything and anything). In this context, as in so many others in life, we simply have to think things over and take responsibility for our actions. The fact that we can inoculate offers us an option rather than a duty. We can choose to inoculate or not to inoculate, rather than blindly immunizing against everything under the sun. Faith is good; blind faith is dangerous. Before we cross the street, we look to the left and then to the right; only then do we put our faith in God and step into the roadway. It would be absurd to place so much faith in God that we did not bother to look both ways. After all, God gave us eyes for a reason! The Sufis have a saying: "Trust in Allah, but tether your camel."

Kindergarten Fun or Preschool Stress?

Although kindergarten was originally intended to serve as an easy transition toward the ever more closely approaching earnestness of life, our achievement-oriented society threatens to change that institution into a high-stress preschool. That is a pity, especially for children who have no siblings since kindergarten gives them a valuable opportunity to playfully practice the rules of the social game and learn how to behave appropriately in a group situation. When kindergarten falls prey to overly ambitious parents or an overly demanding society, it can become a kind of boot camp for new recruits to the rat race. Like the APGAR points for evaluating newborns, if a kindergarten is run according to brownie points earned for achievement, it becomes a way of shortening childhood and is less a "garden for children" than an ordeal and a proving ground for adult vanities. Especially because the rat race is so ever-present in our society, it behooves us to do our best to shield our children from unduly early induction into it.

If we consider society's attitude toward children, we can readily see just how little heed it pays to children and to feelings. From the earliest days of infancy, our children are locked into cages and cribs (euphemistically known as "playpens"). Cages like these shield the children from dangers in their environment, but they also shield us from our children. While our cities have become paradises for automobile drivers, our children are confined to tiny reservations called playgrounds that, in some respects, resemble the reservations established to contain indigenous peoples whom civilized adult society found troublesome. Ancient indigenous societies are good examples of a world in which children are welcome. Their children grew up in natural landscapes rather than in artificial canyons enlivened by gleaming automobile paint jobs. The adults had time to spend with their children because time was not equated with money. We Germans regard the American and Italian societies as especially friendly to children, but they only look this way because our own society is so unfriendly to kids.

A garden can be used "industrially" as a place to grow a maximum amount of *young vegetables*, or it can be devoted to pleasure and the senses, offering plenty of flowers, scents and natural beauties. Metaphorically speaking, only the second type of garden is the right place for *young humans*.

And it should be an especially attractive garden, one that makes the daily farewell from home seem like a meaningful exchange. Even if the kindergarten is in fact very appealing, children still sometimes have trouble taking the necessary step of separating themselves from the familiar nest. Being weaned from the parental bed and from the mother's breast are useful as preliminaries to this next test of courage. Leaving the safe prone posture on Mother Earth and learning to say that first definite "No!" are necessary precursors, as well. Finally, with a solid foundation in primal trust, the child can begin its step-by-step conquest of the outside world.

If children are spontaneously ready to take these steps toward independence, chances are that their previous development has been good. Independent children who do not like to hold their parents' hands and who prefer to run off on their own two little feet are the ones who most clearly show that they trust their parents and know that they can rely on them. Children who anxiously clutch their mothers' apron strings do so less from feelings of love for their mothers than from feelings of dependency and insecurity. When little children angrily strike out at a parent, that is a sign they are absolutely sure of their parents' affection and have no fear of losing it by indulging in an aggressive explosion.

Of course, another reason children may want to boycott their kindergarten could be that the place is inappropriate and that the kindergarten teachers are either too demanding or not challenging enough. If that is not the case, and even if the child succeeds in asserting itself and is not compelled to attend kindergarten, its victory is only temporary since the first day of elementary school is sure to bring the onset of the next crisis. The preschool years can be a valuable time of play, giving the child ample opportunity to enhance its self-confidence and independence. This could begin with corresponding physical exercises that teach the child to fall backward into arms waiting to catch it. Later, it begins to spend increasingly lengthy intervals away from its parents and learns by experience that they nevertheless always return again after some time has passed. Kindergarten offers a community of children where, through play, the children learn to cope with new peers and to venture a few steps further into the world. Afterward, with the first grade of elementary school, they begin to take their first steps into an adult world where people are expected to work.

The First Day of School

This day marks the onset of the *seriousness* of life, although it is sometimes mollified by a preparatory year in kindergarten or preschool. Even the German tradition of sending the children to their first day of school with a huge paper cone full of treats cannot disguise the fact that this is an *earnest* event. The candy tries to put a sugar coating on the farewell to the carefree days of early childhood, to throw a veil over the severity awaiting them in this new phase of life. The cleverest little ones quickly see through the subterfuge and say, "Come on, Mom, let's go home. I don't like it here." But their protests are useless. Sooner or later they all end up in their designated chair in their designated school, where they begin by learning how to act like little adults who have "voluntarily" surrendered the privileges of childhood. Despite all pedagogical disclaimers, despite all "child-friendly" curricula, the fact remains that childhood must now be left behind, playfulness must be tempered with earnestness, and efficiency is the order of the day. "Don't sleep! Don't dream! Stop fantasizing and concentrate!" is the austere tone, with the equally austere consequences that, in time, we lose touch with our playful, creative, childlike skills and become serious, dull adults. The bitter fruits of this (misdirected) education provide plenty of work for psychotherapists who teach adults how to fantasize, dream, restore playfulness into their lives, reawaken the long-suppressed inner child and discover that life is more than concentration and hard work. Some adults even need to be taught how to sleep.

The real task of the early school years should be to add analytical thought to the image-based perception children naturally possess. This should be an addition rather than a replacement, a playful process that shows the child that analytic thinking can be fun. As important as it may be for the child to process and cope with the sober changes that school entails, it is no less important for the school's curriculum to be at least somewhat relevant to the "school of life." The currently instituted nine-to-thirteen year preparatory course leading to participation in our market-oriented society shapes its graduates into conveniently achievement-oriented, efficient, success-motivated workers and consumers. However, as far as their souls are concerned, it degrades them into less than human cripples who, if they want to reclaim their other halves (the feminine half of their souls), have little choice but to seek out costly psychotherapeutic "playgrounds."

If that sounds too severe, we should recall that if the greatest German physicians of the past were required to pass today's medical boards, none would ever have been permitted to practice medicine. The majority of Nobel Prizes for outstanding scientific achievements have been awarded to U.S. citizens, most of whom are graduates of elite schools whose curricula emphasize entirely different criteria that place top priority on creativity. Hordes of business executives are attending psychotherapeutic workshops, ardently hoping they will be able to regain the creativity and playful lightheartedness that engenders the kinds of ideas and visions needed to run a business today. Finally, we ought to bear in mind that the heart attack—the trademark of our high-pressure, success-oriented society—is no longer a stranger to secondary schools.[33]

Private schools are enjoying ever-greater popularity, but they are by no means the best answer for every student. All we can do is hope that the current paradigm shift away from old-fashioned, purely male-style logic will bring a new worldview and a more mature, more comprehensive style of pedagogy.[34] This new approach to schooling would heed the fact that human beings have souls as well as minds, and would integrate this realization into its curricula in practical, holistic ways.

Questions About Childhood

1. How well have I learned to assert myself?
2. How did I experience kindergarten? Or why didn't I go to kindergarten?
3. How independent was I as a child? Was I the sort of child who was content to sit in the safety of its parents' laps or did I yearn to go off and explore the world on my own?
4. How did I experience my first day of school?
5. Did I cope with my school years more or less on my own or did I ask for a lot of help? Could I solve my problems and cope with my tasks without outside help?
6. How eager was I to achieve, both at the onset and at the end of my school years? Did the grades I received in school reflect these attitudes?
7. What is the current state of my imagination and creativity?

Exercises for Children

1. A long-term and highly rewarding option is to allow the child to grow up with a pet animal. This gives the child an early and "unpedagogic" opportunity to assume responsibility for the well-being of an other creature. The child can share its joys and sorrows with its companion and give

the pet its love—a love that is often all the more profound because it must overcome the gap between the human and animal realms. Having a pet also helps the child learn about life's phases and changes, perhaps even confronting the child with death and the need to bid adieu to a beloved companion.

2. The following exercise is also effective, but does not intervene quite so profoundly in the life of the family. Entrusting the child to care for a tree allows the child to care for another living thing and helps her to more consciously experience life's phases in terms of the changing seasons of the year. Like a pet, a favorite tree can become a true friend and a source of stability in life. Similar effects can be achieved by giving the child one corner of a garden to care for. Apartment dwellers might consider allowing the child to take responsibility for an aquarium or terrarium.

5. Puberty

*The laziness of youth
is a dress rehearsal for the inability of old age.*

—Sufi adage

Problems and Symptoms

Rather than finding its unofficial end with the first day of school, childhood ought to find its official end with the onset of puberty. The child (a neuter noun in German) is transformed into the young woman or man (female and male nouns, respectively). In the past and in archaic cultures, this transition marked a decisive and unmistakable caesura in life. We modern people mostly ignore the event and hope the children will get through these "difficult" years without causing too much trouble. We prefer not to notice puberty, with the corresponding result that the children are either told too little about it or else have trouble making sense of whatever scraps of information they are able to glean. It is a peculiar paradox: that, on the one hand, we put an unduly early end to childhood by insisting that little children cope with the demands of school yet, on the other hand, we will not allow childhood to end when the time has come for it to cease.

As usual, the body does not pay much heed to our attitudes, and simply does what is natural and timely. It increases the concentration of hormones, causes girls' breasts to swell, boys' voices to break, and young people of both genders to sprout pubic hairs. Sperm spurts and menstrual blood flows into the no longer naive "brave new world" of late childhood. If the individual's soul cannot keep pace with her body, crises are sure to ensue.

The First Menstruation

Of course, the onset of menarche in a formerly carefree life is by no means the symptom of an illness, nor need it necessarily inaugurate a crisis. But if the girl is unprepared for it, if she has not been adequately informed and adequately initiated into the feminine realm, then menarche can be experienced as a crisis. Even in today's so-called "enlightened" era, there are still some girls for whom the first blood comes without warning. They fear for their lives and imagine that something dreadful has happened to them. Although such cases are less common now than they were in the past, and although the failure to appreciate the needs of pubescent girls is somewhat less egregious than it used to be, the persistence of derogatory or euphemistic locutions (e.g., "filthiness," "bloody days," "indisposition," "the curse") reveals the low regard in which menstruation is held. Attempts to replace neutral locutions such as "my period" or "menstruation" with "moontime" have met with little acceptance. The disrespect shown to this primal feminine event lays the groundwork upon which subsequent menstrual problems thrive. Many such difficulties have their beginnings in puberty, and are frequently associated with unexamined and unresolved problems dating from the experience of puberty.

In recent years, people of both genders are beginning to give greater respect for the feminine pole of reality, and this re-evaluation is reflected in the greater sense of self-confidence many woman now feel. At the same time, however, there is also a contrary tendency to reify old prejudices. Women sometimes cooperate in maintaining these obsolete prejudices. The argument has even been accepted in American law courts that the few days prior to menstruation represent a cyclically recurring interval of unaccountability during which women cannot be held entirely responsible for their actions.

Menstruation contains many mysteries. Alongside its factual, gynecological significance, a woman's period is also the time for her organism to cleanse itself by giving up old blood, thus leading to regeneration and recuperation. Most menstrual difficulties are accompanied by symptoms that more or less compel the sufferer to relax and take it easy. If the body were sure that it would be voluntarily given the necessary respite, there would be no need for it to cause discomfort and force the woman to take life easier for a few days. Women would be well-advised to use these few special days as a period of unaccountability in a deeper sense, as a time when one cannot count on her full participation in the outer world because she is busy taking care of her body's needs.

No doubt the regenerative effects which menstruation has upon a woman's body are one of the reasons women in many societies tend to live longer than men, despite the strenuous lives the women lead. The fundamental reason behind menstrual problems is the body's attempt to compel the woman to give it the recuperative, regenerative interval it needs. If "the period" would ensure that a woman were given free space to be herself, to be unaccountable during these days when no one is *counting* on her, then she would be able to be unpredictable (in the best sense of the word) during the central years of her life.[35] Counting and reckoning are typically male attributes. As long as men continue to call the tune and make the rules in life, unaccountability and fickleness are liable to remain negative attributes and spontaneity will continue to languish in a shadowy limbo.

When the Voice Breaks

When a boy's voice breaks, he suffers one of the more harmless fractures to which flesh is heir. Yet the fact that his voice is suddenly out of tune reveals that something inside the youth is no longer in tune. His vocal cords are undergoing a tune-up, or rather a "tune-down," into a lower register and, until the process is completed, his voice may jump without warning from one level to the other. The old, familiar, high voice is no longer appropriate, but the crow-like caw of the new, deeper voice does not feel quite right either. The deeper voice shows the grounding, the connection to the earth the youth needs now. The embarrassing peeps and squeaks are recurrent returns into the upper heaven of childhood he is now leaving. If change-of-voice symptoms persist, it could be an indication that the youth is having difficulties coping with the transition from boy to young man. The growth of the larynx and enlargement of the Adam's apple as a male secondary sexual characteristic provide the corporeal foundations for the event. The squeaks and breaks in the voice make it clear how far along this event has already come and how inappropriate the old, childish voice sounds in this new, more manly body. Pubescent boys necessarily leave the ranks of the boy's choir, but (unfortunately) do not always leave the realm of childhood.

Youths and their parents alike must learn that along with the new voice comes a new voice in life. Keeping the youth in an artificially extended childhood is quite literally inhumane since it does to the soul what the princes of the church once did to young male bodies: castrating pubescent youths in order to keep their angelic voices for the church's choir. Nowadays we have put an end to this gruesome practice, but the castration of the soul through undue prolongation of childhood is still widely practiced.

Puberty and Acne

The prevalence of pubescent acne makes a clear statement. Instead of exposing pubescent sexuality to the world, what breaks out is a horde of pimples. They rear their ugly little heads like tiny volcanoes, nourished by a continually growing inner tension, until they finally pop their tops and make space for the release of discharge. Adolescents generally cannot wait for the explosion to come of its accord; they force the process by squeezing with their fingers, which leaves little scars as souvenirs of this intensive phase in life. Rather than living out the unaccustomed urges they feel inside them, they quite literally *ex-press* their pimples. And the pimples, appropriately enough, are most prevalent on precisely those parts of the body through which pubescent sexuality ought to express itself. The décolleté exposed by an evening gown with a daringly low neckline is all too often marked and marred by the physical manifestations of the irritations and challenges accompanying this next phase in life.

Acne on the face, décolleté and back performs the tasks young people themselves ought to fulfill. The pimples overcome the boundaries (of the skin), open themselves and openly *express* what their owners' lack. By squeezing their pimples, the young people open the boundaries of their skin and are compelled to give it the attention it now needs. But this attention occurs only on the physical plane, and mostly in an aggressively Mars-oriented style. Venus appears only marginally in the care lavished on the wounds and scars. The warmth of intensive sunlight can help, as can treatment with artificial sunlamps. The best therapy, of course, would be a trip to the ocean with plenty of opportunity for getting a healthy suntan and a healthy flirt, both of which would give the young person's skin the affectionate attention it longs for.

In any case, the acne sufferers must someday leap over their own shadows and surrender to their new urges and instincts.

The rebuttal arguments are as impressive and touching as are their sorrows: one young acne patient lamented, "Who would want to kiss pimples?" Therapeutically instructed to try his luck in a disco, the poor youth's expectations of failure brought him just what he expected: a series of rejections. When he was instructed to return to the scene of the failure, systematically collect ten rejections and document each one in writing, he found himself between the proverbial "rock and a hard place." At his next therapy session, he reported that despite his intensive efforts and despite staying in the disco until three o'clock in the morning, he was able to collect only eight rejections since (contrary to his expectations) some girls actually agreed to dance with him. Requiring him to collect failures called into question his program for failure. The ultimate success came when he was advised to look for a girlfriend who also had acne. Although his initial arguments were vehement and well-founded, he soon fell head over heals in love, which eliminated the source of his acne. No longer compelled to play this proxy role, his acne gradually disappeared. Incidentally, his girlfriend (who never attended a therapy session in her life) also lost her acne.

Puberty and Anorexia

The literal meaning of the German word for anorexia (*Magersucht*) is "addiction to leanness." Like many other addictions, anorexia can be a difficult and dangerous problem. Almost exclusively restricted to girls and young women, anorexia's increasing prevalence in recent decades is symptomatic of our era. Indeed, for decades, the zeitgeist has held (and continues to hold) in esteem the figure of a youthful anorexic woman as the ideal feminine form. By definition, the slender figure has no curves, and curves are what anorexics fear most.

To remain forever lean and lank is a peculiarly childish goal. This is obviously not the grown-up dream *woman* but the immature dream *girl* in the fantasies of so many correspondingly immature men (and, thus, also women). Anorexics are particularly uncompromising in their pursuit of this goal, preventing both their souls and their bodies from developing into those of mature, adult women. Hardly have feminine curves begun to appear when anorexics diet them away through extreme fasting. Menstruation can be preempted through fasting, and even the pressure of hormones that would otherwise cause breasts to enlarge can be counteracted through self-imposed starvation. Either consciously or unconsciously, people who suffer from anorexia do not want to become adults, preferring instead to remain girls (or boys) rather than surrendering themselves to the next phase in development that would ordinarily follow with puberty. They refuse to take yet another step into polarity. In their imagination, they yearn to maintain the clean sphere of an angelic and, thus, sexless existence. Because eating would make them into mature women, it is the most direct route into the realm of feminine sexuality, a realm they imagine to be unclean. If they fall victim to the opposite pole of their pure and sexless asceticism, if they lose faith in the boyish slenderness of their ideal figure and eat normally, they can sometimes feel so guilty that they deliberately vomit what they have just ingested. Afterward they frequently feel a sense of liberation, as if they had regained their purity and lightness.

Bulimia

If the emergency measure of vomiting becomes habitual, the anorexic has crossed the narrow line that separated her (or him) from bulimia. This disorder is a complement or an opposite pole to anorexia and closely allied with that problem. Both ailments are quite rightly described as addictions since they are ultimately connected to the search for the developmental path and the goal of attaining wholeness. At first glance, both disorders seem like an attempt to escape from polarity and the demands of femininity (both of which are experienced as being unclean). The resistance is especially strong when femininity tends toward its maternal aspects. Anything suggesting pregnancy, fertility and fecund vitality triggers revulsion, either on a conscious or an unconscious level since it reminds the bulimic or anorexic of the destiny she has refused.

But because the asceticism and its associated high ideal of purity is based on a refusal to accept the next developmental step, it cannot be maintained. During moments of weakness, the pleasure-oriented opposite pole asserts itself and, the longer and more successfully it has been repressed, the more powerfully and immoderately it emerges. Bulimia sufferers sometimes devour everything in the refrigerator, from the upper left corner all the way to the lower right, paying no heed to the actual contents of the jars and packages they open and ingest. The more intensive this "feeding frenzy," the worse are the subsequent feelings of remorse, and the more powerful is the sense of catharsis (and sometimes atonement) associated with the ensuing regurgitation.

In most cases, the voracious ingestion of huge quantities of food occurs in an orgiastic frenzy that brings neither pleasure nor satisfaction. The term "orgy" is therefore only partly appropriate since it is precisely this orgiastic element in life—the ecstatic element that expresses itself in sexuality and other sensual pleasures such as eating—that is most steadfastly rejected. As a symptom of bulimia, it expresses itself as a caricature of its true self in a greed that, although it remains forever insatiable, nevertheless indicates the path to its own resolution: true healing involves genuine sensuality that sates and ful*fills*. The ultimate goal is the ful*fill*ment of religion that offers the religious lightness and purity that so often touched the hearts of young people who subsequently suffer from bulimia.

Similarly orgiastic outbreaks can also occur in the area of sexuality. First comes the step from rigorous asceticism to devil-may-care lasciviousness, then comes the subsequent remorse. Here again, pleasure is seldom present, and "the morning after" usually brings the resolution to be even more strict with oneself.

There is nothing essentially wrong with the ideals of purity and of overcoming polarity. This is, in fact, the goal of all human development. But wholeness and oneness can only be achieved by transcending polarity, not by seeking to escape from it as anorexics and some bulimia sufferers try to do.

Anorexics desperately need to reconcile themselves with their feminine destiny, and this reconciliation will lead them back to life. They need to leave the ivory tower of disembodied purity and descend into the depths of polar life. The attempt to *evaporate* oneself, to slip away from life, leads through death into oneness, but only remains in that oneness for a brief and unsatisfying period of time. After suicide through self-imposed starvation, the attempted escape is presented in such an unpleasant way that the error of one's ways is unmistakably obvious. The only path toward definitive and lasting wholeness leads *through* polarity and, in this earthly life, through femininity.

As is the case in so many addictions, an overdose can be deadly. This is true for drug addicts no less than for anorexics. These people experience life as extremely threatening. The only real chance lies in their becoming aware that they have rejected their own (feminine) half of life in the hope of someday enjoying the bliss of wholeness.

Those of us who are not anorexic can learn a great deal from those of us who are. First of all, we can learn that the attempt to repress half of reality is ultimately irreconcilable with life itself. Just as breath as a whole is impossible without exhalation, just as light is impossible without shadow, so too is life impossible without its feminine pole. Secondly, anorexics reveal the extreme significance and absolutely indomitable power of the soul's intentions and programs. These young, almost always highly intelligent patients can be intellectually convinced that they need to eat in order to survive. But as early as the very next meal, their soul's pattern proves itself stronger than their mind's understanding, and the food disappears into every imaginable hiding place—except into the patient's mouth. As is the case with all symptoms, the real chance lies in reforming the energy bound up inside the symptoms without suppressing the issue. If the patient understands that the background involves her rejection of the feminine and especially of the maternal principle, and if she agrees that the goal of wholeness can be achieved as a female and that only the path needs to change, then healing and recovery are possible.

The conscious path through the formerly refused pole of femininity is one option for development, as is the offensive attempt to immerse oneself in conscious asceticism (e.g., by withdrawing for a time into a nunnery). Compared to the daily unconscious refusal of life that anorexic patients have practiced thus far, monastic life as a ritualized "avoidance strategy" has at least two distinct advantages. On the one hand, it offers regular spiritual exercises designed to raise the level of awareness and, thus, to reconcile the patient with the backgrounds of her own life and, in the long term, with the feminine lessons she needs to learn. On the other hand, when confronted with the austerities of an ascetic life that closes the doors on unconscious excesses, the previously suppressed, pleasure-oriented side of the personality may assert itself so strongly that it gradually works its way up into conscious awareness. Finally, along a path that seeks to integrate everything, the young woman can learn to accept her own sexual role and begin to see puberty as an opportunity. "Therapeutic situations" of this sort highlight the egregious lack of appropriate rites of passage.

The impending reconciliation with the feminine pole is made more difficult because our culture continues to devalue it. Far too many girls in our society look toward becoming a woman as a not especially tempting prospect, with the result that they unconsciously refuse to become women and compel their bodies to physically express that refusal.

Bulimia sufferers, too, must ultimately reconcile themselves with all those things in life they find so nauseating. The solution is similar in both disorders. People suffering from one ailment can serve as mirrors for those afflicted with the other, and both groups can learn from each other. As always, the symptoms shed light on the problem and on the task. The individuals must learn to *devour* life, to *bite into it* on the figurative level, while simultaneously realizing that uncontrolled bingeing on groceries is a *disgusting* mistake on the physical level. Orgiastic fulfillment is the goal of the learning process, but this fulfillment ought not to be solely equated with eating and not seen as a reaction to an ascetically motivated pleasure blockage. It makes no difference whether the ecstatic experience—everything is within us and we are within all things—is achieved through the monastic path of asceticism or through the everyday experiences of coping with life. One thing is sure: the attempt to achieve this ecstasy by physically devouring huge quantities of food has never been crowned with success. Human consciousness is predestined to absorb the entirety of creation into itself, but the human stomach is most certainly not so destined.

Asceticism originally meant "to work artfully" (i.e., the art of living). Among other things, life means giving and taking in rhythmic alternation. Rudolf Steiner said, "Life is rhythm." Anorexia overemphasizes the crest of the wave and ignores the corresponding valley, while bulimia emphasizes the valley but ignores the crest. Eating is okay and occasional vomiting is okay, too. Eating is necessary for survival, and vomiting can be a great relief when one has eaten something poisonous or something which one cannot digest. Eating, as a form of taking, is okay; and, in emergencies, vomiting is an equally appropriate form of giving away. Anorexics and bulimia sufferers both need to find a happy medium, a middle path where eating in moderation helps sustain life and bring us closer to our goal of wholeness, where giving, as an emergency expedient, helps restore proper balance and is not repeatedly misused. The patients would be well-advised to transfer the whole issue onto a less corporeal level, where it would be much more pleasant for everyone involved. Practical exercises, the goal of which is the middle point (e.g., tai chi chuan, turning clay on a potter's wheel, painting mandalas) would be a great help.

Bulimia sufferers suppress the Saturn aspect in their lives, an aspect they could learn about through rituals of moderation such as fasting and asceticism. Anorexics negate the Moon portion of their lives, and in so doing also negate their own corporeality. They could profit from ritualized sexuality and its accompanying pleasure. In many cases, anorexia is a precursor to bulimia, a transition that reveals just how closely related these two disorders are. Their central issue is identical since neither anorexics nor bulimia sufferers experience satisfying sensuality as a precursor to sensual fulfillment and ultimately to genuine satisfaction.

Rituals of Puberty

Traditional Rituals

The pubescent problems that we have been describing are entirely unknown in archaic societies. Instead of a plethora of crises, these societies have an abundant supply of rites of passage. Thanks to these initiations into the adult world, disorders associated with the refusal to accept puberty are practically unknown, as are the problems that beset a society inhabited by uninitiated, overgrown children masquerading as adults.

Anthropologists' reports about indigenous peoples' puberty rituals often sound terrifying to people in modern industrial countries. Pubescent girls are sometimes imprisoned for several days in dark, subterranean caverns. Boys are often sent into the wilderness, deliberately scared half to death, or visibly wounded. All this sounds awful and gruesome to our soft and "civilized" ears, as does the often uncompromising way that youths are compelled to take leave of their parents. Although the youths are frightened and panicky, it would be unthinkable for their parents to come rushing to their aid. Just the opposite is the case: the entire tribe stands together to ensure that the ancient, traditional ritual is conducted in its proper manner and in the sight of the gods. Older members of the tribe often don bizarre masks that transform them into terrifying spirits, thus creating the necessary panic. Other tribesmen loudly lament the loss of the children and stand beside the parents, who sometimes conduct a kind of funeral as a way of bidding farewell to their children's childhood. The children must die so they can be reborn as adults. After the completion of the ritual, the parents no longer have a daughter or a son, but the tribe has gained one more young woman or man. Grief over the loss is intimately connected to joy over the gain.

Australian Aborigines circulate rumors among the boys who are nearing puberty insinuating that, during the transition into the adult world, demons will come and kill the boys by tearing the flesh from their bones. When the time for the ritual arrives, the tribe's adult men choose a moonless night to steal the children from their parental homes or fireplaces and drag them off into the forest. Blindfolds prevent the boys from seeing where they are being taken. The mothers pursue their stolen offspring to the edge of the village, screaming and lamenting loudly, thus venting their pain and grief in cathartic cries. By taking leave of their sons in this way, the mothers relieve the burden of loss that weighs on their souls and need not carry it with them for the rest of their lives (as is too often the case among "modern" mothers).

While the mothers celebrate a death ritual for their lost sons, the sons are carried to a special cult site in the depths of the forest where they are forced to dig their own graves. Each boy is then buried in his own separate grave. Only the child's head extends above the surface of the soil. The tribesmen abandon the buried boys, but not before promising them that wildly shrieking demons will soon arrive to eat their flesh. The boys lie in their graves and listen to the sounds of the night forest. At first far off, then slowly approaching, the noise from specially constructed instruments played by the masked and costumed tribesmen terrifies the boys throughout the night. Not until the youths' panic has reached its peak in the early morning twilight do the men return, kindle a big fire, disinter the now adult youths from their graves and ceremoniously offer the young men their hands as a sign of their acceptance into the society of men.

We "modern" people can hardly imagine such a rite. Because none of us has ever had a similar experience, we tend to emphasize the ritual's superficially terrifying aspects and are apt to overlook its enormous effectiveness within the context of the field of consciousness that predominates among the Aborigines. The influence of this field is so great that the newly initiated young adults generally do not need to learn the rules of the adult world. Along with their integration into the field of consciousness of adult life, this sphere also naturally communicates to them its wisdom and its customs. In the truest sense of the words, they have been *wholly* initiated into *holy* wisdom, and the adult world influences their minds in a way that transcends causal logic.

Since we "civilized" people tend to overlook the importance of rites of passage (e.g., rites associated with puberty), we tend to overemphasize the severity of the minor injuries that may occur during initiation. Many Westerners are happy that civilization has outgrown such "gruesome superstitions." But how severe is the loss of a piece of a tooth, the suffering of a flesh wound and its lasting scar or the terrors of the rite compared with the opportunity to truly become an adult?

Modern Rites

The "heartlessness" with which indigenous parents sometimes eject their offspring from the parental nest is all too often misinterpreted. We jump to conclusions, unfairly branding the parents as unfeeling or cruel, just as the German language casts unfair aspersions on the innocent raven clan by describing unduly neglectful human parents as *Rabeneltern* ("raven parents"). The fact of the matter is that ravens are excellent parents who take very good care of their nestlings. But if the fully fledged young birds refuse to leave the nest when the time is due, the adult birds simply push the reluctant offspring over the edge of the nest. Depending on the height of the nest, the plummeting young bird has anywhere between five or six meters free-fall time to decide whether or not it wants to be a raven. In most cases, the plunge does the trick and the expulsion from paradise transforms itself into a free flight into the independence of the next phase of avian life.

What we do with our own young (people), who frequently remain far too long in the parental nest, is the real catastrophe. Already decorated with academic titles and mortarboards galore, they stay at home and let their mothers care for them and cook for them. Faced with the coming winter, a raven family could never allow itself such a luxury and, if one looks closely, one finds that human families are not well-served by keeping their nestlings too long either. The offspring never really grow up, and the adults are likewise hindered in their own development. Psychoanalysts describe this situation as an "unhealthy catastrophe." But because there is nothing spectacular about it, the problem often goes unnoticed. As its name implies, the *Matura* exam that marks the end of secondary school in Germany ought to coincide with the student's *maturity*, but it is all too often merely proof of the reluctant nestling's lack of maturity. Another possible test of maturity is the driver's test a young person must pass to qualify for a driver's license. Passing that test gives a youth access to the automotive community, but still does not make him one whit more mature.

In the past, there were a number of rituals during the transitional years of puberty. After completing their apprenticeship, whether they wanted to or not, young artisans were required to wander far from home as so-called "journeymen." Although these years of wandering were often fraught with austerities and tribulations,[36] the young men nonetheless gained a certain measure of maturity, independence and life experience.

Leaving home and taking a job as an *au-pair* girl in a foreign country served a similar purpose for young women. Suddenly in unfamiliar surroundings and on their own, these young women first had to learn to speak a foreign language. For many years, this was used as an excuse to maintain the institution. Nowadays it has become less common for young women to "waste" such a valuable part of their lives.

In the past, young men (who were not yet fully mature) had a chance to become more fully mature in the military. Sent on principle to distant garrisons, they had no choice but to try to cope with life in a less than gentle, all-male community. Of course it is more practical to send the youths to the nearest military base, and this is the practice today. Now they no longer have a chance to demolish the train cars during the long journey home from the base, the federal government no longer needs to pay for their train tickets and the youths are less of a financial burden to the state (and more a burden on their parents). But the current practice does not help them become full-grown adults.

Similar reforms have changed the situation in academia, as well. Conditions for acceptance to German universities have been reformed so that young people are encouraged to attend school close to home and are impelled to complete their studies as quickly as possible. In the past, at least they had the chance to get away from home, to transfer from one university to another, to learn the sights and customs of other cities and perhaps even to spend a few semesters abroad. Nowadays young people complete their university education in fewer semesters. More of them live at home while attending university, thus helping relieve the burden on the nation's already tight housing market. More rigorous admissions standards ensure that the universities run more efficiently. What were once universities have become schools— "tertiary" schools that follow secondary school, not schools of life, and no one becomes a mature adult simply by attending classes there anymore. As in archaic cultures in which rites of passage were part of the cult and were officiated over by medicine men, shamans and priests, in our culture, too, religion once assumed this responsibility. But along with the decline of our *cult*ure, the cult has gradually retreated into the background.

Along with the loss of the cult, the rites of passage that were associated with that cult lost much of their influence and binding force.

In principle, the Catholic rite of first communion and the Protestant rite of confirmation[37] still serve as rituals initiating young people into the adult world of the Christian society. Only after this initiation are first communicants and first confirmands allowed to participate fully in the rites of their respective cult, especially in the ritual of holy communion. But nowadays the desire to become a full member of the congregation is a low priority for most young people and has little or nothing to do with what it means to become a full adult. Most people have forgotten the connection between communion or confirmation and adulthood. Even the priests and ministers tend not to emphasize this aspect. Young people and their families take the events less and less seriously, thus sapping the ritual of its energetic charge and allowing it to deteriorate into a mere family get-together. As such, the celebrations are fine and good. But if a ritual is no longer charged and recharged with the energy of consciousness, it gradually loses its efficacy.

All in all, many old rites and customs have been rationalized away in order to save time and especially money, for convenience's sake or because they no longer seem believable anymore. Everybody is trying to belly up to the feeding trough as quickly as possible, and security is more highly prized than experience. Religion has lost much of its believability, and has consequently come to play a subordinate role. The logical result is a society composed of people who have either not become adults soon enough or who have never become mature adults at all, people who are playing (in often ridiculous ways) at being adults or desperately trying to prove they are mature women and men.

Modern Childish Societies

The lack of ritualized transitions from childhood to adulthood and the simultaneously strenuous and unconscious efforts to make those transitions lead to a sometimes silly, sometimes dangerously childish society. The adults in this society have never grown up, so it is not surprising that they seldom display attributes associated with adulthood. Their childish qualities, on the other hand, frequently turn into unresolved and often dangerous games. C.G. Jung said, "From a psychological point of view, most of humanity is still in a childish state....The vast majority need authority, leadership and laws."[38]

Evidence for the existence of childish societies in the so-called "First World" can be found everywhere, but nowhere is it more obvious than at specially designated sites such as Disneyland. This is a place where the propagation of a (typically American) style of childish world has become a big, money-making business. The corporation has discovered a niche on the market and is thriving. On the one hand, a genuine child's world in an otherwise child-unfriendly environment is like an oasis. On the other hand, with his mixture of childlike naiveté and patriotic American childish ideology, Walt Disney has given a refreshing new vision to a world that is so often paralyzed by bureaucracy: "If we can dream it, we can do it!" But actual children are only indirectly the material basis for this million-dollar empire. In fact, it is the neglected and destitute inner children in the pseudo-adult visitors who, pretending they have come to show their offspring a good time, are actually having the time of their lives allowing their own inner children to have a field day. The fact that love of children is not the sole motivation behind businesses like Disneyland becomes abundantly clear when one considers that the admission fees are far beyond the means of the average child's allowance, that unaccompanied children are not allowed to enter and that the enormous advertising expenditure in such theme parks surely has not been invested with an eye toward luring merely allowance money.

Above all, the *child in the man* is the target of numerous theme parks that, especially in the U.S. but to an increasing degree in Germany, too, are popping up all over the place. The combination of leisure time, ubiquitous boredom and a shortage of rites of passage would seem to promise success and profits for these parks. If one wants to predict the future of such parks in Europe, one should take a look at the U.S., the home of the theme park. Gigantic playgrounds such as "Magic Mountain," "Six Flags over Texas" and many similar places abound in skillfully staged tests of courage for so-called "adults." These are the homelands of enormous roller-coasters with multiple loops and hosts of other adrenaline-pumping rides. The old American dream—the promise that a daringly bravura ride through the Wild West could turn a boy into a man—has been cleverly refashioned, although the rides in such theme parks come nowhere close to fulfilling that promise. In perfectly staged ghost trains with computerized monsters one can let the devil give you the ride of your life, scare yourself half to death in runaway trains or conquer your fears on wildly rocking rafts plummeting down (artificial) whitewater rivers. There are rides in which you can strap yourself standing up into metal frames and allow yourself to be propelled at breakneck speed through futuristic worlds. In other rides you can experience free fall inside metal cages. At "Magic Mountain" you can leave the mundane, efficient, businesslike world behind and allow yourself to be magically transported into a childlike world where, in the nick of time, you survive the most daring tests of courage and emerge as an adult hero. In many cases, the wives or girlfriends who have been brought along simply stand at the sidelines and watch their teenage-men prove to them and to themselves that, yes, these overgrown adolescents have what it takes to become "real" men.

What else but the yearning to face danger and prove oneself a man (or woman) could explain why young teenagers of both genders pay admission and buy tickets for a chance to suffer nausea and cold sweat on scary "adventure" rides? And yet, does not the exaggerated desire to "stand up and be a man" suggest a certain doubt about whether that little man's littler man is able to stand on his own?

What else but a profound need for horror and panic would propel young people into ghost trains where all sorts of tricks are used to make ghostly apparitions appear, where computer-guided bony arms claw at them from clouds of light and where real-looking artificial monsters make one's blood freeze? Now, as in the past, young people have the need to leave home and experience adventure. They will make any sacrifice for a chance to encounter the god Pan, thus unconsciously following the fairytale pattern: the young prince must venture into the wide world, overcome obstacles and emerge victorious from harrowing adventures in order to discover his own limits. This is the only way for him to free himself from the domestic structures of his parental home, gain independence and authority, pass the tests that prove him worthy of his chosen princess and ultimately return home and accept his royal destiny.

There are dozens of examples of such playgrounds for pseudo-adults. Entire cities such as Las Vegas in the U.S. and Lost City in South Africa are devoted to the "adult" desire for play and excitement and to the desperate need to prove oneself. Unfortunately, visits to such parks are unlikely to make one an adult, but are guaranteed to make one a pauper. Folk festivals such as Munich's *Oktoberfest* are similar in their intent, although somewhat more modest in their means. *Oktoberfest*, of course, includes the doubtful advantage of allowing its visitors to imbibe some liquid courage before daring a ride on one of the roller coasters. The lack of existential options in their daily lives is so severe that people (especially Americans and Japanese) travel thousands of miles to sit with their peers on hard wooden benches, deafen themselves listening to primitive "oom-pah" music and swig immoderately large volumes of overpriced beer. In this situation, the test of courage retreats into the background and the foreground is occupied by the wish to numb oneself with alcohol until the world seems round and happy and in order. *Oktoberfest* is one of the few places and occasions in the modern world where excessive drug-taking is encouraged by the state and where modern people can experience a modicum of ecstasy without breaking any laws. The awakening the next morning is apt to be rude and painful because the night's illusion inevitably succumbs to the next day's hangover and because even participation in one of the many, regularly staged fistfights has again failed to make a man out of the drinker. Despite all the night's other attractions (e.g., swinging until the swing flips over the top, flying in rockets and simulated crashes in bumper cars) the fundamental yearning remains ultimately unsatisfied.

For a short time after each test of courage (e.g., after taking the plunge at one of the increasingly popular bungee-jumping sites), the unsatisfied, growth-hungry, half-grown ego feels somewhat better. But in the long run one cannot escape the sobering realization that, once again, facing the dare has failed to make a man of the boy. Bungee-jumping is particularly interesting in this context since it derives from an archaic initiation ritual in which young men tied vines to their ankles and jumped headfirst from high platforms. What no doubt worked in its original cultures has become little more than a cheap thrill in our own society. The difference lies not in the inelastic vines or the real danger of a crash landing, but in the lack of a ritual framework and in the absence of a charged field of consciousness such as those present in the archaic initiation. Our modern version nevertheless has certain advantages since, like its ancient predecessor, leaping headfirst into the adventure of free fall requires the jumper to take a deliberate step into the void.

Similar themes are present in the firewalking ceremonies that have recently become so popular in the esoteric scene. Here again, the modern versions derive from precursors in spiritual traditions where, in their ritual context, they had profound effects on their participants. But taken out of this context and performed without a ritualized framework, firewalking can have only a limited effect on people in our culture. Overcoming one's fears feels great, but neither the high nor the field of consciousness lasts very long, and not even walking across glowing coals can change a boy into a man or a girl into a woman.

The so-called "extreme sports" that have become so trendy in recent years fulfill similar functions. The tests of courage are impressive but even the most spectacular and most death-defying feats (e.g., free-climbing, hang-gliding or whitewater-kayaking) cannot make the young hero into a mature adult because the corresponding ritual field is absent. The yearning for growth remains unfulfilled, with the result that the youths attempt ever more dangerous feats in a misguided effort to accomplish the unconscious goal. The real goal, as described in the chapter on adolescence—namely, becoming a mature adult together with all the discriminating attributes of adulthood—is seldom clear to daredevil heroes. Often it is the desire to impress a girlfriend, the yearning to belong to the select group of "the initiates" or to be accepted into the society of men that occupies the foreground. The escalation to progressively more dangerous feats can become a genuine addiction since the body can become addicted to the adrenaline released in such situations. Ultimately, however, daredevils only show how immature they are since they can only feel truly alive when they are faced with mortal danger.

Eternal Youths and Timeless Virgins

It is in this context that we find the Peter Pan pattern of the eternal youth, a pattern that is quite popular in our childish society. The Little Prince[39] has found a host of imitators, small to middle-aged princes who charm their way through life and who would rather kill themselves in spectacular fashion than face life, adulthood and responsibility. Saint-Exupéry, author of *Le Petit Prince*, imitated his own book's protagonist; Marilyn Monroe and James Dean followed this same pattern and Robert Redford performed it in an exemplary manner in the cult film *Out of Africa*. All of these people preferred to become a legend rather than accept the less spectacular responsibilities of genuine human relationships and the entirety of the hero's journey. Naturally, even eternal youths have their redeeming features, as Exupéry's prince shows in an especially lovely fashion. As always, the problem has to do with fixation. The lightness of being, the childlike qualities of awe and wonder and the refusal to be judgmental all belong among the tasks associated with again becoming like the children. The problem arises when one insists one remaining a child or refuses to become an adult. People who have never become mature adults cannot again become like children.

An especially tedious version of the eternal youth is embodied by playboys and a few playgirls, although the male version is typically more popular. The success[40] of the empire founded on *Playboy* magazine shows just how many men have gotten stuck on this immature level. The entirety of life is marketed in the guise of an exciting, superficial game. *Play*boys see women as playmates and ultimately as toys, as objects. These are men who fear nothing more than responsible relationships with earnest consequences and real commitments. Only a small fraction of the hundreds of thousands of men who read this magazine are actually trapped in the playboy pattern. The vast majority of readers have long since entered into long-term relationships, although they continue to fantasize about this step backward into hedonistic irresponsibility. It is interesting to note that the feminine counterpart (*Playgirl*) has little chance as a magazine or as a social pattern. Filled with photos of naked men, the magazine has never had a corresponding popularity among women and, without its many homosexual male readers, would no doubt never have survived. Woman find it less tempting to remain stuck at this childish level—on the one hand, because there are better chances and/or better rituals to become adult women and, on the other hand, because our society tolerates even middle-aged play*boys* but people tend to view middle-aged play*girls* as vaguely embarrassing. When one considers these people (of both genders) with an awareness of their underlying motivations, one cannot but feel pity for both—the middle-aged playboys no less than the middle-aged playgirls.

The Television Kindergarten

The childishness of the society is, of course, also reflected in its habits of life and especially in the mass medium of television. Ever greater numbers of people are watching ever more hours of ever more childish programming. Many more channels and many more shows are available, but this cannot disguise the fact that what is offered is more and more the same, more and more childishness. So-called "children's programming" really does not end until long past midnight. Game shows make it difficult to know whether the commercials are still running or if this is actually the show. At the show's end, the amateur contestants hardly know why, what or even if they have won. Boring ballgames and horrendous prizes and asinine action films: all this dominates the TV channels and keeps viewers in a permanently infantile state. Action films, the favorite genre of half-grown adolescents of all ages, appeal to a particularly childish sensibility. Every halfway intelligent human being knows what happens to a person who slams his fist into another person's chin: he and his opponent both end up requiring treatment by a doctor or surgeon. But reality is one thing and entertainment is another. The heroes in action films punch their way through ninety minutes of fist fights and no one questions the realism or lack thereof. Despite all its foolishness, the action-film genre does have at least one redeeming feature: more so than any other genre of entertainment, action films confront us with death. These characters die in the most spectacular ways and with a regularity rivaled only by mass-production in factory assembly lines.

The popularity of the fantasy genre per se proves just how much today's overgrown children need fantasy stories of the sort that fill every healthy childhood. The film industry has made enormous strides in the trick-photography and special-effects techniques that make fantasies come true on the silver screen.

Directors such as Steven Spielberg skillfully concoct films that show archetypal dreams to millions upon millions of people. The financial expenditure alone clearly shows the seriousness of the big business with the world of childhood—a world most people have lost yet never let go of.

All this pales in comparison with the cyberspace wave[41] that is soon to break upon us. When it hits, the cyberspace tsunami will inundate us with virtual excursions into fantasies that seem far more adventurous than actual journeys through time and space.

The wave of horror movies, on the other hand, reflects the primal urge to experience fear and fright, as we discussed above. Hollywood helps meet an actual need, although it does not fulfill the real goal of childish yearning. Watching horror movies does not make anyone into a mature adult. Instead, the films simply become increasingly gruesome and the (overgrown) children who watch them become addicted fans of the genre. They remain fixated on their unsolved problems, and repeatedly watch the same motifs repeated in film after film. The yearning to experience terror is alright in itself. After all, even the word "panic" is derived from the name of a god: Pan. The upper half of Pan's body is that of a handsome, flute-playing youth; below the belt, Pan is a lascivious and permanently erect man. After attracting the nymphs with his handsome upper half, Pan's lower half rapes them and sends them into paroxysms of panic. As a nature god, Pan was once a central figure whom the nymphs both feared and sought. The Greek word *daimon*, which means both "demon" and "divine enthusiasm," points toward this same connection.

Along with the ready made and freely delivered entertainment options, a host of more individualized media are in the offing. Video games and computer games allow children (and those pitiful overgrown babies who have aged yet never matured) to embark on diverse hero's journeys. They give their all as virtual knights and astronauts, race drivers and dragon-slayers—but their "all" is by no means enough. Here, to,o a certain addictive potential cannot be overlooked; but no matter how skillful one becomes at playing a computer game, one does not come any closer to reaching the real goal—namely, adulthood.

Children's Food for Everyone

Another field full of indications that we are living in an unconsciously childish society can be seen in the way we eat. The spectrum of foods available reveals the influence of children's tastes, although it does violence to the meaning of the word "taste" to use it in this context since children's taste is seldom equivalent with good taste. A child's bedroom is filled with many different things, but one seldom finds evidence of good taste or discriminating style. The same is true of our modern grocery markets. Fruits and vegetables are larger, prettier and less flavorful than ever, while other groceries are colored and decorated to tempt the shopper. Taste is secondary; appearance is all-important. Here we can see another expression of one of our society's central issues: outer forms are increasingly crucial while inner contents increasingly irrelevant.

Today's restaurants express this superficiality with particular crassness. Even the name "restaurant" is a mockery. As the name implies, *rest*aurants used to have something to do with *rest*, but how can a human being possibly find *rest* in the hectic turmoil of a typical fast-food restaurant where the grossest groceries are catapulted from freezer to microwave to table to dumpster? It is possible to survive on fast-food for a while, but really living (and really dining) demands much, much more. Adults are seldom seen in such eateries since most mature individuals would prefer not to have their chicken precut and preshaped into convenient cubes or "chicken nuggets." Adults can handle a normal potato or a real fish, so they need not have it preformed as a french-fry or fish-stick. Adults generally prefer their meat whole, rather than chopped and patted into uniform patties, squeezed between gummy layers of white bread and topped with industrial-strength sauces that bear no relation to the meat mass beneath them. Where real taste is present, one would hardly opt to pour the same "tomato" catsup over everything and anything. The fact that feeding sites like these are so popular with adults as well as children can be explained when one admits that, when it comes to eating, adults are honest and unabashed, simply allowing their inner child (and its childish tastes) to determine what and where they eat.[42] This is kid's food for immature adults, for people who do not like to chew, who prefer precooked, prechewed, predigested, pudding-like baby food. It makes little difference what it actually is, as long as it *goes down easy.*

The beverage situation is analogous since little more than carbonated sugar water lurks behind all those sodas in all their rainbow colors. Not only are these sticky liquids hazardous to one's health, they cannot quench one's thirst either. All they can do is temporarily pacify, yet never truly satisfy, one's childish urges.

Children's Fashion Paradise

A similar situation exists in the world of fashion. Not only are children's clothes childish, but clothing for adults is childish as well, and there is hardly any clothing available that *isn't* childish. The fashion industry has been quick to follow society's trend toward emphasizing the outer form while forgetting about the inner contents. "Clothes make the man" has been replaced by "clothes make the man into a child." Teenagers ignore the materials of which their clothes are made, but pay a great deal of attention to brand names printed in unmistakably large letters. In the past, manufacturers tried to use the style and look of their collections as a means of attracting customers. Some of the better manufacturers still subscribe to this old-fashioned policy. The vast majority, however, simply use their buyers as walking billboards who pay for the privilege of advertising the manufacturer's wares. Although fashions in colors come and go, good taste in colors was a matter of course for many years. Nowadays, it seems, brighter is better. Here again we can see another reflection of the "children's bedroom mentality." Athletic wear tends to be especially bright and colorful, and this provides further evidence of the influence of childish urges on the world of sports and athletics.

Where romper suits, bib overalls and playsuits dominate in the alternative scene and among exponents of the women's movement, no interpretation is necessary. Rather than trying to hide their own immaturity, these overgrown children actually idealize and celebrate it. The phenomenon is not all that new, as we can see when we remember the erstwhile popularity of so-called "baby doll" fashions in the U.S.

All this may sound like criticism of the fashion industry, but it is not meant to be. We can be grateful to the fashion industry (and to the film industry) for creatively taking up our dominant problems and reflecting them so clearly. If we did not have childish fashions, we would no doubt be obliged to live out the same issue more drastically in other fields. And there are few areas in life that are as harmless as is the playground of fashion.

A fad that has little to do with the fashion industry but that is so unmistakably self-evident that no interpretation is necessary is the trend among young people from prosperous families to wear little plastic pacifiers. Teachers report that half the adolescents in their classes come to school wearing little glass or plastic pacifiers around their necks. And the kids seem quite content with their infantile pendants. What makes the kids so happy and the teachers so annoyed is the exaggerated honesty of the message: "We are basically still babies, and we openly admit it." Like Native Americans, they wear their "medicine" around their necks. In this regard, the pacifier fad is unquestionably honest. It marks a deliberate, remedial attempt to recoup lost childhood—a childhood whose lack makes these kids ill and whose recovery might help to heal them.

The Child in the Executive

The need for puberty rituals is celebrating peculiar victories even in places where one would least expect to find them—for example, among business executives. Anyone who offers training seminars for managers can make her life easy simply by offering exercises designed to remedy this deficiency. The world's high-carat decision-makers like nothing better than being shipped off to the boondocks and abandoned there with neither money nor credit cards. Like young Indians, they do their best to find their way back to the seminar center where, after their successful return, they feel wonderful. But, unlike their Native American models, the ordeal does not make these would-be urban Indians one iota more mature. More awareness would be needed to achieve that goal (i.e., the whole procedure would need to have a more ritualistic character).

But even if those conditions were met, it would still be taking place at the wrong time. Nothing but a great deal of awareness and conscious dedication can compensate for this problem. Consciously or unconsciously, all adventures involving extreme experiences are ultimately working on this issue. Whether one lets those seeking initiation rappel off mountains or hang-glide over the abyss, whether one persuades them to trek across deserts or undergo other emotional or physical hardships, in every case the same yearning is present: the hope that the experience will lead to something. This "something" is almost always the next step in development. The initiates leave their wives at home, and the wives spend the time hoping that nothing (terrible) will happen. But the initiates themselves are desperately hoping that something *will* happen after all these uneventful years, some kind of adventure at least, an adventure that will make the whole ordeal worthwhile and truly satisfying. The greatest adventure of all would be to follow the path of personal development, leap over the puberty hurdle and become a unique, independent, self-confident adult who is no longer afraid that

195

"something might happen" and who, instead, yearns to encounter life and all its challenges.

Childish Alpine Heroes

This context also seems to be the source of that peculiar urge, especially among people from cult(ure)less societies, to climb the highest mountains. For many people, it seems that conquering a mighty peak symbolizes conquering one's own life. Life as a mountain is an old motif; seen from above, from "God's eye view," a mountain really does resemble a mandala with its summit at the midpoint.[43] More than a few people risk their very lives on the slopes of these stony symbols. The greater their demands on life, the loftier are the peaks they attempt. On a single day in 1993, no fewer than thirty-eight climbers met on the summit of Mount Everest. Most mountaineers agree that there are plenty of more interesting mountains, but there is only one that culminates in the world's tallest peak, and that is the goal for climbers who are principally concerned with symbolism. If awareness of the actual motivation were added to the physical feat, there would be no reason to criticize the project and more would result from the effort than merely heaps of trash at the foot of the hill.

Securely rooted in the traditions of their cult and culture, the indigenous peoples who live in the shadows of these giant peaks never felt the need to scale the slopes. They usually felt far too much respect for the mountains per se, which they revered as the dwelling places of the gods. These people also conducted effective rituals that helped them ascend through the stages of life's path. They already felt like mature adults without needing to risk their lives on the cliffs.[44] Only after Western adventurers started arriving en masse did the local people begin carrying the foreigners' baggage up the mountainsides. A gigantic trash heap—discarded equipment left behind by decades of climbers—has since accumulated at the foot of Mount Everest. That heap of trash is like a materialization of the broken dreams that have also been left behind. Nevertheless, *peak experiences* do have some definite advantages: they put an end to illusions and, on the way down the mountain, most alpine "heroes" realize their real lives lie ahead of them—much like an as-yet unclimbed peak. It is to be hoped that the symbolism of the one success can provide the courage for the second and more important attempt—namely, the assault on the summits of life. Peak experiences are genuinely satisfying only when understood in the sense defined by psychologist Abraham Maslow, who coined this phrase to describe those instants of timeless bliss that people can experience during life's most special moments.

Old Babies

The most absurdly embarrassing, but also the most honest manifestations of this issue are the "baby clubs" that have sprung up for so-called "adults" in England. These clubs are the tip of a sad yet comical societal iceberg. These refuges are not so attractive for men who have failed to leap over the hurdle of puberty, but tend instead to draw individuals who have had too little childhood and babyhood. They are so badly lacking this little piece of paradise that they invest large amounts of time and money for a chance to spend weekends and vacations immersed in a "baby world for adults." In return for their money, they get what they are lacking: infantile experiences. They trade their three-piece suits for playsuits and diapers, are given special jumbo pacifiers to suck on and drink milk from oversized baby bottles. They ride on extra-large rocking horses, are rocked asleep to the tune of lullabies, tucked into bed and told stories. They can play with their food to their hearts' content and, for a small extra fee, are even allowed to wet their diapers. Regression is tolerated and encouraged, although the club's directress insists that the big babies refrain from soiling their diapers, which would be going one step too far. It is estimated that there are more than 5,000 such "babies" in England alone, and most of them come from the better classes of society: bank managers and police officers, vicars and above all military men. The estimated number is no doubt too low since an incalculable number of adult babies have yet to emerge from the proverbial closet. No comparable studies have been made for Germany, but there is every reason to suspect that the phenomenon exists here as well.

The Threatening World of Childhood: The Addicted Society

Alongside the silly signs of collective childishness, there are also a number of far less amusing phenomena that include attempts at becoming an adult and proving oneself, and that run the gamut from dubious to terrifying. The threat of addiction appears more than once in the many doomed attempts to reach the right goal by the wrong means. A tendency to abide by the "more of the same" principle can sometimes turn the search into an addiction, as we can clearly see when we consider the problems associated with smoking.

In its original context in Amerindian culture, smoking was a ritual reserved for adults. This, at least, is one Indian aspect of smoking we seem to have accepted in our own society. Children who are ardently eager to become adults are naturally tempted to imitate typically adult behavior. Smoking is a perfect example. On the one hand, children are not allowed to smoke; on the other hand, cigarettes are readily available. Juvenile smoking also includes the test-of-courage aspect since everyone knows smoking is a severe health hazard. Many adults accept the risk and smoke anyway, so children inevitably want to find out for themselves what it is like to smoke. Adults' well-meaning warnings usually only encourage kids to puff since the danger and the risk are precisely what they are looking for. Daring the risks, throwing caution to the winds, they venture forth to face danger in the form of tobacco, unconsciously hoping the confrontation will somehow make them into adults.

When they gather with their peers at a secluded site to conduct the pubescent tobacco ritual, they are often ready for anything and everything. Like heroic little actors, they try to hide the awful physical reactions to their first puffs. The lungs desperately defend themselves with the urge to cough, the colon threatens to discharge its contents, but the would-be smokers valiantly strive to keep their bodies under control. The threat of losing control and soiling one's trousers only makes the whole ordeal more of a thrill. They feel nauseous and dizzy, but they accept the symptoms as just another ordeal in this rite of passage. The dizziness [the German word *Schwindel* means both "dizziness" and "swindle"] and the *Schiss* [meaning both "fear" and "feces" in German] are both entirely honest since, as far as adulthood is concerned, they are both faking it and afraid of it. No matter how intensely the body protests, the neophyte smokers pay it no heed because everything is subordinated to the single, great goal: to seem like an adult, even if that semblance is restricted to a small circle of peers. It is obvious that these attempts cannot make the children into adults, but can easily make them into chain smokers. By the time they realize smoking does not make them one iota more mature, they have already sampled the drug often enough to get themselves hooked.[45]

Juvenile alcoholism is similar in many respects. Again, we are dealing with an addictive substance whose use is prohibited among children. As a typical intoxicating drug with the ability to help its abusers avoid facing reality, alcohol can help overcome inhibitions and anxieties, at least for a short time. Since genuine rites of passage are largely lacking, pubescent juveniles generally have no shortage of inhibitions and anxieties about life, and thus eagerly take advantage of the opportunity to imbibe some courage along with their first sips of alcohol. It is hard to blame them because their situation is difficult and genuine courage is lacking, so what could be more natural than reaching for the bottle filled with our society's most common and most commonly abused substitute for courage?

Here, too, "more of the same" leads to addiction rather than maturity. Advertising sometimes takes advantage of this confusion, for example, in the old slogan "Pushkin [vodka] for tough men." By the time young people have seen through the swindle and realized nothing makes a man impotent more surely than excessive alcohol, it is usually too late. They are no longer young, yet neither are they mature. All they are is addicted.

Tests of Courage in Cars.

When teenagers pass their driving tests and acquire a driver's license, they frequently pose a danger to themselves and to others. They drive out onto the streets to face danger and experience thrills, and all too often end up endangering or harming others. According to a police psychologist, there is no rational explanation for the many automobile accidents that occur during the first year of driving. These accidents are, in fact, readily understandable, but not if one regards them solely from the point of view of automotive technology. When a car slams against a bridge pylon without leaving any skid marks, chances are the accident was caused by a dare gone haywire rather than by the simultaneous failure of the car's brakes and steering mechanism. James Dean blazed this deadly trail in the classic film *Rebel Without a Cause* that featured exciting scenes of teenagers in old cars racing toward a cliff. The winner is the driver who waits longest and comes closest to the abyss before leaping from the speeding vehicle. In the film, there is one victim and one victor, neither of whom emerge from the dare one whit more mature.

With alarming frequency, recent years have seen young drivers speeding down limited-access highways on the wrong side of the road. This phenomenon has little to do with poor driving skills or orientation problems on the road. The real problem involves disorientation along the road of life. The young people are truly, if only figuratively, on the wrong side of the street. Racing against oncoming traffic is a particularly bizarre and obviously dangerous test of courage, all too often the result of barroom dares and boasts in which alcohol combines with gambling to cause dangerous behavior. "Anybody who can drive past two exits on the wrong side of the freeway is a real man...." The fact that the "real man" is really just a poor fool (and very likely to become the perpetrator of vehicular homicide) is usually realized too late since the dare-taker's judgment is blinded by the yearning to prove himself among his peers. Mortal danger is an added thrill, and the chance to read about his feats in the morning paper probably makes the whole escapade even more tempting.

Anyone who thinks that imposing limits on the legal driving speed of first year drivers only reveals how limited his view of the problem is. Any attempt to slow them down is more likely to speed them up since it would probably only enhance the test-of-courage aspect and challenge the daredevil "heroes" to drive all the more rashly.

Seeking Danger for Its Own Sake

The same problem is even more obvious among so-called "train surfers." Long a popular "sport" among youths in Brazil, climbing out the window and onto the roof of a moving train is becoming an increasingly popular activity in Germany. Intoxicated by the speed and the danger, train surfers stand erect atop the train, ducking down at the last possible moment to avoid certain death through collision with overhead electrical wires. This particularly dangerous test of juvenile courage has already led to a number of deaths in Germany.

"Auto surfing" is similar, except instead of standing atop a moving train, the would-be daredevil leaps onto the roof of a moving car and tries to remain there, standing erect, as the car accelerates to ever faster speeds. If no car is available, kids sometimes ride skateboards down steep hills at breakneck velocities. Speeds in excess of sixty miles per hour have been recorded.

When tests of courage backfire and someone gets hurt or killed, the result is usually described as an "accident" or else misunderstood by the youth's relatives as a suicide. Nothing could be further from the truth since the apparent suicide is, in fact, a desperate attempt to step into (rather than out of) life and emerge from the dare as a full-grown hero.

Together We're (Half) Strong

Compared with modern tests of courage, those practiced by Germany's university dueling fraternities seem almost antiquated and harmless. Although they vehemently deny the fact, these post-pubescent students uphold an old tradition and deliberately slash each others' faces while fencing with sabers or daggers. They believe their scars, proudly known as *Schmisse*, do not signify immature stupidity, but are a sign of adult masculinity. Scar-faced old boys like these are surely not grownups, but because they stand shoulder to shoulder in support of each others' career ambitions and because they rely on their mutual camaraderie, they are successful as a group. Here, too, the original intent is not difficult to imagine. After proving his courage and circumspection in a test of courage organized like a ritualized battle, the young warrior is accepted into a circle of men who agree to support one another through thick and thin. Lodges and "climbing teams" like these have an enormous influence on our modern society, a fact that again demonstrates the longing male youths feel for a way to prove themselves as men.

This yearning to belong to a men's lodge is often an expression of problems with maturation. People who join groups like these generally try to overcome the urgent problems of growing up by uniting together and combining their individual energies in a common effort. Students who have exchanged their biological mother for the alma *mater* seem particularly receptive to such groups, as the large number of student fraternities proves.

Germany's equivalent of the Boy Scouts (known as "Pathfinders") reveals this idea in its name. Girls are less likely to join clubs of this sort because they have their own, sometimes more mature, methods of becoming grownup adults.

Groups or clubs seem to have a similar ersatz function. Men who do not feel complete on their own join a group, where the company of likewise incomplete fellows makes everyone feel stronger and gives each one the feeling that, yes, he just might be able to make it on his own someday. No one is maturing and all are suffering from their immaturity, but shared pain is easier to bear. Arguments and intrigues about wholly irrelevant posts and functions within the club can be interpreted as ersatz for ritualized battles. On the other hand, there is also a reconciled level in this context. One person really is stronger when he (or less often) she is part of a community. This experience could derive from humankind's earliest beginnings, when survival outside the group was virtually impossible. Our vague memories of this situation could be the basis for clubs and lodges of this sort—from prosaic groups like the Lions or Rotary to esoteric and powerful lodges like the Free Masons, a fraternity that has had a more formative influence on our civilization than any other comparable group.

The effect is especially obvious on all levels in soccer clubs. We will take a closer look at that here since soccer games are one of European civilization's favorite rituals. Although often only a mediocre staging, the theater is astonishingly effective throughout the ranks, from the owners and captains right down to the ordinary fan in the bleachers. The infighting for the honor of occupying the president's chair corresponds to the struggle for the title of chief trainer and is further echoed by the tumult in the grandstands. All that struggling is far more interesting than the comparatively unimportant contest being waged by twenty-two millionaires down on the playing field. It is well-known that professional soccer players tend to have difficulty with the issue of becoming mature adults. No matter how wealthy or influential they may be, they must still obey their club and its trainer who dictate when they must go to bed and turn out the lights. They are not allowed to voice their own opinions and, if they do, they risk punishment in the form of penalties. When major games are in the offing, it is neither their wives nor the players themselves but the all-powerful trainer who decides whether their wives can be present and whether they can sleep with them. This is precisely the situation that most annoys pubescent men, with the result that soccer players repeatedly "act up" and stage little uprisings. The press exploits these mischievous tricks for all they are worth: after all, soccer is the favorite ritual of the majority of people in Germany.

In terms of sheer numbers, the most significant group in the soccer event is obviously the fans and spectators who finance the whole thing. They share the fever with the millionaire athletes, but actually have nothing but disadvantages since they are the ones who buy the expensive tickets to watch mostly dull competitions.[46] They endure long bus rides to attend matches in distant cities, while their idols, of course, have flown on ahead, leaving their fans struggling along the highway to catch up. The same money that makes the men at the top of the soccer pyramid wealthier is taken from the pockets of their fans, thus making the fans monetarily (and intellectually) all the poorer. But the fans must be getting something for their money, otherwise they would neither book entire railroad cars and sections of the grandstands, nor endure all the hassles of getting there, being there and getting home again. The covert, profound payoff is the hope of sharing in their favorite team's glory, of vicariously becoming state, national, European or world champions along with their victorious team. The yearning to *be somebody*, a champion, a winner is, of course, the flip side of the coin: deep inside, each hapless fan feels like a *nobody*—or at least, like nobody he would want to identify with. The fact of the matter is that being a fan costs time and money and, even if their team wins the championship, the victory does not make the fans into champions—nor into adults. For a glorious and fleeting moment, however, they feel like winners themselves, and the problem of their own childishness retreats into the background, almost invisible in the jostling, howling exultation of victory. The fans' noisemakers and mascots look as if they were taken directly from a child's bedroom. Their desire to win each others' respect and admiration lies behind all these hopeless attempts. Young fans may look silly dressed in their team colors, but older fans tend to look either ridiculous or pitiful or both.

The whole thing becomes dangerous when the puerile soccer horde regresses still further and returns to the phase of infantile spite popularly known as the "terrible twos." When there are no successes to be celebrated, neither in their own lives nor in the life of their team, fans are apt to express their frustration through anger. Some of them never find their way out of the spite phase and, as "rowdies," terrorize entire stadiums. Even worse cases, the so-called "hooligans," misuse soccer as an excuse for an orgy of destruction and warlike battles. The link between joblessness, frustration and aggression is especially obvious. Lacking both self-confidence and maturity, these are people who need to be part of a group, who need to compensate for their failures in real life by successes in club life or in street fights. If enough of them gather in one place, and if they have imbibed enough alcohol-induced courage, they even dare to do battle. Their acts of vandalism and mindless mayhem are an ersatz for entering the fray of life itself.

Afterward, when they stand alone in court before the judge, the erstwhile hooligans shrink into miserable crybabies. Many people who regularly travel to away games to cheer for their teams are aware that soccer-side fights sometimes escalate into full-fledged warfare. The townspeople are duly shocked to see the real background break out in such awful clarity. Things have obviously gone too far when, after a soccer war that claimed the lives of more than thirty Italian fans, a truck in Liverpool was spotted with a bumper sticker that proclaimed "Liverpool 34, Genoa 0". On the other hand, examples like this clearly reveal that what is actually at stake is far more than an athletic contest, but is, in fact, a ritualized war between two countries. Used to vent the steam of accumulated frustration and anger at one's own failures in life, soccer matches can take on nearly military dimensions as surrogate battles.

Similar patterns can be seen among rock fans and in all groups (e.g., rightwing neo-Nazis) whose members desperately try to compensate for their own lack of self-esteem by adhering to aggressive or disparaging ideologies. Like their historical predecessors, the neo-Nazis reveal a sharp discrepancy between the toughness and brutality of the violent mob and the pitiable misery of the individual members. The ranks of such mobs are filled with disadvantaged individuals who are trying to prove they are *somebody* by projecting their own frustration onto somebody else. The attempt always fails, but it nonetheless often costs the lives of the victims and scapegoats.

More Discriminating and Deadlier Surrogate Rituals

Naturally, such phenomena also exist on less primitive levels, although they are less readily discernable when they occur on a higher social level. Much of the phenomenon known as "trophy hunting" has its roots here. Long ago, successfully hunting down and slaying a large animal was truly a sign of adult masculinity .Nowadays, big-game hunting has nothing to do with survival and everything to do with a misplaced attempt to appear heroic and adult. Safely seated in comfortably padded seats inside their off-road vehicles, modern trophy hunters blast the last big-game animals to smithereens from a safe distance and for no good reason. Not until the poor beast is dead do their murderers dare to approach the stricken creature. The hunt's leader holds the animal's head up, while the pitiful hero strikes a suitably heroic pose. What seems so pitiful to others obviously makes the hunters feel worthwhile and important. They regularly pay huge sums for this kind of immature self-aggrandizement, for this moment of killing, for the horns and skin of their victims. They then hang these as trophies on the walls of their own "dens," no doubt hoping the display will win the admiration of naive guests. The fact that some people actually do admire these bloody trophies only proves how many people suffer from a similar lack of self-esteem. Blind to their own shortcomings, they tend to admire the embarrassing wall arrangement.

Of course, the whole issue can be described in grandiose words and even portrayed as a literary event by an author like Ernest Hemingway, but the real issue—becoming a mature adult—remains unaddressed and unsolved. No doubt because it was his own central theme, Hemingway made this struggle the centerpiece of his literary career, writing dozens of tales about bullfights, deep-sea fishing, big-game hunting and war. He was essentially preoccupied with masculinity, and in his private life, too, did everything he could to deal with that issue. The fact that he ended up working with ancient, ritualized patterns like the hunt, battle and wars between clans and peoples only reveals the accuracy and acuity of his feelings for this issue. Upon closer examination, even the bullfight, a spectacle most Germans regard as a primitive form of animal torture, shows its true intimacy with the themes of masculine battle and ritual.

The foreign legions of various colonial powers are a socially irrelevant but nonetheless typical way for frustrated men to wrestle with the issue of becoming an adult. Harshness, readiness to fight, aggression and the soldier's life in general as an ideal of masculinity are openly propagated and lived through. Although war is a classical option as a rite of sexual maturity and coming of age, as long as the corresponding awareness is lacking, the rite's effects inevitably lag far behind the efforts demanded from its participants.[47]

War is undoubtedly the absolutely worst level for puerile would-be men to act out the drama of their coming of age. When youths play soccer with severed heads, when thousands of woman are raped: this is war. An adult man, a man who is secure in his own masculinity, does not need to attack women and injure them with this perverted variety of maleness. A mature human being is simply incapable of the brutality needed to use another human's head as a soccer ball. Only miserable, immature youths are capable of such atrocities. Almost nothing except a wartime situation could provide the background for the lack of inhibitions required to perpetrate such misdeeds. Every humiliation imposed upon another sentient being is always intended to unduly elevate one's own position. And this, in turn, is something that only the lowest people need. All those Rambo clones we see on both sides of the front in Yugoslavia, whom we find throughout the world with bandoleers of ammunition crossed over their naked adolescent chests, are only desperately trying to use violence as a compensation for the misery of their own existence, as a way of making them feel male and mighty.

The fascination war movies and war stories have on so many "men" is surely connected with the issue of the hero's journey. Hardly any other situation gives puerile "men" so many opportunities (both negative and positive) to grow and transcend themselves. Growth, of course, is always what a person yearns for as long as he (or she) is not yet fully grown. What else could explain why, years after war's end, old men repeatedly tell their old war stories, even though no one has asked to hear the tales "one more time." Obviously, these were the most important events in their lives, a time when growth was possible and when, in direct confrontation with death, they felt themselves to be most fully alive. Even men who have had no firsthand experience with war are nonetheless fascinated by video games and, when an actual war is televised live (e.g., the Gulf War), the fascination and excitement are even greater.

In considering all the terrible and gruesome things associated with this theme, one cannot but notice that even among religions, war plays an important role as an event that harbors the chance to gain maturity. "Warrior" is an honorable titles among certain Native American tribes, and the Islamic faith guarantees a place in seventh heaven to soldiers who die while fighting a holy war. Christianity can look back upon more than a few Crusades in which the notion of a "holy war" was similarly propagated. If one believes in the tradition of the Sufis (adherents of an esoteric Islamic doctrine), then the error lies in conflating the

inner with the outer. Holy war, the Sufis say, is an inner struggle during which the faithful individual does battle with her own
demons (ultimately with her own shadow). This war's ultimate
victory lies not in murder, but in enlightenment. This inner war is
the only war that deserves to be described as "holy" since it is
the only one that leads to holiness. It completely transforms the
spiritual warriors, enabling them to overcome their own shadows
with the light of awareness. External wars, on the other hand,
make people anything but complete. If some youths become
mature because of their participation in a war, it is only because
the war has catalyzed corresponding inner processes inside
them. The redeemed level of war is always an inner war, and it
is this inner holy war that is to be highly recommended.

Rituals of Becoming a Woman

Among women collectively, there is far less of a tendency
toward perverted surrogate rituals because pregnancy and the
act of giving birth provide them with a tremendous natural ritual
that, when experienced consciously or even unconsciously, offers an opportunity to become mature in the feminine realm. This
explains why our society has relatively more adult women than
adult men, and it also explains why women tend to give their
daughters more space and more guidance as far as the issue of
feminine maturity is concerned. The fact that so many women
who have had a cesarean section insist on giving birth to their
next baby by natural means (despite the risks) is undoubtedly
related to their intuition of the mysteries surrounding birth and
birthing. This issue was openly discussed in the past. Nowadays, even though most births are regarded solely from a technical and external point of view, the ritual nonetheless remains
nearly as effective as ever.

Experiencing sexual intercourse for the first time is more
often an initiatory event for girls then it is for boys. In "primitive"
societies, we find a great many examples of how this essential

step into adulthood, when taken in a ritualized manner, can be the occasion for celebration. Naturally, there is no fundamental reason this cannot also be the case today. But when one considers the "mating behavior" of today's adolescents, the emphasis on "coolness" in their ersatz rituals leaves little room for depth of soul. Profound feelings are all too often interpreted as weakness and summarily rejected, with the result that the situation remains basically unsatisfying. The sources of the fundamentalists' attempt to get back to the roots may well lie here. Especially in the U.S., for example, we can find youth movements that reject premarital sex and in which (anatomical) virginity is again regarded as a virtue rather than an embarrassment. In most big cities, however, post-pubescent virgins frequently feel compelled to conceal the fact rather than risk ridicule by their peers. Fundamentalism, of course, offers little or no chance for the growth of the soul because the entire movement is much too strongly opposed to development and growth. Nevertheless, more awareness about sexuality would open up far more options. By its very nature, sexual intercourse already contains everything needed for an effective ritual: a threshold is crossed and a barrier is penetrated, the Mars energy of all beginnings enters the fray, and blood flows. Pain is felt, and with that pain comes a new realm of experience that, soon after the ice has been broken, offers opportunities for joy and pleasure. Even though this experience is scarcely honored today as the right of passage it truly is, the natural pattern is still so powerful that—similar to giving birth later on—many girls experience its initiatory character.

Specific feminine threshold rituals are relatively unknown in our culture because the male developmental path has been given far more space and significance in the annals of documented history. Special mention ought to be given to the debutante balls that signal the entry into social life for young girls from well-to-do families. These "gilded maidens" are introduced to polite society at events such as the Chrysanthemum Ball or the Vienna Opera Ball. Old patterns survive since these rituals (like their historical precursors) are official declarations of the girls' adulthood and their availability on the marriage market. The young men who escort the debutantes are little more than stage dressing, although the organizers nonetheless make sure that the escorts also represent something honorable and courteous. Although schools for military officers formerly provided the escorts, nowadays it has become increasingly difficult to find more or less respectable, more or less adult-looking male candidates.

The Search for Surrogate Rituals

Rituals of Searching

As a consequence of the widespread attention currently focused on the lack of puberty rituals, an ever greater number of people in our society are becoming aware of this theme. The tendency to imitate archaic rituals, however, is a rather questionable compensatory attempt since, even when a ritual is identically repeated, it cannot offer access to the original fields and hence cannot create the needed awareness. If, as the gypsies do, one were to trap a youth between the halves of a split tree, the ordeal might lead to the death of the tree, but could hardly be expected to cause the birth of an adult through the symbolic death of the child. If this ritual is to be effective, one would need to spend a long time learning about the world of the gypsies, making oneself at home in their particular style of thinking and feeling and ultimately finding access to the patterns that structure their lives. Homemade constructs that merely borrow a few ancient elements have, at first, no field at all and are correspondingly ineffective. It requires a tremendous investment of awareness to compensate for the absence of the field.

The simplest path for us would surely be to revive the old Christian rites of passage, simply because it would be possible to plug into the two-millennia-old field associated with these rites.[48] Of course, the rituals of confirmation and first communion must be recharged to serve this purpose, and the young people (as well as their adult relatives, priests and godparents) need to recognize the depth, significance and true importance of the rites. Recharging them would mean making space for their central place and value in life, consciously preparing oneself for them and consciously applying the consequences of the caesuras in life marked by such rituals. It would mean that, after the ritual, the confirmands would not only be treated as adults, but would be regarded as full adults. Indigenous people have an easier time of it: without any alternatives, they are simply born into their tribe's traditional cosmic order. Our situation is more difficult because the doubting intellect interposes itself and refuses to believe that a ritual alone can make a person into an adult.

If the return path toward our "tribe's" rituals (i.e., toward the rituals of our own languishing religion) is blocked, it is better to consciously attempt other rituals rather than do without them entirely. In times of upheaval like our own, it seems we simply must tread new paths. With our intellectual development and through the history of the organizations that represent our religions, we seem to have blocked the return path.

Climbing a mountain, for example, can become somewhat like a ritual, but only after we clearly understand what the symbolism of the ascent means. Whether they intend it or not, the climbers inevitably become more acutely aware of everything that happens during the climb, and begin to search for the meaning in these events. A consciousness of symbolism is still deeply rooted in human beings, even if it expresses itself solely in superstition. Only the natural sciences have entirely denied themselves access.

In this way, every journey can become a pilgrimage. This offers viable alternatives to the dearth of rituals and our concomitant helplessness. Young people could embark on a truly *great* journey and consciously experience it as a path toward

212

adulthood. The most appropriate such journey would be one whose length and destination would not be determined in advance, but would become apparent during the course of the journey. This would indeed be a journey whose goal is "to find oneself." During the journey, youths could expect to be given hints about their future path in life, and could more consciously perceive and receive the dreams and "coincidences" that occur during this "voyage of (self-)discovery."

The likelihood of success increases in direct proportion to the strength of the inner intention and expectation of dreaming a "great dream" in the sense of the visions sought by young Indians. The stronger the charge flowing into such a journey of self-discovery, the greater the power derived from the vision once it is found. Everyone experiences important dreams, but we all too often forget them, file them away in the pigeonhole marked "dreams are mere phantasms," or lose sight of them because of our preoccupation with so-called "reality." Every patient undergoing psychoanalysis knows it is possible to ask for and receive the dreams that are important for one's own development. Even people who were seldom or never able to remember their dreams in the past find that a large number of significant dreams suddenly appear during such a charged time period.

Journeys to search for one's path in life or to seek the dream of one's life are, at the same time, a kind of career counseling from one's interior. Finding one's true calling is essential; nothing can take its place. Leaving this central theme in life in the hands of an anonymous civil servant in the employment office who juggles a potpourri of school grades, compulsory training courses and income figures until a career profile emerges is disadvantageous to everyone involved, including society as a whole. The real reason behind all the unfinished training courses and switches from one course of study to another lies in the fact that people are unable to harmonize their career with their true path in life.

The mere thought of sending their children on a journey of this sort is enough to terrify most parents today. Safety and security, they believe, is far more important than liveliness. But every vacation after puberty could offer the possibility for just such a journey. Automatically dragging "children" along on family vacations is not a sign of love, but is an intrusion into their own space and an interference with an essential phase of development, even if the young people themselves do not articulate it as such. Sojourns in foreign countries where the young people can learn about the world and about themselves are called for, and such journeys would be excellent preparation for the ultimate step of leaving the parental nest.

After completing an apprenticeship or graduating from high school, it is entirely possible for young people to embark on an extended journey in order to find themselves again after spending so many years obeying externally imposed educational structures. A free year after this necessary but rather "unfree" time would offer plenty of opportunities for self-discovery. In the past, artisans regularly went "on the road" as itinerant journeymen after completing their apprenticeships, and students commonly spent a year or two at a different university or in a foreign country.

The Jesuits continue to practice a similar custom with great success. After many years of study, each student is free to devote himself to a discipline of his choice, even if that choice entails immersion in another culture on another continent where another religion is practiced. This custom undoubtedly widens the young man's intellectual horizons, raises his consciousness and facilitates his search for his true path in life. The journey, of course, is above all an inner voyage, but it can be simultaneously played out on the great stage of the world.

Rituals to Prevent Addiction

Although the search for rites of passage is more difficult than ever in today's modern industrial societies,[49] one can at least use awareness and courage to try to reduce the danger of the most dangerous surrogate rituals. This would be the job for godparents or other adults who feel a sense of shared responsibility for their godchild's or protégé's path in life.

The First Cigarette

Even if the smoking society is gradually nearing its *last gasp,* it is still urgently necessary to introduce children to the pernicious habit of smoking at an early age, thus preventing them from getting hooked on this mistaken version of a puberty ritual. Nowadays, it is practically impossible to prevent children from coming into contact with cigarettes. Merely alerting them to the harmful effects of smoking does not necessarily prevent them from starting, and it certainly does not help them become more mature. But one could invite them to participate in a smoking ritual, and that invitation should come early, before the onset of puberty, no matter whether the adult is a smoker or nonsmoker. Otherwise, the ritual is sure to take place anyway, most likely without adult supervision and under far less favorable circumstances.

Part of the preparation should include a thorough explanation about the background of smoking. The children should be told just how difficult it can be to become an adult. One should explain to them that many young people try to use smoking in order to seem like adults, since smoking is a habit that is typical of and reserved for adults. One should not blame young people for making this attempt, but it is important to know that the attempt cannot succeed since smoking cannot make anyone into an adult, but can make a person into an addicted smoker. One should not despise smokers, but ought to look upon them with the same compassion one feels for other addicts. After all, smokers have a hard enough time of it with their dependency and general susceptibility to illnesses of all sorts—illnesses that, sadly, are not limited to cancer and heart attack. Since the child will soon take his first puffs, it is a good idea to give him firsthand access to information about the theory and practice of smoking. That is why the initiating adult and child are about to smoke a cigarette together. It is necessary to smoke a whole cigarette, even if it makes the child nauseous or causes diarrhea, and especially if it makes the child feel like coughing. All of these are unpleasant side effects, but there is no other choice and, after all, this is (hopefully) going to be a one-time-only ritual.

After this lengthy introduction, when the two of you finally smoke that first cigarette together, the child is very likely to experience everything exactly as predicted. The child might want to stop the ritual, but in order to be truly successful, it is important to continue smoking. A nonsmoking godparent might have some problems with that cigarette, too. The adult need not inhale, but it is essential that the child take a few deep inhalations of smoke so he can really feel the effects.[50] Godparents who smoke regularly will be able to recount all the more convincingly exactly what they went through in the early days of their smoking careers, when they discovered that smoking cannot make them into adults, but can definitely make them into tobacco addicts. Confessing this, of course, demands a great deal of honesty from a smoker in order to conduct the ritual properly. Afterward, when a child who has already been initiated into the mysteries of tobacco is invited by another child to share what the second child believes to be the other's first cigarette, the initiated child can calmly say, "No, thanks, I already know all about it." The initiate is not likely to feel much temptation, and through her description of what it was like to smoke that first cigarette, she might actually prevent the friend from delving deeper into the smoking enterprise. Sometimes an initiated child might even initiate her friends into this other, healthier version of the first-cigarette ritual.

Of course, the peer pressure to which children are exposed at this age is enormous and should not be underestimated. Even if, after sharing the first-cigarette ritual with an adult, the child does become involved in a nicotine orgy at the next school outing, the ritual was not in vain and can still serve as a stimulus to help the young person put an early end to the smoking habit.

The First Alcoholic Drink

A similar procedure can be conducted with that other socially accepted drug: alcohol. In a society in which alcohol is an integral part of daily life, where not drinking is sometimes even regarded as impolite, where millions of people regularly use alcohol to try to drown their cares, flee from an unbearable daily life, or raise their spirits, it can hardly be expected that a child will long remain untouched by alcohol. It is therefore a good idea to introduce the child to her first whiskey or other liquor at an early age and within the framework of a little ritual. After explaining alcohol's role in our society, its function at parties and the role it plays in notions of becoming an adult, the godparent would then clearly describe alcohol's effects on the body and soul. The few sips of whiskey will not do the child any harm, but will make it abundantly clear that the description is accurate. The child's head swims, knees go soft, and maybe she feels nauseous as well. As in the tobacco ritual, this little alcohol ritual helps prepare children to resist temptation when their peers invite them to indulge in alcohol. The initiated child already knows all about alcohol and need not prove anything to her peers.

Here again, the attempt to introduce children to alcohol in a sensible manner can do no harm, but it can do a great deal of good. After all, alcohol is our society's "contact drug" of choice, and it is nearly impossible to prevent a young person from having at least some experience with it. Only after standing up, clinking glasses and speaking a toast is it polite for bourgeois Germans to use the familiar pronoun and call each other by their first names. Even young people frequently use alcohol as a form of "liquid courage" or to "wash away" their cares and woes. The best prevention, of course, would be to help a child find his own natural courage, so there would be no need for chemical crutches.

The Trap of Intoxicating Drugs

One ought to deal similarly with the cannabis products marijuana and hashish. The first shared and ritually smoked joint[51] can take the place of many subsequent experiences the child would otherwise be obliged to have on her own. Once again, the choice is not whether to smoke or not to smoke, but where and in what context. Some mentors or godparents may need to experiment with cannabis products themselves in order to acquire the experience and feel the effects first-hand so they can competently introduce the next generation to this drug. Many adults will be surprised to discover, contrary to their expectations and prejudices, that cannabis is astonishingly harmless. Indeed, cannabis products are significantly less harmful in their effects on body and soul than are the socially accepted drugs nicotine and alcohol. Of course, as far as becoming an adult is concerned, nicotine, alcohol and cannabis products cannot solve problems, but they can seduce their users into avoiding life.

After the children have tried cannabis themselves and discovered that the information they got from their godparents or mentors matches their own experiences, the mentors acquire (in the children's eyes) the necessary competence and trustworthiness needed to talk about other drugs (e.g., heroin). The children are more likely to believe them when these adults warn that hard drugs are so dangerous one ought not try them even once. The very word "heroin" (from the Greek word *heros* meaning "hero") puns on the idea of the hero's journey. But heroin trips always lead to a dead end, and all too often to death itself. No one ever used heroin to help him (or her) master the trials of one's personal hero's journey. The heroic feelings the drug elicits are purely illusory. Instead, heroin tends to provoke total refusal to embark on the hero's journey through life. Its users end up hooked and enslaved. They vegetate and ultimately lose everything. The most certain way to protect one's children from this awful fate is to be as honest as possible early on. An adult who drinks alcohol but simultaneously claims that all marijuana

218

users will surely end up in the gutter will inevitably be exposed as a liar by her children or godchildren. The proof that marijuana does not necessarily lead to the gutter is being smoked daily in every German schoolyard. Children who have been lied to once (about marijuana) are apt to assume that all the information adults give them about other drugs is likewise false. Hypocritical warnings and inadequate information are a dangerous trap for many post-pubescent youths who are apt to run off the road (of life) at the first hairpin turn.

The Necessity of Rebellion

Despite all these well-intentioned, ritualized attempts from the adult side, it behooves adults to bear in mind that puberty and the teenage years are always associated with upheaval and rebellion. Hence, these rituals ought not to be conducted with the aim of preventing subsequent crises, but with the intent of encouraging the crises to take place—within the bounds of certain "road signs" furnished by the initiating adults. This is why it is better when godparents rather than parents play the role of helper. Young people find it difficult to take advice from their own parents since this is the time when they are trying to achieve independence from them. A mother or father can do little to support her or his own children's rebellion. The more understanding a parent has for the youth, the more difficult she makes the situation for that young person. The hippie generation needed only wear their hair in (still rather orderly) Beatles-style hairdos, needed only light a joint or two and they had already succeeded in arousing their parents and testing the limits of teenage rebellion. A generation later, young people eager to shock their parents must pierce their ears with safety pins, dye their hair bright green and inject heroin. It is hard to imagine any further stages in this escalation, but we can rest assured that each new generation will undoubtedly invent its own form of rebellion.

This is also the reason cruel stepmothers and terrible parents in fairytales make life easier for the fairytale heroes and heroines.

These parents are easier to provoke and easier to abandon. Liberal, permissive, understanding parents are a greater problem. Their children have to bring out the heavy artillery (i.e., heroin) in order to provoke them. Parents would be well-advised not to pretend to be more liberal than they actually are, and not to deny their principles in a last-ditch attempt not to lose all ties to their rebellious offspring. Good contact with one's children must, for a time, be lost or temporarily severed. It is certainly more sensible to do battle on the issues where opinions differ rather than push one's children toward extreme or rash acts. On the other hand, there is no reason to pretend to be more authoritarian than one actually is merely in order to provide "friction" and limits for one's teenage children. If the youngsters cannot find appropriate adversaries within their own families, they will look elsewhere, find them and rebel against them.

Ecstasy

The issue of ecstasy is an important point, and one whose consequences can relate to drug problems. The whole field relating to ecstatic experiences is a taboo in our culture. Archaic cultures, on the other hand, regarded ecstasy as a natural component of social life. In their rhythmical stamping dances and long mantric chants or in trances and rituals such as fire walking, members of archaic societies experienced ecstasy spontaneously and also experienced their connection to that inner core of being where every person is hale, whole and holy. This experience is an important part of becoming an adult because it reveals a goal that must someday be attained. As soon as a person has discovered a really big goal, all the smaller steps (even those that seem huge when viewed one at a time) are much easier to accomplish. Young people who have seen the ultimate goal have an easier time coping with intermediate goals along the way. Although the quest for ecstasy has sunk into the shadows, it nevertheless lies behind the increasingly serious problem of addiction and the desire so many young people have to see life's goal without having to do much work in return for that glimpse. They use chemicals to try to blast open "the doors of perception." But drugs always offer only one part of the vision, and that alone is enough to make a person addicted—especially in a society that no longer has a functional cult to provide a meaningful framework for drug-induced experience.

Where spaces and exercises to experience ecstasy are no longer available, drugs become a danger because they provide (or seem to provide) ephemeral, chemical access to these experiential spaces. In this context, it is interesting to note that our society tries to prevent even the most harmless approaches leading to ecstasy. Rather than being pleased because our children need to go to discos and dance themselves into ecstasy (or at least blow off steam), many parents do everything they can to prevent their children from treading this essentially harmless path. Our experience with athletically inclined youths has shown that young people who regularly exhaust themselves through strenuous physical training are extremely unlikely to abuse hard drugs such as heroin. By providing moments of complete exhaustion and total dedication, athletics allows athletes to experience ecstasy. Young people who frequently dance themselves into ecstasy and thereby receive positive stimulation for the hero's journey satisfy similar needs. The best way to prevent addictions is to lead people toward ecstatic experiences, enable them to confront what they are seeking and initiate them into the mandala's pattern of life where the various stages and the ultimate goal are clearly recognizable.

The dangers of ecstasy are readily apparent. The whole issue has acquired negative connotations simply because ecstasy is almost always experienced in the context of drugs in our culture.[52] The ancient world still had the cult of Dionysus, a religion whose adherents intoxicated themselves with wine as a way of experiencing orgiastic feelings. Or course, in those days, society did not have a widespread alcohol problem because the intoxicating drug alcohol was ritually integrated within the context of the religious cult. This example helps us see that the problem is not drugs per se, but the un*cul*tured surroundings and lack of ecstatic experiential frameworks. This point shows just how misguided our society's policies are with respect to drug-related issues.

Ecstasy allows people to step beyond their egoistic limits and experience themselves anew. That is why ecstasy is the most impressive option for transcending the narrow limits of life and penetrating to the core of essential reality. The narrower the limits, the more urgent is the need to escape and erupt into ecstasy. On the other hand, inadequate or entirely absent limits can also encourage a person to seek ecstatic experiences. This would seem to be the reason the two groups that are most jeopardized by addiction are the bourgeois children of overprotective parents and lower-class children who grew up in chaotic familial surroundings.

Questions About Puberty

1. How did I experience my first menstruation/my first ejaculation of semen?
2. How did I experience the onset of puberty in my life? Did I have orgasms from the start? How did I learn "the facts of life"? What was the mood during that lesson?
3. How much unresolved childishness remains in my life?
   - Do I eat and drink like an adult or like a child?
   - Which childish games interfere with my career?
   - What conclusions about this issue can be drawn by considering my clothes?
4. What role do dares and tests of courage play for me?
5. How do I feel about (same-gender) groups? How do I feel within such groups?
6. What rebellions have I struggled through in my life?
7. How do I feel about asceticism and hedonism, fasting and feasting? Have I found my center, the "happy medium," in this context?
8. Do I experience moments of ecstasy? What is my relationship to ecstatic feelings and intoxicating drugs?

222

Exercises During Puberty

1. *Puberty festival:* The parents of a girl who has just experienced her first menstruation can organize a big party for their daughter. All her important friends and acquaintances would be invited. If this custom were to become more prevalent, the aura of embarrassment currently surrounding menarche would quickly disappear.

   A similar festival can also be celebrated within the circle of the family. This gives the parents an opportunity to make it clear that, from now on, the daughter is able to and has a right to take the mother's place in certain situations. They can also use the festival as an opportunity to explain what it means for them to begin relinquishing their parental role and what it means for their daughter to begin assuming adult responsibilities. It is especially important for the parents to clearly announce that it is good and right for their children to surpass them in many respects. A similar festival, of course, can be staged for boys on the threshold of manhood.

2. *Puberty journeys:* Journeys of this kind provide incomparable chances—for the journeyers no less than for the adults who remain at home. The voyage offers both groups an excellent opportunity to come to terms with the new situation and with their transformed roles. Children leave the nest to try their wings and learn how to take responsibility for their own lives. One can send them off with two stories: the myth of Icarus as a warning and the epic of Perceval as an encouragement. Backpacking trips have the added advantage of compelling the young adventurers to carry their own weight, take responsibility for the necessities of life, budget their money over a period of time and see to it that they themselves meet their own needs. Independence, self-reliance, courage and the pleasure of conquering new vistas in life are all

part of the backpacking trip. Earning the necessary money to finance the journey deepens the meaning of this ritual even further. A sojourn as an *au pair* can likewise be ritually charged and used as a chance for a new beginning.

Important precursors to such a journey include completion of childhood duties, giving away stuffed animals and other favorite childhood toys and bidding a general farewell to everything that remains behind in the land of childhood at home. All this must be taken care of before the young adventurer can embark on his voyage of self-discovery.

3. *Parents' journeys:* Of course, it is also possible to turn the tables and send the parents away on a journey, leaving the children behind to take care of the house. While the young people are at home playing at being adults, the "old folks" can enjoy a second honeymoon, taking as much time as they desire to look back at the active life they have had as parents.

4. *Tree ritual:* One can celebrate the onset of puberty by planting a sapling. This tree will continue to grow along with the girl or boy, reflecting in its own seasonal cycles the life phases of its human "sibling." Trees such as the walnut that need many years before they begin to bear fruit are especially appropriate.

5. *Medicine-wheel ritual:* The traditional Amerindian medicine wheel is well-suited for diverse rituals of orientation. The mere construction of a mandala of this sort—a task readily accomplished in appropriate natural places—can have a profound ritual character. The east represents the little girl; the west stands for the adult woman; the south symbolizes the little boy; the north signifies the adult man. The simplest exercise is to meditate while seated at the place of the youth and then at the place of the adult, and simply observe and take note of the images that emerge there.

6.   *Hot-air-balloon ritual:* This ritual can be staged as an actual
     journey in a hot-air balloon, a journey in which each mo-
     ment's winds carry the traveler wherever they may chance
     to blow. Since the only control the balloonists can exercise
     is in their choice of altitude, a journey of this kind is an espe-
     cially clear mirror of life's journey as a whole. As in the bal-
     loon journey, so too in life's journey we are free to choose
     our level, but have little or no influence on the pattern.

     A similar, albeit somewhat more childish. Ritual can be
     staged using an especially beautiful helium-filled balloon.
     The child can decorate the balloon with wishes for the next
     segment in life, and the parents can use the balloon as a
     symbolic means of granting their child freedom. Watching
     the balloon disappear into the sky is the final meditation in
     this poetic ritual. Competitions between children (whose
     balloon will travel farthest?) can be preparations for actual
     journeys and ascents in later life.

7.   *Ritual for the parents of pubescent children:* This is a
     shared meditation on the two great tasks for parents as
     formulated by the American journalist Hodding Carter:
     first, to give the children roots; then to allow their wings
     to grow. If both parents begin early and then regularly
     embark on inner journeys with this theme, the inner im-
     ages and the depth of the trance will no doubt help them
     cope with questions about child-raising and caring for their
     offspring.

8.   The phases of typical puberty rituals include:
     * leaving the family and the home,
     * bearing hardships, tests of courage, ritualized quests,
     * group ritual to celebrate the new identity of the newly adult
       young person,
     * roots phase: introduction to the rules of the new phase
       in life.

6. Adolescence

People are not born on the day
their mothers give birth to them,
but on the day
when life compels them
to give birth to themselves.
—Gabriel García Marquez

You ask me, "What shall I do?"
And I tell you, "Live wildly and dangerously, Arthur!"

When they reached puberty, young people in archaic cultures were physically and emotionally capable of taking the final step to separate themselves from the parental nest. For modern youths, on the other hand, this seems no longer to be the case. They are far ahead of their "primitive" brothers and sisters in certain respects yet, in other respects, today's young people lag far behind their archaic counterparts. The phenomenon of acceleration[53]—the constant increase in the speed of physical development—seems to be balanced by a corresponding decrease in the rate of emotional and psychological development. Today's youths reach puberty at an earlier age than ever before, even as they fall further behind in their degree of spiritual development. Scientists believe that abundant supplies of protein and vitamins are responsible for the first phenomenon. If a better diet is decisive for accelerating physical development, then it seems likely that the deceleration in spiritual development is due to the poor nourishment "fed" to the souls of today's young people.

Abundant proof of this is available. Instead of getting the "soul food" they need, youths receive nothing but "fast food" —enough to live on, but not the sort of stuff from which mature adults are made. An evolutionary deficit is the logical consequence. Even survival itself is no longer so certain, and the high suicide rates in "culture-less" societies include a large percentage of suicides among young people. In archaic cultures, on the other hand, suicide was practically unknown.

In any case, today's young people are entirely overwhelmed by the prospect of "severing the umbilical cord" at puberty, and thus adolescence moves into the focal point of events. The interval between puberty and full physical maturity provides the chance to complete the difficult process of severing ties. In many respects, this second great severance from the parental nest corresponds to the first major severance (from the maternal womb). The first cutting of ties with the nest more or less coincides with the first day of school. What begins with puberty ought to come to an end with adolescence, otherwise it threatens to interfere with the subsequent evolution of both generations.

As far as severing ties with the parental home is concerned, women generally have an easier time than men, precisely because the women's path looks like the more difficult one. According to a custom firmly anchored in our culture and in many others, the young woman leaves her parental home and follows her husband into his house. What is generally experienced as a personal hardship has a variety of advantages over the long run. Even if the new bride has merely exchanged subservience to her parents for subservience to her husband, she nonetheless automatically experiences a severance of the parental umbilical cord. Her husband, on the other hand, has had only a short interval of freedom during which he has sought and found his bride, followed by a long period of return to yet another cozy nest, where he is confronted with all the old patterns. This is one of the reasons male offspring are so avidly sought in many archaic cultures. The clan has more to gain from males in the long run because males stay at home. Women, on the other hand, almost always leave their parental home and often leave their villages and familiar region.

Although this pattern remains largely unchallenged in many parts of the world, it has become more or less obsolete in our latitudes. But if one looks more closely, one discovers the ways in which it continues to function and how difficult it is for even the most self-aware young people to shake it off. Even if both partners have severed their ties to their parental homes at an early age, traditional roles and patterns often persist, appearing in new but equally influential guises. No doubt in our culture, as in many others, wives tend to suffer more under their mothers-in-law simply because wives tend to be more closely tied to the home and cannot so easily escape from it. Children tend to bind the young mother to the close confines of the nest. Women who have fully divorced themselves from patterns of this kind during the course of their emancipation often confront problems similar to those that generally face men.

The second essential advantage on the female side lies, as already mentioned, in the option of bearing children and thus escaping from the Venus pattern that corresponds in many respects with the playgirl and playboy style of loving. By becoming mothers themselves, they enter the maternal sphere where motherly love naturally allows a more mature variety of affection to express itself. Experiencing a birth is the most important step of all since it almost always brings (along with the new baby) a new step in the mother's maturity. It also offers her a chance to re-experience her own birth trauma. Above all, bearing her own child is the paramount initiation into the sphere of full adulthood. At the same time, it also compels her to move from the egoistic "I" to the "Thou" of relationship.

In terms of temporal sequence, adolescence is the last appropriate chance to become an adult. But what does that really mean? Is it the attainment of legal age, whose threshold we lowered not so long ago from twenty-one to eighteen years? The move was no doubt correct, since eighteen-year-olds have already got their driver's licenses and have thus already acquired full membership in the (auto)mobile society. In the past, reaching the age of twenty-one added little more than the right to vote and run a business. In any case, neither a driver's license, the right to vote nor the right to run a business have much to do with maturity and adulthood, although all three presuppose maturity.

It is obvious that there are some people who are already quite mature at age fifteen and others who have reached the age of fifty without coming any closer to adulthood and maturity. The quantity of lived time is a poor basis upon which to define adulthood, although social life offers us scarcely any other choice. If we really wanted to institute tests of maturity, it would be difficult or impossible to agree on the criteria of adulthood and it would be entirely impossible to supervise their fulfillment. Clearly, then, it is not the quantity but the *quality* of lived time that determines when and whether a person has achieved adulthood. Quality, of course, cannot be measured with a yardstick but only judged by those who can appreciate it. The lack of objective criteria makes it impossible to test for maturity, and thus such critically important things as the freedom to start a family and exercise power over other human beings remain unregulated. Nonetheless, there are certain criteria that help a person judge whether she has come close to resolving the issues associated with becoming an adult. Of course, these criteria cannot but remain subjective in nature and ought therefore be considered as a whole rather than as individual points.

A resolved attitude toward the issues of adulthood includes the following basic points:

- readiness to give up childish notions of a world seen "through rose-colored glasses,"
- willingness to stop expecting others to take care of oneself,
- the ability to anticipate and accept the consequences of one's own actions,
- acceptance of responsibility for oneself and for others,
- understanding that the environment is a mirror, which means putting an end to the mechanisms of projection,

- orienting one's life according to wholeness rather than solely according to prosperity,
- subordinating oneself to the mandala's pattern of life.

A resolved attitude toward adulthood also includes the pleasure to be experienced through:

- personal growth and evolution,
- confronting boundaries and transcending them when necessary,
- searching for and accepting ones calling in life,
- recognizing and enjoying the best time of the day and the zenith of ones life as a whole,
- recognizing ones own maturity.

In terms of partnership with another person, a resolved attitude toward adulthood includes the willingness:

- to devote oneself physically, materially, spiritually and intellectually to the other person,
- to see one's partner as a mirror in good times and bad times,
- to stay together and move through crises rather than simply changing partners,
- to strive for a relationship based on wholeness rather than on material prosperity,
- to develop oneself from "I" to "Thou."

About Adolescence

1. How free am I from my parents?
   - Where do I spend the fixed points in life (e.g., Christmas and Easter)?
   - How voluntarily do I come home?
   - Where is my home? Have I gone so far as to create a home of my own? Or is my home still identical with my old home, my parents' home?
   - How often, and in which situations, do I think to myself, "I never want to become like my mother/my father"?

2. Can I relax, let go and let life come?
   - Do I remain in relationships only until challenges and difficulties arise, or do I persist?
   - Do I tend to play the role of the eternal boy or the eternal maiden?
   - Can I follow my career path? Or do I resign myself to failure and give up when problems arise?
3. Do I have addictive tendencies?
   - Have my habits become compulsions?
   - Do I become anxious if I do not get certain things?
   - Do I experience moments of ecstasy?
   - What role does the quest for my path in life play for me?
4. Can I feel as though I am part of a same-gender group?
5. Do I openly and directly encounter people of the opposite gender?
   - Is my sexuality on an adult level? Or am I attracted only to fatherly men or motherly women?
   - Do I continually feel the need to prove myself through new sexual conquests?
   - Is my sexuality fulfilling and satisfying?

7. Marriage

You were born together,
and together you shall be forevermore.
You shall be together when the white wings of death
scatter your days.
Ay, you shall be together even in the silent
memory of God.
But let there be spaces in your togetherness,
And let the winds of the heavens dance between you.
Love one another, but make not a bond of love:
Let it rather be a moving sea
between the shores of your souls.
Fill each other's cup
But drink not from one cup.
Give one another of your bread
but eat not from the same loaf.
Sing and dance together and be joyous,
but let each one of you be alone,
even as the strings of a lute are alone
though they quiver with the same music.
Give one another your hearts,
but not into each other's keeping.
For only the hand of Life can contain your hearts.
And stand together yet not too near together:
For the pillars of the temple stand apart,
and the oak tree and the cypress grow not
in each other's shadow.

—Khalil Gibran, Of Marriage

Marriage per se, of course, is not a crisis in life, but it can often mark the beginning of one. Insofar as a marriage is misused as a way to escape from one's parental home, the wedding bells are quite likely to double as the starting gun for a long-term crisis. As far as its crisis-engendering potential is concerned, it makes little difference whether one marries early to escape from being treated as a child by one's parents or whether one marries late in life as a last-ditch effort to finally escape from the parental nest. The problem in such situations is exacerbated by the tendency to marry the first one who comes along, or at least the first one who seems more or less acceptable. Few people will doubt that a purely utilitarian marriage (e.g., marriage to an asylum-seeker to help the refugee escape from a despicable national regime) is not likely to succeed. Why should a marriage whose true purpose lies in an attempt to escape from the overly narrow constraints of one's parental home be any more likely to thrive? The purpose of such marriages is fulfilled by the wedding itself; afterward there is no further reason for the couple to remain together. If they nevertheless do stay together in order to preserve appearances, the growth that is essential for every relationship is largely blocked. Often only one partner pursues a certain goal and either consciously or unconsciously pretends to fulfil the other partner's reasonable expectations for shared life and growth. In this wider sense, under closer examination, marital fraud is much more common than is generally believed.

To sum things up, we can conclude that if the step up to the altar is dishonestly motivated, sooner or later one's partner will detect the fraud, which will then provide volatile fuel for a potential explosion. Speculative marriages motivated by dowry, influence, status or other advantages tend to become prisons that hinder rather than encourage evolution and development. If a ritual seal (e.g., the ecclesiastical sacrament of marriage) is added, the trap slams even more ineluctably shut.

The notion that a ritually sealed bond could be dissolved according to one's whims by a court of law or by the affixing of a signature is a widespread illusion based upon a naive underestimation of the power of ritual. Countless couples suffer under this mistaken impression. Even many years after their separation, they continue to define themselves as the partner of their first spouse from whom they have not yet succeeded in emotionally divorcing themselves despite time and legal divorce. The Jewish religion, sensibly enough, makes provision for a divorce ritual. The Catholic Church has a similar institution, although the mechanism is more in the nature of a bureaucratic act than a genuine ritual, and in practice the annulment is only available to the wealthiest and most influential of the faithful.[54]

On the other hand, the number of ritually sealed marriages is decreasing rapidly, with the consequence that the couples can no longer keep what they have promised at the wedding. This phenomenon is especially obvious in countries with an atheistic state ideology. But even in such countries, grotesque imitations of church-like ceremonies are staged, no doubt because of the suspicion that marriages without a ritual seal simply do not endure.

The less thoroughly the partners have overcome life crises in the past, the greater are the debts they bring to married life. Even in so-called "marriages for love," one sooner or later discovers attributes in one's partner that one detests in oneself. At first, one falls head over heals in love with all the wonderful character traits one sees in oneself, or one would dearly like to see in oneself or one would hope to develop. As time goes on, "familiarity breeds contempt" and one begins to notice all those traits one had never in one's wildest dreams imagined to be present in one's spouse. These are the selfsame traits one has denied in oneself, the ones we do not like to admit and prefer to overlook, the traits we find so repulsive that we have suppressed them. Their emergence in our partner is particularly irritating and annoying. Basically, we would prefer a partner who never reflected our shadow and who always illuminated nothing but our own best sides. This desire corresponds to the likewise illusory dream of perennially falling in love. Partnerships of this sort can provide many opportunities for pleasure, but few opportunities for learning.

Jungian analyst Adolf Guggenbühl-Craig[55] divides relationships into two basic categories. He talks about the "partnership for weal," that tends to run a pleasant course and does not constantly compel us to confront our shadow. He contrasts this with the "partnership for healing," in which nothing further can be accomplished without serious work on one's shadow. Two old folk sayings about partnership express the same ideas. On the one hand, we have the adage "Birds of a feather flock together," alluding to the weal kind of relationship without strong tendencies for personal development. On the other hand, there is the saying "Opposites attract," describing the heal kind of partnership in which shadows constantly emerge and are dealt with (i.e., demand integration).

In so-called "weal" relationships, both partners expect their spouses to take care of their own well-being. This frequently leads to the creation of a superficial harmony that is nourished by the partners' similarities and threatens to deteriorate into the mere semblance of harmony. This sort of relationship is built on the illusion that a marriage ought to present an image of harmonious togetherness or to create heaven on earth (i.e., the quest for an external heaven). Genuine harmony is more difficult to achieve, but more likely to develop in the "heal" type of relationship. True harmony takes time to develop and is in no way superficial. It is allied with the goddess Harmonia, daughter of the love goddess Venus and the war god Mars. One can feel how genuine harmony is nourished by both divinities—the loving no less than the warring principle.

This pattern ought to be repeated in our own marriages, at least in the Christian ones that are sealed by a sacrament and represent a holy bond. A marriage that strives to be healing and holy needs to be oriented according to "heal" more than "weal." The fundamental idea is that true matrimony is sealed in heaven and both husband and wife are linked with God. Heaven and

God both represent unity and wholeness and this, in turn, corresponds to the "heal/whole/holy" type of relationship.

In practice, most marriages are mixed forms on a continuum between the extremes of "heal" and "weal." As time goes on, love marriages tend to develop into "heal" relationships, while utilitarian marriages based on reason (the sort of marriages parents are so fond of arranging) are more likely to develop into "weal" relationships. The greater the differences between the two lovers, the stronger must their love be in order to bridge this gap. Falling in love means moving into resonance, coming in tune, learning to vibrate on a new, shared level. The further one needs to go from one's familiar state of vibration toward the new, mutual level, the more powerful the feeling of falling in love is likely to be. This is also the reason the most ardent love affairs so often reverse their polarity and become the coldest of animosity and hatred.[56] When the person whom we love so ardently begins to show her other side, when the relationship is not used as a chance for shared growth through the integration of parts that are lacking but is instead misused as a screen for projections, an explosion is likely to ensue. The idiomatic expression that describes one's partner as "my better half" is accurate insofar as the partner reflects another side of reality, a side that is foreign to, and thus more important to, one's mate. The hotter the love at the outset, the greater the chances for maturation and growth within the context of the relationship. But ardent love at the beginning also increases the danger that projection will transform love into hate.

In marriages based on reason rather than love, the gap to be bridged is usually narrower since we tend to seek (or ask others to seek on our behalf) a partner who is likely to suit us. But the feeling of falling in love, if it is present at all, is generally less strong. Likewise less strong is the potential for hatred and the opportunity for evolution. In a society characterized by the avoidance of personal development and by a ubiquitous tendency to misuse projection mechanisms, such relationships tend to last longer since they harbor less explosive potential.

The more shadows have formed in the course of one's life thus far (e.g., through nonintegrated developmental steps) just that much more likely is it for the partnership to bring those shadows to light. This means the relationship is likely to be both difficult and full of chances for growth. From the point of view of spiritual development, integration of the shadow is the principal goal of partnership.

If primal trust has not developed (e.g., during the intrauterine phase), then trust in general is likely to be minimal. To compensate for that lack, one is apt to seek trust within his partnership and, at least in the earlier years, may well find it there. But, as time goes on, the unavoidable shadow will surely make itself known and the person will begin projecting the lack of trust onto his partner. For example, a man who has seemed to be so boastfully self-confident may suddenly begin to show his anxious side and give his wife precisely those feelings of insecurity she married him to avoid. In any case, it is destiny that presents us with this lesson: if fate chooses to do so via one's partnership, then the passion for projection is particularly enflamed. If a natural catastrophe such as an earthquake triggered the insecurity, most people would be able to recognize the machinations of destiny and resign themselves to it with a shrug, a sigh and the words, "That's fate! There's no way to change it." If an economic crisis were responsible for the insecurity, many people would project their unease onto the politicians and try to place the blame there. But if it is one's spouse who introduces the next lesson in life, the majority of people tend to use projection mechanisms—even though the situation is essentially identical to the aforementioned cases. The real challenge, of course, is to recognize and confess to the existence of something inside oneself that one has hitherto neither recognized nor admitted.

If one has not dealt with the feelings of claustrophobia, narrowness and anxiety suffered in the birth canal, marriage can soon begin to feel uncomfortably narrow and constrictive. Naturally, every partnership goes through bottlenecks that can make this latent issue an urgent crisis. A relationship can potentially confront a person with all the particularities of his own birth pattern. Problems arise wherever such themes have not been dealt with. The individual's responses are apt to reflect his reactions at birth. A person might confront every challenge by turning sideways or turning away and opposing it, or the habitual pattern could be a rash and headlong attack. Or the person might tend to delay facing the problem for as long as possible. Other potential patterns include allowing one's partner to drag one through all sorts of difficulties, or always expecting one's spouse to help without making any independent efforts to help oneself.

Unresolved puberty issues put an even more serious burden on a relationship. It is only natural that a person who has never matured into a full-fledged adult is not going to be able to behave like a mature partner in a love relationship or marriage. If he has chosen a similarly childish partner according to the "birds of a feather" principle, the two of them can play together and enjoy one another only until one of them begins to evolve and mature. In constellations of this kind, psychotherapy frequently explodes the whole system. The game is much more exciting, on the other hand, if the immature partner chooses an "adult" mate. In most cases, he will not find a real adult, but will opt instead for someone who is willing to play the role of parent.[57] While the "child" unconsciously searches for his own future in the partner who is simultaneously fascinating and frightening, the "adult" partner will be appreciating his own lost childhood in the mate and will be searching for his own future in the sense of Christ's exhortation to "be converted, and become as little children" again. The partnership can succeed if the one partner matures and becomes adult by integrating what she lacks and sees reflected in the mate, while the other discovers the "golden" child within in the form of creativity, spontaneity, courage and vitality that she has been lacking and that the mate, albeit on an unresolved level, so obviously embodies. The danger is that the child partner will feel overwhelmed by the adult mate and will project that unease according to the motto "Leave me in peace with your exaggerated demands and stop trying to ruin the joy and fun in my life with your supercilious, know-it-all attitude." The adult partner could lose interest in the naiveté and childishness of the spouse and, rather than seizing the chance for personal growth, might project the task onto the mate according to the motto, "First of all, you have to grow up; I won't have anything more to do with your childishness."

A person who has achieved only an external separation from mother and father by marrying a double of a parent lives with the constant yearning to complete a genuine separation and finally become free—and free from the relationship, too. Sooner or later, such people will "see through" their spouses and discover all those things they found so annoying in their parents—not necessarily because the mates embody those attributes, but because those annoying traits remain unresolved within the beholders themselves. The only healthy and timely step is forward, which represents an acute threat to the relationship. The only hope would be to begin the relationship anew on an entirely different level. In this case, both partners would need to work hard, with a diligence that presupposes a great deal of consciousness and dedication in both people.

An adolescence that has not been used to sever the metaphoric umbilical cord often shows itself in the pattern of exchanging one's parental home for one' spouse's home, where one soon feels equally unhappy. A lack of personal responsibility for one's self is the underlying theme. Wives ask their husbands for money to run the household just as they used to ask their fathers for allowance money. The old Christian wedding ritual further strengthens this basic pattern by exhorting the groom to treat his childish bride as a father would treat his daughter and by exhorting the bride to obey her husband as a child would obey its parents. The suitor asks the bride's father for her hand, after which, in the course of the wedding ceremony, it is typical for the groom to receive his bride from her father's hand, whereupon the groom takes over the old paternal role.

The reverse situation has become increasingly common. A mature woman helps a child groom "fly the coop" and escape from his parental nest. From an erotic point of view, the pattern is quite popular among adolescent boys since it allows them to take their first tentative (sexual) steps while the experienced older woman assumes most of the responsibility. In the ancient world, this situation was accorded official status. Temple priestesses known as "vestals" initiated young men into the mysteries of physical love. Ensuing millennia have brought such a severe decline in the status of such a career that this option now exists only in exceptional cases. But the pattern nevertheless continues to survive in a certain sense because girls, who are generally more mature than boys of the same age, take the erotic initiative far more frequently than the dominant ideology would lead us to believe. When constellations of this sort develop into long-term relationships and even into marriage, the problem lies in the fact that, if the less mature partner begins to evolve, the evolution itself tends to interfere with the delicate balance of the relationship. Couples caught in this pattern tend to avoid growth and evolution rather than call their relationships into question.

Alongside these specific themes, partnerships can also bring to light a host of other problems that have been left unsolved in the course of the partners' previous development. Whenever we discover a new and unpleasant side of our spouse, we have a wonderful chance to recognize and learn to integrate a part of our own shadow. That is the theoretical advantage, although in practice we are more likely to demand that our spouses stop manifesting these annoying traits, and we may even threaten to leave our spouses and exchange them for mates who do not display such aggravating behaviors. For example, when unexpected jealousies arise, partners who mistakenly imagine they have evolved so far as to no longer feel possessive of other human beings will likely project their own jealousy upon the spouses who have cheated on them or who are contemplating cheating on them. Instead of being grateful to their spouses for bringing to light this difficult, denied and as yet unresolved issue, the jealous mates project their own disappointment in themselves onto their spouses and try to place the blame there.

In reality, however, the partners were merely the triggers who catalyzed an as yet unlearned lesson. Rather than gratefully recognizing their disappointment and disillusionment with their (allegedly) unfaithful mates as an end to illusion and self-deception, they often behave as if the problem lay with their mates. It makes no difference whether the mates really were unfaithful. Even if the incriminated spouses never ended up in an adulterous bed, they have still served as the trigger for their partners' jealousy.

Marital crises are invariably opportunities to become honest and to make honest decisions. Will I project the problem and flee from my own development, or will I use the difficulties as an opportunity for growth? Every crisis offers us the chance to come to terms with unresolved developmental issues. This helps to explain why, when we have weathered the storm and overcome a crisis, we generally feel stronger and feel our relationship has grown more mature.

In place of jealousy, the reader can insert any of several issues (e.g., the striving for power, craving for recognition, or miserliness) and reach the same results. The only things that can annoy us about other people are issues that relate to unresolved themes within ourselves. The things that disturb us most deeply are those that concern us most and contain the greatest chances for growth.

Because of all the dangers and chances that marriage affords, it is not surprising to learn that various rituals have been used to prepare young people for this major developmental step. Relics of these rituals can be still be seen today, for example in the so-called "*Polterabend*," a wild party on the evening before the wedding when the couple and their guests smash old crockery in accord with the old adage that "shards bring good luck." Breaking the old so the new can begin may well be one motivation for this orgy of shards, together with the chance to "live it up" one last time before the serious business of married life begins. This latter pattern also expresses itself in typical bachelor parties. It is hoped that allowing the disorderly and potentially destructive energy to discharge itself shortly before the wedding will help to calm the waters in the marital harbor. That might also be the reason the groom-to-be's friends at some parties chip in and rent an especially attractive call girl for him to enjoy. If, despite this temptation, he is ready to take the step across the threshold and into married life, then he is no doubt going to be a faithful husband. On the other hand, the planned wedding could well be canceled at short notice if, contrary to plan, the bride-to-be somehow finds out about this "ritual." In that case the call-girl ritual would truly be a test of maturity—a test the groom would have failed.

Questions about Marriage

1. In what respects does my marriage repeat patterns in the relationship between my parents?

2. Have I found *my* partner? And have *I* found my partner?
   - Did my parents have an (un)official voice in making the decision?
   - What were my feelings when I introduced by fiancé(e) to my parents? How important to me was their acceptance of my chosen spouse?
   - Have I married a person who is very much like my mother/father, or have I chosen someone who is exactly their opposite? What sort of similarities/dissimilarities exist between my mother/father and my wife/husband?
   - Do I tend to play the role of father or mother for my spouse?

3. Do I strive for a trouble-free, rosy world in my "weal" marriage or am I willing to face the risks of a "heal" partnership?

4. Can I fill the requirements of the mother/father role?
   - Do I often allow myself to fall into childish patterns?
   - Am I, in certain respects, my husband's eldest daughter or my wife's eldest son?
   - Why do I have (no) children? What do they give me? What do I give them?

5.   Am I ready to make an emotional investment in my relationship?

6.   What are the dominant role patterns in my relationship? What roles do I delegate?

7.   How far am I willing to compromise? How much am I willing to accept conflicts? Is there anything like a "culture of strife" in my relationship?

8.   What is the central point about which my marriage revolves?

9.   What do my children mean to me? What sacrifices would having children entail for me?

Ideas for Divorce Rituals

1.   Perform the essential points of the relationship as a theater play. Relive once more how you met one another and fell in love, the first disappointment, the beginning of the end, and so on.

2.   Conduct a ritualized separation in the same church where you were wed. Take off the wedding rings and give them back, cut or untie a sash tied between your hands as a visible expression of cutting the ties or untying the knot between the former marital partners.

3.   Divide and share. Begin by dividing the photos, each of you taking the ones you want. Then divide the personal items, the valuables, and finally the material possessions.

4.   Conduct a ritual of inward separation in a ceremonial context. Spend a quarter of an hour painstakingly cutting a wedding photo into two parts. Then consciously destroy both halves; for example, by burning them and returning the ashes to nature, burying them and planting a tree or seed of hope on the spot (do not plant forget-me-nots or pansies). Alternatively, mail the ashes to your former partner.

5.   Consciously remove your ex-partner's belongings. At the same time, consciously remove her from the uppermost place in your heart and put her in a new place. If the two

243

        of you have a child, it makes little sense to ban her entirely because if you try to do that she will find a new and extensive home for herself in the shadowy realm of your own soul's landscape—where her presence will be much more unpleasant.

6.   Melt your wedding-rings and use the gold to make something new.

7.   Ritually dispose of certificates attesting to your marriage, either by burning or burying them.

8.   After the separation and divorce have been completed, conduct a ritualized "burial of the tomahawk," (e.g., by burying some object you had often argued about or fought over).

9.   After the separation, allow yourself time for an interval of wandering in no-man's land.

Ideas for Wedding Rituals

    Ideas for wedding rituals are abundantly available in every culture. The diversity of possibilities strikingly contrasts with the scarcity of divorce rituals, and once again shows the importance of rituals per se. Even in wholly irreligious societies such as those of the former Communist countries, a great deal of effort is expended to stage pseudo-rituals. In the offices of justices of the peace in the Western world—a world that is increasingly losing touch with conscious rituals—everything from organ music to smoke machines is available to provide a semblance of "cult" atmosphere. Even secular, modern couples want to have the feeling that the step into marriage is an important and binding decision. They do not want it to exist solely on paper. An especially large spectrum of elaborate (but not particularly charged) wedding ceremonies can be had in Las Vegas, where practically every gambling casino has its own wedding chapel right next door.

8. Career

You work that you may keep pace
with the earth and the soul of the earth.
For to be idle is to become a stranger unto the
seasons,
and to step out of life's procession,
that marches in majesty and proud submission
towards the infinite.
When you work you are a flute through whose heart
the whispering of the hours turns to music....
Work is love made visible.
And if you cannot work with love
but only with distaste, it is better that you should
leave your work
and sit at the gate of the temple
and take alms of those who work with joy.
For if you bake bread with indifference, you bake a
bitter bread that feeds but half man's hunger.
And if you grudge the crushing of the grapes,
your grudge distils a poison in the wine.
And if you sing though as angels, and love
not the singing, you muffle man's ears
to the voices of the day and the voices of the night.

—Khalil Gibran, *Of Work*

I slept and dreamt that life was joy,
I woke and saw that life was duty.
I did my duty and saw
the duty turn to joy.

—Rabindranath Tagore

Career crises can also encourage the growth of the soul because, as is the case with crises in a relationship, career crises illuminate typical developmental issues. As in a partnership, a career can also become too narrow, feel too constricting and reveal that the real, underlying issue has to do with responsibility. Bosses at work are often substituted for mother or father figures, just as husbands or wives at home often end up playing these roles. We struggle against them not because the boss or spouse is objectively so bad, but simply because or own inner children are still battling with the projections of our parents. Coworkers can play the role of siblings. Competition between old veterans and new arrivals mirrors the rivalry between older and younger siblings, especially when the elder sibs (coworkers) feel that the newcomer is getting too much attention or threatening to usurp them and their familiar position in the family (or business). It is no mere coincidence that we use the word "family business," that the *familiar* atmosphere is praised, or that bosses like to describe the firm as "one big happy family."

If the people involved are able to see through such complications, the workplace situation can be used as a therapeutic opportunity. Instead of resigning from one job only to encounter the same problem elsewhere, one can accept the lesson and solve the unresolved conflict with one's elder brother by resolving it with one's department manager at work.

Fate can be awfully clever: if we try to flee from unlearned lessons, destiny is liable to present them to us in new guises until they are finally learned. We can see this fateful mechanism on the job and in our relationships. Hardly has one split up with one partner when a new one comes along, and because we are so head over heals in love, we feel certain we will not make the same mistakes again. It is often only a matter of time before the dreaded issue rears its ugly head again. This re-emergence, of course, represents an opportunity to learn—without the need for psychotherapeutic help. When the same problem arises for the umpteenth time, at least a few people might begin to suspect that the responsibility for the repetition does not lie solely with the other people. Consequently, the moment one stops resisting and resigns oneself to the process is always the most important moment in therapies, relationships and career situations. This is the moment when essential lessons can be learned; but also the most difficult and crucial moment.

Businesses, like families, sometimes need therapy. And, as in a family, some are ready and willing while others resist. In business situations, often only a few of the coworkers are ready to take this step. Society, businesses and the family can be transformed as institutions, but substantial steps only result when the individual members begin to raise their own consciousness. The vanguard individuals are those who are ready to recognize and begin to work on the deeper problems in their own developmental history as they are reflected in various hierarchical structures. Naturally, this recognition is not meant in the sense of "the society is the culprit" as sociologists and some politicians tend to misinterpret it, but entails recognizing hierarchical structures as mirrors and using them as catalysts for one's own growth. Consciousness is always the underlying force. Even if the impetus for change comes from the top of the hierarchy, chances are that the impulse derives from raised consciousness in one of the decision-makers at the top. Although we so often blame everything on "society," the fact remains that every society is made up of nothing more than many individuals.

Serious conflicts often arise when people fail to follow their own real callings and opt instead for the last (or first) straw or for the career their parents intended for them. If one's parents have already written definitive plans for one's life, it can be difficult to pursue one's own true path. Daughters and sons have difficulty freeing themselves from the image of the ideal partner that their parents instilled in them. Young people can experience corresponding difficulties when they try to derail themselves from their parentally planned career track. If the family insists that their daughter become a seamstress and their son become a baker, there are usually only two possible options: the offspring can either assent to or oppose their parents' wishes. In both cases, the parental intent continues to play a formative role in the offspring's decision. Access to one's true path in life is frequently blocked by the existence of a family business that the next generation is expected to take over, or by a vocational training program the young people have begun at an early age. In cases where everything seems programmed in advance and little or no freedom of choice exists, it can sometimes be better to follow the beaten path (at least for a while) and then begin to grow beyond the bounds of the existing and all-too-narrow concept rather than blindly revolt and oppose the whole project. If one has succeeded in freeing oneself from a constrictive corset, one can be sure one has also resolved the underlying issue. Blind opposition, frequently the tack chosen by strong-minded young people, often leads to the paradoxical situation of allowing one's parents to determine the course of one's entire life because one automatically does exactly the opposite of what one's parents would have judged to be correct.

Compensations of this sort are not always easy to recognize. One client of mine—a professor at a German university—defined himself as "not an electrician" because he had refused to take over his family's electrical business. Listening to his stories, a trained ear could not fail to notice how often and how significantly the electrician theme cropped up in appropriate and inappropriate moments. The client obviously identified himself more with the electrician's career that he rejected than with the professorial career he had chosen.

Another client was supposed to take over his family's bakery. Despite certain misgivings, he acquiesced to his family's wishes, learned the trade that had been practiced by the men in his family for many generations and duly earned his certification as a master baker. But because of his interest in health, he soon transformed the traditional operation into one of Germany's first natural-foods bakeries and established a new kind of business from which even his parents could learn a thing or two. When that venture likewise proved too narrow for him, he earned his high-school diploma in night school, studied dentistry, franchised the bakery and became a dentist. This career also soon proved overly restrictive, so he studied first medicine and then naturopathy. As a physician and dentist versed in the latest holistic approaches to medicine, he realized the important role played by a healthy diet. Thus, the wheel came full circle: back to bread, the staff of life, where it all began. This type of path is long, demands much energy and courage, but is also highly rewarding, especially if one is not all that certain at the outset.

Questions about Career

1. How did my career choice come about?
2. How much "calling" is there in my career?
3. What does my career have to do with parental desires?
4. Is it related to my parents' careers? Is it diametrically opposed to their careers?
5. As a child, what did I always want to be "when I grow up"?
6. Is there such a thing as a career dream?
7. Or a dream career?

9. Spiritual Crises

God dwells in the heart, in the unconscious.
There lies the source of anxiousness about the
unspeakably
terrible and the power
to resist that terror.

—C.G. Jung

Spiritual crises[58] are difficult to delimit in terms of time and contents. They can appear in early youth, but in most cases arise sometime between adolescence and midlife. The familiar "midlife crisis" can also take on some of the characteristics of a spiritual crisis. Christina and Stan Grof were instrumental in removing these crises from the field of psychiatry. Nevertheless, it is not easy to differentiate them from psychiatric problems, especially in Germany, where psychiatry evinces but little understanding for spiritual issues and psychiatric hospitals are like depots that administrate human misery, which is frequently related to spiritual problems. Our unconscious way of coping with death-related issues creates a variety of psychiatric problems. Finally, people whose ailments are difficult to identify or whom society finds unduly problematic are frequently shunted off to the psychiatric wards, the populations of which include patients ranging from hardened criminals to spiritual seekers.

Apparently innocent diagnoses sometimes conceal spiritual problems. Many years ago I treated a five-year-old "autistic" girl who, although she had spoken in the past, had severed all verbal contact with her surroundings. From the start of our sessions, measurements of her skin's resistance to electrical current showed she was aware of everything I said, and that the stimulus was most lasting when I told her fairytale stories about nature. After I had elaborated on those tales and fantasized ever deeper into the realms of elves and fairies, the long-awaited moment suddenly came when my little patient broke her silence. At first with extreme hesitation, she cautiously asked me if I had actually seen all these creatures. After I explained to her that I was unfortunately able to see them only in my mind's eye but that there were some people who can perceive such entities outside their minds and in the world of nature, she finally revealed her well-kept secret. She told me that she could see these and other unusual creatures and things, but that no one had understood her. Instead of praising her sharp-sightedness, she had been scolded and ridiculed. The insult had prompted her to withdraw into her own inner world, where she had remained for more than a year. Naturally, this was by no means a case of autism. But if the spell had not been broken at an early age, it is quite possible she would have been drawn into the abyssal vortex of a psychiatric career. A psychiatrist had already written the condemning diagnosis.

Extreme alertness is recommended before one unquestioningly accepts any psychiatric diagnosis. When one looks behind the scenes of superficial ideas about mental illness and gazes more deeply into the soul, even classical pathological categories such as schizophrenia and cyclothymia frequently are found to overlie a variety of spiritual issues. The American psychiatrist Edward Podvoll has documented his pioneering work in this field in his illuminating book *The Temptations of Madness.*

Finally, spiritual crises can also include phenomena of possession, unresolved crises following experiences of death, as well as addiction and substance-abuse issues deriving from failed quests. We should also add all of those paranoid ailments evoked by suppression techniques (e.g., positive thinking[59]) that have followed in the wake of the esoteric movement.

What most interests us in this chapter is the phenomenon that the Grofs call "the kundalini process." Although the vast majority of people in our society have too much resistance to the processes of the soul, a few individuals are immoderately receptive to these processes. Naturally, many people in the esoteric scene are members of that latter group. They have either voraciously consumed every possible technique or have become inextricably caught up in one particular technique. A sensitive person need only begin with an effective meditation technique that offers little or no grounding (e.g., a mantra meditation such as Transcendental Meditation).[60] After experiencing the first pleasant journeys into her inner world, and after ignoring all of her teacher's warnings, such a person can soon "lift off" and "flip out" in ways that terrify her friends and family. These negative side-effects are by no means the fault of the meditation technique taught by any particular school, but prove only that the technique is too effective. If we exaggerate, things that begin as wonderful can soon acquire awesome (and awful) dimensions. People who immoderately practice exercises designed to dissolve the ego without correspondingly working to ground themselves should not be surprised if they lose contact with the ground beneath their feet and begin drifting off into psychotic experiences.

The specific details depend upon the peculiarities of each individual's soul and its inner landscapes. Wonderful experiences can alternate with gruesome visions of the soul's shadow side. Euphoric moods can bear the person aloft on the wings of bizarre dreams into emotional realms of overwhelming intensity, or threatening clouds can darken one's path. In essence, the inner images assume power over the individual and overwhelm his unprotected soul. It is often possible to detect the spiritual components that underlie a patient's experiences, but merely explaining this to the patient seldom does much good. A therapist's lectures about the meaning of nothingness and the role of the void in Buddhism are more or less useless to people who feel drowned by overwhelming feelings and catapulted into nothingness, dissolved by the wind or afraid of dissolving into space. As long as such images continue to dominate the patient, it is more or less irrelevant for a therapist to try to interpret those visions. To explain them as deriving from a past life is likewise inappropriate. Outsiders may be fascinated to observe patients whose empathy with others borders on clairvoyance or to hear tales told by patients who can feel others' moods as if they were their own. If one is adequately grounded and endowed with clear ego boundaries, these can be beautiful experiences along the spiritual path. But for the patients, these experiences are more often the frightening symptoms of a lack of boundaries. The openness so naively worshipped by the esoteric scene (and, until recently, perhaps by the patient, as well) becomes a curse. One feels oneself reminded of the warning to "be careful what you wish, because wishes can come true!"

The much-praised kundalini energy that gives the phenomenon its name and that is so ardently sought (especially by those who have never experienced it) can emerge in powerful waves that rob one of sleep and sometimes cause the body to twitch and spasm in ways that frighten or even terrify the spiritual voyager. The individuals no longer feel like the masters (or mistresses) of their own house, and this loss of control is drastically demonstrated. Gopi Krishna describes how even ice-cold baths could not cool the inner heat. For many people, the most frightening thing is the mixture of images and feelings that usually begins as an undifferentiated collection of personal memories, archetypal themes, mythical and religious patterns. Depending on the preceding history of one's personal soul, this mix can include crazed ideas of sin and guilt and a wild array of unpleasant complexes. Even inherently pleasant experiences of light and moments of unbelievable insight cannot be enjoyed because anxiety and fear overshadow everything else. This fear can become the central issue and worst part of the situation. The complete immersion in another world that accompanies some psychoses may be lacking, but so too is the temporary relief such submergence brings. It may sound strange, but the loss of nearly all contact with reality that occurs in a profound psychosis frequently protects the psychotic's soul from the worst suffering. The spiritual crisis compels the soul to embark upon a nightmarish journey, and the trip is all the more awful because the individual still possesses enough awareness to suffer from manifold apparitions and acute fear of the loss of self. Finally, the individual is plunged into panic, afraid of the imminent dissolution of his ego. The ego lives by setting limits, and must always sort things out and arrange them into orderly patterns. It only feels well when it can differentiate itself from everything else. In the attempt to transcend the ego (which really means nothing more than to become healed and whole), the individual has encountered his own shadow. That is perfectly alright in itself, since the shadow is an essential part of the whole person. Self-realization means integrating one's shadow. But self-realization is a long path that requires secure guidance and should not be rushed.

Encounter with the shadow is an essential step along one's spiritual path, but it should be taken abruptly. If it is, one is likely to "blow one's fuse" and fall victim to one's own shadow. The fault does not lie in the techniques and exercises, nor even in the mind-expanding drugs that frequently trigger such phenomena. The real responsibility lies only in their misuse and in the frequent lack of secure frameworks to accompany the journey on this risk-ridden path. One must learn to progress safely, gradually allowing one's nervous system to become accustomed to such experiential spaces. Only then can one can dare to take the appropriate steps forward. In several places in the Bible, it is written that man cannot see God face to face. Not even Moses, Israel's most highly initiated prophet, can gaze without danger at so much radiance; he too must avert his eyes. Naturally, this does not mean God or the light is dangerous or bad, but only that one needs to use the right methods, follow the right guidance and choosing the appropriate moment for contacting God and the divine light.

As is the case with symptoms of many sorts, the experiences associated with spiritual crises are entirely benign. They simply belong to a higher state of consciousness, a state in which the ego has been transcended. Once that has occurred, we no longer feel fear when we experience that we are nothing, that there are no boundaries and that time and space are illusory. Socrates first had to become wise in order to bear the weight of the experience that he knows nothing.

To relive such states and then not merely bear them but actually enjoy them, one must first be sure that one can safely return from the dark journey. In most cases, the individual must have enough experiences in the depths of the soul and be happy to recuperate from this psychic overdose by engaging in mundane activities. Everyday activities also provide a welcome opportunity for grounding during the crisis. Compared with the overabundance of energy (the element of fire), the depth and intensity of feelings (the element of water), and the flightiness of the thoughts (the element of air), it is obvious that the element of earth is in short supply.

Concrete contact with the soil (e.g., by working in a garden) can be a wonderful way of grounding oneself. The individual, however, generally has little desire to work the soil at first, and are likely to need encouragement and motivation. Simple handicrafts and other activities that place minor demands on the intellect but that nevertheless help to focus one's attention and prevent the mind from wandering off into a (momentarily) unhealthy journey are recommended. Any activities that, through movement, cause mild perspiration can likewise be helpful. One should, however, make sure that the patients do not try to suddenly wash away the unwelcome feelings in an inordinate flood of sweat. Symbolic acts such as cleaning house are useful, as are long walks in nature. Everything should focus on contact with the earth and the material world.

The same is true of diet, which ought to be heavier and heartier. Vegetarian cuisine and sensitizing diets of raw foods are not at all appropriate and should be temporarily exchanged for healthy but heavier foods. In such cases, roast pork is better than raw fruit. The "food" served to the mind and soul ought likewise be somewhat heartier than usual. Spiritual exercises that aim toward lightness, especially exercises practiced with closed eyes, should be abandoned for the time being. When conducted with the proper therapeutic guidance, even a tough form of meditation such as zazen (in which one gazes open-eyed at the floor) can be helpful. Drugs should definitely be avoided. Psychedelic drugs such as LSD and peyote can trigger psychotic episodes and would be dangerous to use. Drugs such as nicotine and alcohol are never good these two are perhaps the least damaging if the patient cannot do without escapist drugs altogether. Smokers can veil themselves in blue clouds of tobacco smoke and drinkers can fill themselves with alcohol, but everything that leads to intoxication is directly contrary to progress. It is also usually best to do without medication since medicinal drugs generally do not shorten the experience, but merely serve to suppress and thus lengthen it. In some cases, however, sedatives or sleeping pills can be indispensable.

An important aid is a good relationship with a partner involving intense physical contact. Bodily contact is usually experienced as pleasant since it communicates the feeling of being in one's body and being present in the here and now. Sexual intercourse is likewise recommended, although it should not be engaged in with "tantric" intentions,[61] but rather practiced with the goal of releasing and discharging accumulated energies through orgasm.

Protected by this sort of grounding and within a secure therapeutic context, one can try to create order in the chaotic world of images that is making the patient ill. This attempt is especially relevant toward the end of the crisis since this is when patients frequently yearn to begin organizing and accepting the lessons to be learned from earlier experiences. Methods such as those used in reincarnation therapy are useful; however, exercises such as rebirthing or other techniques that tend to stir up more energy are not recommended.

The best way to prevent such crises is to maintain a healthy balance between experiences of presence and experiences of transcendence. Relaxation and activity should be alternated in proper proportions. This means learning to properly evaluate the merits (and demerits) of the various techniques one has learned along one's spiritual path. The simplest path is not always the safest path. The shadow should not be suppressed, but must be illuminated. Positive thinking combined with a tendency to suppress and deny is one of the most effective "ejector seats" for catapulting a spiritual seeker into the madness of paranoia. As a general rule of thumb, my advice is not to rush ahead too quickly, but not to fall asleep in the middle of the road either. The Native Americans have a helpful image: they believe one's roots must be deeply anchored in Mother Earth before one can raise one's head to Father Sky.

10. Menopause and Midlife Crisis

Verily I say unto you,
Except ye be converted, and become as little
children,
ye shall not enter into the kingdom of heaven.

—Jesus Christ

Many paths lead to becoming conscious,
but all of them obey certain laws.
Generally, the beginning of the transformation
coincides with the onset of life's second half.

—C. G. Jung

I f we have lived up to the Biblical injunction to "replenish the earth, and subdue it,"[62] then we have reached the outer limit of the mandala. The only constructive option at this point in the pattern is to turn around. The decision to be made at this critical juncture depends on whether we consciously return or whether we remain unconscious and wait for fate to forcefully compel us to return while we insist upon clinging desperately to the edge of the mandala. The option of simply continuing with the status quo is not viable, even though so many modern people persist in that course. We can see this most clearly when we consider the mandala itself: no path leads beyond the circle of life. No human being ever went beyond that boundary, nor will anyone ever succeed at some time in the future. Those who insist on continuing in the same old direction suddenly find themselves with their faces to the wall, gazing out into a black void. The path seems lost and everything seems meaningless. It is not uncommon for this inflexibly stubborn attitude to lead to depression.

In a lecture entitled *Lebenswende* ("Life's Turning Point") delivered in 1930, C.G. Jung used the sun's daily cycle as a metaphor: "The decline begins at noon. And the decline is the reversal of all the values and ideals of the morning." In the same lecture, Jung lamented that "the worst of all things is when clever, well-educated people live purposelessly, without knowledge of the possibility of making such transformational changes.... Profoundly unprepared, we arrive at life's noon, or worse, we arrive there under the false assumptions of truths and ideals that we have unquestioningly accepted thus far."[63]

The mandala pattern explains why this transition into midlife can become a catastrophe for so many people. The Greek word "catastrophe" means "reversal." Indeed, we have the choice to consider this time period as a reversal or turning point and voluntarily undergo transformation, or else to resist the inevitable change and suffer a catastrophe in the ordinary sense of the word. A certain amount of suffering is unavoidable since transformation always entails sacrificing and letting go of something old and familiar. In this case, it means letting go of the direction in life that we have been pursuing for many decades. Just as even the best planned and most optimal "gentle" birth is painful so too must we suffer certain pains during this new birth at midlife. The severity and dimensions of this painful reversal, and above all the length of time we spend pilloried upon the critical point, all depend upon our inner attitude and readiness to decide.

There are a number of reasons the crisis at life's midpoint looms above all of life's other crises. The necessity of changing direction is surely the most significant reason. In all previous crises, we have made changes in the level of the subsequent path, but the direction has remained unchanged. Now, at the midpoint of life, we cannot continue onward: we must turn back.

Change of life involves a fundamental *change of direction,* and that change can be difficult simply because it is so basic. In the Swiss dialect of German, what Germans call the *Wechseljahre* ("years of change") is known as *Abänderung* (literally "alteration" or " amendment"). Indeed, midlife alters everything: for better or for worse. A change must ensue because nothing can remain as it has been in the past.

Another reason the issue inherent in this problem is so difficult to resolve lies in the necessity of balancing one's life thus far with the tasks facing us in the future. After having lived half one's life, we have accumulated much more "stuff" than we had at life's beginning. "Unfinished business" is the phrase Elisabeth Kübler-Ross uses to describe the accumulated baggage. Midlife is the time when unfinished business comes to light. Its contents can range from relationships we never had a chance to live out to an unfulfilled yearning to have children of one's own.

Perhaps the most important reason for the threatening feeling associated with midlife is the urgency of the insistence that we jettison excess ballast. Materialistic people find this demand particularly unpleasant. The years leading toward life's midpoint have been devoted to acquisition and accumulation, and now the time has come to begin leaving things behind, abandoning everything that might hinder the soul on her homeward journey. Evolution in the true sense of the word is needed. Up to this point, everything we described as "evolution" was really more in the nature of involution and convolution. Leaving behind the convolutions of life—the nets and knots that tie us to the world and that we have spent so much time and effort knitting and tying—is actually a beautiful task and one that archaic people are able to appreciate. We modern people, on the other hand, often hate even the thought of divesting ourselves of positions, prestige and possessions.

The divestiture would not be so painful if we could learn to appreciate the time of maturity and harvest and the pleasures that time can bring. It is astonishing to see how earnestly some people spend a lifetime yearning for certain things, and it is downright shocking to see those same people become absolutely helpless when the time finally comes for them to enjoy those acquisitions. Midlife is the ideal time to take that long-postponed vacation and finally use that "vacation home" for the purpose implicit in its name. Now is the time to read those worthwhile but demanding books we never found time to read amid the hustle and bustle of mundane affairs. Now is the time to sail that sailboat, ride that horse and enjoy that garden. Now is the time to begin the life we have been dreaming about all our lives. Activities of this sort are not the solution to all our problems, but they can offer us leisure time and thereby increase the likelihood of our making a major breakthrough. It is interesting to note how difficult it is for many of us to accept things that are obviously easy and pleasant. After a life spent in striving and amassing, many people are overwhelmed by the switch to sensuality, introspection and the search for meaning. The word "climacteric" is derived from the same root as climax, the high point at the end of the ladder, and this phase of life is intended to embody just such an acme. The word "menopause," on the other hand, emphasizes the "pause" and, by this stage in life, we have earned the right to take a just such a breather.

Businesses make things involuntarily easier for some people because there is too little work and therefore executives are sometimes given a generous "golden parachute" and impelled to resign when they reach their early fifties. Relieved of their career responsibilities and rewarded with huge sums of money or stocks, these former managers and executives now have abundant leisure to enjoy their lives as they wish, and gradually to begin thinking about the mandala's "homeward path." But because they have spent a lifetime on one track, both privately and in their professional life, many find it difficult to adapt to the changes of early retirement. Instead of feeling enthusiastic about the opportunities offered to them, many react to this paradisiacal situation by becoming melancholy and depressed. They feel as if they are no longer needed and do not want to accept that they had become superfluous in their old position.

Above all, they tend to overlook the more important tasks that lie ahead. Other retirees are at a loss for ways to spend their time. Sheer desperation drives them to rearrange their wives' households, transform their backyards into formal gardens or seek psychotherapeutic help. Of course, altruism is by no means the reason that motivates business and industry to help so many people begin a peaceful, meaningful second half of life. Since this often happens unintentionally, far too few retirees are able to make the best of their retirement, and they simply continue living life as they had lived it before. This persistence, of course, is senseless when one considers where their lives are headed. A person who is so extremely fixed on one direction is sure to suffer when it becomes clear that no further progress is possible without a change of direction. Attempts to begin a second career frequently fail because this is not the season of life for that venture.

On the other hand, it could well be the proper season to find a field of activity that is more of a true calling and less of an occupation to keep oneself occupied. The contents of that calling should be related to themes of return, reversal and the homeward path. In the Christian context, we are familiar with the great conversions that transform everything in life and bring an entirely new direction into the game of life. Even if the new calling sometimes seems to have its greatest effects in the outer world, the inner attitude is still far more decisive and essential. This inner upheaval corresponds to the old adage about converting from "Saul to Paul" and to the reversal experienced by St. Francis of Assisi who turned away from the life of a playboy and began to live the life of a saint.

Well-meaning advice for people who have chosen the unresolved side of the crisis and who feel depressed and unhappy is of no avail if it encourages the sufferer to continue with "more of the same." This is not the time to begin a new career, build up a new business, acquire more cars or more real estate. It is the time to draw the line, take account of things and cast off ballast rather than accumulating more.

When an Amerindian reaches this season of life, the problem is usually insignificant. In his culture, old age is held in high regard and death is regarded without fear as a stage of transition into another world. When he feels that his time has come, he voluntarily takes a step back, allows younger men to take his place and joins the council of wise elders. Like elderly Indian women in the same situation, he has nothing to lose and everything to gain—not only in terms of personal growth, but also in terms of the esteem he receives from his tribe. Indian women know they will become mothers when the flow of menstrual blood temporarily stops, and that they will become Great Mothers when the flow permanently stops. The first interruption is a cause for rejoicing and the latter interruption is a cause for still greater rejoicing.

The same holds true in the majority of archaic cultures. In our society, however, stepping back has negative connotations, as if it were tantamount to failure, giving up, relegating oneself to the scrap heap. Re*sign*ation is regarded as entirely negative, despite the fact that it means taking back one's *sign*, one's signature and seal, and that it can be very timely in certain situations. Caring for material concerns has become superfluous, and resignation in the positive sense is needed. In another sense, old age is a time to set one's sign (*signum*) and seal, to be significant, to give and have meaning. The ancient Egyptians used the same hieroglyph to signify both "age" and "meaning."

Independent of these considerations, hardly anyone can avoid dealing with the low esteem in which our society holds the post-menopausal or post-midlife portion of a person's life. This low status is especially clear in the slang titles given by youths to older people. Even if the words are used in jest, such designations as *Grufti* ("tomber") for people over forty and *Verwesi* ("decayer") for those over fifty express scant regard for this phase of life.

In the past, our society had rules for an orderly retreat from the front lines of life's battle, a retreat that offered better chances for retiring elders and advancing youngsters alike. This transition sometimes still functions today in rural areas. When the time is ripe and the hard work becomes too much for him, the old farmer gives the farm over to his son and retires to that portion of the farm property reserved for him and his wife. From a legal point of view, he has handed over the entire property to his successor so that he and his wife retain only the right to occupy their retirement dwelling. This spatial separation may entail tremendous material sacrifices, but it is nevertheless relatively strictly observed, and even the state recognizes its value over the personal interests of the older farmer. For example, in a region whose zoning regulations prohibit further construction, the erection of a retirement dwelling for an old farmer is generally permitted as an exception to the prohibition. Now that caring for the needs of their home and farm is gradually coming to an end, new themes automatically begin to occupy the elderly couple's attention. Walks over the former *field* of work can become part of the play of life, and some of the rural elderly attend daily church services. The issues of power and responsibility are resolved, and the father now asks for his son's advice and consent before beginning even a relatively minor task around the farm.

In the executive levels of large businesses, the transfer of power from one generation to the next can be especially drastic if the business is in a crisis and is ruthlessly searching for scapegoats. In the harshness of the struggle for existence, veteran employees are best suited to play the part. Rather than voluntarily resigning at the right time, these older executives are often shoved out of the organization and off to their homes with not very gentle pressure. Structural crises in business and industry tend to bring what looks at first glance like bad luck to decision-makers at all levels. But, if they would look again with a greater degree of spiritual openness, they might realize that the apparent misfortune is in fact a blessing in disguise.

At least as far as their timing is concerned, deliberate or crisis-related changes in life's plans bear astonishing similarities to patterns of life such as those upon which classical Indian culture was based. Assuming an ideal life span of 84 years, the first 21 years would be devoted to growth and learning, the next 31 to the establishment of one's family and career, the third 21 to the strengthening and consolidating of these structures, and the final 21 years solely to spiritual development. People who had reached the age of 63 separated themselves from everything and set out toward Benares, where they would devote their remaining years to spiritual and intellectual pursuits along the shores of the holy Ganges River.

C.G. Jung said that people who discover spirituality prior to midlife are apt to encounter problems and that people who do not discovery spirituality after midlife are likely to fall into severe crises of meaning. The first part of Jung's statement applies to the first half of life and to the experience that an early interest in spiritual themes can lead to premature "dropping out" and avoidance of the lessons one has yet to learn in life. Meditation is no substitute for maturation! Everything has its proper time, and the selfsame practice that can be as good as gold at the right time can represent a dangerous sidetrack at the wrong time. If it is discovered too early in life, esotericism can easily be misused as an excuse to avoid life. Rather than facing life, with all its task and lessons, such people may hide themselves in an ashram. Rather than first securely anchoring themselves in polarity, they flee to "Cloud Nine." In Eastern cultures—the homeland of the ashram—that flight is not a big problem because experienced gurus are on hand to ensure that spiritual life does not become too idyllic too soon, and that only those people remain in the ashram who really belong there. This has become more difficult in the wake of the Western esoteric wave, since the competition for disciples among certain self-proclaimed gurus[64] has led them to accept anyone and everyone who comes along.

But even in India the classical patterns of transition for divorcing oneself from external affairs and from the outwardly directed life no longer function as well as they once did. In our society, they are highly exceptional or absent entirely. Family businesses and politics make this lack obvious. In situations where power and influence take precedence over all other values, the older generation tends to cling stubbornly to the reins of power. For the most part, our world is currently ruled by elderly dotards who have long since outlived the moment when they ought to have stepped down. If their fear of being deposed prompts them to thwart the development of any possible successors, the situation can become dangerous. Clinging to power for too long can exclude an entire generation from politics and lead to the creation of power vacuums such as occurred in post-Tito Yugoslavia and post-Mao China. Increasingly many gerontocracies can be found in firms and families, to the detriment of older and younger generations alike.

Swiss author Max Frisch describes a politician who bears the marks of age: "...as his ability to experience physical lust declines, political life becomes a kind of last resort, a refuge where an old man can still feel powerful and in charge. No longer tempted by spontaneity, his age-dimmed brain is immune to annoyances, so he can readily make political decisions—not through rashness, but through senility. He functions like a machine that neither loves nor fears risks. He is old enough to have survived one or more bad decisions in the past. The loss of his ability to imagine and envision allows him to objectively weigh all the factors without feeling any terror from their consequences. The lives of others no longer seem so important to him since he has so little of his own life left to lose. The older he gets, the better suited he becomes for serving as the leader of a country."[65]

Of course, having missed his chance to withdraw from the field of mundane power and daily affairs also makes it more difficult to accept spiritual power in the sense of a change of direction (e.g., joining the council of elders in an archaic society and accepting the concomitant spiritual authority).

England's royal family currently provides a clear and publicly accessible example of what can happen when the transfer of power from one generation to the next is delayed too long and develops into a classical conflict of generations.[66] If a person's entire childhood and young adulthood is devoted to learning how to be a prince and king, and if that person is then deprived of the promised fruits year after year, it should come as no surprise when that prince begins to cause mischief and unconscious acts of sabotage. Without a long and intensive training during the first two decades of life, it is almost impossible to behave oneself while waiting for the throne, as we can see by considering the behavior of the prince and (late) princess of Wales. Full of cares for the future of the empire, the queen waits longer and longer before turning over the crown to her son, and the situation becomes increasingly hopeless with each passing year. She has waited so long that there are now good reasons to shift the transfer of power to the third generation, bypass her son and give the crown directly to her grandson. The longer she delays, the more she deprives her son of his life's meaning in two senses: first by robbing him of his childhood, and then by robbing him of his calling. She also deprives her grandchildren of their grand*mother* and deprives herself of allowing her own soul to embark on its rightful homeward journey. Rather than accepting responsibility for this delay, she no doubt projects it all onto her son, his (late) wife and their lifestyle. Projection is a quality she shares with all other powerful people who cannot let go at the right time. They can always find reasons for their own insatiability—all they need to do is search intensely and desperately enough for those reasons.

In a society that does everything in its power to ignore the pattern of life's mandala, some people applaud irresponsible behavior of the sort described above. The applause is even more likely to come when the incumbent makes it look as though her clinging to power is motivated solely by altruism and by a noble personal sacrifice for the greater good of the nation, the party, the business or the family. Such behavior is ir*responsible* because it means that the incumbent is unable to adequately *respond* to the demands of the life pattern. The further one strays from one's own path, the more gravely one loses the ability to respond adequately, the more unresponsive and irresponsible one becomes. The suffering one inflicts upon oneself and upon everyone involved in the situation is proportional to the severity of one's own error and confusion.

Essentially, everyone who reaches midlife no doubt feels the quality of this time, and feels time itself calling for reversal and transformation. The likelihood of ignoring this natural tendency to return is directly proportional to one's fear of letting go (and ultimately to one's fear of death), to one's overestimation of oneself (which can culminate in the feeling of being irreplaceable and indispensable) or to one's sense that one will have no future after surrendering one's hard-earned position.

Diversionary Tactics

Outsiders who have not yet mastered this transition themselves cannot be expected to offer understanding or useful advice. Like society as a whole, they are most likely to advise the midlifer to found a new business, start a new project according to the same old pattern or search for a new challenge. The new "project" is then spawned by the illusory notion that this time everything will be better and nourished by the desperate certainty that this is one's last chance to experience whatever one has missed thus far. In most cases, nothing changes: the same pattern and same mistakes are simply repeated once more.

In a few exceptional cases, however, the individual who has done his duty succeeds in reaping the rewards and actualizing his heart's desire. This is similar to the behavior of older people who feel life's gates closing upon them and react with desperation, greedily grasping at whatever life (still) has to offer, but never really making any fundamental *changes* inside themselves. In such a situation, a reversal of direction would be the greatest and only truly satisfying change. Nothing else can solve the real problem.

People suffering from midlife crisis will remain despondent and be unable to find meaning in life until they begin to orient themselves in the correct new direction. All other more convenient or superficial attempts will fail to satisfy their souls. Outsiders find it especially easy to see through the variant embodied by middle-aged men who feel time closing in on them but who misinterpret the Biblical injunction to "be converted, and become as little children" in a materialistic and convenient manner. They buy youthful clothes in the nearest boutique, buy a sporty convertible car and *acquire* a young girlfriend. Nevertheless, all this only makes the midlife sufferer look childish, and only reveals what an immature head sits atop the elderly shoulders. It certainly does not solve the problem. Mis(s)relationships of this sort may function for a while, especially if the girl involved has a father complex and is searching for a paternal mate. Such women are apt to accept the offer in the form of an experienced, older man with graying temples. It is a deal of sorts that, although not a solution for either partner, can sometimes bring the people one step further—assuming they survive and learn from the disappointment and disillusionment that is likely to ensue. The girl generally accepts financial support from the man and, in return, plays along with his pseudo-youthful self-confirming trip. It is a situation in which unresolved problems from an earlier phase cause a man to get stuck at a subsequent juncture.

The same pattern, albeit with gender-reversed roles, is also possible. A woman who has not adequately lived through this issue can react to the threat of incipient menopause by finding herself a younger boyfriend. He might provide her with the illusory impression that she herself is young again and still has her whole life ahead of her. In the age of "equal rights," some emancipated women believe that finding a youthful boyfriend is more or less the duty of a mature woman, according to the motto "Anything men can do, we can do better." Certain Hollywood stars, who have plenty of money to support this extravagance, serve as role models by living this pattern. Even though they are unable to grow old in dignity because they lack the real content and depth to support that step, they continue to put their trust in external and superficial things, and continue to enhance the popularity and the acceptability of the "May-December" pattern.

Of course, relationships with much younger partners can also have their bright sides, as long as the soul feels fulfilled and genuine love is present on both sides. They can even help make up for deficiencies in the "sensuality account" before the final reversal in life's direction. The only problem lies in the illusion that a relationship with a younger person will make the older person young again and give his life a deeper meaning.

The irreversible physical changes that accompany both male and female menopause can intensify the "now or never" panic and blur the boundaries between illusion and reality. In the past, an aging king would take a virgin to bed, hoping her youth would somehow "rub off" on him. The insane Rumanian dictator Ceausescu put his faith in transfusions of blood from newborn babies. Of course, becoming "as little children" does not mean becoming childish. The exhortation applies to the soul and the spirit, and refers to the soul's homeward path.

But what are the criteria of this mature yet childlike state that is so eagerly sought by all those who are questing for their inner child? Mythology mentions the "golden child" who dwells within every person regardless of their age. We commonly praise infants by describing them as "good as gold." Christ says that this child is the goal of our lives. As we already mentioned in our discussion of mature adulthood, the actualization of the inner child cannot be measured in terms of individual attributes, but must be recognized by perceiving the soul's total state. Nonetheless, we can only approach a definition of the "inner child" by examining individual traits. We might be able to form at least a vague idea of what Christ meant when we consider how loveable little children usually are.

The attributes and special traits of people, both young and old, who embody resolved "childlikeness" include their:

- Ability to live in the moment,
- Spontaneity,
- Unconditional openness, their open hearts,
- • Blithe (and blissful) trust,
- Courage,

- Honesty and freedom from artificiality,
- *Joie de vivre* in all things,
- Ability to rest calmly within themselves,
- Tendency not to judge, evaluate or pass verdicts,
- Ability not to allow externals to impress them,
- Readiness to grow unconditionally,
- Ability to find meaning in everything, to find the magic in everyone and everything,
- Readiness to experience learning as a pleasure rather than as a chore or duty,
- Simplicity and their uncomplicated nature,
- Pleasure they take in movement and flow (gleefully destroying the sandcastle after spending hours building it),[67]
- Lively emotions: brief, intense, changing rapidly,
- Readiness to forgive and to accept apologies,
- Oneness with every game, without forgetting that it is "only a game,"
- Natural balance between activity and relaxation,
- Natural connection to the numinous.

Symptoms of Midlife Crisis

Depression

Depression, which often accompanies midlife, is increasing to epidemic proportions. Statisticians claim that the risk of suffering from depression is three times greater for individuals born after 1950 than for their grandparents. The word "de-pression" means pressing something down, and the vital energies are what is pressed down. But life's energies cannot be suppressed indefinitely because they always return the pressure. Whatever we suppress long enough becomes oppressive, which helps explain why aggression plays such a significant role in the total picture of depression. Scarcely any Mars energy can be detected by an outsider because this vital energy is almost entirely directed inward, against the depressive individual. The most logical therapeutic step would be to help clients rediscover their vital Mars energy. It is a sign of progress (albeit a potentially dangerous development) when, as a first step out of depression, clients begin to direct their aggressive energies toward their surroundings. By directing their vital energies against themselves, they have largely deprived themselves of life. Conversely, when they redirect the charge toward their environment, other people experience the change as unpleasant and perhaps even threatening. Fortunately, it is possible to transform such energies into constructive forces and make them available to one's path in life. In the case of a midlife depression, this means using them for a courageous reversal and for challenges on the homeward path.

One could also quite literally interpret the word "de-pression" as meaning "away from pressure." Like all other symptoms, depression expresses the right thing: it compels the depressive individual to relax and let go on the physical and thus also on the problematic level. "Away from pressure" can also be understood as a hint to turn around and begin moving toward the center of the mandala, toward the point where there is no tension, where there is nothing but the perfect peace of the center. At the acme of life, on the periphery of the mandala, the tension of polarity is at its maximum. People who have accumulated treasures live in the constant fear of losing them. If they want to prevent that, they need to administrate their valuables and remain rooted in the polar world. The tension along the periphery of the mandala, at the summit of life's midpoint, has reached its maximum. As we move closer toward the center, the tension declines and approaches zero. Returning to the center and to peace, moving away from the periphery and its tension, is our post-midlife destiny.

The depressive person also aims for relaxation, but does so in a problematic way, unconsciously stretching out all four limbs in spread-eagled passivity and simply "hanging loose"—all *too* loose! The elasticity and tone of body and soul can atrophy so much that the depressive individual no longer feels the slightest motivation or vital energy. Physicians frequently have difficulty extracting blood samples from depressed people because the patients' veins are so lacking in tension that the blood vessel slips away from the point of the needle. In both a literal and a metaphoric sense, the flow of life energy has all but ceased. Depression is a way to "play possum," to seem dead, a suicide attempt that has not been physically lived out.

Like all symptoms, the thoughts of death that often accompany depression are appropriate in their own peculiar way. It is necessary to take a long, hard look at death, the next great crisis in life. Suicidal thoughts, then, actually direct our gaze in the right direction and toward the next major issue. But the issue of death can be approached in far more positive ways than by brooding over suicide, as we shall see later in our discussion of this final crisis.

A therapist working with a depressive client should first determine which of the two themes is primary. If the issue is suppressed aggression, then the therapy ought to challenge (and channel) the patient toward a healthy explosion. If the principal issue is the need to release inner tension on the level of the soul rather than on the level of the body, then the therapist ought to work toward precipitating an implosion, in the course of which the client's energies will turn inward. In either case, the therapy ought to involve a confrontation with the Saturnine theme of death and the need to reduce things to their bare essentials.

Typical medical treatments of the problem pursue an allopathic course, prescribing psychotropic drugs that contribute nothing to the patient's path in life and that, rather than encouraging the patient to progress along her path, may in fact hinder that progress. A person who suffers from midlife depression feels no motivation to pursue their path, and that lack of motivation is fundamentally good and appropriate. She has been moving with much too much momentum in the wrong direction and needs to "step on the brakes" in order to find the peace and quiet to focus on the real issue and discover the real task at hand.

273

People suffering from midlife depression experience no pleasure in the company of others and in the usual diversions, and that lack of pleasure is exactly what they need at the moment because a certain loneliness is appropriate and overdue. To prescribe chemicals in tablet form designed to increase motivation is not the right therapy because it does not bring the client into order (and toward the cosmic order of the mandala's pattern) any faster, nor does it do anything to cure the client of the underlying depression. Such medications can even exacerbate the problem since they supply the lacking motivation but do nothing to change the orientation, and the patient may well resume her familiar and misguided route. This kind of "therapy" can become a threat to life when the patient's energy is flowing in what is essentially the correct direction (i.e., toward death) and the patient uses the chemically induced motivation to succeed in a suicide attempt. Prescribing one drug is not enough in such cases, so the responsible physician is compelled to prescribe even more psychotropic medication. In addition to the drug that increases motivation, it becomes necessary to prescribe another one designed to brighten the patient's mood.[68] But the latter drug distracts the individual from confronting the real theme (i.e., his mortality) and ultimate aloneness. From this point of view, it is not surprising that depressed individuals are often advised to continue swallowing their pills indefinitely. There is a German saying that reflects a folk wisdom: "delayed isn't made." As long as the depression's underlying issue remains untreated, it will continue to press upon and "de-press" the individual.

Of course, this is not intended to mean that a regime of psychotropic medication is never the right course of treatment. Drugs of this kind can save lives by preventing suicide among people who can no longer bear themselves and the issues weighing upon them. But we should remember that psychotropic drugs cannot cure depression. Sometimes, however, when the pressure of the symptoms is unbearable, it can be helpful to approach the oppressive issues through psychotherapy while the patient is under the protection afforded by the medication.

Like every pattern of symptoms, depression has its good sides and teaches essential lessons. One could understand depression as the soul's emergency brake that slows us down when we are traveling too fast in the wrong direction. It compels us to retreat from situations that have become inappropriate and leads us to seek out the fundamental aloneness we need to existentially confront ourselves and death as life's final goal. In many cases, nothing but a depression can push one's life back into the midpoint where it belongs, enabling the depressed individual to let go of the compulsion to satisfy everyone else's expectations, providing space for sadness and grief, allowing him to spend time alone and at last "do nothing" in a life that has otherwise been overly full of business and busyness.

Finally, we ought not forget that there can be no summits without their corresponding abysses. Not only the weather is comprised of highs and lows. A permanent high would dry out the earth, while a perpetual low would drown it. That is why one high necessarily causes the next low, and the low prepares the atmosphere for the next high. An especially long-lasting low may well be the precursor of or compensation for an equally long high. The ideal lies in the middle. Beginning with the middle of life, our primary task is to find that middle in every sense, and that includes finding the golden middle in our moods.

Involution Depression

A later version is the involution depression, whose very name contains clues about its meaning. Involution is the natural regression of the physical body that accompanies aging. This type of depression is associated with the time of regression, when the theme of death draws increasingly closer. Childhood and youth were principally times of growth for the body, although the soul and mind of course also grew along with the body.[69] The growth of the soul is the chief theme for the phase of life from adolescence to midlife, while the body's growth is reserved for pregnancies or less pleasant showplaces (e.g., when warts or other uninvited growths appear). After the "change of life," growth occurs mostly in the spirit while physical growth ceases or even reverses itself. Each of the great phases in life begins with a kind of birth. The first birth relates to the birth of the body; the second, puberty, relates above all to the soul; and the third, which occurs during the climacteric years, is directed toward spiritual growth.

During the involution phase that accompanies aging, less tissue is regenerated than dies off and the body gradually atrophies. Ideally, however, this decline of the physical body is more than offset by the increased rates of spiritual and mental growth. Intellectual growth leading to wisdom and maturity far outweighs the degeneration taking place in physical structures. The body's physical capacities become relatively unimportant because they are less in demand. Unused muscles naturally shrink. The physical degeneration is only dangerous if little progress is made on the spiritual level. If one's body is the only thing one has and the only thing to which one clings, its degeneration can be experienced as a catastrophe. Psychosis is often an attempt to escape, usually from a reality experienced as unbearable. When one no longer has any hope of coping with life, when one sees no further possibilities, psychosis can seem (at first glance anyway) like a more pleasant alternative.

Aging people who try to use athletic achievements[70] to prove to themselves and those around them that they are immune to the effects of old age are sure to suffer a metaphorical shipwreck, as are those who refuse to believe in any sort of continued existence after physical death. If the threat posed by physical degeneration becomes an existential danger and if these people can find nothing else to cling to, the aging process can trigger an unconscious flight into depression or psychosis. For all human beings, the decline of the body symbolizes the fundamental decay to which all material things are subject. This realization, of course, is most threatening to materialists. The deeper meaning of involution depression is twofold: it can help us realize that the body, like all material things, is ephemeral; and it can prompt us to seek and find something to hold onto, something that can give us permanent strength on another level. To a greater degree than midlife depression, involution depression involves the Saturnine principle of reduction—namely, that the only things that matter are the essentials (e.g., the immortal soul and the timeless, holy spirit).

Swollen Prostate Gland[71]

This symptom occurs when physical growth begins at a time and in a place where it is inappropriate. Problems with the prostate gland affect a part of the body most men find extremely sensitive or even embarrassing. The problems generally appear during the second half of life, in the years of mature adulthood, when the man is ripe (i.e., ripe and ready for a change in his life). For many men, prostate problems ruin their riper years. In its healthy state, the prostate surrounds the urethra in a "loving embrace." As it begins to swell, however, the embrace becomes a vice-like grip that reduces and ultimately throttles the flow of urine, causing unbearable pain and difficulties passing urine. The symbolism is clear. The prostate sufferer can no longer bear the situation. Unable to pass his water, he is threatened with drowning in his soul's own fluid. A more drastic method could hardly be imagined to show a man that his soul's energies are blocked and that he has painful problems with the feminine pole, which is currently putting pressure on him (and his urethra). There is no escape except to drain off and release the blocked elements of the soul. Enhanced awareness at this point can significantly reduce the oppressive burden of the physical situation.

If urination is still possible at all, it generally requires a great deal of (pressing) effort to squeeze past the clutches of the swollen prostate. Releasing urine becomes a strenuous labor, and every urination is like a little birth. Since the bladder can no longer be emptied completely, the gestation periods between these annoying *water births* grow increasingly short, finally interfering with the prostate sufferer's sleep. This, in turn, can lead to a deficit of dream phases and the subsequent mental disorders discussed in the chapter about nursing mothers.

Even if the difficulty passing urine is moderate and has not yet developed into a serious physical problem, the symptom can nonetheless create problems for the soul. Urination was formerly a pleasure as the fountain of urine gushed skyward in a proud arc. Now urination is a cramped struggle that results in little more than a humble trickle. One's childhood pride is over and done with. The remaining trickle is unimpressive and surely not going to win any contests. Public urinals suddenly become battlefields the sufferer does his best to avoid. But that is not always possible, especially because of the continually partially full bladder and the consequent constant pressure.

The interpretation may seem ridiculous to people unaffected by prostate problems, but men suffering from this syndrome often interpret the weakness of their urination to mean they will not be able to get very far in life and that "it's all downhill from here." Urologists' assurances that this interpretation is medically unfounded fall on deaf. And, of course, these men are right: the path of life has long since taken a downward turn. The acme is passed and now lies behind them. The stream of urination is no longer what it was in youth, and neither are the man's aura and appearance as youthful and dynamic as they once were. Every urination can bring the redeeming insight, so each urination represents fate's therapeutic efforts on the man's behalf. As time goes on, fate (and a full bladder) prescribes increasingly frequent therapy sessions. The prostate sufferer can view this as a bitter joke played by destiny, or can turn the tables and realize that fate is doing its best to ensure the welfare of his soul.

The impressively masculine posture formerly assumed while urinating—legs apart, the pale yellow fountain streaming forth in a powerful arc—has become a humiliating ordeal that differs only in negative aspects from its trouble-free feminine counterpart. In the past, *he* was finished with his "business" much quicker than she, but now *she* is the one who must wait for him. The so-called *weaker* sex, accustomed to urinate in a humble sitting or squatting posture, has become unmistakably more powerful in this situation. Our bodies stage this impressive and vivid depiction of the animus-anima situation. The time has come for him to discover his anima, his feminine aspect, and the time will soon come for her to discover her animus, her masculine aspect—but more about that later.

A man who cannot correctly interpret the signs of the times may react to the swelling of his prostate gland by swelling up his own ego and attempting to recoup elsewhere the losses he has suffered on the "pissing" front. The reader will pardon, I hope, my use of this vulgar expression, but I do so with good historical foundations. No less a personage than Martin Luther used the verb "to piss" in his translation of the Bible, and he seems to have used that expression where urination is meant to demonstrate one's power.

As always, the symptom reveals the task at hand. The pseudo-masculine, self-aggrandizing fantasies that began with childhood peeing contests and were subsequently adapted to suit each new phase in life have failed. The masculine urination, like the masculine *emanation*, no longer reaches very far. The time has come for a man to approach his feminine pole, the anima.

The genesis of prostate swelling contains another aspect—namely, that the prostate is the gland that produces the fluid that provides the lubrication needed during sexual intercourse and that nourishes the sperm cells on their journey into the depths of the feminine cave. Hence, the reservoir of liquid in this gland is reduced with each ejaculation of semen and this, in turn, explains why urologists frequently prescribe sexual satisf-*action*. An additional benefit lies in the massage to which the gland is subjected during sexual activity. When the gland is left for too long with nothing to do, it swells and calls attention to itself. If the patient refuses to follow his doctor's recommendation, the physician has no choice but take things into his own hands. The finger she inserts into the patient's anus puts pressure on the prostate gland and expels its contents, albeit without the pleasurable feeling of release that ordinarily accompanies ejaculation. In the

Arab world, where caring for one's harem requires a man to continue his sexual activity even at an advanced age, prostate problems are comparatively unknown. On the other hand, the problem can also be caused by impotence, in which case the gland produces fluid secretions that accumulate because they are not discharged.

The cure lies in more sexuality, and thus more intimate contact with "the second sex." Especially since certain changes in sexuality are likely to take place after midlife, it is recommended for a man to develop an erotic relationship that includes contact with his own feminine side. As time goes on, the erotic focus shifts from sexual encounter to encounter with the anima per se. The physical level remains important insofar as it was neglected or isolated from the emotional level in the past. Sexuality without love is form without content, and form alone is fundamentally unsatisfying.

The essence of the lesson lies in the need for the man to turn his attention to his own feminine side—although, as he does, he will no doubt encounter any unfinished issues that remain in the masculine realm. As in every crisis, the imminent and urgent new issue is always accompanied by the need to deal with unresolved themes. Readers eager to find out how a man can extricate himself from this unpleasant situation should refer to the corresponding chapter in *Krankheit als Sprache der Seele* (*Illness as a Language of the Soul*).

Hair Loss

Hair loss is another symptom that commonly occurs during this phase of a man's life. Thinning hair and baldness are like losing one's feathers (i.e., one pays the price for something received by giving up the symbols of freedom and power). If, for example, a man has perse*vered* too long in an obsolete situation, *seve*rance from his own hair may be the price. The symptomatic loss of essential status symbols shows that the man is no longer lord and master over his fate. Nudge becomes push, and push comes to shove, as destiny urges the reluctant individual into the right direction, which is, incidentally, the only route still open to him.[72] Once again, the decision that is typical of crisis situations appears: will I consciously release my grip on external badges of power and freedom, or will I be compelled to release my hold unconsciously? In the latter case, destiny makes sure that the issue manifests on the stage of the body because the issue must be given space to express itself somewhere. The balding pate is part of the destined path back toward becoming a child, but it appears on the clumsy bodily level where we began as bald-headed babies.

As long as women are protected by estrogen, they are not subject to loss of hair and the corresponding loss of their symbols of power, freedom and beauty. As long as they are still potentially able to bear children, fate leaves them every chance to attract the mate they need and thus allows them to remain fetchingly hirsute. As the flood of estrogen ebbs during menopause, the same bald fate begins to threaten women. If a woman refuses to surrender enough of her power, freedom and desire to be beautiful on the physical level, the corresponding symbols appears upon her head and compels her to surrender.

Tumors

In this case, too, the process of growth has erred in place and time. Children are meant to develop within the uterus, but not after a woman's change of life. Tumors that can swell to the size of children's heads are clear symbols of an unconscious, unlived or not adequately manifest desire to have children. Tumors are obvious expressions of a woman's clinging to biological womanhood and her refusal to accept the fact that she is now too old to bear children. The gynecological "therapy" of removing the uterus is essentially a step in the right direction, but in the wrong plane. There are far simpler and healthier ways for a woman to take leave of her childbearing abilities than by allowing (usually male) surgeons to physically remove the physical organ. The best way for her to cope with the feeling that she has become infertile is to express her innate creativity in another productive field. In any case, her task is to take leave of sexual fertility and find the solution by being productive elsewhere.

Even if a woman has borne several children, she may still yearn for one more, perhaps for the "golden child" she always wanted and to whom she could now wholeheartedly devote herself. Like all other symptoms, tumors are problematic expressions of reasonable tendencies. The issue involves bringing real children into the world, but it is obvious that metaphorical "brain-children" rather than flesh-and-blood offspring are appropriate at this phase in life. Implanting the ovum of a younger woman into the womb of a fiftyor sixty-year-old "mother" is a perversion of nature perpetrated by gynecologists. It is evidence of the inability to find one's proper place in the pattern of life. The hour hand on life's clock points to a much later hour than the post-menopausal mother is willing to admit.

Rather than trying to have a late-in-life child to devote herself to, she is better advised to channel her devotion toward her own projects, paintings, sculptures, books or toward whatever work requires her to invest her heart and soul. Intellectual interests related to religion are particularly helpful in dealing with this issue because they can lead to intellectual and spiritual growth. In any case, the growth must take place on a different plane— namely, it should move up from the womb into the heart and head. Another alternative is for her to transform her unconscious but nonetheless real yearning to have a child into love for her grandchildren—the children of the next generation—so that this grandmother can truly become a *grand* mother.

The archetype of the grandmother has declined, and this decline has been detrimental to grandchildren, mothers and grandmothers alike. The essential cause of the decline lies in our incapacity to cope with life's transitions at the proper time and in our tendency to limp along many years behind the times, learning our natural lessons too little and too late. Old mothers create superannuated grandmothers for whom too little time remains to grow into the archetype of the Great Mother. If the tendency toward delayed motherhood continues in the same direction, if the interval of regeneration increases from twenty years to forty years, then women will not become grandmothers until the age of eighty and will not become great-grandmothers until their 120th birthdays.

The growth that expresses itself in every tumor is essentially alright, but has merely occurred too late and on the physical rather than the intellectual or spiritual plane. The task is to lift that growth upward into its proper plane. A woman can become a grandmother (and a grand or Great Mother) in a metaphorical sense by adopting all the world's children as her own grandchildren. Motherly love draws its life from a woman's lunar aspect; grandmotherly love is more related to the solar aspect, less tied to the familial pattern and to everyday life, and therefore more generous and wise. Miranda Gray[73] believes that the destiny of a post-menopausal woman is to become a spiritual leader who regards all pre-menopausal women as her daughters and all post-menopausal women as her sisters. This attitude agrees with C.G. Jung's call for the post-midlife woman to begin paying more attention to her animus, the masculine part of her soul. As a spiritual teacher, she should take care of the essentially masculine intellect, and as a leader, she should play an archetypal masculine role, but she should play these roles in her own feminine way.

Hysterectomy

It is difficult to say whether the incidence of uterine tumors has rapidly increased in recent years, but there can be no doubt that the surgical removal of such tumors has snowballed. A rather uncommon procedure twenty years ago, hysterectomies have since become a more or less routine part of a gynecologist's trade. The justifications for such operations are sometimes hair-raising and, in a deeper sense, contrary to proper medical practice. One of the favorite arguments used to convince woman over the age of forty to assent to a hysterectomy runs something like this: "You'd be better off having your uterus removed; the tumor isn't very large, but it's better to be safe than sorry; and once the uterus is out, nothing inside it can possibly become malignant." If a woman who has been subjected to (mis)advise of this sort dares to ask another doctor for a second opinion, she generally wants to be assured that her uterus cannot develop a malignancy. The physician can assure her that a myoma (muscular tumor) cannot become malignant, but there are essentially no guarantees in the medical field, and surely not with respect to what may or may not happen to other structures within the uterus. After hearing this (admittedly equivocal) verdict, chances are her uterus will soon belong to the charlatan whose fear-inducing advice represents a misuse of physician's authority impelling his patient to assent to a needless operation. The women patients of such a quack ought to urge their surgeon to have his ears amputated as a prophylactic measure—after all, a myoma could develop there, and it is better to safe than sorry.

Some doctors unscrupulously exaggerate the size of the tumor, hoping to frighten their patient into assenting to its surgical removal. Simply asking for a second opinion from a gynecologist who has no need to precipitate unnecessary operations can, to the embarrassment of the scalpel-happy would-be hysterectomist, cause a myoma to suddenly shrink from the size of a fist to the size of a pigeon's egg. The best protection against unnecessary surgery is to find a gynecologist who has no desire to accumulate surgical experience. The deliberately fear-inducing insinuations uttered by unscrupulous physicians are one of the worst offenses with which doctors sully their profession's reputation. The accusation may sound harsh, but facts are facts. In the past decade, uterine amputations has been more prevalent in Germany than in practically any other country in the world. Some cynics even suggest that the number of superfluous operations increases in indirect proportion to the gynecologists' workload. The worst part of all this is that some uteruses really do need to be removed. How can a woman know whether she is sitting in the office of a virulent quack eager to cut, sew and earn money on his anti-uterine crusade or whether she is had the good fortune to find one of the many responsible and trustworthy gynecologists?

The pseudo-argument some specialists use (i.e., that an older woman's uterus is as useless as a goiter) simply does not ring true. Even a goiter has its *raison d'être* because it fulfils a function, albeit an unpleasant one. Above all, this argument has encouraged surgeons to become overeager in recommending surgery. Portraying hysterectomy as an absolutely harmless operation, gynecologists for decades brushed off hysterectomy patients' complaints about climacteric symptoms by laconically reminding them that their symptoms are impossible because their fallopian tubes have not been removed. Decades later, medical researchers finally discovered that typical hysterectomy operations tie off important blood vessels and thus reduce circulation to the fallopian tubes by as much as fifty percent. This throttling of the blood supply is not unlike a partial castration. Surgical procedures have been improved since then, but these subsequent improvements are of little use to the women who underwent the operation before the newer methods were implemented. These patients are generally regarded as hypochondriacs and are frequently dismissed without therapy. The history of gynecology has not been especially praiseworthy in its handling of hysterectomy patients, but it seems as though the future will bring greater respect for life and for the biological structures upon which life is based. If the uterus really were entirely superfluous in this phase of life, the organism would automatically cause it to atrophy as it does with other unused muscles and as it partially does with the uterus.

Along with the disadvantages described above, women who have sacrificed their uteruses on the altar of scientific medicine have the advantage of being free of this problematic showplace for growth-related conflicts. Consequently, however, it becomes all the more urgently necessary for them to find another stage upon which to enact life's subsequent growth processes.

Complaints Associated with Menopause

These symptoms are above all related to the issue of taking stock, and they generally point toward missed chances and overdue tasks. The expression "unfinished business" hits the nail squarely on the head: the "business" it refers to is not objective tasks, but rather unfinished projects within the landscape of a woman's soul. There is nothing inherently wrong with hot flashes and sudden sweats. Both are normal, for example, during sexual intercourse. When they occur at the right time, they can be pleasant and exciting for everyone involved. But when they suddenly occur while shopping, they can be quite annoying. And occur they do, at the least opportune moments and in the most inappropriate situations. The organism is working on unfinished issues, and it will continue to work on them until, in one way or another, it has finished this work.

A look at the medical background of these symptoms can be illuminating. The hypothalamus (an important coordinating center within the brain) causes a rapid decline in the body's temperature. Inside, the organism feels as though it were freezing, which means that, compared to its inner core, the outer layers of the body are too warm. Blood vessels in the skin enlarge in order to give off excess heat, leading to a reddening of the skin (so-called "flush") and to perspiration. The latter reaction helps to reduce the body's temperature through evaporative cooling. In the later phases of a "hot flash," some women experience shivers and develop *goose flesh*. The real roots of the problem, then, lie in erroneous regulatory behavior on the part of the hypothalamus (i.e., the right reactions occur at the wrong times). Once again and on several planes, the body is revealing the real issue: the time is indeed ripe for a woman to cool off a bit (i.e., to become somewhat more peaceful inside and to keep a cool head). Outwardly, she needs to radiate a bit more warmth in the sense of warmhearted feelings, self-surrender and dedication to a task. Perhaps she needs to admit that she did not fully live out the season of her life when ardent sensibilities were appropriate and that now, at the wrong time, these heated feelings are seeking an outlet. Her task is to allow them to express themselves, even if the situations are not entirely appropriate, rather than ignoring them and allowing them to overwhelm her when she least expects it.

Dry, burning hot mucous membranes are unpleasant, but they nevertheless reveal that this person still feels herself to be a *hot*, indeed a *red hot*, woman. If the issue can be restored to consciousness and lived out on the appropriate level, the burden is correspondingly reduced on the physical stage of the body. Physical expression is only a "last resort," an expedient to which the organism has recourse when important issues are not manifest elsewhere. The accompanying dehydration (drying out) of the entire body contains additional messages that need to be interpreted. Along with the loss of weight, dehydration also leads to so-called hemoconcentration (a reduction in the volume of blood and a corresponding increase in the concentration of the blood). The vital energies in the blood ought not be reduced in their essence, but only in their amounts, so that the essential part (i.e., the hemoglobin that gives the blood its color) becomes all the more evident. A reduction in turgor (the interior pressure within each cell) also occurs. This reduction, in turn, expresses itself in a less plump, somewhat wilted appearance of the skin. When the pressure within each of her cells declines, a woman ought to reduce inner pressure in general.

Urinary incontinence is related to the issue of letting go and/ or holding back. A person who continually feels the need to urinate is being urged by his organism to allow the body's water (a symbol of the soul) to flow unimpeded. What seems so unpleasant on the physical level would be extremely pleasant if it were lived on the proper level (i.e., the plane of consciousness). All these symptoms appear in order to draw one's attention to the fact that vital self-realization or transformation is urgently needed. Only after the necessary changes have been made do the symptoms become unnecessary. Again, the healing step lies in conscious reversal, turning about on the path of life. After all, urinary incontinence, when the urine is allowed to flow without restriction, is typical of the first years of life. The task is to become like little children—not, of course, by wetting our beds, but on a metaphorical plane.

The same remarks apply to weakness of the sphincter, which leads to repeated loss of control over one's defecation and thus to a return into the diapers of infancy, where it all began. This type of incontinence not only relates to the idea of "becoming like little children," but also has to do with the issue of letting go in the material realm because feces symbolize material treasures and possessions.[74] As in weakness of the bladder, in which the task is to replace the release of urine on the bodily level with release of blocked energies on the soul level, in this case the challenge is to continually let go of material possessions and thus relieve the sphincter of the need to play a proxy function.

The reduction in the amount of growth hormone in the blood follows a similar pattern and points in a similar direction. The message is that growth on the bodily plane is no longer appropriate. For women, the growth hormone is the substance that most directly encourages muscle growth, so it would seem that muscular growth is no longer the proper response at this stage in life. It also fits the overall pattern to note that the growth hormone catalyzes protein synthesis and that this synthesis likewise declines with reduction in the amount of growth hormone. The body receives less of this important raw material and lipolysis (the breakdown of fat) increases in its place. This is yet another expression of the general tendency to reduce things to the bare essentials. Artificially adding estrogen to the system would preempt all these symptoms by preventing the change of life from happening and tricking the body so that it fails to recognize the real situation.

One effect of this trickery is that estrogen reduces the threat of heart attack. During the fertile years, the body's own estrogen reduces the level of "bad" (LDL) cholesterol and raises the level of "good" (HDL) cholesterol. This is nature's way of protecting the female organism during the phase of life nature regards as most important. After menopause, estrogen protection wanes and the rate of heart attack among women gradually begins to approach the rate among men. As we will discuss in greater depth later on in the chapter "Animus and Anima," the real issue here involves the masculine pole in a woman's life. If her attempts to actualize this issue are as unsuccessful as they are among many men today, then she naturally runs the risk of developing the same symptoms.[75] The best way to prevent angina pectoris and heart attack is to attend to one's heart, both literally and figuratively, by paying attention to one's heart and to heart-related themes early rather than waiting until one feels pain on the bodily level.

When we consider the change of life, its various symptoms and their interpretations, it seems that the advice to enjoy ardent sexuality is the most controversial prescription since it seems to stand in obvious contradiction to the necessary reversal in the path of life. One should bear in mind that we are dealing with a phenomenon that relates to taking stock. Basically, the time has come to concentrate on the essentials, to collect and budget one's vitality, to become cooler and clearer inside. If sexuality did not find adequate expression during the first half of life, it may try to find a "quick fix" during the second half. But there is no need to hurry things since sexuality is by no means at an end merely because a woman is no longer able to become pregnant. Sexuality during life's first half draws its vitality above all from the tension between the genders. During the second half of life, the theme of sexual union rather than sexual tension gains in importance. Of course, sexuality is far too comprehensive an issue to be divided into two parts, but the simplification does help to make some things clearer. The outward path in life's mandala leads us from oneness toward the maximal tension of midlife, while the return path leads away from this tension and toward the union of the center. In every phase of life, sexuality represents an ideal way for a couple to ritually express their current station on life's path. When the mucous membranes begin to produce less lubricant, the message could be "less is more."

The body is helping to make it clear that the orientation ought to be toward greater quality rather than quantity in sexuality, and that erotic life ought to be elevated to a higher plane.

Alleviating the symptoms by consuming estrogen pills would represent a clinging to an earlier phase in life. Although artificial consumption of estrogen (and especially its long-term consumption for years on end) ought to be avoided, short-term therapy with hormones is justifiable to provide temporary relief from massive symptoms. Hormonal therapy should not be misused to allow the patient to continue living as before. Instead, she ought to use the symptom-free interval the medication has provided as an opportunity to truly make up for what she may have missed in the past, to genuinely live the life of a *hot* woman on the appropriate level. Even it this may not seem like the proper age for such behavior, we should bear in mind that we have been tardy in taking many of life's developmental steps. The adulthood that ought to accompany puberty, for example, is usually delayed until late adolescence. Since we can only let go of things we have truly experienced and fulfilled, it is alright to give ourselves the space and time (even late in life) to live out urgent and unfilled issues.

Taking our time and living life fully is fine, but we ought to bear in mind that the final crisis (death) is not likely to wait until we feel ready for it. Intensive medical care promises to delay death, but the promise is soon debunked as illusory. The *Everyman* tale is an exhaustive literary treatment of this issue. Rather than granting ourselves generous postponements, we ought to be more thrifty with our time by midlife (if not before).

Nevertheless, a certain degree of postponement is appropriate at midlife, as long as it does not become a complete refusal to turn around and begin moving back toward the center of the mandala. Unhealthy postponement is all too likely in the context of a "therapy" that seems so natural and pleasant. Doses of estrogen seem pleasant because they can eliminate all the unpleasant climacteric symptoms and hormonal "therapy" seems natural because the body produced these same hormones for many years and is therefore accustomed to their effects. This form of therapy seems to have brought us somewhat closer to the fulfillment of one of humanity's oldest dreams: the fountain of youth. Voluntarily choosing not to drink from that fabled fountain because one prefers to fulfil life's pattern as fate intended it for us is a choice that requires a great deal of consciousness and, nowadays, a large measure of courage.

The Estrogen Madness

Its Effects on Women

There are still some women who make their way through mid-life without annoying symptoms and without suppressive measures, but this seems to be the exception rather than the rule for women today. Gynecologists describe it as malpractice when one does not offer one's patients the typical symptom-suppressive estrogen therapy. They talk about a menopausal "estrogen deficit," a phraseology that implies that nature or God made an error in the construction of all female beings. The suppression of climacteric symptoms is only one pleasant side effect of such "therapy": the principal purpose of estrogen treatments is to prevent osteoporosis (a weakening of the bones caused by decalcification). But upon closer examination, the "logic" used to justify the therapy turns out to be astonishingly illogical.

A naive person might assume that because calcium is lacking, one ought to prescribe calcium. In most cases, the body does not want to accept doses of calcium. It excretes the added calcium and continues to decalcify the bones. That is why gynecologists resort to the estrogen trick. If levels of feminine hormones are kept artificially high, the organism does not notice that menopause has occurred. Duped into believing it needs to strengthen itself for childbearing, the body begins again to deposit calcium in the bones. Thus women can hide the fact of the climacteric from themselves and the rest of the world. But they are working against the achievement of their goal in life, manipulating their biochemistry so they can continue to cling to the periphery of the mandala. If the focal point of her life lies in action and sports, in proving to her mate or to society how young and active she is, then this therapy is perfect for her. But essentially, it is nothing more than the attempt to bear children at age sixty—an error in timing and a failure to take advantage of one's real opportunities on life's path. This biochemical postponement of menopause is the worst possible preparation for death—the final crisis in life. The complete prevention of menopause (overly eager physicians continue to prescribe these medications for older women and even for eighty-year-old women[76]) obviously interferes with a woman's progress along life's path. Hers is only half a life because its progress has been artificially halted at midlife, and half lives of this kind usually end horribly. It is only natural that death is terrifying when it comes unexpectedly to a body that has been duped into believing itself to be young.

Blinded by the universal euphoria accompanying estrogen therapy, it is difficult to see things in their natural relationships. At first glance, "carpet bombing" with estrogen seems to bring nothing but advantages to everyone involved. The women are no longer troubled by menopausal complaints and are no longer reminded of the unpleasant issue of aging. The gynecologists have plenty of work to do, although (especially rural women) still manage to cope with menopause and their lives without the assistance of gynecologists and their medications. Last but not least, the pharmaceutical industry is pleased as punch over the magnitude of this opportunity to offer chemical help. A naive observer might wonder how billions of women, from Eve all the way to those of the last generation, managed to cope with menopause without the benefit of hormonal therapy. Gynecologists are ready with massive justifications: never before have women lived so long! First of all, this assertion is factually false, since the life expectancy for forty-year-olds is no longer climbing, but has begun to decline slightly. That life expectancies are increasing overall is due to the continuing decline in infant mortality. Secondly, in the past, countless women lived long enough to experience menopause and grew old in dignity without developing the characteristically rounded "witch's" or "widow's" back that typically accompanies osteoporosis.[77]

Some gynecologists use these and other justifications as their chief arguments to frighten women (a tactic they have already used successfully in their campaign for hysterectomies). Without estrogen, they say, an older woman will surely become a hunchbacked witch. Threats like these can frighten even the most rational woman into obedience. A hunched back can develop in old age through the collapse of overburdened vertebrae. Such collapses do occur, but surely not as frequently as the estrogen prophets would have women believe. Furthermore, the spine is not the only organ that shows the effects of osteoporosis. The neck of the femur as well as other bones are likewise vulnerable. No other part of the body is better suited than the spine for inducing fear. When the spine curves into a hump, everyone can see just how many years a woman has "carried on her shoulders," and nowadays most women would prefer to conceal (or at least not to emphasize) their true age.

Although osteoporosis has been so frequently diagnosed in recent years, there is good reason to doubt that the ailment is a new phenomenon. It seems likely that the disease has always existed and caused similar symptoms, but that no one conducted research designed to reveal its presence. In any case, a sudden increase in the number of elderly people developing hunched backs did not occur in the years prior to the introduction of estrogen therapy. It seems more likely that bodies that had reached the climacteric phase naturally began casting off ballast in order to make their homeward journey easier. The tasks at hand in this phase of life do not require such a sturdy and weighty skeletal framework. The fact that elderly bodies do not assimilate calcium supplements lends support to this idea. The organism is not suffering from a lack of calcium; rather, the body has a surplus of calcium for its age that it removes and excretes.

Only through deliberate misleading and through attempts to imitate an earlier phase in life with hormonal supplements can the body by tricked into assimilating calcium and building heavy bones again.

If a person fails to comprehend her own situation in the pattern of life and fails to understand the necessity of casting off ballast at midlife in order to ease the burden for the homeward journey, then the body can jump in to fill the gap and compensate by making itself unduly light. If that happens, the individual has a problem. This cannot be solved by lying to oneself about one's age, but can only be solved when one begins to take account of one's true age and starts living accordingly. Chemically preventing the body from manifesting the problem will only lead it to appear elsewhere since it must express itself somewhere. Making it impossible to manifest the problem cannot lead to its solution. Somewhere and somehow, the individual at this stage of life must cast off ballast and learn to let go. In some cases, she will be forced to let go in a metaphorical sense, compelled to surrender things that previously seemed important but are not essential for the homeward journey. Destiny will do everything in its power to teach the individual the lessons of letting go and turning about. The question will soon arise: isn't it much easier and more pleasant to yield to the natural pattern and pay one's tribute at the site where it was originally demanded?

Of course, this problem also affects men at midlife, but they have the good fortune that our society has far fewer "andrologists" than gynecologists. If there were more "men's doctors," we would no doubt find that older men's bones also suffer from a certain degree of decalcification and that a profitable business could be developed by selling the corresponding therapies and medications. As a side effect, androgen supplements might help combat the loss of motivation and the waning of sexual desire that frequently accompanies "male menopause." If sixty-year-old women are still able to bear children, perhaps something should be done to help sixty-year-old men? Fortunately for the men, it is well-known that, although androgen supplements can help shrink a swollen prostate, they can also trigger prostate cancer. Estrogen supplements increase the likelihood of breast cancer, but gynecologists combat that side effect by simultaneously prescribing progesterone supplements.

Basically, the regressive tendency is quite understandable. If a person cannot cope with greater demands, he is likely to react by retreating to the next lower level where life was easier to handle. Unborn babies react similarly when, shortly before birth, they turn themselves around and aim their heads toward the familiar safety of the womb. Boys and girls on the threshold of puberty display corresponding behavior when they suddenly discover that children of the opposite gender are stupid and silly, and that it is much more fun to play childish games with peers of their own gender. Teenagers manifest the regressive tendency when they find dozens of plausible reasons to justify their decision to delay moving out of their parents' houses. Regression is a favorite tactic among people facing midlife crisis, too. As a transitional step and accompanied by an alert mind, hormonal supplements can be a reasonable measure. But it is a sad situation when physicians, of all people, conspire with their patients by helping them refuse to make the essential reversal.

In our society, it is common for people to suddenly stop progressing after reaching the midpoint of their lives. The most grotesque aspect of this is that we refuse to halt or take a breather in other fields of life. The tendency is fundamentally wrongheaded, of course, because destiny and the wheel of life continue to turn inexorably onward, irregardless of whether we comprehend what is happening. A few human beings have always sought to cling to certain points in the natural developmental cycles but their attempts have never succeeded for very long, nor can they succeed. Our era is characterized by an unprecedented addiction to life, a collective addiction that includes the widespread refusal to confront the entirety of the developmental path. When one considers how many years went by before the medical establishment abandoned its nonsensical attempts to chemically reduce cholesterol levels[78] (a reduction that brought comparatively few advantages), we can expect the worst with respect to the estrogen fad. It is likely to endure for a long time, leading people astray and diverting them from facing the facts. The few medical doubts are played down. At gynecologists' conferences one sometimes overhears people admit that hormonal protection loses much of its efficacy by the seventy-fifth year of life, the age at which most bone fractures occur. In the meantime, medical opinion has progressed still further and recognized that "the administration of estrogens alone is not indicated, at least not for women who have not had hysterectomies, because estrogens encourage constant proliferation along the endometrium."[79] In other words, if estrogen supplements are taken by women who, for one reason or another, have thus far refused to submit to the removal of their uteruses, they are likely to experience a continual build up of tissue along the mucous membranes inside their uterus because the womb continues to prepare itself for the implantation of a fertilized egg. To prevent this undesired buildup and to reduce the risk of breast cancer associated with estrogen supplements, gynecologists generally prescribe progesterone along with estrogen. This reduces the risk of cancer, but causes the resumption of menstrual bleeding. Since this bleeding finally makes it clear to women that something is not in order, Professor Husmann suggests that the two medications should be administered separately "to those women who prefer not to experience the resumption of menstrual bleeding."[80] In this case, the uterus' mucous membranes should be regularly checked with ultrasound tests. "If bleeding nonetheless begins, an *abrasio* (scraping) is unavoidable."[81]

Progesterone, however, causes even more side effects than estrogen which, although gynecologists are loathe to admit it, leads to a generalized weight gain[82] and to swelling and a sense of tension in the breasts. "Progesterone can cause nausea, dizziness, discomfort and headaches. But these complaints can be minimized if the medication is taken before going to bed."[83] A detailed interpretation of these symptoms can be found in *Krankheit als Sprache der Seele* (*Illness as a Language of the Soul*).

Basically, the appearance of these symptoms shows that this form of therapy is a *swindle* (the German words for "dizziness" and "swindle" are identical). The advice to take these symptoms to bed with them—where they can sleep through them and supposedly not notice them—is understandable, but also reveals just who the father of such a "therapy" truly is. In any case, this is a therapy that will not leave physicians out of work in the future.

Naturally, it is only the more sensitive women who must struggle with such symptoms. They have a particularly difficult row to hoe, since menopause also causes a reduction in the level of endogenous opioids (the body's own "opium"), which in turn makes these women more sensitive to pain and discomfort. Like all other changes in life, this enhanced sensitivity can be experienced as both a burden and as an opportunity.

Effects on the Environment—Ecological Burdens of a New Sort

Since therapy with female hormones brings (superficial) advantages to everyone involved (i.e., to the women, who are now free from symptoms and able to ignore the fact of menopause; and to the gynecologists and pharmaceutical industry, who thereby create work and income for themselves; to the husbands of the patients, who can keep their familiarly docile and low-care housewives), it would seem that this ill-conceived custom will continue to be a fixed feature of a genre of medicine whose prime goal lies in avoidance. The only foreseeable help could potentially come from environmental activists because modern medicine's estrogen madness affects the environment and, through the environment, is beginning to affect human beings to an increasing extent. Along with the vast quantities of hormones ostensibly prescribed to discourage osteoporosis, another major source of hormones is in the contraceptive drugs taken by so many women. Since the female body does not entirely absorb and neutralize these hormones, the substances pass into the women's urine and from there, via wastewater, into the environment. Over the years, people whose faith in progress is less than complete have warned that these hormonal emissions are not entirely harmless. More recently, hard facts have begun to accumulate. Naturalists are distressed to discover that the bald eagle, the national bird of the United States, is no longer able to reproduce and that alligators in Florida are suffering the same fate. Both of these species will become extinct in this generation. The highly alarming cause of the infertility lies in peculiar mutations in the sexual organs of the males of these species. The situation becomes all the more frightening when we learn that many biologists trace the cause of the mutations to pollution of water with female hormones. It is only a matter of time before human beings will be affected.

In fact, it seems as though that time has already come, although the negative effects are most evident in animals that rely solely on marine life for their food. The average sperm content in male ejaculations has declined by thirty percent since 1940 (i.e., from 113 to 66 million spermatozoa per milliliter). Professor R. Dougherty from Tallahassee University in Florida believes that by the year 2000 approximately half of all American men will have become infertile. At present, more than twenty percent of the men in industrialized nations are already infertile. There are three million infertile couples in Germany alone. Despite the fact that in most of these cases, it is the man who is responsible for the couple's inability to conceive children, far more women than men are treated for infertility. This discrepancy is not solely due to the greater number of doctors who specialize in women's health than men's, but is partly due to the fact that women are more likely to seek help when they feel they may be infertile. Infertile men are less likely to suffer from childlessness than from fears that their masculinity is threatened. As a result, they tend to avoid doctors whose medical tests might confirm those fears. In many cases, *she* has already had her fallopian tubes cleared more than once before *he* finally agrees to have his sperm count tested. The latter procedure requires no surgical intervention, but only a brief and painless return to the masturbation habits of puberty.

Undoubtedly other factors also play a role but, in the face of incontrovertible clinical evidence, the attempt to attribute the whole problem to the effects of stress (the universal scapegoat for a host of ills) is simply no longer believable. Stress is nothing new. Paleolithic man, cowering in his cave and poorly protected from savage predators, suffered from environmental stress, too. However, despite that stress, he proved eminently able to father offspring—an ability to which we owe our own existence. In general, we would do well to absolve stress of its thankless scapegoat role and begin looking more carefully at the situation. Is it not a tremendous stress on a male organism to try to maintain his masculinity in an environment that has become artificially saturated with female hormones?

Rather than facing the world with feminine thinking, we inundate it with feminine hormones. Our dealings with femininity per se have fallen much too far into the material plane. If we do not wake up soon and quit interfering with the balance of nature, infertility could provide an unexpected solution to the worldwide problem of overpopulation. We are currently hard at work solving that problem, albeit unconsciously, through global contraception that follows a surprisingly roundabout route from the pharmaceutical industry, through women's urine, into the water supply and ultimately into male gonads.

Animus and Anima

The reversal in the pattern of life applies not only to the direction of the route, but also to gender roles. C.G. Jung believed every woman should attend to the needs of her soul's male component (the so-called "animus") and that every man must learn to accept his soul's feminine aspects as they appear in the form of the so-called "anima." This integration of the opposite pole is hardly an important theme during the first half of life since, at that phase, both genders already have enough trouble coping with the role into which they were born. In the second half of life, however, the time comes for reversal. The inborn gender role has (hopefully) been integrated; and the individual faces the task of integrating the opposite gender aspects of the soul. Only people who already feel secure in their inborn roles and who adequately live out those roles will have the ability to actualize the opposite role within themselves. This is the goal esoteric philosophers describe as the "alchemical wedding."

Serious problems arise when individuals turn toward their opposite poles too early (i.e., before they have adequately manifested their same-gender aspects). Men degenerate into softies and even emancipated women (whose emancipation these men originally championed) find softies unattractive. The reason is simple: soft men tend to remain soft through and through, a situation that brings little pleasure to her or to him, at least not in primal masculine parts of his anatomy. Women who fail to adequately embody their same-gender archetype degenerate into amazons whom neither men nor women find attractive. Outwardly, they stand tall, face life "like a man" and deny every feminine weakness within themselves, but they frequently overlook the fact that their true strengths lie precisely here. In the end, this process usually fails to achieve genuine masculine toughness, but leads only to the loss of feminine softness.

The ideal situation would be to wait for the right time and then, without hesitation, courageously follow the impulses rising from within the depths of one's soul. The task tends toward the image of a hermaphroditic soul that harmoniously unites both poles, masculine and feminine, within itself. From a physical point of view, such an individual would be a pitiful creature, neither fish nor flesh, but from a spiritual point of view, the hermaphrodite represents the acme of development.

If people refuse to accept this task in life, the issue (as is often the case) descends into the body and makes itself unpleasantly apparent. Beards begin to sprout on women's faces and their facial expressions grow more severe. The phenomenon is so common that the Germans have an idiom ("lady's beard") to

describe it. The battle against the emergence of masculine energies only proves that the message has arrived and that its
recipient refuses to accept it. She individually plucks each hair
with a tweezers as if it were her personal enemy. But destiny is
resolutely determined to insist upon the pattern of life, and the
hairs continue to sprout. Men in this situation begin to develop
breasts and their facial expressions become softer. Idiomatic
phrases describe them no less accurately than disrespectfully
as a "womanly old man."

The solution is easier in theory than in practice. In a spiritual
sense, one must grow into one's opposite pole. In the relationship with one's mate, that means moving toward a switch in
roles—for which the limits are quickly evident. If *he* continues to
insist on being the only one to "wear the pants," her evolution
toward her animus is a potential threat to the partnership. Unless
both partners simultaneously embark on the search for animus
and anima, severe animosities are likely to emerge.

Husbands who oppose their wives' evolution are another
group that benefits when their wives are treated with estrogen
therapy. Estrogen is, in a manner of speaking, the feminine part
of the feminine sex hormone. Both genders have both poles
within them, and they also have hormones of both genders. A
woman who takes estrogen is getting a dose of an emphatically
feminine hormone. The effects of progesterone, on the other
hand, are more in the male direction. Both substances, however,
are ultimately female hormones. Estrogen has the upper hand
from puberty to menopause and progesterone begins to dominate and gradually leads to changes in the soul that pave the
way for a woman's conquest of her animus. Her conquest of her
own masculinity can pose a challenge to her husband if he insists on standing his ground and refuses to proceed with his own
evolution. Estrogens keep women pleasantly supple and peace-
able; the decline of their influence on her can be interpreted by
her husband as a threatening new development.

The complementary situation (i.e., when a man begins to devote his attention to his anima despite the fact that his wife is

unready to accept responsibility for her male pole) can confront her with the unpleasant and unaccustomed challenges of making her own decisions and asserting herself. She may no longer feel as protected and defended by him as she felt in the past. When he discovers his soft side, his martial instincts decline. She may welcome the disappearance of his cockily masculine strut, but might also have to accept a collateral loss of chivalry in his behavioral patterns.

On the other hand, if both partners are willing to grow *with one another*, this developmental phase can provide enormous opportunities for growth. A teen's innocent question of a prospective sweetheart, "Will you go steady with me?" develops a far more profound meaning when mature spouses ask it of one another during this phase of life. Each can guide the other into the new territory his mate is about to enter and explore. In the ideal case, each has already fully explored the same-gender archetype and can therefore serve the other as a guide. He already knows the animus that is so new for her, and she is already familiar with the anima that he is in the process of discovering. In the best case, their inner planes grow progressively similar. The understanding they show for one another leads to unquestioning trust in each other. Each has already discovered everything within his own self, and the remainder of their lives together is pure luxury. Because they no longer need one another, the pleasure they derive from being together is greater than ever before.

This process of becoming more and more alike can also manifest as a problem: having settled on the least common denominator, the partners may cling to one another and exclude everything and everyone else. The basic mood in this case is one of anxious resignation rather than courage. Such couples stick together like fire and smoke, whereas open-minded couples leave more space in their relationships and enjoy correspondingly more room for shared growth. They do not experience their spouses' progress as a personal threat since they are aware that a spouse's advance into new spiritual territory will ultimately help to expand *both* their horizons. One spouse's progress helps to expand and enrich the life both spouses share.

Reconciliation with one's opposite pole frequently comes only after, for whatever reason, a spouse has been left alone. Left on her own, the lone individual suddenly discovers the tasks and challenges implicit in all those areas of life that had previously been the exclusive and unquestioned province of her spouse.

Questions about Midlife Crisis

1. How do I deal with the middle of my day?
    - Do I allow myself the luxury of an afternoon nap?
    - Do I take a long lunch break?
    - Do I give myself time to regenerate?
    - Or is my midday break just long enough for quick "fast-food style" interruption?
2. How do I react when I'm on vacation and realize that half of the vacation is over?
3. What does "halftime" in sports mean to me?
4. Do I have the tendency to bring things to completion?
5. Do I have a good sense for knowing when the time has come to turn around—for example, while hiking, biking or mountain climbing?

Exercises

1. A festival to celebrate arrival at life's midpoint.
2. Consciously taking stock: celebrate what one has attained and become consciously aware of as "unfinished business."
3. Clarify one's goals for the future.
4. Study the map of life's path and especially the route leading back to the center of the mandala; draw or paint the important episodes of the outward path within the initially empty circle of a mandala.
5. Mandala exercise:
    - Draw or paint a mandala from the periphery toward the center (choose the colors blindfolded?)

- Draw or paint a mandala together with one's partner from the periphery toward the center; the partners alternate, each drawing one concentric layer. Draw or paint simultaneously and observe your reactions when you feel that your boundaries have been trespassed upon.

6. Take a long, sober look at the return path; strive to achieve an orderly retreat.

7. Exercises to strengthen equilibrium and the center: meditation, tai chi, working with clay as it turns on a potter's wheel.

8. Meditation on issues that have not yet been adequately lived out, especially on related to the opposite-gender pole.

9. Give away or give back your work clothes; give away or give back the tools and symbols of your trade.

10. Ritualistically pass along responsibility: pass the conductor's baton, the scepter, the deed of ownership or the torch to the next generation.

11. Give your old sporting equipment to a younger person.

12. Consciously remove or update old name plates or office signs.

13. Consciously sacrifice the symbols of life's first half; find new symbols for the second half of life.

14. Rituals of taking stock: recognize and complete those items your ambition tells you are still unfinished.

15. Climb small hills and celebrate the ritual of reversal when you reach the peak; experience the midpoint of the stroll as the high point of your walk.

16. Learn to enjoy a break or nap at midday.

17. A deliberate sojourn in solitude can complement the phase of wandering through no-man's land, a phase that is stronger during midlife than during any other crisis. Meditate and introspect about life's progress; give yourself plenty of time.

18. Use the yin-yang symbol as the center of a daily meditation.

19. Reserve one room in your house for issues related to regeneration and the homeward journey.

20. Go without sleeping an entire night and observe the transitions that occur in nature: the gradual decline of daylight in the evening and its steady return at dawn. As the night darkens in the early evening, your meditation can focus on the things you must leave behind; as dawn begins to brighten the sky, allow those issues to emerge within you that can fill and fulfill your future years.

21. Cast off ballast: lose excess pounds through fasting; shrink yourself down to a healthy size for the homeward journey.

22. Modify your diet to emphasize lighter foods that are more appropriate for a less strenuous lifestyle.

23. Midlife exercises for people who own a garden:

- Cultivate a plot of ground, but do not sow seeds yourself: simply wait until next spring and see what plants appear.

- Dig a hole for a pond and then just let it be: allow life and nature to run its course; use the site as a place for contemplation.

- Partially or entirely transform a vegetable garden into a low-maintenance flower garden; give "weeds" a chance to grow.

- Stop pruning trees and let them follow their own "unproductive" path; stop cutting the lawn and allow a flowery meadow to grow in its place.

11. Old Age

Human beings wouldn't live seventy or eighty years
if this longevity made no sense for our species.
Hence, the noontide of our lives ought to have a
meaning and a purpose; it cannot be merely a pitiful
appendix
clinging to life's morning.
The meaning of morning is undoubtedly
our development as individuals, our anchorage
and reproduction in the outer world and our caring
for our offspring....
Anyone who takes the law of the morning,
(i.e., the natural purpose of the morning) and
needlessly
drags it into life's afternoon, must pay for it
with one's soul.... Earning money, social life, family,
offspring are mere nature; they are not yet culture.
Culture transcends the necessities of mere nature.
Could culture be the meaning and purpose
of life's second half?
In primitive tribes, for example, we see
that it is almost always the elders who safeguard the
mysteries
and laws; and it is above all through them
that the tribe's culture expresses itself.
What is the situation in our own culture?
Where is the wisdom of our elders?

*Where are their mysteries and the visions of their
dreams?*
—C.G. Jung, The Turning Point in Life

After the crisis of midlife and the time of harvest comes the conscious or unconscious leave-taking we call "old age." Because most people try to deny it, this bidding adieu is more likely to take place unconsciously. Almost everyone in our society wants to live a long life, but no one, it seems, wants to be old. This contradiction inevitably leads to problems.

Since despite numerous attempts we have been unable to prevent aging, we use every means at our disposal to fight its effects and erase its traces. No one is supposed to get the idea that she is elderly. Being regarded as *old and obsolete* is just about the worse thing that can happen to a person. As soon as an unmistakable sign of age appears, we rush in to retouch it or paint it over. Cosmetics that "cover everything" and leave the old skin to suffer its fate beneath a youthful patina are the mildest treatment. The cosmetic industry cleverly capitalizes on our fear of the bugbear called "old age" and sells so-called "age-control creams" to gullible consumers. The notion that smearing such salves onto one's face can control (i.e., put a stop to) aging is as patently ridiculous as the idea that buying life insurance can increase the span of one's life. The global war on wrinkles unites the entire Western world. Seen from the viewpoint of the power and honor old age ought to entail, the daily reports of new breakthroughs and victories against wrinkles are debunked as ridiculous. Nevertheless, subcutaneous injections are still administered to smooth out individual wrinkles; panaceas of all sorts are applied to (irreversibly) aged skin; and dozens of facial masks try to relax and resuscitate one's face, only to find that the *good old days* are here and now in one's *good old face*.

If all these cosmetic approaches have not helped make us any wiser, we can visit a plastic surgeon and have our face's sagging skin stretched a little tighter. This works well enough once or twice, but after one too many face lifts, the facial skin has been stretched so taut it becomes difficult or impossible to close our eyelids. Nature and our biological clock are telling us that it is time to relax and "hang loose," but we and our plastic surgeons apparently have something else in mind.

Whatever we have allowed to go slack can be surgically lifted, and those lifts are not confined to facial skin. If our muscle tone no longer suffices to maintain the tension in one or another part of the body, plastic surgeons are eager to jump in and fill the gap. They stretch the skin on our foreheads taut as a drum, although a couple of thoughtful wrinkles really would not look all that out of place. When the furrows on our cheeks etched by a lifetime of smiles are excised and smoothed over, does it mean that the days of cramp-free laughter are also gone? Life's traces are surgically erased. The unwept tears that have collected in little bags under our eyes are amputated and we are, quite literally, cut off from the sorrow we have not yet lived out.

Excess fat, accumulated during the years we used material abundance to compensate for our soul's undernourishment, is vacuumed away. Gone are the double chin, the "spare tire" belly, the Rubens buttocks and other ample things.[84] Postural training helps hide the years that have accumulated on our shoulders and, if all else fails, we can support the old organism with elastic corsets. If the accoutrements of eternal youth threaten to fall out (as they so often do on men's pates), then toupees, implants or hair weaving camouflage the bald truth with a hirsute falsehood we vainly believe is more handsome.

Anything that ages and loses its youthful shape must be replaced, or at least be so well restored that no one will notice its real age. Those who know horses also know that the surest way to judge a horse's age is by looking in its mouth. Aging humans (and dentists) know this, too, so they do their best to imitate youthful teeth. A jaw that is, in fact, a graveyard can be dressed up to look like a new playground. A mouth full of youthful, radiantly white teeth in an old face may seem rather out of place, but who cares? Worn-out joints can be replaced before their owners allow themselves and their rusty joints a well-earned rest. When cataracts[85] lay a gray veil over our eyesight and life's vivid colors begin to grow dim, we hurry to the surgeon and exchange our cloudy old retinas for limpid new ones. If necessary, kidneys, livers and hearts can be removed and exchanged for newer organs. Most of these spare parts come from cadavers—a fact that might help us take a step toward honesty if we were not so eager to enjoy our new organs rather than brood over their macabre origins. Although their original owners are long dead, we refuse to let them die. They live on inside us, where they help enliven the deathly impression we make.

If we imagine old age without all the fakery and without all the prostheses (from the Greek word *prosthesis* meaning "to append, show or pretend")—the technical ones such as eyeglasses, dentures, artificial joints and artificial heart valves, as well as the organic ones modern medicine borrows from cadavers—then old age would again show the genuine, frightening face that we put it. Lameness and decrepitude would surround us, continually holding the mirror of our own mortality before our eyes. Of course, this is only an imaginary experiment. It does not mean it would be better to dispense with all the aids and prostheses, and stop visiting our dentists or orthopedists. It is only meant to emphasize the magnitude of our struggle against old age. It is perfectly reasonable to get a good set of "third teeth" — as long as we do not allow our dentures to seduce us into ignoring the real tasks facing us in this phase of our lives.

We can more or less camouflage the effects aging has on our bodies but, when it comes to the soul, each of us must directly confront old age. The more we try to hide the exterior trappings of our real age, the harder it hits us inwardly. There is no reason an old Amerindian woman who has learned to wear her wrinkles with dignity cannot become young at heart once more. But because we deprive old age of every chance to express itself outwardly, we are all the more vulnerable and terrified of age as it manifests in an unresolved and ugly form.

The commandment to honor the elderly dates from a long-gone era when advanced age and old people represented something special. Nowadays we "honor" old people, if at all, with patently transparent lies, assuring them that things are not all that bad *yet*—a phrase that indirectly asserts our certainty that it will get bad *later* and that the time will come when they will be ready for the scrap heap. The culprit is the monosyllabic modifier "yet": "You don not look old *yet,*" "You don't look your age *yet*" or, worst of all, "He's still got the mind and spirit of a boy." This last statement places puerile immaturity above maturity and ripeness, a value judgment that is, unfortunately, as typical as it is ridiculous. We no longer respect old age, but revere instead the skill some elderly people use to avoid revealing their real age.

Our society is so out of kilter that it is not uncommon for people whose children have just borne children to become depressed rather than take pleasure in the honor and new challenges that accompany being a grandmother or grandfather. They equate being a grandparent with being old, and may even be annoyed with their children for having made them into "premature grandparents." It comes as no surprise to find that grandparents' relationships with their grandchildren are likely to suffer from the oldsters' anxieties about growing old. The intimacy between grandparents and grandchildren ought to foster the process of becoming "like little children." The two generations can encounter one another on a more profound level in life's mandala. Although they are each moving in opposite directions, they nevertheless meet in the same sphere. This is also why the understanding between these two generations is often deeper than what exists between parents and children. Parents and children are moving in the same direction, but they occupy completely different locations in the mandala of life.

The similarities between life's beginning and its end are strikingly profound. These two phases adjoin one another in the mandala. One issues from, and the other returns to, the same central point. Both phases directly transition into one another on the mandala's spiral. If it were not for the wonders of modern dentistry, what began without teeth would very likely end without teeth. This means that the capacity for aggression must gradually push its way through our gums and into the world soon after our life begins, and that the capacity for aggression gradually diminishes before life's end. Aggression is the power behind every new beginning. It should grow strong at the outset of life but, by life's end, it has already served its purpose and we have less need of it.

Homeopathy frequently prescribes the same medications for infants that it prescribes for geriatric patients. Elderly people do indeed move through the same stages of development infants experience, but they do so in the opposite direction. This process of "becoming like little children" can take place on the non-reconciled (and hence unpleasant) bodily plane or in a reconciled manner on the spiritual/intellectual plane. Physically, the tottering gait of a young child who is learning to walk can resemble the shuffling gait of the elderly before they lie down for the last time. Garbled speech occurs at life's beginning and at its end. The diapers that are necessary during the first months of life may again be needed in its last days. The immune system that was weak at the beginning may again grow weak toward the end.

Certain similarities are also evident on the plane of the soul. Chatterbox little children cannot keep still while elderly people sometimes maintain a permanent soliloquy. Both our youngest and our eldest citizens drool at mealtime. However, the same behavior we pardon or even find charming in infants is generally viewed with far less pleasure and compassion when it is exhibited by the elderly.

An essential link between the beginning and the end lies, for example, in the absence of the compulsion to achieve and in relief from the enormous pressure built up at the periphery of life's mandala. Even in a high-pressure society, when a person nears the center of the mandala, life becomes much easier. Old people once again have time to tell stories, and young children still have time to listen to their elders. These are the phases in life when the seriousness of life either has not begun or has already come to end—the seasons when fun and joy can be relished most fully. There is no schedule yet, or no schedule any more, so introspection and a midday nap are possible whenever one wishes. Those around us who are still torturing themselves with the earnestness of life may even be happy to see us napping since the hardworking folks between infancy and old age are glad to be free from the youngest and the oldest who make no material contributions but so readily throw sand in the gears of busy life. Like tiny infants, old people have plenty of time to gaze in rapture at the miracle of creation—with old eyes that seem young once more.

The marks of age we regard as our enemies can, in fact, become our best friends. When we look at photos in a family album that remind us of important events that have left their marks on us, we do not generally regard those pictures as our enemies. But as long as we continue to view aging as an adversary, we will never reconcile ourselves to our childhood since those two phases belong so close together.

We do not yet take children all that seriously and we do not take the elderly seriously anymore. Perhaps that is why the hard-won, humane laws and rules of society are often called into question when the time comes to apply them to the unborn or the very old. Even as we (falsely) accuse archaic peoples of having exiled and abandoned their elderly to a lonely death, we ourselves do precisely that to our elderly. The artificial extension of life in old-age homes is little more than a euphemism for banishment and abandonment. Seldom do the elderly feel *at home* in these so-called "homes." Far too often, the institutions are merely holding tanks that satisfy their inhabitants' material needs but ignore everything that is truly necessary. Their chief task is not to care for the elderly, but simply to get them out our way, take them off the shoulders of their younger relatives and keep them somewhere where we do not have to look at them. People who fear aging themselves prefer not to be confronted

with old age in the faces of their elderly relatives since the encounter only reminds them of the ill-suppressed certainty of their
own mortality.

"Storing" and ultimately exiling our youngest citizens into
day-care centers, nursery schools, kindergartens and the like
follows an essentially similar pattern. Just as old-age homes
seldom help their residents to close accounts with the life that
lies behind them, nurseries seldom help their little charges to
open accounts with the life awaiting them. More often than not,
nurseries are little more than legal and socially acceptable ex-
pedients for temporarily getting the toddlers *out of our way* because they so often get *in the way* in our achievement-oriented,
production-oriented society. And since the tots do manage to
learn a few things "in storage," we need not have a guilty conscience about having dropped them off there. The reconciled
and non-reconciled planes intersect here.

The issue becomes even clearer when we consider how we
sometimes deal with human beings during still earlier or still later
phases of their lives. At the outset, when accepting a new life
may seem inconvenient, we are more or less at liberty to abort it
as we wish; near life's end, on the other hand, we are somewhat
less direct, although we may catch ourselves thinking about how
to put an early end to the misery. Abortion and euthanasia both
relate to the same area in life's mandala.

Symptoms Associated with Aging

Phenomena that are typically associated with aging need not
always manifest themselves. We note their absence in some
of our German aged, as well as in elderly Native Americans or
Africans. Phenomena such as farsightedness in old age[86] or
nearsightedness in youth are typical only for our era and our social system. This symptom compels young people to look more

closely at their immediate surroundings. Rather than gazing into the future, the nearsighted young person is more or less forced to take whatever lies nearest at hand as his task in life. The distant future, toward which he all too idealistically yearns, is blurry and out-of-focus. At the same time, nearsightedness also casts a gauzy veil over the future so that young people are free to dream their unrealistic dreams without being disturbed by a clear perception of life's hard edges and sharp corners.

Farsightedness literally takes the daily newspaper *out of the hands* of the elderly. Are their eyes failing or their arms getting shorter? The elderly need to hold an object at arm's length (or further away) in order to see it clearly. Their task is to separate themselves from the immediate vicinity and allow their gaze to peer into the distance, where they can get the "big picture." Rather than brooding on close-lying trifles, the elderly are better advised to evolve synoptic outlooks for life as a whole. Farsightedness makes the nearest things appear blurry and indistinct anyway. The idea is to divorce themselves from worrying about mundane details and leave petty, sublunary affairs to the younger folks. The old farmer who has handed the farm over to his son no longer needs to worry about his "daily bread." Because younger people are taking care of that, his realm need no longer be entirely on this earthly plane. In any case, daily chores and cares are no longer his problem.

This attitude ought to be shared by retired people and pensioners in general. In the ideal case, they have planned for their old age, and the government or company they once worked for is taking care of their material needs, thus leaving them time and leisure to focus on other, more important issues (e.g., the well-being of their immortal souls). Although ophthalmologists and opticians vainly struggle against it, farsightedness is the body's attempt to enhance the soul's ability to *see far*. Unfortunately for us, most old people in our society are too unaware to consciously confront this issue since honestly dealing with geriatric farsightedness would entail honestly accepting their advanced age and all its consequences.

When we consider the issue more closely, we see that geriatric *forgetfulness* follows a similar pattern and points in a similar direction. Old people tend to forget those things that are nearest in time, while events in the distant past are more likely to remain clear in their memories. A typical example of this is the old man in a store who has forgotten what he came to buy but who can still recall every detail of his old war stories. These symptoms are trying to tell him that he ought to divorce himself from immediate trifles and turn his attention to the decisive events of his life. It may seem strange or sad, but the fact remains that tales of their wartime experiences often rank among the best things elderly men have to offer. Far from home and in existential danger, the soldier's life gave them a sense of vitality that many have not felt since. Even if loss of memory is caused by senility, cerebral sclerosis or Alzheimer's disease, the amnesia generally progresses according to the same pattern: the trivial details of daily life are forgotten first while the larger, overall scheme of life persists much longer. This pattern is especially clear in morbus Alzheimer, the most serious form of the ailment. This disease confronts us with an accelerated and often premature intensification of the aging process. Its sudden increase in our society is yet another indication that we have a collective problem with aging itself.

All these illness and their accompanying symptoms embody the loss of egoistic capabilities. As the brain's strength gradually declines, the ailing individuals are progressively forced into the present moment. The lack of distance reveals the breakdown of ego boundaries in the most extreme way. Just as spiritual crises reveal the kinds of problems that can arise when one rushes rashly ahead on the spiritual path, symptoms associated with senility show that the time is overdue to begin surrendering the ego and that the body has stepped in to sacrifice the ego's corporeal basis. In this case, as well, it would be far better to tread the path voluntarily on the level of the mind and soul rather than letting physical decline compel us to tread it with our bodies.

Arteriosclerosis[87] of the brain exacerbates forgetfulness and gradually leads to a loss of many other cerebral functions. Phylogenetic development is retarded as the elderly individual is cast back into the world of emotions and feelings where, it seems, she must do remedial work on issues that were neglected earlier. On the other hand, the saturnine qualities of hardening and ossification are reconciled through clarity, structure, simplicity and a return to essentials. For the individuals and those around them, the task of learning these emotional lessons is often a burdensome imposition in our mostly cool and intellectual modern world. The old-age home is frequently the only option for rescuing the situation, even though such institutions are not able to truly rescue old people. The hardness and the structure of limestone are clearly evident in the symbolism of sclerosis, as are the lessons of clarity and structure that must be learned. Saturn (the principle of time and old age) uncompromisingly demands the tribute he will inevitably receive in one form or another.

The hunched spine that sometimes accompanies aging clearly shows how severely life and its burdens have bent the old person under their weight and the extent to which the individual has acquiesced to them. It indicates that the weight fate (or we ourselves) have placed upon our shoulders has caused us to bend or even break. Inadequate flexibility, harshness toward oneself and the demands of life all express themselves in this symptom. A person who voluntarily bends under the burden is apt to be less severely bent or broken by fate. In any case, the hunched spine shows that pride has been defeated. Of course, the body itself cannot tell us to what degree this outward expression of humility corresponds to an inner attitude. It does, however, reveal the underlying theme with unmistakable clarity.

Fracture of the neck of the femur suggests unduly wild leaps and, since it is always caused by a fall, this break also alludes to the primal human issue of falling. The spectrum of falls can run the gamut from original sin to an unprepared plunge from the career ladder. The accident imposes rest and immobility, and gives the person time to think about any metaphorical accidents he has not yet recognized and understood. Only *old bones* are susceptible to so-called "fatigue fractures," a fact that suggests that one's bones need to rest and conserve their strength for the inner evolutionary work that lies ahead. More clearly than any other fracture, this typical geriatric symptom reveals the breakdown of a rigid form and posture. A pattern of living or a concept about life that has run on the same old track for decades is abruptly interrupted. The lesson could not be more clear: the time has come to abandon old structures. By compelling the individual to remain physically inactive, it gives the person a chance to get things moving again inside. As far as the location of the fracture is concerned, the symbolism suggests that the issue involves walking and thus one's path. A person with a broken hip cannot "step out of line" or overstep certain boundaries guarded by Saturn. On the other hand, when the fracture makes it impossible to take another step in the outer world, it can open a path for inner progress.

The decline or complete failure of the organs of the senses suggests that the time has come to divorce ourselves from the outer world and turn inward, focusing our gaze on inner images and visions.

Blindness compels us to devote ourselves to introspection. Both the mandala and traditional Christianity agree that, at this stage in life, all solutions lie within. Jesus says, "The kingdom of God is within you" (Luke 17:21). When the colors of the outer world begin to fade, it is time to look at the "inner colors," the primordial vitality inside oneself. Mythology offers many examples of blindness among great seers (e.g., Tiresias, who prophesied Odysseus' fate). Blind to the appearances of the outside world, they were able to look within, into the otherworld that lies behind external phenomena. Old age and the approach of death point toward the otherworld. The task is to move from mere looking to true *seeing*, to develop the introspection that has less need of physical sense organs because it is independent of the outer world.

Deafness means that one must listen to one's inner voice, which is more important for one's subsequent evolution than all outer voices combined. If it is experienced with resistance and unconsciousness and without understanding, deafness can cause depression and desperation. But if it is freely and consciously accepted, loss of hearing can catalyze a profound contact with one's inner essence. It can be the best preparation for life's final crisis, when all essential advice about the path comes from within. A person who has learned to gaze within, to listen inwardly and to obey the inner voice is well-equipped to confront this last crisis. The threat of deafness indicates that the individual needs to work on the issue of listening to, and obeying, the urgings of the inner voice. Deafness jeopardizes people who cannot listen and obey as well as people who have only listened to sounds in the outer world. The solution lies in attending to and obeying the inner voice. By obeying that voice's wise guidance and counsel, the individual is free to continue on her true spiritual path.

The sense of taste also becomes less acute as we grow older. In a metaphorical sense, this is sometimes evident in the charming "tastelessness" of the furnishings in elderly people's homes that can rival or even exceed the poor taste with which children furnish their bedrooms. The tendency to crowd the home with collections of superfluous things can be a sign the individual has not sufficiently heeded the advice of Saturn (who embodies the principle of old age) to begin paring things down to the bare essentials. The ultimate issue is not one of taste, but one of reduction and simplicity. Memories need to be internalized rather than mummified as souvenirs in a showcase. The external counterparts of whatever cannot be kept alive within oneself ought to be let go of or given to one's grandchildren. After all, whatever is still alive and vital inside us cannot be given away on the outer plane. The kingdom of the aged is no longer in this world: it lies within—where, according to Christ, the kingdom of God is to be found.

As the outwardly directed senses decline, so too does the world of *maya*,[88] whose two great illusions (i.e., space and time) decline in importance. When these sources of illusion are deposed, inner evolution can proceed more easily. When the veil of Isis[89] drops away from things, they can appear within us in their true forms, and their genuine essence can manifest more clearly. No longer distracted by the objects of the outer senses, it becomes easier for us to penetrate to the essence. The task is to move away from sense impressions and sensuality: to abandon the *senses* and discover the *sense*—the meaning of it all. Transformation of the outer senses leads toward inner meaning. The gradual decline of one's sense organs propels us inward and facilitates this discovery, although we can also search for inner meaning voluntarily, without having to suffer a decline in the acuity of our five outwardly directed senses.

In addition to the specific meaning in the soul's corporeal vocabulary, illnesses and complexes of symptoms that appear solely or with particular frequency in old age (e.g., Parkinson's disease, St. Vitus' dance, and to some extent cancer) involve the issues of taking stock and turning homeward in the mandala's pattern. Although cancer can also strike younger people, it occurs more frequently among the elderly. The issue in this case is to live one's life and even to make errors. A "good" little life, free of errors simply because we never dared to risk anything that might have led to an error, can cause us to overlook our true lessons. It can lead into a cul-de-sac—a dead end that ends with death by cancer. One could also say that cancer takes stock and determines that one's path thus far has not been identical with one's true path. People who survive cancer are often impelled to make profound "course corrections" in the trajectories of their lives. Having been off course (i.e., not on their own true path) and headed for a dead end, they realize the error of their ways in the nick of time.

Each of these grave geriatric illnesses offers the opportunity to understand illness *as a path* and the chance to make the best of it. When a crisis appears late in one's mandala pattern, the pressures it exerts tend to be strong and threatening, but so too are the opportunities it can offer for learning and reorienting oneself to one's true pattern.

Along with the ailments typically associated with old age and the illnesses that threaten to shorten this final phase in life, there is a series of relatively harmless signs associated with aging. If we can properly interpret the symbolism inherent in these signs, they can provide us with useful clues about the patterns that remain to be reconciled.

Harmless "messengers of aging" include, for example, age spots on the skin. We can battle vehemently and resolutely against them, but they simply cannot be eliminated. Time has put spots on our hide, and no amount of cleansing, no bleach nor any trick can make the old leopard change his spots. The whole struggle to remove them is more than merely superfluous: try as we may, no one can turn back the hands of time.

Geriatric warts and other minor epidermal growths are readily understood and relatively harmless. We have "saved our skins" throughout our long lives, and that process has left its tracks and scars. Little boys (including the overgrown little boys who belong to certain student fencing fraternities) proudly display their scars, but older people may be ashamed and try to hide time's traces. Warts bring dark, unacknowledged characteristics to the surface and remind us of our magical roots in childhood, another phase of life when warts typically appear. We know about warts from the image of the witch with a wart on her nose, and we can successfully use magical remedies to make them disappear again.

Hair, too, begins to play strange tricks on us in old age. The hair on our heads we were so proud of as a status symbol grows thin or disappears altogether, only to reappear where we would rather not have it (e.g., in our ears and nostrils or between our eyebrows). Sometimes our orderly eyebrows suddenly begin to get out of hand, the hairs sprouting and twisting in unexpected contortions. Elderly individuals may still keep themselves under strict control, but their hair seems to go crazy, as if it were enjoying a final chance to play out all the wild options a lifetime of good grooming and good behavior has denied it. The task so clearly symbolized by these symptoms is to accept the games one's body is playing and grant oneself the chance to step out of line, dance to a different drummer and enjoy a bit of geriatric eccentricity. Hair is a symbol of freedom and power and it is no mere coincidence when one's hair begins to live a life of its own since neither baldness nor wild growth occur without their underlying reasons.

The Archetypes of Old Age

In his diaries[90], Swiss author Max Frisch developed an ironic typology of aging in the form of a three-stage system. Each of us will no doubt readily recognize the phase most closely corresponding to our own present situation. Frisch distinguishes between the pre-marked, the marked, and the elderly.

Frisch writes about people in the first category:

> *The pre-marked individual enjoys it when people underestimate his age, even if the estimate is only one year of. Then again, he also doesn't enjoy it. After all, he is forty years old anyway....In athletics (e.g., skiing) he tends to ski faster than he really feels comfortable whenever young people are nearby.*
>
> *Lack of tact is a sure sign that an individual belongs to this group. When he talks with people who are several decades older than he, the pre-marked man emphasizes the fact the he is no longer as young as he used to be. In conversations with younger people, he loves to call attention to all the great things he achieved in the past. The pre-marked individual always brings up the issue of age.*

He always refuses to allow you to help him into his overcoat. If there is a shortage of chairs at a casual get-together, he is sure to be among those who sit on the floor. He never uses the ladder to get into a swimming-pool, but prefers to dive in. At black-tie affairs, he is always the one with his hands in his trouser pockets, demonstrably trying to look like a teenager. On hikes with younger people, he will insist on carrying the backpack. On the other hand, he is sure to call everyone's attention to his first gray or white hairs, as if the most natural thing in the world were a unique and sensational event....He detests the kind of off-color jokes old men typically enjoy. He does not want to hear them told by others, simply because he is already starting to think of them on his own.

He once survived a grave accident, and he never tires of telling the story of his near-death in all its boring detail. The pre-marked man knows all too well that things will soon change and that he will no longer have the chance to narrowly escape a tragic death at an oh-so-early age.

It is more difficult for the pre-marked man than for the marked man to accord due respect to younger colleagues in his specialty. He tends to describe anything suggested by a younger person as "mere fashion," although that concept begins for him precisely at the point where, despite all his efforts to keep pace, he can no longer keep up.

P.S.—The marked man tends toward the opposite extreme: confronted with something that is merely an ephemeral fashion, he will mistake it for an epochal innovation and put himself in the role of its self-styled exponent.

Moving to the second category, Frisch writes:

The man who is marked by age knows that he has become a marked man when he notices that no one envies him, even if he enjoys a good reputation or has a lot of wealth (that is, when he has options open to him that they, the younger people, don not have). Nevertheless, no one wants to trade places with him....The man who is marked by age begins to envy his contemporaries less and less for their achievements, more and more for their late births— he envies the years they still have in store for the future.

The marked man notices, or perhaps does not notice, that his presence inhibits other people. They shake his hand when he arrives, and it need not necessarily be a wasted evening, but it will be a different one than it would have been if he had not come at all. The presence of a marked man has immediate consequences: something is vaguely strenuous—he does not want us to treat him gently and it is not really a question of special treatment....The obvious and most annoying change: wherever he goes, whether on business or as a social occasion, the majority of the people there are younger than he—maybe not all of them are younger than he, but especially the ones who interest him are.

The marked man begins his sentences with phrases like, "After all, we've all had the experience at one time or another...," "We, too, once...," "If you've ever known what it's like to...," "In my day...,"[91] "In our era...," "Nowadays everyone supposes...," "When I was your age, you know, I would have been ashamed to...," "In my experience, there can be only one...," "One really ought to give the younger folks a chance...," and so on.

The marked man distinguishes himself by a new kind of boredom. If he was bored in the past, it was usually only because of circumstances: school, the office, the army...In the past, he could always imagine another situation, one in which he would not feel at all bored. The new aspect now is that even thinking about making his wishes come true bores him.

If someone makes a witty remark, his laughter comes after a brief delay, during which he checked to be sure the quip was not at his expense; afterward he laughs a bit too much, and that is what betrays him.

The marked man finds himself waking up before the break of day—at the hour when prisoners face the firing squad. He awakens because he is not at all tired. He becomes an early riser—but for what purpose?

The marked man insists on idiosyncrasies that, at least in his eyes, make him feel like a man with a strong and definite personality; if it does not convince those around him, he persists in it all the more, if only out of spite. Geriatric peculiarities.

"How could you," he thinks disapprovingly, "lie around doing nothing for days on end!" The marked man could never do that: but his ability to enjoy pleasure is no longer strong enough to allow him to do nothing other than pursue pleasure.

Frisch writes the following about the third and final stage in this escalating series that culminates in death:

The outward appearance of the elderly man is well-known. He shuffles, scarcely raising his heels off the floor. He hesitates as though he were walking on slippery ice. He spreads his legs when he sits in an upholstered chair, and he looks vaguely improper. All of his movements—the casual as well as the urgent ones—have the same tempo. When he has drunk a beer, he cannot contain the liquid very long. He does not care whether or not he can hear what people are saying at the table around him. Not only must we speak louder so that he can understand us, we also have to simplify our speech so he can understand and, when he has finally understood, it only confirms his certainty that he had not missed anything important to begin with. When he chews, we lose our appetite for whatever it is he is eating....When several elderly people sit together, we are involuntarily reminded of amphibians; they have nothing to do with us. One feels uncomfortable when one tries to help an elderly man across the street or up a flight of stairs because one is not eager to touch his body. In his sleep, he looks like a dead man. That is the time when we feel sorry for him. He does not bother us if he is sitting on a bench in the park. If he is someone whom we knew when he was younger, we feel distracted when we talk with him now because we can only see him from the outside: the veins in his hands, the watery eyes, the lips....

Frisch's subtle observations clearly show that, simply because we do not like aging, half our life revolves around that issue. And the most unpleasant part of it all is that the misery begins long before actual old age. Let's move on and examine the typical archetypes of old age in their reconciled and non-reconciled versions.

No doubt the best-known and best-loved archetype is the *wise old man* or *wise old woman*. This is an archetype that, especially in the West, plays a severely subordinate role and is only seldom encountered. Nonetheless, this archetype is the goal in life for a great many people. Incidentally, archetypes are valid for both genders, even if they are presented here for the sake of simplicity with pronouns of one gender or the other. The mandala contains the path toward becoming an old and wise human being. The path toward wisdom is open to us all, so long as we have accomplished our tasks on the outward path, consciously withdrawn ourselves from polarity and focused our energy on the return journey to the midpoint of the mandala. Wise men and women have divorced themselves (at least inwardly) from material possessions and from all inessentials, becoming far more concerned with the inward voyage. Following in Socrates' footsteps, wise men and women realize that, despite all their wisdom, they really know nothing. They know wisdom grows from simplicity. Their thoughts leave the surface behind and penetrate the depths where the pattern of the world is woven from primal principles and where unity can be seen shining through the veils of polarity and its constructs. Wise people not only possess an intellectual knowledge of things, but also live those experiences with their innermost being. They experience their essence as clarity, purity and beyond polarity. They no longer "act" in our sense of the word because they live in an attitude of spirit Buddha called *upekkha* (meaning "equanimity"). Like the sun whose rays shine upon beauty and ugliness alike, the old wise person can look at everything without having to evaluate or judge it. Peaceful and easy in themselves, they gaze knowingly and benevolently upon the world, secure in the experience that everything follows the grand cosmic order.

This is the main reason for our difficulties with this archetype. Our prosperous Western society has amassed a tremendous trove of knowledge. Our physicists have reached limits where their scientific discoveries begin to confirm ancient wisdom teachings. But Western civilization has consistently failed to create (or even maintain existing) experiential frameworks within which this wisdom could be experienced and kept alive inside us. The East has a far greater number of such practices, mediations and exercises, which is why so many Westerners who are searching for wisdom turn their gazes to the East. The old wise man (or woman) has become like a child, one who lives in wholeness and whose eyes can penetrate the illusion of time. He has reached the midpoint of the mandala and left the world of polarity behind, even if he still abides for a time here on earth in a physical body.

If the attempt to grow old *and* wise is only partially successful, or if that goal has been lost sight of at an early age, it is quite common for a person to develop into a caricature of the old, wise archetype. In this case, we find the old fool, the doddering oldster, the *absent-minded professor* who has amassed a hoard of knowledge but never truly gained wisdom. Slowly but surely, the superannuated professor is losing clarity and contact. Or else the unresolved archetype can appear as the chronically dissatisfied senior citizen, a person who is stuck in his projections and lives in an unceasing battle with the world. These people are unable to see through their own game and, for lack of wisdom, desperately cling to material possessions. Fortunately, the other, reconciled aspect is always implicitly present, even in the unresolved versions of this archetype. The task comes clearly to light when we consider the symptoms exhibited by the learned but absent-minded oldster. He has been metaphorically short-sighted for years, and now he has also become farsighted from an ophthalmic perspective. The challenge is to learn to see the whole picture, from near and far, thus discovering wholeness inside and out. Such a "modern wise one" would be wise in the traditional sense of the word, like an old seer or an old natural philosopher.

Another aspect of the reconciled version of this archetype manifests as the *good old fool* who has found freedom within and now no longer feels the need to prove himself to anybody. Dozens of stories in the Zen Buddhist tradition recount the instant when the practitioner suddenly attains liberation from the world (of polarity) and becomes a master. It is not uncommon for the world to echo his laughter in such moments when the new master finally realizes everything has always just *been* and sees just how ridiculously dumb he was behaving in the past.

During the Middle Ages, a few gifted individuals were called to a career as *court jesters*. Equipped with the proverbial "fool's license," these professional merrymakers were exempt from all prohibitions. As long as they chose a funny way of saying it, they were even allowed to confront kings and emperors with unpleasant truths. Native Americans had a kind of tribal fool (the *heyoka*) who was always present in the council of elders and who always asserted the craziest ideas. It was his task to play the devil's advocate, always championing the opposite of what everyone else agreed to, and arguing in favor of his wild ideas in the craziest way possible. This had the enormous advantage of constantly keeping the opposite pole alive in the conversation rather than ignoring it and allowing it to take the tribe from behind or by surprise. In the ideal case, court jesters and *heyokas* always kept an eye on the deeper truths, uncompromisingly ignoring everyday positions and superficial prejudices. Of course, only highly intelligent and extremely alert individuals where able to play these roles with the necessary humor and appropriate depth of insight.

Then as now, this type of person is worth his weight in gold. Just imagine a modern-day fool in the hallowed halls of the legislature, blithely aloof from partisan infighting and narrow-minded quibbling over money and vested interests, his incisive fool's mind devoted to the whole picture—and clever enough to utter the unspeakable, to disguise the unthinkable in the veils of a joke, to break the taboos, to laugh at the world and at his own foolishness. Politics could again become interesting and fun. An old fool could have a similarly refreshing effect on business. When everyone else is worrying about dividends and about the outlooks for the next millennium, the fool's capers could shatter the board of directors' rigidity and(perhaps even bring the business back into the cosmic order. Even as the power brokers and power vultures (the latter is a commonly encountered archetype in our culture) desperately try to maintain their composure, the corporate jester could dip the annual report to the shareholders into her hot chocolate and joke about the old codgers' fear of losing their positions to younger colleagues.

When the process that ordinarily leads to the creation of an old fool comes to an unduly early halt, it can create the *wrinkled owl-like curmudgeon* who lives in his own peculiar world and whom no one understands because the poor fellow has entangled himself in the threads of his own idiosyncrasy and lost track of the path. As time goes on, these people begin to believe their own little plot of ground is the whole wide world. This archetype is well-embodied, for example, by people who are so involved in their collection (e.g., of postage stamps, beer coasters or whatever) that they ignore everything else in life.

An equally unattractive caricature of the old fool is the *old malcontent* or *old complainer* who knows better but usually cannot *do* better. If he had ever really done better, he would have scant reason for his chronic dissatisfaction. Rather than stimulating others with his unconventional thoughts (like the good old fool), the old malcontent becomes a notorious annoyance and aggravation to all. He gnaws at and knows better about anything and everything. He is always eager to give you a *good piece* of his mind, even though what is left of his mind is neither *good* nor at *peace*. He takes himself all too seriously, and no one can make much sense of what he is so earnestly trying to say. We are not sure whether to laugh or cry when we see him coming in our direction. Unlike the court jester or the Amerindian *heyokah* (who know they are playing the fool), the old complainer is fooling himself in the worst sense.

The person of equanimity, who recognizes the cosmic laws acting in all things and who has made peace with those laws as they affect him, is a person who has found a personal center. A good example of this type of person is the old Zen master in the following story. Afraid that she could not keep it alive any other way, a poor woman in a nearby village falsely accused this Zen master of having impregnated her. When the baby was born, the indignant villagers give the infant to the Zen master, who accepted it with the words, "So, so." Three years later, when the child's mother finally told the truth about the child's paternity, the villagers returned to the Zen master, apologized profusely and demanded he return the child. As he surrendered the healthy, happy child into their hands, the Zen master again said, "So, so."

The *good grandmother* who has revitalized her inner child and who, from this perspective, treats all forms of life with mercy and compassion has found her way back to the midpoint of the mandala. She is the best thing that can happen to children, who may meet her on her homeward path as they embark on their journey toward the periphery. Her dark sister is the *old maid*: an overripe maiden who is still waiting for her prince to come, an elderly Sleeping Beauty who has resigned herself to the fact that no one wants to awaken her with a kiss.

The *good shepherd* and wisdom teacher who passes along the wisdom he has discovered and actualized within himself is far less common than the religious zealot and fanatic whose hot breath scathes everyone exposed to it. Avoided by all, the zealot is an annoying missionary and a tormenting persecutor. The fanatic's worst sin may well be that he misuses the name of God for the petty purposes of his egoistic little game.

It is no surprise that our patriarchal culture is most familiar with the four reconciled archetypes in their male versions as masters, old wise men, wise fools and good shepherds. Of course, we could just as well clothe those characters in feminine garb: the mistress, the wise woman, the wondrous old lady and the Great Mother. Each of these archetypes, in its reconciled and non-reconciled versions, also appears in many mixed versions. Of course, there is only one midpoint, and liberation is surely found there. The four patterns result from the various shades and colorings the four elements give to them along the path: of course, the wise fool is also able to teach; the good shepherd can embody the clarity of the wise man and the mercy of the Great Mother; and she, for her part, can also have the licentious freedom of the fool and the purity of the wise woman.

The non-reconciled variants likewise appear in many varieties. Each is a more or less obvious reflection of its reconciled counterpart. Sometimes faintly, sometimes more obviously, the positive qualities of its resolved counterpart always shine through. In a certain sense, the old man who stalks through life as a *lone wolf* nourished by his own bitterness represents an inversion of the good old fool. Whereas the old fool cannot take himself and the superficiality of the world seriously anymore, the lone wolf doggedly pursues all his affairs with bitter earnestness. This proud old warrior is generally ignored or outvoted by people half his age, which only adds to his bitterness and disappointment. Rather than humorously exaggerating the absurdity of the situation, he is completely entangled in it and in his personal problems, regardless of whether he is an old thief sneaking his way through life or a lone warrior fighting for some righteous cause or against some imagined enemy. In many cases, the lone wolf has lost touch with reality and has spun himself into the cocoon of his own illusions. In the political arena, we can find examples of this archetype among the Gray Panthers who, in voices even louder and more strident than those of their younger counterparts, vehemently fight for the rights and status of the elderly. If the lone wolf would only look more closely at his *alone*ness, he might find the solution and discover that *all* is indeed contained within *each*.

The *confirmed bachelor* who strides through life inflexibly and without ever questioning the truth of his self-made illusion of respectability is yet another variant. Irreconcilable and harsh toward himself and the world, he is ruthless with himself and imagines himself to be in the right—right up to the bitter end. His goal, if he could only recognize it, would be to transform his stiffly upright posture into authentic righteousness and sincerity.

An exciting and amusing version is embodied by the *old fox*. A good example of this figure is the German TV detective nicknamed "Der Alte"—a cunning sleuth and an indefatigable scourge of televised criminals. On a more reconciled level, this figure also appears as the gray fool who frightens others. In one of his lectures, Alfred Ziegler described this character incomparably well as "the foolish old man."

The *old witch* or bitter *old maid* who sees herself as the victim of a cruel world and has become spiteful and nasty herself is captured with particular clarity in projections. Just as the Inquisition projected every evil of its petty clerical world onto the "witches," this bitter old maid projects her own failures onto the screen of the world as a whole. Poisoned by her own bitterness, she spits poison at everything she sees and is convinced everyone else has either done her harm or is planning to do so. She is particularly envious of vivacious youths, the sort of young people for whom she sets her traps in fairy tales no less than in real life. To become like little children ought to be her goal. Her error lies in the attempt to become like them by devouring them rather than through inner transformation.

In certain respects, the *old miser* is similar to the old "power vulture." The miser's soul, however, is addicted to material possessions rather than to power and influence. He is quite correct to feel terribly afraid of the imminent end since it will also put an end to all his illusions. And he has been vaguely aware of its approach through all the terrible years of his unenviable life. Consequently, he suffers the tortures of hell long before he actually dies, simply because he has mistakenly imagined outer gold to be a substitute for inner gold.

The *good-old-days* type has obviously gotten stuck in the past. He is constantly whining about the good times and golden opportunities that are irretrievably gone. He often feels as though he has wasted his life because the good old days with all their fantastic opportunities will never return. The present day or the future could not possibly be good enough to persuade him to open up and accept them; or perhaps he never was open to them because, by definition, the good old days are always in the past. Until the ultimate goal is recognized as lying within ourselves, our quest for the Golden Age is doomed to remain as hopeless as the Conquistadors' quest for El Dorado, the mythical city of gold.

The *old washerwoman* washes other people's dirty laundry in public. She is also known in a similar variant as the *old gossip*. Talking about others rather than developing oneself is her pattern. She is always waiting with her unsolicited advice about how *we* could do things better, but she is never ready to take the initiative, pitch in and actually do something herself. In order to avoid looking at herself, she keeps her disparaging gaze fixed on everyone else, imagining them to be every bit as bad as she herself feels inside. The solution for her would be to understand that the outer world that occupies her undivided attention is nothing more than a mirror of her inner world.

The *old globetrotter* knows the world better than he knows himself. He refuses to grow old and has made the journey toward ever-new horizons into his personal "trip." Together with younger people, he drifts around the world, an overripe hippie forever running away from himself. He is proud that no woman nor any country has been able to make him settle down, and he fears nothing more than another person who would stay with him as a permanent mirror in whom he would be compelled to recognize himself. As he drifts around for better or worse (mostly worse), the time remaining for him to live his own life grows ever shorter. The pride he takes in his freedom from ties and responsibilities only blinds him to the fact that other people—the ones who are not always on the run—actually enjoy more freedom than he does. A late stage in this pattern is embodied in the *old hobo* who, loathe to admit that he is just a bit of driftwood on the shores of life, abuses alcohol in a desperate attempt to hide from the truth. The salvation to this fleeing that has become an addiction would be to rediscover the quest whose goal is one's own center.

The *horny old goat* is the pitiful remnant of the eternal youth who, although he has not been able to find an elegant exit or escape from life, nevertheless cannot give up his old pattern. He still tries to prove his masculinity through sexual conquests. As he grows older, such conquests become more difficult to achieve and, once achieved, earn him progressively fewer accolades from those around him. He is liable to expend much of his time and energy on toupees, dentures and elaborate rituals with anti-impotence pills. The *face-lifted lady* is the feminine counterpart of this archetype. Like the old goat, she has not been able to accept aging and its role in her life. Instead, she has made her body into a field for experiments in medicine and cosmetology. Despite her self-sacrificial dedication, the aging playgirl has a tougher time of it than her inverse sibling, the hoary old boy. Sooner or later (and most likely sooner), no new young playmates will want to play with them anymore, not to mention refusing to allow these aging Don (and Donna) Juans to play the same old games with their young flesh. The lesson aging playboys and playgirls need to learn is to become one with the opposite pole. As is so often the case, the only problem lies in the playperson's unduly one-sided sexuality.

As in all other solutions, this last situation aims inward, toward the individual's own center. The exterior factor (i.e., the form) is only a means to an end. As soon as it is allowed to become an end in itself, it begins to create sorrow and confusion in life's pattern. One's own midpoint corresponds to the midpoint of the mandala, the one point toward which all development, whether reconciled or non-reconciled, tends at this stage in life.

Questions About Aging

1. What are my feelings at sundown?
2. How do I cope with the last few days of a vacation?
3. How do I behave at the end of a game? Is it easier or more difficult for me to score the final points?
4. Do I always eat everything on my plate? Or do I tend to leave some scraps?
5. How do I deal with farewells? Can I separate myself easily and drive away gladly? Or do I suffer when the time comes to bid adieu? Do I delay (necessary) farewells?
6. Do I know when the time is due—or overdue—to say goodbye?

7. Do I enjoy bidding farewell to others? Do I escort them to the train station or the airport? What are my feelings while I wave goodbye?
8. How much attention do I pay to the issue of bringing things to a harmonious conclusion?
9. How happily and how often do I move to a new dwelling, and what are my underlying motivations for the move?

Meditations to Prepare for the Great Letting-go

1. Imagine floating in the midst of the open ocean: does pleasure or anxiety occupy the foreground?
2. Imagine floating all alone in outer space: can you enjoy the freedom or are your frightened by it?
3. A hike in the mountains as a model of life's pattern: what ideas and feelings do you associate with a hike in the mountains begun shortly before sunup?

-   Imagine a project of this sort, beginning with the moment the alarm clock rings at an unfamiliarly early hour to begin the adventure. Experience your feelings when the sun rises above the horizon while you climb the mountain that represents this day and this life.
-   How do you behave at the summit? Can you enjoy the acme (of life) and the view from the top (midlife crisis)? Do you allow yourself a pause to relax at the top?
-   How do you feel as you begin the homeward trek? How do you feel about climbing down? Do you experience as much pleasure in the descent as in the ascent?
-   How do you feel when you arrive at the foot of the mountain? How will you feel in the evening, after the hike, when the time comes to go to bed?
-   Can you imagine transforming this imagined journey into an actual hike?

Exercises

4. Conduct a farewell ritual to bid adieu to superfluous things. Afterward, actually give them away. Get rid of inessential items.

5. Consciously surrender whatever is no longer appropriate at this phase of life. For example, give your sports car to your children or to an orphanage.

6. Write your last will and testament:
   - for material possessions
   - from an intellectual and spiritual viewpoint: what part of me do I want to bequeath as a legacy?

7. Conduct prophylactic farewell rituals for things that are still needed (house, apartment) and make it clear to yourself that death must also take these away from you.

8. Consciously pay one last personal visit to places that mean a lot to you.

9. Meditate about what you could take along at the end of life.

10. Make friends with the Saturn archetype.
    - get to know it theoretically
    - experience it through exercises that emphasize austerity and simplicity, through fasting, or in a monastery with strict, simple meditation

11. Make life easier for yourself, take things easier (e.g., a cane as a symbol of accepting help).

12. Clarify the chief issues of old age:
    - learn to cope with loss: consciously attend the funerals to which you seem to be invited with increasing frequency; recognize the decline of health and physical strength as a symbol; plan for the unavoidable loss of external rank and status. Wisdom is most likely to grow from consciously dealing with loss.
    - Finish things off with yourself, bring things to a harmonious conclusion: self-knowledge, work on the shadow.

Valuable help is available in William A. Miller's *Der Goldene Schatten* (Munich 1994).

- Become aware of the great whole and subordinate yourself to that wholeness, discover your proper place in creation, recognize higher values: what reaches beyond me?
- Become like little children, regain lost innocence. Use confession as a preparation, as emancipation from everyday affairs. Give more priority to the heart than to the head (as was the case during childhood), return to the land of myths and mysteries, build a bridge to the dreams of ideals of youth.

12. Death

You would know the secret of death.
But how shall you find it unless you seek it
in the heart of life?
The owl whose night-bound eyes
are blind unto the day cannot unveil
the mystery of light.
If you would indeed behold the spirit of death,
open your heart wide unto the body of life.
For life and death are one, even as the river and the
sea are one.
In the depth of your hopes and desires
lies your silent knowledge of the beyond;
And like seeds dreaming beneath the snow
your heart dreams of spring.
Trust the dreams, for in them is hidden the gate to
eternity.
Your fear of death is but the trembling of the
shepherd
when he stands before the king whose hand
is to be laid upon him in honor.
Is the shepherd not joyful beneath his trembling,
that he shall wear the mark of the king?
Yet is he not more mindful of his trembling?
For what is it to die but to stand naked in the wind
and to melt into the sun?
And what is it to cease breathing,
but to free the breath from its restless tides,

*that it may rise and expand and seek god
unencumbered?
Only when you drink from the river of silence
shall you indeed sing.
And when you have reached the mountain top,
then you shall begin to climb.
And when the earth shall claim your limbs,
then shall you truly dance.*

—Khalil Gibran, *On Death*

Dying in Modern Times

F ew themes trigger as much terror in us as does the issue of death. Death and time belong to the same primal principle, and all time ultimately runs toward death or, as Meister Eckhart said, "Whatever touches on time is temporal and mortal." In Greco-Roman mythology, this theme is represented by the figure of Chronos Saturn who, with his sickle and scythe, symbolizes harvest and finitude. Both tools indicate that we will harvest what we have sown and die as we have lived. Only what is most essential in us will remain. In the mythos, Saturn devours his children, just as time devours its children because whatever was born must someday also die.

We know this, but generally suppress the knowledge in our unconscious. Nonetheless present as a vaguely disquieting premonition, awareness of our own finitude impels us to fall for a large number of tricks that relate to time. We desperately try to save time, as if saving it today would allow us to have more time at the end. If we do end up having plenty of spare time near the end of life, we are generally less than delighted by the surplus time on our hands, and we try to "kill time" by distracting ourselves with one diversion or another. If only we would realize that it is time itself and its primal principle that can help us solve this dilemma. Since time, death, the guardian of the threshold, return, reduction to essentials, depression, problems with bones, sickness in general and regression all belong to the same principle, we have a choice: if we intensively and consciously occupy ourselves with thoughts about reversal and return in life, and if we voluntarily focus on the essentials, then we are relatively safe from the other, unresolved variations of this principle.

In our society, old age has become a season of illness. That is, of course, one way to spend this phase since it corresponds to one level of the fundamental principle, but it is not the only way and certainly not the cleverest. The Saturn principle demands tribute in the form of attention, but the particular currency in which we pay that price is mostly a matter of our own free choice. Saturn accepts payment in the typical symptoms of geriatric illness, but he will also accept it in the form of conscious restriction and humility, voluntary reduction of needs, self-imposed aloneness, introspection about the essentials in life and a return homeward. Rather than paying the principle its due tribute, we mostly try to escape from its unpleasant representatives (especially death). If we had our druthers, most of us would opt to cheat death of his prize altogether. Our attempts in this direction range from worthwhile literature (e.g., *Everyman*) to grotesque denial. In the U.S., it has even become customary to put rejuvenating makeup on cadavers so their next-of-kin will not have to confront the marks of death face-to-face. The elaborate effort, all the cosmetics and medicine, is ultimately motivated by the fear of death. That terror is so powerful that it can even seduce us into the most tasteless behavior and can make us lose touch with our inherent humanity.

According to Professor Student, between eighty and ninety percent of the deaths that occur in our supposedly humane and highly evolved society take place in the exile and lonesomeness of hospital bathrooms and hallways. Although surveys show that the majority of Germans would prefer to die at home, ninety percent of the urban and sixty percent of the rural population spend their last days in hospitals or old-age homes. Only one in five succeeds in dying within her own four walls. Fear of death is so ubiquitous that there are hardly any people left who are willing to grant their moribund relatives' last wish—to die at home. Before the time comes for death to claim them, a medical reason or some other excuse is found for shipping them off to a hospital. Perhaps a role in this is also played by the irrational hope that medicine will somehow vanquish death at the last minute.[92] Since the majority of people do not have expensive private health insurance, the hospital assigns them to multi-bed rooms where, when one of the patients begins to embark on the path into the Great Beyond, his roommates realize what is going on and they panic. Their fears of succumbing to the same fate prompt them to ring for the nurse, who rolls the dying person's bed out of the room. Most German hospitals do not have rooms especially reserved for the dying, so there is often no other place to put the bed and its moribund occupant than in a bathroom or hallway. Because the nurses are generally so overworked, they are not likely to have time to spend at the dying person's bedside. Instead, they call the individual's next-of-kin who, for one reason or another, often arrive too late. The physicians, educated to do battle against sickness and death, are seldom eager to be present at their own defeat. If one of the few remaining nursing nuns (who can still reconcile the fact of death with her own worldview and is able to look death squarely in the face) is not on duty in this ward, then often no one is present to accompany the dying person to the threshold of this great transition.

In his *Studien zur Geschichte des Todes im Abendland (Studies of the History of Death in the West)* French historian Philippe Ariès talks about a decay and decline of cultivation in the customs relating to our dealings with death. He identifies three salient points to support his thesis:

1. *Dying is hidden, denied and isolated in our society.* Dying people are hidden out of public view. One could raise the objection that action films and news broadcasts deliver images of dead and dying people to our living rooms every evening, but these media only show us death in its most abnormal forms. The spectator is (usually) correct in assuming that this type of death

surely will not claim her. Our unconscious assumption is that *no* type of death will ever befall us.

2. *The dying person is lied to and deprived of the right to decide.* A survey of nursing personnel in 70 German hospitals revealed that although eighty-four percent of the staff wanted to speak candidly about death with their patients, only thirty percent felt that such dialogues actually took place in their hospitals. Professor Student, a pioneer in the German hospice movement, is convinced that dying people are rarely informed about their situation early enough. Since their next-of-kin are almost always informed, downright grotesque situations frequently arise. Terminally ill people often realize what is happening, but no one takes their fears seriously. Their worries are ignored or played down by their relatives because the family (in accord with their doctor's advice) generally wants to "spare them" the bad news. The terminally ill patients sense the barrier and withdraw into silence—like children who are not permitted to know everything but who clearly sense the truth nonetheless. Against this background of fear and denial, dying people are deprived of their rights "for their own good." Physicians claim that most patients would rather not know the truth and that telling them the bad news would only worsen their illness, but these arguments are really little more than attempts to protect the physicians themselves.

Surveys show that fear of death is much stronger among nursing personnel and physicians than it is among people in non-health-related occupations. Fear leads to denial and aggression. Physicians and nursing personnel who work with the terminally ill tend to suffer from an above average rate of ill health. Is this (as Professor Student believes) a job-related consequence or does it derive from the law of affinity? We will leave that question unanswered. In any case, it does reveal the intensity of the problem as it affects health-care professionals. Not only do they deny the fact of death to their patients, they also deny it to themselves, and what remains is resignation. The aforementioned survey also documents the extent of this resignation: Seventy-five percent of the caregivers described their hospitals' conditions for dying people as degrading and burdensome, above all because they had too little time available to devote to dying patients. The caregivers also complained about inadequate hospice-related training, inordinate use of medical technology and excessive use of life-prolonging measures for terminal patients. Fifty-one percent of those surveyed felt this situation could not be changed—a statistic that reveals the profundity of the resignation they feel in the face of this last great crisis in life.

3. *The abolition of grief.* Plenty of proof can be found for Ariès' third point. Rituals and customs relating to grief and mourning play a less and less important role in our society. The classical year of mourning that, for example, traditional Jews subdivide into three days of pain, seven days of mourning, thirty days of gradually getting a grip on oneself again and eleven months of remembrance and recuperation seems to be going out of fashion. In our society, there is hardly any time for immediate grief, simply because the preparations for the funeral take so much time and attention. This leads to an unnecessary prolongation of the initial state of shock. Some people remain in this unhealthy and often tearless, dry-eyed situation for several months. If loss is not processed through grief, the body's immune system can collapse, and it is not uncommon for cancer to develop. Statistical studies of the bereaved show that their mortality rates exceed the population's average by forty percent and that their suicide rates are five times higher than those for the population as a whole. Survivors who cannot mourn are also more likely to become addicted, all too often with the help of their doctors, who unnecessarily prescribe tranquilizers. These medications are meant to chemically suppress grief because we have forgotten how to bear this situation of the soul and because so many physicians have little more than chemicals to offer their bereaved patients. Fortunately, an ever-increasing number of colleagues (like Professor Student) has chosen this issue as their sphere of interest.

Most people, however, still make life even more burdensome for the mourners with advice such as: "Empty the dead person's room, get rid of all their personal effects, dispose of everything that reminds you of them—it'll make life easier for you." The survivors often work like possessed people, in a state of shock, never really dealing with the loss but nonetheless reaping praise from the people around them—people who are likewise unwilling or unable to mourn. Weeks later, when they awaken from their shock, all the traces have been erased and their souls have missed an essential opportunity. Even worse advice: "Keep him in your memory just the way you knew him because now, after the accident, you wouldn't be able to bear the sight of him." Following this ill-conceived advice robs the survivor of the chance to bid farewell and all too often leads the survivor to harbor irrational doubts: did the family member or friend really die in the accident? Because the survivor has failed to confront the fact of death, there is no way for him to know for certain.

Tears of grief are the best thing that can happen to survivors. If, however, grief has been abolished or hindered because the survivors must return too quickly to the sphere of normality, tears of grief frequently remain unshed. Professor Student views grief as a lifelong process. Grief becomes a part of us, gradually moves into memory and finally loses all its terrors. As is almost always the case in life, it is better to confront tough experiences at the moment when fate presents us with them. Denial, suppression and stagnation are poor alternatives. Suppressed grief not only makes us physically ill, but can also lead to emotional disturbances and *dis-ease* in the soul.

Nevertheless, no (modern) person wants to have much to do with death because each of us knows (or vaguely suspects) that we will fall victim to "all-devouring death" soon enough. People who deal with death as part of their profession (e.g., physicians) see themselves as death's adversaries. For better or worse (mostly worse), they have been taught to fight death with all the weapons at their disposal. In this context, it is no surprise that hardly any physicians have learned to love their enemy. Worse yet, physicians do not even know death since they run away when death approaches. Even in cancer wards, telling patients the truth is not considered to be a good idea, despite the fact that most patients know full well where they are and why. But the medical establishment insists that these patients could not cope with the truth. One cannot help but suspect that it is really the doctors rather than the patients who cannot cope with the truth and who refuse to honorably accept their defeat.

A young leukemia patient, who had already been subjected to three cytostasis treatments and who had been more or less "written off" as incurable, once asked me if she would have to die soon. When I responded to her question by asking how she arrived at that question, she said that her doctors spent so little time at her bedside when they made their rounds. It was sad but true: her impression and conclusion were correct. Since nothing more could be done for her from a medical standpoint, the doctors generally spent no more than a few embarrassed moments by her bed, exchanged a few polite but empty phrases with her and hurried away.

As a general rule, no one likes to confront his own failure, and physicians are no exception. The only difference is that death puts a final seal on physicians' defeats. Their denial mechanisms are often so extreme they refuse to even use the word "death." The patient is not a "dying" patient but merely "moribund;" and rather than actually dying she merely makes an "*exitus*" (the Latin word for "exit"). In the typically laconic language of hospital slang, they say, "The patient in 14 has gone *ex.*"

In intensive care units (where the illusion that death can be defeated is often indulged), the staff will go to extreme lengths to banish death, but they never achieve more than a delay. Of course, postponing death can be enormously important for individual patients. Physicians and nurses who work in the ICU have become quite careful ever since medicine has earned the questionable reputation of being able to torture people for weeks by attaching them to life-support machines rather than allowing them to die in peace. If the tables were turned, many of these caregivers who so courageously campaign against this kind of medicine would no doubt be very glad for the options it can provide. Intensive care has its shadow sides and (like broad areas of medicine in general) is largely motivated by the fear of death. Although it cannot heal, it can grant terminally ill people a stay of execution, and that is often what gravely ill patients want.

Doctors do not have an easy time of it in their dealings with death. Patients have become very sharp-eared. Many patients have begun to distrust the idea of fighting death at all costs, although this distrust does not necessarily mean they have gained a greater measure of trust in death. When the situation turns grave, most of them call for the selfsame medication or treatment they rejected earlier on. This puts doctors in increasingly uncomfortable positions. Their dilemma is no longer confined to the problem that they do not really know death, but now includes the difficulty of determining when death has occurred. In the past, heart stoppage was an unambiguous indication but, in the era of open-heart surgery on exposed and motionless hearts, brain death has become a more significant indicator. Despite it all, there are many doubtful cases (e.g., when people spend months in a coma or are kept alive for a long time through permanent attachment to life-support machinery). Transplant medicine that, as we described above, was developed as an means of avoiding death, has changed many things for doctors. If they belong to the teams whose job it is to remove the donor's organ, they may be obliged to wait beside mortally wounded patients until other physicians[93] finally declare the donor "dead enough" so the scavenger team can begin its work. Their job is not made any easier by the low regard some people have for these "corpse robbers." Yet chances are good that the very same people who look down their noses at them would be all too eager to receive a donated organ if and when their own lives depended on it.

Nowadays, patients feel that they should enjoy certain rights in their dealings with death—after all, they have paid their health insurance premiums! If and when they need an organ transplant, they suddenly feel that the shortage of donors is a scandalous situation. Rather than humbly accepting God's gift and grate-fully acknowledging the physicians' achievements in prolonging their life span, some patients behave as if they had a right to it. Arrogantly and impudently denying death its due is ultimately a sign of anxiety and narrowness. We lack the collective willing-ness to affirm the necessity of death as the goal of our lives. C.G. Jung said, "As a physician, I'm convinced that it is health-ier to regard death as a goal toward which we ought to strive; struggling against it, on the other hand, is unhealthy and abnor-mal because the struggle deprives life's second half of its goal. From the point of view of the soul's hygiene, I would say that all religions with an otherworldy goal are extremely reasonable.... As physicians of the soul, we would do well to understand that death is only a transition, one part of an unknown, grand and lengthy process of life."[94]

The problem is so severe that even in the esoteric scene there are movements, motivated by fear (of death), that are searching for an escape in the promise of physical immortality. They assume that human beings die only because of beliefs and programming. This view may be worth discussing in theory, but it becomes rather ludicrous when clubs like these try to rescue as many people as possible from death's clutches by going out and convincing them that death is unnecessary. Either they have the feeling that there are not enough people on earth already or else their fear of death is so extreme they cannot bear even the thought of death and therefore yearn to repeal it. Despite all their efforts, Death himself seems entirely unimpressed with these "immortality groups," whose members typically manifest unmistakable signs of (sometimes premature) aging. The law of polarity rears its head once again.

In our society, people whose professions require them to deal with the dead (e.g., morticians, gravediggers) are well paid for accepting this "unpleasant imposition." This is another expres-sion of our aversion to everything associated with this theme.

Death himself preserves his inherent dignity despite all our ri-diculous attempts to ignore him, despite all our strategies and all our bending over backward to avoid him. Death can comfortably afford to endure our disrespect; the real question is, can we afford to ignore death? Whatever one's personal answer may be, the fact remains that death always wins *in the end.*

Thanks to their pioneering work in death research, physicians such as Raymond A. Moody and Elisabeth Kübler-Roth have taken us a decisive step closer to understanding death. Their discoveries turned out to be identical with the reports that have been recorded for centuries in "books of the dead" belonging to various of the world's cultures. The Tibetan and Egyptian books of the dead and the Mayan *Popul Vuh* leave no question unanswered about death and dying. But we Westerners have faith in nothing other than our own empirical research and must therefore discover everything anew. Despite these discoveries, death researchers still have a hard time since the statements that these physicians record from patients who have been "reanimated" (recalled to life) are apt to sound strange to Western ears.

The vast majority of "reanimated eyewitnesses" report that their dying was not at all terrifying. In most cases, they experience it as a dignified act of letting go. Luminous beings arrive to escort them toward an indescribably intense light. In the Western tradition, the centuries-old *ars moriendi* has reported very similar images and descriptions.[95] As the fruits of new research began to more closely resemble the ancient wisdom teachings, the official medical establishment began to distance itself from this discipline and relegate it to the "spiritual scene." Because of the arrogance that currently reigns in the scientific ghetto, other scientists need not take anything (including death researchers' results) in the "spiritual scene" seriously. That is a pity because death research would offer a simple way for Westerners to begin assuaging the fears of death that detract so much from the quality of their lives.

Nearly all wisdom teachers have realized that the fear of death is the most essential hindrance to life. Angelus Silesius wrote,

Die before you are compelled to die....
If you have not died in life, then when you die
You will rot forever....

Goethe said the same thing in different words,

And as long as you do not grasp this:
Die and become!
You are naught but a dreary guest
On the dark Earth.

Seneca is reported to have said,

In order not to fear Death
I constantly think about him.

Knowledge about death is a matter of course in the East. Tagore said,

Death belongs to life, just like birth. Life occurs in the
upbeat and downbeat of the poetic foot.

Despite many similar approaches by mystics such as Meister Eckhart, by saints like Teresa of Avila and Francis of Assisi, the art of dying and death per se remain a taboo in our culture. The Catholic Church plays a significant role in maintaining this taboo since it cleverly uses people's fear of death to uphold its own power politics. In principle, it makes little difference whether one extorts the faithful to purchase indulgences (as the Church did in the past), advises the flock to write wills that might contribute to the likelihood of their salvation or imposes good behavior by threat of hellfire (as it does now). As inhumane Chinese "experiments" on Tibetan Buddhists clearly show, people who are aware of the eternal rhythms of life and death are far more difficult to manipulate.

Dealing Consciously with Death

Other cultures can give us some valuable hints about how to have a freer and more relaxed relationship with death. In many respects, Angelus Silesius is correct when he asserts that life only begins after one has fully encountered and profoundly reconciled oneself with the fact of death. Many "reanimated" people confirm this view. Having already encountered death, many of them report that they no longer fear death and that the confrontation has impelled them to begin a new life—a life many of them emphatically claim to be their *real* life.

Amerindians and Eskimos—the selfsame peoples whom we falsely accuse of abandoning their elderly to die of exposure and starvation—enjoy a profoundly reconciled relationship with death. Many even regard death as a brother. When the elderly tribesman feels death's approach, he begins, without external compulsion, to prepare for life's last great transition. This preparation is easier because Native Americans who still live in traditional ways have *no doubt* they will meet Manitou (the Great Spirit) and that their life will by no means come to an end when they enter the Happy Hunting Grounds. Their notions of life after death are not all that different from our Christian concepts; the only difference is that the Amerindians really *believe* in it, and this faith gives them courage and confidence.

The old Amerindian would apprise her family about the imminent transition to the next plane and, according to tradition, the family would help build a last "raised hide" or other appropriate campsite. She would gather together personal totem objects—which, although they have no material value, are endowed with tremendous spiritual significance—and await death's arrival with dignity and patience. The elderly Amerindian has totems for the journey, but no physical food and drink. This is by no means a reflection of her tribe's miserliness, but derives instead from the understanding that the dying individual no longer has any need for material nourishment. Materialistic Western researchers fail to understand that this ritual is much more than a picnic!

Similarly, an old Eskimo is left alone and without food in his last igloo not because the tribe is cruel or heartless, but because he is embarking on the Great Journey—a journey for which nothing but spiritual nourishment is needed.

The benign nature of these rituals is also evident in the fact that an elderly tribesman who has mistakenly embarked on the last journey too soon is wholeheartedly welcome to rejoin the tribe and return to tribal life until he again hears the call and is transported into the afterlife. Compared to dignified and meaningful rites of passage such as these, it is not the indigenous peoples but we ourselves who allow our dying relatives to starve because we deny them essential spiritual nourishment.

People in India devote the last quarter of their lives to the preparation for dying. To us, this may seem like an astonishingly respectful attitude toward death. We shudder to think that they surrender everything and make a pilgrimage on foot (i.e., in humility) to the holy Ganges where they wait for death to claim them while helping to cremate those who have preceded them to the pyres on the ghats. Most Western tourists gaze in dismay and without understanding at what they mistakenly assume to be primitive Indians conducting a bizarre death rite. Too many Westerners look askance at what they consider to be uncivilized and barbaric customs, all the while ignoring the fact that no culture in the world is more barbaric than our own in the way it *disposes* of dying people.

We can observe the most impressive way of dealing with death and dying among the Tibetans who, steeped in Vajrayana Buddhist philosophy and equipped with their *Book of the Dead*, spend half their lives preparing themselves for the other plane. And, of course, the lama continues to escort those who have passed away on their subsequent paths through the so-called *bardo* (intermediate states after death). Despite, or perhaps *because* of, their intensive interest in death and dying, the Tibetans are a strikingly cheerful people. Western-style depression (representing another level of paying one's dues to the Saturn principle) is unknown there. Depression is a phenomenon of our modern society that, rather than dealing consciously with this archetype, prefers to deal with it unconsciously and thus in a non-reconciled manner.

Voluntary Death

Against a more open and receptive background, it becomes easier to comprehend phenomena such as the choice to consciously seek death. The immolation of widows in India still persists as a barbaric ritual in a patriarchal society. Although the practice has been prohibited, some women still leap onto the burning pyre to join the their husband's cadaver—thus displaying a fearlessness in the face of death that has little in common with the countless suicides in our own culture.

The Japanese even make an art form (called *hara-kiri*) out of ritualized suicide. In full awareness of his actions and in a precisely determined manner, the people who practice hara-kiri plunge a special, long knife into the belly's *hara* center and then, with their last remnants of concentration and awareness, pull the blade upward toward the heart. It is against this background that we can understand the *kamikaze* flights flown by young Japanese pilots during the Second World War. In a society in which death was respected rather than feared and in which emperor and empire took precedence over everything, it was honorable to crash one's plane as a "divine wind" (the literal meaning of "kamikaze") into the enemies of the empire. When they started their engines and took off on these suicide flights, these young heroes had already celebrated their funerals in the circle of their families, were already wearing their funereal shrouds and their blessed shawls around their necks.

The fearlessness, indeed the yearning for death, exhibited by some young Moslems can be similarly understood. They have no doubt that anyone who dies while fighting in a so-called "Holy War" will inevitably enjoy the postmortem bliss of seventh heaven. Of course, from an esoteric point of view, they are making an egregious error since they believe that the Holy War is an event in the material world. The Sufis, who are aware of the esoteric tradition in Islam, know that "Holy War" refers to an inner struggle. Finally, this category of voluntary death includes many Christian martyrs, at least those early Christians who chose to die rather than betray their faith.

In these and similar genres of voluntary death, the fear of crossing death's threshold is reduced because the candidate's religion or philosophy convincingly guarantees the certainty of life after death. The souls of people who commit ritualized suicide probably experience relatively little confusion because the death has been so consciously chosen and because the individuals expect their souls to survive the suicide. But even in these cases, a confrontation is unavoidable on the next level of existence with all the errors made during life.

Suicides in our society, on the other hand, are almost always motivated by fear of life and seldom have a ritualized element. Whenever fear of life outweighs fear of death, suicidal tendencies can jeopardize an individual's life. The vast majority of suicide attempts in Germany are serious, but are not meant to succeed because help (rather than death) is their real intent. Desperate people attempt suicide as an expression of the emergency within them, or want to use violence against themselves as a way of punishing others. When suicide attempts are successful, the deceased individuals are those whose fear of life was so gigantic that it outweighed a tremendous fear of death. Furthermore, most people who attempt suicide do not realize that killing themselves will only make their situation worse.

Experiences with reincarnation therapy show that escape into suicide does not bring relief. Just the opposite: the situation becomes much worse after suicide. Basically, possessing a body is a great advantage, and one that is often underestimated as long as one continues to have a body. Especially those people who do not believe in a life after death are utterly astonished to discover that their perceptions do not cease with their suicides and that they remain fully aware of what is happening around them, yet unable to make anyone notice their presence or establish contact with living, incarnate people. The majority of suicides in our society belong to this category. After "death" they generally have problems finding the right path. Poor souls like these often hang around an incarnate person, desperately trying to make contact and exert influence. The cares that plagued them prior to their deaths continue to torture them, making their disincarnate existence into a veritable hell on earth—or rather hell in that intermediate realm where their souls have become stuck. Not knowing where to go next, under pressure from a situation that has now truly become a "dead end," these confused souls instigate a series of phenomena our society generally assigns to the psychiatric field, despite the fact that conventional psychiatry can neither explain nor handle them. Phenomena such as haunted houses, demonic possession and the like have their roots here. Would-be therapies typically prescribed by academic psychiatrists (ranging from poisoning with psychotropic drugs to electroshock therapy) are unconsciously aiming at making life in the "host" body so unbearable that the "stuck" soul is driven away. Therapies like these may even prove temporarily successful.

Crises After Death

The problem we have been discussing has brought us to crises that occur on the other side of life's boundary. Postmortem crises have many traits in common with conception—that first crisis that begins prior to incarnate life and that so many people underestimate. Most *mere mortals* have no idea of the misery that can reign after death. We typically avoid thinking about the subject, steadfastly denying it until its existence can no longer be denied. If we are compelled to enter this sphere, we are apt to experience complete and utter disorientation. The reality of the postmortem sphere offers us three alternatives: we can accept its existence, we can struggle against accepting its existence, or we can ignore it. Regardless of which alternative we select, the fact remains that the sphere indeed exists and affects us.

A society whose members are so fixated on mundane life and who have no hope for life after death unknowingly creates irreparable confusion and endless misery in the realm beyond death. Anyone who dies unprepared and without any idea of what is waiting on the next plane lands in awful chaos. People who die suddenly and without time to prepare themselves are particularly hard hit. The soul of a young and life-affirming victim of a high-speed automobile accident may discover that her soul, which has been catapulted out of the car, is wandering the landscape at a great distance from the scene of the accident.[96] It may take time for the soul to find the accident scene, look at the wrecked car and dead body and realize that a fatal accident has occurred. Once she becomes aware of her own death, she generally does not know where to go or what to do next. American physician Carl Wickland has documented his work in this field in a book entitled *Thirty Years Among the Dead*. Wickland's studies provide abundant testimony about this plane and offer a certain degree of insight into the misery that reigns there. It is likely to be quite some time before psychiatry (the only discipline that seems to be more or less charged with investigating these phenomena) even recognizes the existence of this field. At the moment, psychiatry continues to wrestle with phenomena that derive from planes whose existence psychiatrists deny. It is no wonder, then, that their therapeutic success rate is anything but convincing.

Possibilities for Becoming More Intimate with Death

The biggest problem about dying in our situation is the scandalous dearth of knowledge about it. The particular ways in which we compensate for this lack are relatively unimportant compared to the fact of our compensation per se. For many Westerners, it may be sensible to begin with the realization that time is ultimately an illusion and that, on a more profound level of reality, the linear form of time with which we are familiar does not really exist. We can form at least some small impression of the subjective way that we perceive time through experiences with profound concentration, meditation, or even while watching an exciting movie. "Time flies" when we are having fun, but seems to stand still when we are suffering from boredom. The new physics has discovered scientific parallels to this subjective experience: time is relative, and by no means as objective and independent as the old physics had always claimed. Since our perception of time is relative anyway, the step toward a cyclical concept of time (like the one archaic peoples hold) is not such a big leap—even the thought of return in the sense of reincarnation becomes conceivable.

Death researchers such as Moody and Kübler-Ross have collected an abundance of material that can provide us with some initial, tentative insights into the land *beyond* the threshold of death. There is something downright convincing about the striking correspondences between the eyewitness reports given us by so many different "reanimated" people from so many disparate cultures. The logical next step—studying ancient cultures' books of the dead—would lead us further and cast more light on the landscapes of the after-death worlds. Understanding these texts, however, requires us to penetrate the mythological symbolism in which their messages are couched, and it requires us to take the notion of reincarnation seriously.

Reincarnation research like that conducted by the American researcher Ian Stevenson is a good place to begin. Thanks to his work, it is now possible to get a feeling for this theme without the need to abandon one's critical mode of thought. When one begins to study the issue, one soon discovers that the arguments in favor of the existence of reincarnation are much more plausible than those that try to deny its reality. The amount of collected material has grown so large and so comprehensive that even the most skeptical readers can scarcely continue doubting the truth of the best-documented cases. Of course, it is quite difficult to prove that reincarnation exists, and fundamentally impossible to prove that it does not exist.

It is only a small step from the books of the dead to the philosophies and religions of cultures regard reincarnation as the most natural thing in the world. These cultures include all archaic ones as well as the majority of the great religions. When one considers that nearly all the world's cultures agree on this point, one begins to feel peculiarly isolated in one's adherence to the Western worldview. Buddhist philosophy, which explicitly regards itself as a *weltanschauung* rather than as a religion, makes it especially easy to understand reincarnation within the context of the wheel of rebirth. The Buddhist concept is one version of the pattern of life as expressed in the familiar mandala.

People who prefer not to stray too far afield from Christianity can also find potential access to the idea of reincarnation in that context. The first great Fathers of the Church (e.g., St. Augustine) regarded reincarnation as axiomatic. There are even some verses in the Bible that remain wholly illogical unless one interprets them in terms of reincarnation. The best known is the verse in which the apostles ask Christ whether or not he is the reincarnation of the prophet Elijah. This question would make no sense unless the idea of reincarnation were known and accepted by the apostles. The Nazarene and Essene sects, which were widely distributed at the time of Christ and represented the esoteric version of Judaism, both believed in reincarnation. Christ's answer to the question casts no aspersions on reincarnation: the man whom the apostles have in mind, Christ says, has already come. There can be no doubt that Christ is alluding to John the Baptist. A number of facts suggest the Bible was not "cleansed" of passages alluding to reincarnation until the 5th century at the behest of the pope. Even from this standpoint, the notion of a cycle of rebirths is by no means as far fetched as it may seem at first glance. A closer look at the Christian context *ars moriendi* serves to deepen one's understanding of this theme.

If one prefers to rely solely on one's common sense, one soon finds this route, too, leads directly to the realization that death is not the ultimate end. Since physicists and mystics alike are in full agreement that everything in the universe is vital vibration, would not it be peculiar if human life were the only exception? Everything vibrates in its own unique rhythm. These cycles are often too large for us to perceive them from our limited human viewpoint, but that is no reason to deny their existence.

After an intensive study of the aforementioned sources, one gradually begins to lose the feeling that the burden of proof lies with the adherents of the reincarnation idea. Their worldview is so much in harmony with the old traditions, while the latest scientific discoveries are so logical and reasonable, and so comparatively free of contradictions that not they, but their opponents, are the ones from whom one wants to demand proof that reincarnation *does not* exist. Anyone who claims that human life is an accidental event and out of rhythm with the rest of the cosmos ought to be required to provide proof for this improbable and outlandish position.

New Approaches for Becoming More Intimate with Death

Thanks to the aforementioned work by Elisabeth Kübler-Ross, the German-speaking countries (and especially Switzerland) have seen the burgeoning of the hospice movement as a highly therapeutic approach to the task of liberating death and dying from its taboos. People who feel called to this profession accompany the dying through this last segment of life's journey. Companionship makes the entire process much easier for the dying individuals, and also helps the escorts reconcile themselves to this difficult and challenging theme. For society as a whole, this latter effect may eventually prove most significant since it is creating a group of people who, rather than fearfully avoiding this issue, are able to approach death and dying with respect and competence.

The hospice movement, which enjoys widespread support from the general public in Germany and is gradually gaining credibility in medical circles, also provides reason for optimism. The hospice movement is still just a "stepchild" compared with the profound escort and support for the dying provided by a culture such as the Tibetan, but at least it represents a step in the right direction. Western medicine's strict separation of body, soul and mind makes the issue more difficult for us. Archaic cultures, on the other hand, regard all three as a natural unity. As long as our society lacks a priest-physician figure like that in the Tibetan Buddhist tradition, providing competent escorts for dying people will likely remain a difficult task.

Death Rituals in Our Society

The phenomenon of extreme unction shows the importance of a ritual for this last and most important transition, and also shows the depths of its anchorage in our souls. Although this ritual is commonly understood and used as a death sacrament in Germany and in predominantly Catholic countries, its real intent is quite different. First of all, *letzte Ölung* (meaning "last oiling")—the typical German name for this rite—is misleading since the correct term is *Krankensalbung* (meaning "anointing the sick"). Ever since the days of the apostles, the Church has understood this as a sacramental act to be performed for ailing people whose bodies and souls are weak. It has its roots in the healing promised in the Epistle of James (James 5:14-15), where it is written: "Is any sick among you? Let him call for the elders of the church and let them pray over him, anointing him with oil in the name of the Lord: And the prayer of faith shall save the sick, and the Lord shall raise him up, and if he have committed sins, they shall be forgiven him."

Especially in the Western Church, the needs of the people and pastoral practice have transformed this act of healing the sick into a sacrament for the dying and thus invented the "last oiling." Despite several attempts by the Church (e.g., at the Council of Trient and in the more recent catechisms) to rectify this misunderstanding, the notion of extreme unction as a final prayer for the dying person has persisted. Attempts to correct this have expressly emphasized that the intent of the rite is not to prepare for the imminent end of life. Rather than being understood as a precursor to death, extreme unction should be understood as a rescue. The sacrament of extreme unction should be given to people suffering from any serious illness that has shattered the integrity of human well-being. It can also be received more than once in the course of one's life, and can even be given several times during the course of a particular illness.

The Catholic Church thus has an official sacrament for sick people, but neither it nor the Protestant Church have a sacramental rite of transition. Nonetheless, the lack of such a rite cannot prevent the faithful from (mis)understanding the anointing of the gravely ill as a last oiling for the dying. Because of this persistent misunderstanding, the anointing of the ill (as extreme unction) has taken on the character of a rite of passage. In most Catholics' field of consciousness, the whole situation looks more or less like this: dying people ease their conscience by making a (last) confession of their sins and, in return, receive extreme unction as an initiation prior to crossing the threshold into the next world.

After the individual has crossed over, the physical body that remains behind is taken care of through ritual. Most people in our culture continue to perform this ritual, although a ritualized escort for the departing *soul* would be far more important than elaborate care for the inanimate *body*. Our undue concern for the physical remains is yet another obvious expression of the exaggerated emphasis we place on material reality. The threat of being denied a Christian burial is even misused by some representatives of the Church in a last-ditch effort to prevent disappointed Christians from leaving the Church. The anxious soul asks itself, "If not a Christian burial, what then?"—and generally remains, more or less unwillingly, within the fold of the faithful.

It seems likely that the fear of departing from accepted conventions is an essential reason for the continued strength of the official churches. They maintain their worldly power (and their tax base) in Germany thanks to the "silent majority" who no longer actively participate in ecclesiastical life, but who nonetheless quietly continue to pay their church taxes. People prefer not to dispense with churchly protection altogether, even if that protection is solely restricted to disposing of one's mortal remains. Although most materialists cannot provide a rational justification for it, the majority still feel that it is important to have a ritualized framework for their final departure. There actually is profound wisdom within these ancient rituals, although often even the priests who conduct these rituals are only marginally aware of their deeper meaning.

Although Protestantism has preserved much less relationship to ritual in general, it also does not dispense with a final blessing over the cadaver. In an intact culture, this is above all a ritual for the survivors: the soul of the deceased is long since in good otherworldly hands, but the ritual helps the dead person's next-of-kind reconcile themselves to the fact of death. In our culture, funerals are also useful for the soul of the departed since the disoriented soul tends to tarry near its corpse and does not fully realize that its body has died until, observing the burial from the Great Beyond, the soul finally grasps this fact. It is therefore not a good idea to unduly delay the funeral and burial. In addition, the phrase "ashes to ashes, dust to dust" provides poetic closure for the circle of life on the material plane. A striking similarity between baptism and burial rites is the meal the participants share after the conclusion of the religious service. There is an undeniable joy to both meals, as anyone who has attended an Irish wake can testify. Is the meal after the baptism a welcome and the meal after the burial a farewell? Or vice versa? The answer depends entirely on one's perspective. Baptism is a welcoming to this world and a farewell to the otherworld. Burial is a farewell to this world and a celebration of welcome into the world beyond.

Customs such as dressing the cadaver in its finest clothes or in a special shroud prove that we still preserve some remnants of the idea that the dead person is about to embark on a journey. We should not scoff at the Chinese custom of erecting comfortable houses in cemeteries for their departed relatives and filling those houses with food and good-luck charms. Such houses give the survivors a physical room where, in their thoughts, they can regularly meet with their departed relatives and, in so doing, reconcile themselves to the inevitable fact of their own deaths. So-called "primitive" peoples sometimes preserve the bodies of dead relatives and allow the mummies to "live" with them in their homes for a while. This may seem macabre to us, but it is really nothing other than a more conscious variant of our inhumane tendency to emotionally cling to our dead, despite the fact that this clinging only hinders their progress through the various spheres of life that follow physical death. Especially in esoteric circles, it has become popular to pester the dead by employing mediums to seek out the souls of departed friends or relatives, rather than letting go of them and allowing them to depart in peace.

As is the case during baptism (as an entry into this world), so too during the funeral (as an exit from this world), all four of the classical elements can be used. Interment in the *earth* is still typical, but cremation with the help of the element of *fire* is becoming increasingly popular. Burial at sea (the element of *water*) is another traditional method. Only *air* burial is still unknown in our culture, although it has been practiced for many centuries by the Parsees in India and by various other cultures in the Himalayan region. Simply because it is unfamiliar is not a valid reason to reject or disparage it. There is nothing inherently more unaesthetic about the vultures in Bombay arriving to carry off parts of a body from the tower where the corpse has been laid than there is about the worms arriving to do their subterranean work after the gravediggers and mourners have gone home. Each of these elemental funeral rites emphasizes a different aspect of the whole. Interment makes bidding farewell to the body the central point; cremation emphasizes cauterization of the soul, as it separates itself from the body like a phoenix from the ashes; burial at sea emphasizes the soul's return to the primal ocean; air burial accentuates the resurrection and ascension of the soul-bird.

Requiem masses during the interval after death are the Christian version of escorting the soul as practiced in many archaic and Eastern cultures. The energy that is built up during the ritual is definitely able to reach the soul of the departed and to offer it support during the next transitions. Requiem masses thereby provide a kind of protective escort for the next phases of the soul's journey. Tibetan Buddhist lamas provide a similar (albeit far more intensive) escort service for the departed soul as it continues on its path through the various sometimes threatening levels of the bardo. Westerners are apt to underestimate the value of such service, simply because they have little or no access to the subtle energetic levels of the soul. We are, of course, free to ignore an area of reality, but our ignoring it does not make it any less real.

The idea that everything ends in the cemetery is only true for the body which, at least for a certain period of time, does indeed rest in peace. The soul, on the other hand, faces a transition that, depending on the details of its life thus far, can be quite strenuous. People who are unprepared for this situation and who have lived their lives without much interest in a higher authority are apt to encounter a big surprise after death. It is no coincidence that many people in our culture harbor doubts about the peace of the cemetery. Even the most rational, most logical people devise all kinds of superstitious denial strategies to avoid walking alone through a cemetery at night. The "soul of the folk" knows that the likelihood of finding peace there is by no means guaranteed. Too many souls continue to tarry near their old, now moldy cadavers. Even the body experiences only a temporary rest since the active processes of decay begin as soon as a soul has "shuffled off this mortal coil."

Death from a Spiritual Point of View

Experiences in reincarnation therapy—in which it is quite common to relive the events before, during and after one's death in a previous life—largely coincide with descriptions of death and dying in various Eastern religious traditions. As the last crisis in life, dying really is the acme of life: everything else leads to this culmination. One can, in fact, view one's entire life as a preparation for dying. Death is the real test of maturity because this decisive moment puts whatever we have learned over the years to the ultimate test. The fear of death, then, is like the anxiety students feel before an exam. And since this is life's biggest—and quite literally its "final" —exam, it can generate the greatest fear. Especially for people who have gone through life claiming not to be afraid of death, this moment is the ultimate test.

Many myths feature this motif of death as a test. In classical antiquity, the image of Hades or Pluto (god of the underworld) presiding in his dreary palace and passing judgment over the souls of the dead was a well-known motif. In ancient Egypt, it was the goddess Maat who weighed the hearts of the dead to determine whether their hearts were too light or too heavy. Christians are familiar with the notion of the Last Judgment, although for them this "final exam" is postponed until the end of time.

When a person dies consciously (i.e., slowly rather than suddenly, for example, in an unexpected accident), the separation of soul from body is usually experienced as a spiral suction drawing the soul out of the body. During this process, the soul still remains anchored in the ethereal body, which is like a body composed of electromagnetic fields. This ethereal body is usually cut off from its old energy supply (which ran through the physical body) for a brief period of time and must draw its energy from whatever sources it can find. This is why people who felt close to the deceased person and who keep a vigil near the dying person sometimes suddenly feel weak and de-energized. In this situation, the dying take the energy they need from the living. This is yet another reason dying people ought not be left alone and without companions during this transitional phase. Although this donation of energy does not do any serious harm to the donors, it helps the dying person very much. It is also a good idea to light candles and put fresh flowers in the room where a person is dying because candles and flowers can also supply the ethereal body with ethereal energy. Since this is only a brief transitional period in which the soul is still close to its former body and is freeing itself from its last material ties, there is no need to exaggerate such efforts. The idea is not to detain the soul, but simply to facilitate its passage out of this world. If a soul insists on remaining in this world, ghostly apparitions may appear, and these "spooks" will continue trying to acquire ethereal life energy for themselves.

On the other hand, it might be a good idea to draw the curtains in the death room or to prevent too much sunlight from entering the room since sunlight would dissolve the ethereal body too quickly and thus give the soul too little time for this first transition. Precautionary measures such as this are unnecessary when the dying person has been suffering from a long, slow illness since in such cases the ethereal body has already separated itself adequately. Its dissolution ought to take place as quickly as possible, but not so fast that the soul becomes totally disoriented. Mournful wailing or loud weeping is customary in some cultures and can even include the employment of professional mourners who caterwaul over the deceased although they feel no personal grief at the death. The goal of such loud weeping is to drive away evil spirits. It would make more sense to stand by the dying person with prayers and thoughts, or to play a requiem as accompanying music. Help of this sort, which can include reading aloud the appropriate passages from a book of the dead, can serve as "road signs" for the soul to help it find its proper path.

At the same time, the ethereal body separates from the material body on the physical plane. The material body can then begin to decay since it is the ethereal body's energetic field that maintains the physical body in its stable form. The moment a person dies, breathing and the energy supply are both terminated and the ethereal body and soul begin to separate from the physical body. The soul rests within the ethereal body, and it begins to sink into a sort of unconsciousness. One should not try to contact the soul at this point, but rather leave it to peacefully slumber in its ethereal sleep. Ideally, when the soul awakens from this sleep, it has already freed itself from the ethereal body and has left the material world behind. The soul awakens in the same state of mind it had before its body died. If, on the other hand, the soul is awakened while it is still within the ethereal body, this can cause "spooky" phenomena because the confused soul *haunts* the surroundings.

After the final separation from matter, the soul begins to "dream" in the astral realm. This is the world from which all of those spectacular reports come, and it is also the realm where the famous "life film" is seen. Still close to the images of the life it so recently left behind, the soul can witness that life pass in review. A person who has been bound by the dimensions of space and time may find this difficult to imagine, but these two great sources of illusion have no power in the astral realm. We are familiar with this situation from the realm of dreams that prepares us each night for the experiences that await us on the astral plane. If we regard sleep as death's little brother, we have a useful analogy that even includes the resting phase experienced by many souls on the other side. In Greek mythology, Hypnos (sleep) is the brother of Thanatos (death), and both are the sons of Nyx (night).

Like space and time, so too must the logical mind surrender its sovereignty in the astral plane. Thus, the soul is confronted with the mirror of its deeds—without the intervening intellect and its familiar rationalizations that have helped us worm our way out in the past. The soul sees itself, face-to-face with its past deeds, measured solely in the spiritual terms of its highest vibratory level—the self. The further the soul separated itself from this highest level during its previous incarnation, the more severe the struggle will be during this retrospective vision of life.

Various religions describe this field of the Beyond with images of purgatory and hell, but in the strictest sense it really is not a place at all: it is a state of consciousness, a purifying and cauterizing fire for souls. This situation is wholly subjective and entirely dependent upon one's personal experiences in the life that has just come to an end. A Christian's purgatory would differ from a Muslim's hell; and, beyond that, each Christian would have his own heaven and own individual hell. He has already constructed that heaven or hell during the course of life, and now, after physical death, is free to take possession of this self-made realm. On the other hand, these states of being are likely to have many archetypal similarities, just as all religions share a common essence and all human beings share common primal experiences (e.g., lust, hunger and thirst).

This is the place where souls must look truth in the face. This confrontation can assume purgatorial dimensions or be experienced merely as a brief transitional stage. In any case, the soul learns a karmic lesson: you always reap what you have sown. Even though this state of consciousness has more similarities with the world of dreams than with our familiar physical reality, the "dreams" here are so vivid that it is no longer possible to escape from them (as many modern people prefer to do each night). We would be better advised to take advantage of our nightly dreams as preparatory exercises. Since time plays no role in the after-death worlds, endless repetition is the mildest and most merciful method of teaching life's lessons.

Since we are not dealing with a "space" in our sense of the word but are instead experiencing fields of consciousness that correspond to the soul's patterns, souls who share a particular type of problem are likely to congregate in the corresponding field. To be in a field together with all hatred or envy or greed is a cauterizing experience in itself. Together with all other souls who share a similar pattern, each individual soul must confront precisely those areas and issues where it got stuck during the life it has just left behind. The size of the group enormously increases the pressure of realization. Despite the large number of fellow sufferers, each soul must proceed through this learning experience on its own and without outside help. Neither prayer nor Mass can or should spare us the need to wander through the circle of our own images, although both activities can make that passage easier for us since they send us noticeable energy for our onward path. If we have lived a courageous and fulfilled life, we are already familiar with this process of moving from one level to the next since we practiced it in the world as we evolved from one stage of development to the next.

Just as mundane fire cleanses infected wounds, the astral fire of realization cleanses the wounds of life. The pain can be overwhelming, but this only means that healing is all the more certain afterward. This fire has nothing to do with torture or penalty, but is entirely directed toward purification and realization. According to Dion Fortune,[97] the astral fire "neither punishes nor pardons—it heals."

Not unlike the way the soul experiences the cauterizing fire as a rueful field of consciousness, there is also a complementary pole—a field of consciousness where dreams come true—that we commonly assume to be heaven. It can also be a lesson for the soul to experience the fulfillment of dreams that never came true in the world. It is therefore sensible to fulfill as many dreams as possible here on earth and thereby learn the corresponding lessons. Whatever we have realized and understood but not yet translated into actions during our worldly lives can be learned in these intermediate realms. If we return to earth again in a future life, we bring these experiences and realizations with us as talents and inborn tendencies.

Dying is usually a long process rather than an abrupt step. As we move toward the other side, one curtain of consciousness after another closes in the world. Meanwhile, on the other side, one veil after another is drawn aside. Analogously, one body after another dies away: first the material body, then the ethereal body, then the astral body, and finally the mental body. It is like slowly fording several streams. Helpful entities—luminous figures or angels about whom we are hearing increasingly many reports nowadays—await us on each new shore, where they lovingly welcome us as new arrivals. This "welcoming committee" also helps us with our first steps in the new surroundings, before we are obliged to continue the journey on our own.

From a spiritual point of view, the body that has been left behind on the material plane is the least important factor and should be returned as rapidly as possible to the elements of which it is made. It is characteristic of our materialistically oriented society that we expend so much time and energy dealing with the physical remains: inviting relatives to the funeral, publishing death announcements, catering the wake, selecting the coffin and the wreaths, and choosing a gravestone and an appropriate inscription. In most cases, the funeral and burial put so much stress on the family they have little or no time left for the essentials—namely, for taking care of the soul and helping it on its path into the Beyond.

For example, it makes little or no sense to continue to imagine the deceased person as a corporeal entity still tied to its old, familiar and usually worn-out body. Neither does it help to distribute portraits of the deceased in her old familiar form—a form the soul has just left behind. It would make much more sense to sit in silence and contemplate the immortal soul itself. Consequently, it is likewise nonsensical to preserve the body for as long as possible. Neither mummification with formaldehyde nor a sturdy coffin of solid oak are necessary or appropriate. Cremation is the fastest and most direct way to return the body's matter to the various elemental realms. Dust should again become dust—as soon as possible. Dion Fortune therefore believes that cremation followed by scattering the ashes is the most sensible alternative. Experiences in reincarnation therapy have shown that the soul who has passed into the Beyond is not at all interested in the details of the burial ceremony. The soul is uninterested in the body it has left behind, just as we take no further interest in a worn-out cloak we have given up. Funerals and burial ceremonies are only useful for souls who have trouble finding the path into the Beyond or for souls who cannot believe their bodies have indeed died. In such cases, the funeral ceremony can help the soul to realize that its bell has tolled.

Exercises for Dealing with Death

1. Stroll across a cemetery as evening twilight falls.
2. Observe a period of mourning for relatives who have passed away; keep this interval free of other duties; wear black; attend requiem masses and make friends with this transition.

3. Withdraw from everyday concerns and concentrate your mind on giving spiritual escort to the deceased, knowing that you, too, will follow them soon; learn to be a companion to dying people in the sense popularized by Elisabeth Kübler-Ross; read her books and the books of the dead from other cultural traditions.

4. Rituals of farewell in the circle of survivors: each person tells a story of personal importance that reminds him of the deceased.

5. Portray events you have shared with the deceased: write prose or poetry, paint, write a letter to the deceased—as long as these activities are carried out as a way of letting go rather than binding yourself to the deceased.

6. Rituals of farewell in the context of gestalt therapy: imagine the deceased person seated on an empty chair beside you; tell the person everything you always wanted to tell her while she was alive but that you left unspoken until now.

7. A memorial celebration with candles and the deceased person's favorite music or favorite poems; memorial minutes; periods of silence.

8. Plant a tree each year on the anniversary of the person's death. Celebrate the anniversary of the death as you used to celebrate her birthday. Make cemeteries into forests. Graves are the expression of a possessive way of thinking that is outmoded; they are even more limiting than allotment gardens. If you cannot do without, you may want to hang a memorial plaque on the tree.

PART III

1. The Day as a Reflection of Life

According to the *pars pro toto* principle, we can find the whole within each part. Consequently, we can also find our entire life within each day. When we compare how we Westerners spend our day with the way Eastern or archaic peoples spend theirs, we can clearly see differences in the emphasis placed on death and on other cardinal points in the course of life.

Most of us sleep through sunrise and thus miss the start of the day altogether. This daily behavior corresponds to the unconscious way in which our society generally deals with conception and birth. Eastern societies obviously pay more attention to the needs of the newly arriving soul. Asian wisdom traditions know that the available ethereal energies are strongest at sunrise, which is why Eastern people are happiest when they can greet the new day with meditation or prayer. We Westerners, on the other hand, having overslept the dawn of life and thus gotten off to a poor start, are obliged to chase after life, desperately trying to catch up with it. The later we begin to face each day (and our lives as a whole), the more hectic the subsequent hours and years are liable to be.

Unlike Mediterranean people, Central Europeans are seldom able to enjoy the luxury of an afternoon siesta, but frantically try to make up for lost time, sometimes even eating lunch in a fast-food *restaur*ant where we sacrifice the last shreds of our chances for actually *restor*ing our diminished energies. Our midday crisis parallels our typical midlife crisis: both are characterized by a lack of awareness and by the absence of a pause to relax. All too often, midlifers ignore or overlook the change in life that is due. Just as a hectic lunch hour unfavorably affects the rest of the day, so too does the failure to adequately confront midlife unfavorably affect the issues that need to be faced in life's second half. If we would allow ourselves a midday (or midlife) siesta, we would no doubt be better able to cope with the second half of the day and the second half of life with undistracted concentration and with our minds at ease. Unfortunately, most of us allow the second half to become a hectic sprint toward the finish line.

When we finally come home late in the evening, we are quite right to feel that we have gotten too little from our day or our life, and we tend to search for some escape from that unpleasant feeling. If we would take sundown as a signal for beginning the regenerative phase that comes with sleep (as archaic peoples no doubt did), we would not feel as though we had been cheated out of life altogether, especially because most of us underestimate the significance of night. Rather than learning to appreciate night per se, we make night into day and exploit the nighttime hours for whatever we can get out of them. The majority of Westerners spend their evenings watching movies on TV. Fully absorbed in this world of illusions and appearances, they vicariously experience the more exciting life stories of others—and these stories typically stop long before midlife (i.e., when boy finally gets girl and the happy couple shares their first kiss). To call this pattern a "happy ending" represents a severe abridgement of life's pattern, since a couple's first kiss is, at best, little more than a "happy start." Nonetheless, we are so disinterested in the remainder of their lives together that the tale is seldom the stuff of which films are made. The bottom line is downright depressing: we sleep through the beginning, we do not get fully involved until after puberty and most of us switch ourselves off before we even reach the middle. When we consider the childish character of typical TV programming, there is not much left to lift our spirits.

Many of us know and most of us can feel that the last minute, now-or-never panic that comes upon us in the evening of our lives and in each day's evening stands in direct contradiction to the peace and quiet of the night. It reflects the panic so many Westerns feel at the end of an unfulfilled life spent in hard, unsatisfying work. Nightlife is the mostly unsuccessful attempt to live out the masculine half of the day during its feminine half. We stay up late, even though we know that the healthiest sleep occurs during the hours before midnight. But we cannot treat ourselves to that well-earned rest because we have not yet come to terms with the day and with our lives: we simply do not know when to admit that enough is enough. Whereas archaic people use the nighttime hours for rest and for surrender to the world of images conjured by the dreaming soul, we prefer the world of images conjured for us by Hollywood and the media moguls. Since the images they offer are generally alien to us and have little or nothing to do with the day we have just lived through, it is no surprise that they are far less profound than our own eidetic and oneiric imagery. Rather than rounding out and completing the day, they merely confront us with new problems.

In striking contrast to Hollywood films, the "film" we see at the end of life when our lives pass in review is made entirely from our own images. A corresponding and highly beneficial exercise would be to spend a few minutes each evening reviewing the images of the day that has just come to an end. The more consciously we experience the daily transition between wakefulness and sleep, the easier it will be for us to move through that all-important transition at the end of life. It is no coincidence that we use the phrase "the evening of one's life." A little bit of life comes to an end every evening, and the setting sun is an indication of this. The extraordinary degree of attention we pay to sunsets is evidence of an unconscious preoccupation with this central theme in life. Hardly any other (natural) event is so frequently photographed and so enthusiastically admired. But if we habitually use our evenings to distract ourselves from real life, we run the risk of slumbering through the grand exit at life's close. If we are accustomed to unconsciously allowing ourselves to slip into the embrace of the little brother (sleep), we may find ourselves suddenly swept away when big brother (death) arrives to claim us.

Many people in our society would prefer to die in their sleep (i.e., unexpectedly and unconsciously). Equally many would prefer a sudden, quick death to a long process of slowly dying. The medical establishment therefore sees nothing wrong with the common practice of allowing patients who have been suffering from chronic pain to slip unawares from anesthesia into death. This spares the patient a certain amount of physical discomfort, but ignores the significance of sleep and the critical importance of the final transition out of this life and into the Beyond. Many people in Germany confuse sleep with unconsciousness, and these are usually the same people who overlook the opportunities inherent in the process of dying and in all of life's other significant transitions. Healthy sleep is by no means an interval of unconsciousness, but is filled with vivid and lively dreams. The distant goal—like that to be attained in yogic sleep—is to maintain wide-awake awareness throughout the entire night. On the larger plane, this would correspond to total awareness during the postmortem phase as we transition through all the tests leading to our next conscious incarnation. Life's film, in which the important situations of the past pass in review before our inner eye, is nothing other than a stocktaking of the life we have lived thus far, and is essentially no different than the stocktaking that accompanies every other critical transition in life. Here, too, as in every other crisis in life, the opportunities for learning are tremendous.

It is only natural that the final stocktaking (the "bottom line" as it were) is more important than all of the "subtotals." But this final inventory can prove to be more unpleasant than the intermediate ones, especially if those intermediate ones were propped up on borrowed "cash" and if the gap between body and soul continued to grow wider with each successive transition. On the other hand, if a person has mastered life's phases and preserved the harmony between body, soul and mind, that individual is usually also willing and able to leap this last hurdle without encountering any major problems. But if a person feels she has been cheated of certain segments of life, has failed to live out essential phases or learn decisive lessons along the way, that individual is apt to have difficulty letting go at the end because unfinished business weighs upon her shoulders. In this context, errors and deficiencies that reveal vacancies and deficits become obvious. Things one may have done wrong in the past are usually a much smaller problem than missed opportunities. Most people find it easier to pardon a failed attempt than to pardon someone who has never attempted to find a passage through a crisis because of inadequate self-confidence, or has steadfastly refused to make an essential decision. The primordial pattern we observed in the parable of the Prodigal Son is likely to reappear at this point: we must dare to live our lives, and failure is no disgrace.

Situations in which we have given priority to our heads rather than our hearts can also exacerbate the difficulties encountered in the final transition of death. People who allowed rational arguments and a lack of self-confidence to dissuade them from pursuing a great love can find themselves suffering the consequences decades later on their deathbeds. The heart has a healthier and more courageous relationship to life's challenges than does the intellect. Instinct and "gut feelings" would have been the most natural guide, and would have most fostered the person's spiritual development. Most people in our society are even less likely to heed their instincts than they are to heed the stirrings of their hearts. It is above all the intellect and the reasoning faculty that have led us astray and prompted us to dispense with rites of transition and rituals of initiation. The intellect mistakenly assumes we can do without everything that lies beyond the narrow scope of reason's ken. The ideal would be a person with well-developed "gut feelings," an individual who has learned to use the intellect but is still able to let the heart integrate the various competing factors and make the final decisions.

We have evolved quite a long way from the primal pattern; and this evolution has not been solely to our disadvantage. Prehistoric people lived in close affinity with nature, and they experienced puberty and adolescence as one and the same thing. After that phase had been completed, the prehistoric human being was an adult. He had reached life's midpoint (when the sun reaches its zenith) at midday. And just as he went to sleep at sundown, his life did not last beyond this point. Life expectancy was generally less than forty years. By contrast, modern human beings take longer to grow up and have longer lifetimes during which to do so. We no longer become mature adults at puberty; at best, we might gain some measure of maturity during our adolescent years. Thus we reach midlife not at midday, but significantly later. We no longer go to bed at sundown because our work goes on even though the workday has come to an end. Having more time allows us to differentiate more. We took the step from nature to culture, yet it seems that nowadays we are preparing to abandon that hard-won culture. Despite the extra time we have gained, too many of us are unable to cope with life's tasks.

If only we took advantage of it, our privileged situation would offer us excellent opportunities for reconciling ourselves to the day and to life as a whole. We could start each day at sunup, awakening refreshed after the *re-creation* of sleep. This early hour of the day is naturally filled with plenty of energy. It is the ideal hour for morning meditation and prayer, and for preparing ourselves to meet the new day. The morning toilet is a classical ritual of purification—all we need to do is recognize it as such and recharge it with that energy. Everybody knows the old saying: "The early bird catches the worm." This is why, in a monastic schedule, dawn is the time to sing and celebrate the new day. Morning vespers above all include the spiritual bread to be shared. We could enjoy a corresponding feeling of joyous gratitude as we leave our homes after having taken our break-fast and broken the night's fast.[1]

A kind of threshold ritual like those that are still practiced in the Buddhist tradition occurs every time we cross the threshold and step out into the world. In the course of a lifetime, this step corresponds to puberty—the critical transition that demands all our energy and all our courage to master the difficulties on our path. In the course of a single day, this step corresponds to the time when we take our work into our hands and create the necessary breakthrough. Creative achievements can grow and goals can be reached when we draw upon this abundant res-ervoir of fresh energy. We are coming closer to the best hours of the day, the hours of vitality and enthusiasm when work is a pleasure. At midday we can enjoy a well-earned rest as we eat our lunch and retire for a pleasant nap that fully regenerates our vital energies.

After resting and crossing the midpoint of the day, the time comes for introspective work. The overview we gained during the morning hours enables us to decide the next steps needed to deal with essentials. Five o'clock tea brings a pause, after which we can begin thinking about tomorrow before concluding our work for today. "Conclusion" means finding an end, bring-ing things to a point where we can leave them as they are and where we need not take them home with us. It is quitting time at the evening of a long day or time to retire at the evening of a long life, and both situations are worth celebrating. The journey home and the retirement from work are joyous events that lead directly to leisure time. Leisure ought to be consciously experi-enced as an opposite pole to work. Early evening is luxury time: it ought to be fun and it ought to be enjoyed. It is time for culture in the sense of evening meditation, music and good food. The German language still uses the phrases "musical culture" and "dining culture," both of which suggest the originally profound link between cult (i.e., religion) and each of these areas. It really has not been such a long time since all music was sacred music and every meal was framed between prayers.

Evening twilight and sunset make the day and one's life older. They give us time to do whatever it is we have been looking forward to all day (or all life). There is no reason that simple pleasure cannot sometimes take the form of watching a well-chosen film. Even the more or less unaware fans of action films have a chance to acquaint themselves with death—they will face it themselves sooner or later—although these films do not bring death into relation to their own situations and the situations of the day. Late evening should be devoted to preparations for sleep and for reviewing the day that is about to end. It is time to take stock, perhaps by writing a few lines in one's diary. At the same time, it is also the moment to consciously let go of whatever ties still bind us. Because the evening toilet is the ritual that concludes the day, it is no mere coincidence that it involves ablution and cleansing. We wash off whatever remnants of the day are still clinging to the surface of our skin, and simultaneously let go of superfluities that have no lasting value for our souls.

As we crawl into bed and drift into sleep, our awareness turns toward the future, toward the realm of dreams. Falling asleep at night means encountering the god Hypnos (sleep); dying means encountering his divine brother Thanatos (death). Both encounters correspond with one another in many ways. The brothers' mother, Nyx (night) has her phases and stages, even if we generally pay little attention to them. Scientific experiments have shown that the hours of sleep before midnight are especially healthy and refreshing because this is the phase of deep sleep that is so important for detoxification and regeneration. After midnight, phases of deep sleep alternate with dream phases. This is the time for deep and essential dreams, for visions and lucid experiences. The soul embarks on journeys into the astral plane. Total awareness in this area would correspond to yogic sleep. In colloquial German, the time after midnight is called the *Geisterstunde* ("spirit hour"). Morning twilight and the crepuscular hour of the new day frequently coincide with dream or REM phases. The themes of these dreams are generally more superficial, as indicated by the sexual dreams that commonly occur during this phase. The themes involve coming to terms with day-dreams we have been unable to live out, and the dreams generally revolve around lusty or anxiety producing images such as those Sigmund Freud and his students were so fond of analyzing. This is a kind of preparatory hour for the coming day, albeit on a largely unconscious level. It ends when we wake up and start the whole cycle anew.

At this point it becomes easy to understand why Eastern people use their morning meditation to help them evolve in a profound spiritual sense and use their evening meditation for regeneration and recuperation. Perhaps it will also become clear how day follows day, year follows year, and life follows life in an eternal rhythm that embraces all living things. Or, as Manfred Kyber says,

Again, again and ever again
you descend to this Earth,
to womb after womb,
until you have learned to see by the light
that life and death are one
and all times are timeless;
until the tireless, tiring chain of things
curls itself into a ring
within you—then
the will of the world is in your will,
stillness is in you—stillness—
and eternity.

2. The Proper Time and the Proper Sequence

To every thing there is a season,
and a time to every purpose under the heaven:
a time to be born, and a time to die;
a time to plant, and a time to pluck up
that which is planted;
a time to kill, and a time to heal;
a time to break down, and a time to build up;
a time to weep, and a time to laugh;
a time to mourn, and a time to dance;
a time to cast away stones, and a time to
gather stones together;
a time to embrace, and a time to
refrain from embracing;
a time to get, and a time to lose;
a time to keep, and a time to cast away;
a time to rend, and a time to sew;
a time to keep silence, and a time to speak;
a time to love, and a time to hate;
a time of war, and a time of peace.

—Ecclesiastes 3:1-8

2. The Proper Time and the Proper Sequence

All critical transitions have their due time. They cannot be accomplished too early; and if we delay them for too long, they become very difficult. The moment of our conception usually lies beyond the bounds of our responsibility and is therefore not a problem for us. But difficulties begin as early as birth. Birth, too, has its proper time: labor and delivery are never easy, but if they come at the right time they can be much less difficult. If physicians and their drugs induce labor too early, both mother and child are apt to have a difficult time of it. If the pregnancy continues too long, the delay allows the fetus to grow too large and delivery can be difficult and dangerous. The crisis of puberty will never again be as easy to cope with as it is between the ages of twelve and fourteen. Subsequent attempts at age thirty or even at fifty may provide income for psychotherapists but they seldom provide much pleasure for the clients. The midlife crisis is more difficult to localize in time, but it also has its own proper moment, which can vary from one individual to another. Once the well-known symptoms appear, we can be fairly certain midlife's proper time lies in the past. On the other hand, midlife and its critical symptoms can occur too early and cause much damage to young people who have retreated from life and into ashrams at too young an age. Death also has its own proper time. Hurrying death with well-meaning euthanasia will always be problematic, while delaying death with intensive medical treatments usually leads to undue misery.

In an archaic culture, it was easy to conduct the right rituals at the right times. Securely embedded within the tribe's field of consciousness, everyone in the tribe reached the various stages in life's pattern according to the same schedule. In addition, tribal societies had medicine women and medicine men who could sense when the time was ripe for a particular transition and its corresponding ritual. As this ability to sense the quality of time began to decline, rituals of transition were assigned to specific chronological ages in the life of the individual. It would have made more sense to link these rituals with particular events such as menarche or defeat in a battle. Struggles for power within a tribe often had the effect of showing the defeated (ex-)chief that the time had come for him to reorient himself and begin his homeward journey.

Nowadays, if we take these decisive transitions at all seriously, we generally couple them with chronological age, and this expedient is all too likely to fail. There is no such thing as an "average" human being. The whole situation becomes especially problematic when people who never overcame earlier crises in life try to compensate for those deficits at a later date through esoteric initiations. Even a successful career in a spiritual community is no substitute for the failure to cope with the transition of puberty.

Even the right rituals in the wrong sequence are of little use. It seems there is a hierarchical, ordering system in the depths of our souls, just as there is such a system in our bodies, where the sequence of evolutionary steps is strictly enforced by the development of the body's hormones. Everything has its proper time and proper place. This is an unpleasant truth for us, since we no longer have time and have only a few remaining places of power where rites of transition can be conducted. Recognition of this lack is the first step toward regaining a foothold in the pattern of life and beginning to search for new paths. Time will pass before collective energetic fields can be recharged, and until then we have no choice but to seek out our own individual paths and, insofar as it seems reasonable, orient ourselves according to ancient collective forms.

3. Perspectives

Recognize God in yourself as the Existent One
Who transcends before and after, transformation and
change
so that the moment dilates to eternity in you –
to that non-time which is God.

—Hilarion

Criteria for the Timing of Individual Transitions

The following criteria indicate that the proper moment has come for a new transition:

- sudden and unexpected tensions appear;
- you feel an inner uneasiness that can no longer be calmed by recourse to exercises that helped in the past;
- the feeling that you are sitting on a powder keg or are about to face an acid test;
- the appearance of an incalculability;
- a driven feeling without a clear goal;
- a sudden loss of interest in things that were important to you in the past;
- long-standing relationships and friendships break up; you no longer have anything to say to one another;
- you no longer take pleasure in work you found fulfilling in the past;

- you feel inner and outer resentment for structures that never bothered you in the past;
- rebellion for its own sake;
- you enjoy breaking norms you previously accepted and enjoy ignoring prohibitions you formerly abided by;
- surprises and craziness enter your life;
- the feeling of not knowing where to go and what to do with your energies.

Tools and Building Blocks for Some Rituals of Transition

Kathleen Wall is an American therapist who works especially with rituals. In her highly recommended book *Lights of Passage*, she writes, "Reading about rituals stimulates the mind; performing rituals stimulates life." Rituals are like a time-out-of-time that makes it possible for us to step out of the linear flow of time, establish contact with our innermost needs and recognize and seize the chances inherent in new phases of life. An exclusive place is a precondition for being able to enter this special *time-space*. In practically every fairy tale, myth or legend, the protagonist gains insights at an especially challenging place that is located beyond life's familiar, familial framework. An exclusive time is also important: all other mundane affairs must remain outside. In some rituals, regularity and rules also play a role the importance of which should not be underestimated.

You can determine when the moment has come for this kind of time-out-of-time by attending to the flow of life and being aware of the aforementioned criteria. The adequacy of our performance of the ritual depends above all on our own motivation. The danger lies less in the way the ritual is conducted than in our inner sluggishness in the face of novelty and in our "hopefully nothing bad will happen" mentality. When faced with doubts, most people opt for a familiar problem and against an innovative solution.

The Phases of the Ritual of Transition

Analogous to the alchemical scheme of dissolution and co-agulation (*"solve et coagula"*), most rituals involve three distinct steps. It is generally a good idea to include the following three steps in any ritual you devise or perform:

The dissolution: This phase corresponds to the letting go an old person must accomplish: the conscious abandonment of things that were familiar and customary in the past. One should be clear about exactly what aspects need to be surrendered from old roles, postures, behavioral patterns, habits and options. Symbolic phases of letting go are:

- burning in *fire* and strewing the ashes to the four winds;
- burial in the *earth* and surrendering what you bury to the processes of decay and/or dissolution;
- sinking in *water*;
- letting it fly and surrendering it to the realm of the *air*, for example, with a helium balloon.

Along with these classical paths of the four elements, other options might include: tearing, shredding, cutting apart, crushing, pounding (alchemical mortar), pulverizing and strewing.

The transition itself: This phase can be compared to wandering in a no-man's land between the fronts and between the times, where disorientation and polarized impulses reign. The seeker feels pulled back and forth between opposed poles. The positive aspect could be a trial period during which one learns that all growth is based on contradictions. During this interval, it is important to create enough space for negative emotions and feelings. If we try to escape from challenges, they change into demons whom destiny sends to pursue us; but if we accept challenges, anxiety and narrowness are transformed into openness and expansiveness.[2] The consequences and costs of the transition should be estimated, and responsibility for them should be accepted.

1.   Symbols of this phase include the empty chalice; the empty bowl or cup and the scooped out but still empty hole in the ground.

Exercises

• Polarity games: "Taste" both possible sides of a decision, either internally on the level of inner images or physically in the outer world. Trying out both options allows you to decide based on the more appropriate results.

• Crazy meals as an expression of a *crazy* situation: Cook and serve a dinner composed entirely of black and white foods, or use food coloring to dye everything blue in recognition of a "blue" phase (i.e., including blue napkins, blue candles).

The reunion with the new: This often begins with the discovery of a new vision that emerges from the mists of the second phase. Profound longing and passions for which there was no space in the old situation can become conscious and begin to express themselves. The second part of this phase is devoted to integration. The new vision must become firmly fixed and deeply rooted in one's life.

The symbols of the new should be given places of honor in one's life and environment. Appropriate symbols include pictures or sculptures (especially those one has made oneself), as well as collages, poems and any other objects that symbolize new departures, new awakening and novelty per se.

Exercises

- Ritually charged meals with foods symbolize a new beginning (e.g., seeds, bamboo sprouts, eggs, nuts, fruits). Ceremonies are not fully "digested" until their subsequent banquet has taken place (e.g., a wedding dinner, post-baptismal buffet, wake, business lunch after signing a big contract). A ritualized process of cooking and dining together is possible in preparing Christmas cookies, birthday cakes and so on. Potentially appropriate modern mealtime rituals include fondue, raclette, hot stone, Chinese wok and a buffet.

- A deliberate and conscious assignment of seats at the dining table is an important part of such rituals. A particular seat is often associated with a particular role (e.g., at a festival to celebrate menarche, the daughter might sit in the seat ordinarily occupied by her mother). Create an appropriate framework for the start and finish of the ritualized dinner (e.g., prayer, introspection, music).

- Use care in selecting the themes for discussion and be careful not to combine attempts to solve problems with the ritualized meal. It is better to confront problems in a roundtable ritual (as in political negotiations). Like the round table around which King Arthur's knights sat, each person in the circle enjoys equal status to contribute to the discussion.

- Parties with dancing: Many dances have a ritualistic element (e.g., line dances and waltzes, ecstatic trance dances).

- Rituals with plants: Sow seeds; plant trees, flowers, bushes or hedges (to symbolize setting limits). Observe their growth and consider how their growth is linked with your own.

- Regenerative rituals: Underwater massages, (thermal) baths, polarity work, shiatsu, yoga, tai chi.

- Special clothing: Ritualistic garments.

- Special lighting: Ritualistically kindle candles and extinguish them after the rite (e.g., the light of life on the birthday cake, the candles on the Christmas tree).
- Play appropriate music.
- Use scents that match the mood of the ritual: aromatic oils, incense.

Possible Building Blocks and Sequences of Exercises

1. Ritually take stock of prior phases in life that have occurred since the last major transition:
   - Emotionally: In your mind's eye, progress through the important stages of the past. Reread diary entries dating from those stages. Look at old photographs. Bring unfinished business and incomplete tasks to a conscious conclusion. Bid farewell to issues and objects that are obsolete and can be left behind.
   - Physically: A voluntarily imposed period of fasting.[3]

2. A ritual to cleanse yourself of past failures:
   - Conduct a ritual that is like a confession at which you speak to the people who were directly involved in your failure or to another appropriate individual (e.g., a priest).
   - Put an end to unresolved conflicts through forgiveness, confrontation.

3. Generalized exercises for purification:

   - Emotionally: Conduct rituals of elemental purification[4] (on the plane of inner imagery).
   - Physically: A conscious sauna ritual (purification by fire, "sweating it out"). A conscious bathing ritual (water ritual). A conscious breath ritual in the form of a session of

intensive breathing. Physical purification through fasting or by eating nothing but fruits to detoxify yourself.

4. Ceremonies that are appropriate for your own feeling about life (in external reality): Choose a special place for the ritual where you are certain not to be disturbed. Select the time of day that corresponds to the particular crisis in life (e.g., a puberty ritual might take place in the morning, a midlife ritual at noon, a ritual of returning home at sunset). Include only the right people, and be sure no one intrudes on the rite. Use all four elements. Invite people to witness the ritual. Use symbols whose contents are charged with meaning and energy (e.g., pictures, shapes, colors, sounds, movements, gestures). Practice the desired choreography in advance. Plan to include meditative time before and after the rite to prepare for it and digest it.

Additional Exercises

-   Thematic strolls: Encounter the elements of air and earth.
-   Earth ritual: Rest inside Mother Earth (e.g., in a mud bath). Regain your trust in the earth.
-   Pilgrimages to power spots associated with the particular crisis.
-   Medicine-wheel meditations: Each cardinal direction has its own special meaning.
-   Search for symbols in nature: An object to symbolize something that you are happy to let go of, another for something you regret letting go of; a third to symbolize something you definitely want to keep and a forth to represent the new dimension you want to actualize.
-   Find stones for unfinished business and put them to ritualistic uses.
-   Write (endless) letters and ritualistically burn them.
-   Make collages that emphasize a particular aspect (e.g., the future or the three phases of a particular transition).

- Try out (first on the plane of inner imagery and then in external reality) the life you will lead (e.g., in the vague no-man's land that precedes a decision). Live one day as if you had divorced yourself from your spouse, live another day as if you both had definitively decided to stay together, spend the third day in meditative retreat musing on what you experienced during the two preceding days.

4. Outlook

There are a number of reasons it is problematic to borrow rituals from foreign culture and use them in our own, even though it is tempting to do so since so few rituals survive in our culture. Unfortunately, we have neither the exterior nor the interior spaces needed for such rites, and the depths of our souls feel little or no kinship with their unfamiliar symbolism. Building up foreign fields in the depths of our souls is a long process that usually takes more time and patience than we have at our disposal.

Our chances for success would be better if we transfered our journeys from the outside world to the inner world. Carried aloft upon the wings of our thoughts and inner images, we can not only travel to other countries and other cultures, but can also travel in time. This makes it possible to experience rituals from various cultures and especially from our own cultural milieu's distant past. Reincarnation therapy has shown that such experiences are readily accessible during critical situations. They tend to appear almost automatically, rising to the surface of awareness as if of their own accord. If we are able to re-experience them consciously, such images can make valuable contributions and help us to master current crises.

The mechanism is not easily understood from a purely intellectual standpoint. It seems that the old experience highlights the momentary situation in the mandala of life and, vice versa, the present state of affairs once again evokes the old situation. More energy flows into the issue and, assuming that the individual possesses enough openness and readiness, she is better able to accept and digest the current transition. As I suggested at the outset, the pattern's effectiveness is independent of time and space, and its consequences extend into the present moment. Merely looking at patterns of this sort can evoke astonishing effects. A potential parallel to this situation might lie in the new physics, where it is well-known that every observation influences the process under observation.

Psychotherapeutic practice has shown the importance of working through problems in the proper sequence. Even with therapeutic help, it is difficult to cope with the midlife crisis unless the client has already dealt with her puberty. To consciously re-experience the proper sequence and thus build up the right stages one atop the other has a healing effect and makes it possible to bring a stagnant situation into motion. It allows the client to resume participation in a developmental process that has become stalled. This is one reason re-experiencing conception and birth plays such an important role at the outset of every reincarnation therapy. How we start something often determines the course of further development, and this principle is especially valid with respect to conception and birth since these processes lay the groundwork for basic patterns throughout the rest of our lives. It is even more important to re-experience the ways we dealt with crises in the earliest months of life. The rest of our life is basically nothing more than a series of births, and it is no coincidence that Germans have an idiom that literally means "it was a difficult birth" that they use when they have finally completed a difficult task.

Because our options on the exterior plane are limited, the inner plane becomes all the more important. Fortunately, we are comparatively free to do as we please on the plane of inner imagery. Even people who have long since stopped remembering their dreams and who have lost practically all contact with their anima can regain access to their inner imagery in as little as one week's time. Of course, therapy is only a surrogate for functional rituals, but it is the best substitute we have at the moment, especially when therapy enables us to regain access to ancient and effective rituals.

Help with a first and a second step in this direction is provided by the audio cassette[5] that augments this book. It features a guided meditation that first helps to shed light on the situation in one's own mandala of life and then goes on to familiarize listeners with the pattern of a universally applicable ritual of transition. By providing a pre-made beginning, the tape makes it easier for listeners to construct their own personal structures—a task that can be difficult without help getting started. It can be even easier to return to existing rituals (e.g., confession, assuming access is not too deeply buried or barricaded by emotions against the institution that stands behind the confession).

Far and away the best solution would be to make daily life into a ritual. A person who is carried through life by conscious awareness will no doubt recognize the onset of imminent transitions, and paths will likely appear for that person to ritualistically cope with those critical themes. He will live life in harmony with his inner imagery, and his external symbolism will be full of opportunities for realization and growth. The environment will function as a mirror and fate itself will serve as the best of all possible therapists.

Appendix

Index

Endnotes

Introduction

1   Rüdiger Dahlke, *Herz(ens)probleme,* Munich 1992; Rüdiger Dahlke/Robert Hößl, *Verdauungsprobleme,* Munich 1992; Rüdiger Dahlke, *Gewichstsprobleme,* Munich 1989; Rüdiger Dahlke/Margit Dahlke, *Psychologie des blauen Dunstes,* Munich 1992.

Part I

1   See: chapter 2 in: Rüdiger Dahlke, *Krankheit als Sprache der Seele,* Munich 1992.

2   In practice the pattern is often that, for masturbating ten times, you must say five Lord's Prayers and five Ave Marias. It is hard to imagine that Christ would have intended the Lord's Prayer (the only prayer he gave directly to his disciples) as a punishment following confession.

3   Jürg von Ins, *Ekstase, Kult und Zeremonialisierung,* doctoral dissertation, Zurich 1979.

4   Rupert Sheldrake, *Das schöpferische Universum,* Munich 1991.

5   In this context it would be a good idea to recall what the historian of religion Mircea Eliade calls the "holy time beyond polarity." Eliade differentiates between our modern

linear idea of time and the cyclical concept of time as experienced by ancient cultures. This circular time is always related to the midpoint of the mandala and thus tends to move away from polarity. The archaic individual experiences the decisive points in the annual cycle in a ritualized form. He or she is usually in trance and has thus transcended the polarity of space and time. Within this holy time, his or her experiences are free from the limitations imposed by polarity. This situation can be compared to "seeing our life pass before us" in near-death situations when space and time no longer play a role.

6   Paul Rebillot/Melissa Kay, *The Call to Adventure: Living the Hero's Journey in Daily Life*, San Francisco 1993.

7   An introduction to the idea of polarity can be found in: Rüdiger Dahlke/Margit Dahlke, *Die spirituelle Herausforderung*, Munich 1994 as well as in Rüdiger Dahlke, *Der Mensch und die Welt sind eins*, Munich 1991.

8   The best-known monument of this kind is the gigantic circle of standing stones called Stonehenge in southern England. Among its other purposes, this structure seems to have served as a calendar. It was used to determine the four "corners" of the year.

9   The equinoxes are the dates when day and night are equally long. They occur twice each year—once at the beginning of spring, once at the beginning of autumn. Summer solstice occurs on the day in June when the noontime sun has reached its highest annual elevation above the horizon. Winter solstice occurs on the day in December when the noontime sun has descended to its lowest annual elevation above the horizon.

10   A comprehensive introduction to esoteric laws can be found in: Rüdiger Dahlke, *Der Mensch und die Welt sind eins*, Munich 1991.

11   The esoteric tradition begins the year at the vernal equinox (i.e., 0° Aries) because this is the moment when the

day's light hours begin to exceed its nighttime hours. January 1st, which occurs just a few days after the winter solstice (on December 21st), is also a good date for a symbolic beginning. The winter solstice corresponds to conception; vernal equinox corresponds to birth. In principle, though, one could describe both dates as new beginnings, just as we commonly say that life begins at birth although we know it has already begun at conception. Strictly speaking, neither birth nor conception are actual beginnings since we are dealing with a cyclical process. It can also seem confusing because Christians associate Christmas with birth, although if we look more closely we realize that Christmas actually celebrates the birth of Jesus. Christos, the anointed one, does not come into play until later when, after his initiation, he begins his work. One could regard Jesus' birth as Christ's conception since from this moment on he begins to grow into his appointed task. Except for the mention of the twelve-year-old Jesus in the temple, we have no other reports about this period in his life.

12   For more information about this see: Miranda Gray, *Red Moon*, Shaftesbury 1994.

Part II

1   Neophyte means the "newly planted" one. The idea of initiation is associated with the notion of being planted in a new country where the neophyte can continue to grow on a new plane.

2   This relates to experiences from a past life terminated by abortion or to attempted abortions the individual survived in this lifetime.

3   From a scientific point of view, the increased frequency of genetic defects can be traced to the fact that the ova, that have been present within an older mother's body from

the beginning, have been exposed to potentially damaging environmental influences for a longer period of time than the ova in a younger mother.

4   In view of the fact that we would prefer not to have to answer for our actions, one is tempted to ask oneself why the word "response" is contained within the word "responsibility," which obviously means (or meant) "the ability to respond."

5   Stimuli and help are available in the picture book *Die vier Elemente* by Bruno Blum/Rüdiger Dahlke, Munich 1995 and in the accompanying audio cassettes (Bauer Verlag, Freiburg 1995).

6   Damage caused by academic medical techniques is often not discovered until much later. There is no compelling reason to allow oneself or one's unborn child to serve as guinea pigs, especially since fewer examinations would suffice. Especially for parents who would not consent to abortion in any case, there is no reason to undergo many gynecological exams during pregnancy.

7   In this context, see: Rüdiger Dahlke, *Reisen nach Innen*, Munich 1994.

8   In his book *Natürliche Wege zu einem langen Leben*, Leon Chaitow proves that the life expectancy of experimental animals that are fed the "normal diet" of a civilized human being is reduced by 33 percent. The animals usually die of one or another "civilized" disease.

9   Refusal to quit smoking during pregnancy is not caused by ill will, but derives from the psychological patterns in which the parents are caught. Further help and information about the background of this problem is available in: Rüdiger Dahlke/Margit Dahlke, *Psychologie des blauen Dunstes*, Munich 1992.

10   Women in so-called "natural" cultures (that we so readily and so wrongly assume to be "primitive") are usually aware of the moment of conception. Sensitive women in

our own culture may also be able to perceive the moment when conception has occurred.

11   Only inessentials are lost when one fasts. And if one loses a few pounds, one probably has not lost anything worth keeping. The whole process only serves to make us more essential.

12   After the discovery of the x-ray, physicians routinely x-rayed everything and anything (e.g., feet were x-rayed before buying shoes; schoolchildren were x-rayed once a year). It is only common sense, born of experience, for physicians to adopt a cautious attitude and to take seriously even the first hints of a potential danger.

13   APGAR is an acronym constructed from the first letters of the German words for breath, pulse, muscle tone, appearance and reflex. When a newborn wails, it turns red and breathes more deeply; redness and deep breaths earn it points on the APGAR scale. Screaming can also help it score a few more points in the pulse test. If the torture really enrages the infant, its muscle tone and unmistakably vital appearance earn it still more points.

14   Birth is entry into the world of polarity. As Christ expressly stated during the Last Supper, the world of polarity is ruled by the devil. It is only a small exaggeration to say that physicians are therefore acting in accord with the mythological role of the devil. The point is not to discontinue the practice of drawing blood from the infant's heel, but perhaps it is unnecessary to do so immediately after the baby is born—a decidedly unpleasant way to welcome the little fellow into our world.

15   Even in primal-scream or primary therapy, which might seem at first glance to be a training and an exercise in screaming, the genuine primal scream only issues from a situation of the most profound inner tension and urgency. It discharges an inner need that has been building up for a long time. The accompanying feeling of relief is often experienced as joyful and triumphant. But there is

no need to provoke such screams by slapping newborn babies on the buttocks.

16   This phenomenon is not so astonishing and not restricted to gynecology. Wherever doctors have gone on strike, there has almost always been a simultaneous and obvious decrease in the population's mortality rate.

17   Rebirthing means being "born again." This technique can help people relive the experience of their own birth. It is especially useful for people whose as yet non-reconciled birth trauma is forcing its way into their conscious awareness. A certain degree of caution is recommended, however, because there are a great many dubious practitioners operating under the label "rebirther." More information about reliable rebirthing may be obtained by writing to Heil-Kunde-Zentrum, D-84381 Johanniskirchen, Germany.

18   Dr. Robert Mendelsohn's *Male(e) Practice,* Chicago 1981 documents the fact that the pressure of labor pangs is greater when the birthing mother is in a squatting position.

19   Afterward, the specialists in attendance at the birth are sometimes surprised to discover that the infant's blood is not at all overly acidic. This should not come as a surprise since the mother's deep breathing has kept the baby's blood more than adequately supplied with oxygen and/or life energy

20   Although academically trained physicians are notoriously loathe to give up the illusion of their own infallibility, they are often overly eager to place blame on alternative medical approaches. Many things that go wrong in the course of a conventional medical procedure are routinely overlooked and hushed up. Few things in Germany are more difficult to prove than allegation of malpractice against a physician. Infallibility is part and parcel of most doctors' self-images; and what cannot be overlooked or hushed up can be justified by recourse to the latest scientific

research or, if all else fails, perhaps things can be arranged to prevent the error from being documented by a competent witness.

21   The example is not entirely accurate since our birth involves a striving to leave the watery element and enter life in the ocean of air.

22   A similar phenomenon can be observed in surgery, where every surgeon must prove that he has performed a certain minimum number of operations. More appendectomies are performed in Germany than in any other country.

23   Al Siebert, *The Survivor Personality,* Portland 1993. The German translation of this book is available from Hugendubel Verlag, Munich.

24   REM is an acronym for *r*apid *e*ye *m*ovement. It refers to the speedy motion of the eyeballs that occurs during dream phases. The motion of the eyeballs is easily measured with a simple electrode fixed to the corner of the eyelid. If the patient is awakened every time she begins a REM phase and is then allowed to fall asleep again, she can get enough hours of sleep but never have a chance to immerse herself in a REM phase because each REM phase is preceded by a phase of deep sleep.

25   This phenomenon is well-known by physicians and biologists, who describe it with the phrase "phylogeny recapitulates ontogeny." Esoteric philosophy regards each individual's repetition of the great evolutionary processes as an illustration of the *pars pro toto* principle, that asserts that the whole is contained within each of its parts.

26   Our most unmistakably "human" attributes are the double arches in our feet and our erect spines. Marine mammals (e.g., dolphins and some whales) have larger and more differentiated brains than do human beings.

27   There is not adequate space here for an in-depth discussion of reincarnation. Nevertheless, we are convinced that life follows life in a long series of incarnations.

Experiences in reincarnation therapy readily and convincingly confirm this conviction. For more information see: Margit Dahlke/Rüdiger Dalke, *Die spirituelle Herausforderung,* Munich 1990

28 Sometimes the German verb *zahnen* (meaning "to teethe") is also used to mean "to laugh." Laughing and weeping are closely related to one another, a fact that is evident in colloquial expressions.

29 For more information about this theme, see: Irina Prekop, *Der kleine Tyrann,* Munich 1992 and Irina Prekop, *Unruhige Kinder,* Munich 1994.

30 See the corresponding chapter in: Rüdiger Dahlke/Robert Hößl, *Verdauungsprobleme,* Munich 1992.

31 A whole series of suggestions for access and hints about how to move more quickly and more effectively through the depths of one's inner imaginative worlds can be found in: Rüdiger Dahlke, *Reisen nach Innen,* Munich 1994.

32 The "pusher" is a piece of cutlery for children that is especially popular in northern Germany. A pusher makes it easier for the child to persuade a reluctant bit of food onto a spoon.

33 Two students suffered heart attacks some years later, in the same high school where I had spent a relatively peaceful few years prior to my own graduation.

34 This would also mean that public schools would have to have smaller classes in which teachers would be able to deal more effectively with each student's individual personality. But smaller classes cost more money, and those funds are not available.

35 Rhythmical, alternating elements are a fundamental aspect of the feminine archetype. Our culture clings to masculine ideals and therefore tends to disparage alternation as moodiness and incalculability. Every religion and wisdom tradition warns against trying to calculate everything and emphasizes the importance of living spontaneously and experiencing each and every moment as it passes.

36 Shocked by these conditions, Adolf Kolping founded the so-called "Kolping houses" as local clubs for journeymen.

37 The idea of strengthening one's faith is explicit in the word "confirmation" since it contains the Latin word *firmus*, meaning "strong" or "firm." Communion contains the Latin word *communio*, meaning "community," and emphasizing the idea of community with Christ and his church.

38 C.G. Jung, *Grundwerk, Band 3*, Olten, Freiburg 1984, p. 122.

39 See: Marie-Luise von Franz, *Der ewige Jüngling*, Munich 1992.

40 The fact that this magazine's readership has been declining of late does not necessarily mean that its readers have evolved so far that they no longer want its contents. Just the opposite seems to be the case since many of its erstwhile readers now buy pornographic magazines instead.

41 This involves modern computer technology that provides access to so-called "virtual reality." Helmets and data gloves full of sensitive electronic equipment combine with miniature video monitors to simulate experiences in an artificial world through which the cyberspace journeyer seems to travel. Many people in the U.S. are already more fascinated by virtual reality than by actual reality.

42 Unfortunately this does not happen consciously since the rediscovery of one's own inner child could be a tremendous boost to personal development and serve as a reliable foundation for attempts at becoming an adult.

43 Many cultures have holy mountains. Indonesia's Borobudur Stupa, for example, is built upon a natural mountain that has been terraced to create a holy mountain shaped like a visible image of life's path. The spiral route leads past countless statues of the Buddha, each representing a particular situation on the path of life. The goal

is the summit of the mountain, which is also the center of the mandala and the site of a special Buddha statue. Stations of the Cross serve a similar purpose in the Christian tradition.

44   On the other hand, from a symbolic point of view, they live in the center of the mandala and it is possible that the whole outward path lies ahead of them. This makes them important for us as an image, but not as an idol to be imitated.

45   The issue of smoking as a compensatory behavior is comprehensively discussed in: Rüdiger Dahlke/Margit Dahlke, *Psychologie des blauen Dunstes,* Munich 1992.

46   If soccer devotees feel that this description is unduly critical, they ought to consider that, according to sport moderators and soccer trainers, on the whole most games are not very good (i.e., are not very interesting). Even in the good games, the exciting scenes seldom last more than a few seconds, and it is these brief highlights that are endlessly replayed on "children's television" the next day.

47   For more information about rituals of manhood, see: *Vom Mannwerden* (Munich 1993). American author Ray Raphael's discussion of modern men's attempts to become mature men brings to light a great deal of exciting and sobering material.

48   The annual decline in membership that continues to afflict Germany's two official churches (the Catholic and the Protestant) is proof of this defeat, as is the increasing difficulty many people have accepting churches whose entire histories embody a mockery of the church's own holy scripture. At the moment, it is above all women who still attend church services. As women's consciousness continues to rise, we can expect them also to abandon the church in ever greater numbers since it is women who have suffered the most (and who continue to suffer today) under the church's policies. The official churches

are so unmistakably the bastions of ossified patriarchal power structures that they can hardly expect self-aware women to feel at home within them. If women were to abandon the churches, there would be no one left to maintain the rituals. An additional factor is that we are living in an era of secularization and disenchantment, two tendencies that have a severe impact upon the churches. It is no coincidence that former cult sites are frequently converted into museums.

49   Ray Raphael's book *Vom Mannwerden* (Munich 1993) includes both positive and negative examples.

50   If you hesitate to insist that the child inhale cigarette smoke for fear of harming the child's health, you should understand that chances are nearly 100 percent that the child will sooner or later smoke a first cigarette and that this one cigarette is far less dangerous than the fate that threatens addicted smokers. For more information about this, see: Rüdiger Dahlke/Margit Dahlke, *Psychologie des blauen Dunstes,* Munich 1992.

51   Marijuana cigarettes are called "joints" because they are passed from one smoker to the next (i.e., they are "jointly" smoked).

52   According to surveys, more than 60 percent of all adult Germans are familiar with intoxication and ecstasy as effects of drinking alcohol. Fewer than 20 percent have experienced corresponding feelings in their sexual lives.

53   This applies to youths in civilized societies. People in archaic societies generally have a much shorter life expectancy, sometimes becoming sexually mature at even younger ages than our "accelerated" youths.

54   It may seem rather farcical, but when the right people pull the right ecclesiastical strings, a marriage (e.g., Princess Caroline of Monaco's marriage) can be retroactively declared "never consummated" and annulled with papal blessing. This option is seldom or never available to ordinary Catholics, who must either stay together or risk

excommunication after having been granted a secular divorce.

55 Adolf Guggenbühl-Craig, *Die Ehe ist tot, lang lebe die Ehe,* Munich 1990.

56 In this context, see the detailed discussion of resonance as the basis of love in: Rüdiger Dahlke, *Der Mensch und die Welt sind eins,* Munich 1991.

57 Children often enjoy playing roles they will one day be called upon to play in earnest. When they play house, assigning each other the roles of father, mother and child, they may quarrel over which child gets to play the adult role with the most promising future.

58 The concept was first articulated by Christina and Stan Grof, who wrote a book about this theme. See: *Spiritual Krisen. Chancen der Selbstfindung,* Munich 1993.

59 This refers to the naive method that attempts, above all by means of affirmations (positive statements), to cover up shadowy areas such as the symptoms of various illnesses. This method, like the allopathic medicinal approach on which it is based, unfortunately functions rather well. The symptoms are covered up and the shadow grows correspondingly larger. For more information about this issue, see: Margit Dahlke/Rüdiger Dahlke, *Die spirituelle Herausforderung,* Munich 1994.

60 Transcendental Meditation was propagated in the West by the Indian yogi Maharishi Mahesh Yogi during the 1960s and 70s and still has many adherents.

61 The word "tantra" is somewhat incorrectly used in this context to refer to a sexual practice that attempts to avoid orgasm. This use of the term is not altogether correct since the term "tantra" embraces a much wider field.

62 From a linguistic point of view, we could understand this injunction in a more discriminating way. "To subdue something" also means "to put oneself above something else." The Biblical phrase, then, could also be interpreted as urging us to put ourselves above (i.e., to transcend)

the polarities of the world and evolve toward unity and wholeness.

63 *Das C.G. Jung Lesebuch,* Olten, Freiburg 1983, pp. 156, 158.

64 In this context, it is hard to overlook the fact that some erstwhile disciples in this scene have tried to solve their midlife crises by the simple expedient of declaring themselves to be gurus and thus regarding themselves as the measure of all things. Rather than recognizing and dealing with their own shadow and its power-related issues, they have elevated it into a program in its own right. The consequences are all too obviously embarrassing. But even "gurus" of this ilk succeed in attracting disciples of their own, especially among people who are desperately searching for authority figures. Rather than solving their own hang-ups, the would-be disciples only become hangers-on.

65 Max Frisch, *Gesammelte Werke, Band 6, Tagebuch 1966-1971,* Frankfurt am Main 1986, p. 246.

66 It is worth considering whether the increased violence and brutality that social scientists have noted among today's young people might not be related to the fact that youths are seldom voluntarily given the space for development they need. This creates a vicious circle since the older generation can argue that such violence-prone young people are all the more unworthy of being given the power of decision that their elders refuse to give up.

67 The similarity to "primitives" is quite clear here. Amerindians or Tibetans treat their mandalas much the same way children treat their sandcastles: "enjoy and destroy" is the motto. They spend hours or days painstakingly creating a structure they then jubilantly wreak.

68 This creates a tremendous danger since practitioners of alternative medicine can incompetently advise the patient to stop taking a particular medication. If the antidepressant effect wanes before the motivating effect, the

combination can practically drive the patient into a suicide that he never could have committed without the motivation provided by the latter medication. Anyone who deals with medicated patients ought to be very well-informed about these drugs, their synergies and side-effects. Most academically trained physicians are adequately informed about this. It is common in modern psychiatric practice to link both types of drugs (i.e., prescribing both or discontinuing both at the same time).

69   If, for whatever reasons, physical growth has been prevented or interfered with, compensatory growth sometimes occurs on the plane of the mind or soul.

70   An athletic discipline (e.g., marathon running) that includes the archetypally saturnine theme of old age might have a certain chance here, although it cannot provide a solution.

71   From a medical point of view, this could be either a harmless tumor (e.g., a prostate adenoma) or a malignant tumor (e.g.,. a carcinoma). In the latter case, all of the comments found in: Rüdiger Dahlke, *Krankheit als Sprache der Seele,* Munich 1992 would be applicable.

72   A comprehensive interpretation of hair and the symbolic significance of hair loss can be found in: Rüdiger Dahlke, *Krankheit als Sprache der Seele,* Munich 1992.

73   Miranda Gray, *Red Moon,* Shaftesbury 1994.

74   See also the relevant chapter in: Rüdiger Dahlke/Robert Hößl, *Verdauungsprobleme,* Munich 1992.

75   For more information about the interpretation of heart attacks, see: Rüdiger Dahlke, *Herz(ens)probleme,* Munich 1992.

76   The situation becomes quite crazy when women who have left menopause many years behind them begin taking estrogen as part of a merciless battle against osteoporosis. Nevertheless, some gynecologists stubbornly refuse to see the light, even when seventy-year-old women begin menstruating again.

77   The fact that medicine has granted us so many bless-
      ings does not mean that every innovation and every new
      trend is necessarily sensible, and it certainly does not
      mean that everything in the past was bad.

78   Also see: chapter IX.2 in: Rüdiger Dahlke/Robert Hößl,
      Verdauungsprobleme, Munich 1992.

79   The quotation is a translation of a statement by Prof. Dr.
      Friedrich Husmann in: *Gyne – Fachzeitschrift für prak-
      tische Frauenheilkunde und allgemeine Medizin,* p. 5.

80   Ibid

81   Ibid

82   Typical arguments usually suggest that the weight gain
      caused by the biochemical effects of estrogen (e.g.,
      water buildup) is seldom more than one pound. Any addi-
      tional weight gains, they claim, are due to changes in the
      patient's overall living situation. Whatever their causes,
      each additional pound still weighs 16 ounces!

83   The quotation is a translation of a statement by Prof. Dr.
      Friedrich Husmann in: *Gyne – Fachzeitschrift für prak-
      tische Frauenheilkunde und allgemeine Medizin,* p. 5.

84   More about the deeper meaning of this fatty pillow can
      be found in: Rüdiger Dahlke, *Gewichtsprobleme,* Munich
      1989.

85   A comprehensive interpretation can be found in chapter
      15 of: Rüdiger Dahlke, *Krankheit als Sprache der Seele,*
      Munich 1992.

86   All these and other typical geriatric symptoms are dis-
      cussed in greater detail in chapter 15 of: Rüdiger Dahlke,
      Krankheit als Sprache der Seele, Munich 1992.

87   See also: Rüdiger Dahlke, *Herzensprobleme,* Munich
      1992.

88   Certain Eastern philosophies claim that everything we
      believe to exist in the concrete, created universe is really
      illusion, or *maya.* Space and time, according to modern
      physics, are by no means as objective and secure as the

scientifically oriented West assumed them to be during the past two hundred years.

89   The ancient Egyptians described *maya* as "the veil of Isis."

90   Max Frisch, *Gesammelte Werke, Band 6, Tagebuch 1966-1971,* Frankfurt am Main 1986, p. 107 ff., 126 ff.

91   The speaker's frequent use of phrases such as "in my day" or "in our day" reveals that she no longer regards the present day as her time (i.e., the speaker's time is lost in the past).

92   This applies to all those American patients who have arranged for their bodies (or, in the cheaper version, only their heads) to be frozen in the hope that someday medical science will be able to find a panacea that, after the body (or head) is thawed, will save them from death. Cryogenic escape clearly indicates just how desperately afraid of death these people are, and also shows that we generally get whatever it is that we most fear—in this case, death. The drama is exacerbated because these souls typically have a difficult time separating themselves from the hopes (and/or cadavers) that have been put "on ice" for an indefinitely long period of time.

93   Legal regulations specify that the moment of brain death must not be determined by the team of organ removers, who are likely to be interested in the rapid death of the organ donor. In other words, even official lawgivers no longer fully trust physicians to impartially determine when death has actually occurred.

94   *Das C.G. Jung Lesebuch,* Olten, Freiburg 1983, pp. 162.

95   The battle for the soul waged by the devil and the angels is represented in vivid, Medieval images.

96   Claude Chabrol focused on this theme in his highly impressive film *Alice.* As one would expect, this film was not a box-office success, but it nonetheless offers people who are unfamiliar with this theme a wonderful introduction to the postmortem situation.

97   Dion Fortune provides a comprehensive discussion of the postmortem situation from an occult point of view in her book *Durch die Tore des Todes zum Licht* (Neuwied 1990).

Part III

1   The English word "breakfast" (i.e., "to break one's fast") makes this quite clear.

2   See the cassette *Angstfrei leben* by Rüdiger Dahlke, Edition Neptun, Munich.

3   See: Rüdiger Dahlke, *Bewußt Fasten*, Neuhausen 1993.

4   See the meditation cassette *Elemente – Rituale* by Rüdiger Dahlke and Shantiprem, Bauer Verlag, Freiburg 1995.

5   Cassette by Rüdiger Dahlke, *Lebenskrisen als Entwicklungschancen*, Edition Neptun, Munich 1995.

We thank the following persons and publishers for their permission to publish quotations from the following works:

Hermann Hesse: *Stufen. Ausgewählte Gedichte.*
©Suhrkamp Verlag. Frankfurt am Main 1976.

Khalil Gibran: *The Prophet.*
©Alfred A. Knopf Publishers, New York 1952

Rainer Maria Rilke: *Gedichte aus den Jahren 1902 bis 1917.*
©Insel Verlag. Frankfurt am Main 1983.

C.G. Jung: *Vom Wachsen und Erwachsenwerden.*
©Walter Verlag AG. 1991.

Die schönsten Geschichten von Hellmut Holthaus.
Josef Knecht Verlag. Frankfurt am Main 1970
©Angelo Holthaus, Staufen.